FIGHTING THE COLD WAR

A SOLDIER'S MEMOIR

GENERAL JOHN R. GALVIN, USA (RET.)

Foreword by
**GENERAL DAVID H. PETRAEUS,
USA (RET.)**

 UNIVERSITY PRESS OF KENTUCKY

Scholarly publisher for the Commonwealth,
serving Bellarmine University, Berea College, Centre College of Kentucky,
Eastern Kentucky University, The Filson Historical Society, Georgetown
College, Kentucky Historical Society, Kentucky State University, Morehead
State University, Murray State University, Northern Kentucky University,
Transylvania University, University of Kentucky, University of Louisville,
and Western Kentucky University.
All rights reserved.

Editorial and Sales Offices: The University Press of Kentucky
663 South Limestone Street, Lexington, Kentucky 40508-4008
www.kentuckypress.com

Cataloging-in-Publication data is available from the Library of Congress.

ISBN 978-0-8131-6101-3 (hardcover : alk. paper)
ISBN 978-0-8131-6102-0 (epub)
ISBN 978-0-8131-6103-7 (pdf)

This book is printed on acid-free paper meeting the requirements of the
American National Standard for Permanence in Paper for Printed Library
Materials.

Manufactured in the United States of America.

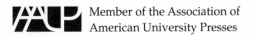 Member of the Association of
American University Presses

To Isomve and Kata

Contents

Photographs follow page 248

Foreword

General Jack Galvin has been many figures to many people. And beyond his exceptional accomplishments in and out of uniform, that is why he stood out from his contemporaries and was a model and an inspiration for so many of us. It is also what makes this book so special.

Fighting the Cold War revisits the many fields of General Galvin's achievements.

He was, of course, a great soldier, highly decorated on the battlefield in Vietnam, who rose to the pinnacle of command as a Cold Warrior, and who was known for his thinking, his integrity, and his forthright advice—as will be clear in the pages that follow.

In his final military assignments, as commander of a corps in Germany, as commander-in-chief of U.S. Southern Command in Latin America, and then as NATO's supreme allied commander in Europe through the end of the Cold War, Jack Galvin proved to be an exceptional statesman as well.

Beyond all that, he was a scholar, the author of three books, a professor at the United States Military Academy, a frequent contributor to military and national security debates of the day, and, after taking off the uniform, the dean of Tufts University's Fletcher School of Law and Diplomacy. Not surprisingly, he was also a voracious reader with a wonderfully inquiring mind and a keen intellect.

This book would be worth reading for his reflections from those roles alone.

But Jack Galvin was more than just a great soldier, scholar, and statesman. He was also a keen observer of his times, with a delightful, quick sense of humor and a sharp eye for actions that inform one about others. He was a lover of writing and literature (and a student of languages, fluent in Spanish and German). His graduate degree was in English, the subject he taught at West Point, and he was constantly scribbling notes and ideas for future writing.

He was also an extraordinary conceptualizer, one of those who stood out in his generation for thinking out of the box, for developing the new big ideas. Moreover, he had the courage of his convictions when he fleshed out a change whose time had come, and he was willing to "speak truth to power," as the saying goes. He was even a superb artist and cartoonist, finding humor in the pressures and peculiarities of West Point—and beyond—with a devilish, wry wit.

Finally, Jack Galvin was a proud son of an Irish bricklayer from a small town outside Boston and a devoted family man. He was particularly devoted to his "girls"—his wife, Ginny, and his four daughters—and, ultimately, to their husbands and partners, and then to their children. And he was an extraordinary friend and mentor to many, one who went out of his way (and out of the little time his schedule afforded) to stay connected with friends and those with whom he had served in the past.

Interestingly, all of these great qualities were packaged in a man who was invariably considerate of others and had a surprisingly small ego, despite the lofty accomplishments, decorations, honors, and acclaim. In part, this was because he never forgot his roots and he returned to them on a regular basis.

It is General Galvin's additional qualities that give this book its extraordinary range: representing an impressive commentary not only on his times, but on timeless issues like leadership, strategic thinking, family, and relationships. It is the joy he takes in observing, commenting, and writing—with his wonderful sense of humor and a measured sense of himself—that comes through in the pages of this engaging memoir.

I was privileged to serve directly for General Galvin in three assignments—first, as his aide when he was a two-star general; then as a temporary duty special assistant when he was commander-in-chief of U.S. Southern Command; and finally, as a military assistant (speechwriter) in his first year as NATO's supreme allied commander. In each of these tours, and beyond, I benefited enormously from his mentorship and from his friendship, ultimately through a correspondence that has lasted for decades. Ours has been, in my mind at least, a truly special relationship, one that I believe both of us treasure. And in a day when one sent actual letters back and forth, our correspondence was extensive, one that remains very enjoyable to reread to this day. In some respects, this foreword is a continuation of our decades-long collaboration in thinking and writing about issues central to the U.S. military and to America's situation in a rapidly changing world.

General Jack Galvin spent four decades in the U.S. Army, including fourteen years as a mid-grade, and then senior, officer in Europe at the height of the Cold War and another handful of years in several tours in Latin America, decades apart in a region facing innumerable crises. After retiring in 1992, he spent eight years at work in academia, reflecting and writing throughout that period and in the decade that followed—and distilling his experiences into this compelling memoir.

Jack Galvin recognized relatively early in his career the dynamic qualities his eventual role in world affairs would require. As he put it, "Mere military experience has never been enough." That awareness also explains why he situates the apex of his military career as but one period in a very full life and in a succession of experiences that shaped the wonderfully grounded leader and man that he was.

The arc of General Galvin's career followed the rise and fall of a pivotal, contentious opposition of world powers through a dramatic and unpredictable outcome. "We were," he notes, "trying to act our parts on the stage while the stagehands changed the scenery around us." And this story maps his development as a youth and then as a young officer, describing the mentoring that proved formative and essential and the ways in which he sought to emulate those who shaped and challenged him.

Fighting the Cold War does not hesitate to recount the author's share of failings and missteps, decisions made and not made, with costs and implications for his career and more. In many ways, it is typical of the man—lacking in bravado, though every inch the forthright, introspective soldier.

It is easy to be drawn into General Galvin's firsthand accounts from remarkably different vantage points ("bottom-up and top-down") and in commands ranging from the "counter-superpower strategic environment" of Western Europe to the "coalition for democracy ambience" of Latin America. Whether he is describing what it was like to march in Eisenhower's inauguration in 1953 (craning as a young cadet to see if the president was wearing his West Point ring) or to brief the Joint Chiefs of Staff as a four-star general in the "tank" (a "windowless room deep in the belly of the Pentagon"), General Galvin gives readers a firsthand account and a vicarious sense of the people and places: traveling the "warrens" of the White House, briefing the vice president aboard Air Force Two, huddling in an anteroom with the president before a pivotal NATO summit, and describing the numbers and ranges of our nuclear weapons to another president who was "appalled by the realities of the nuclear standoff," and who would soon make it his mission and legacy to draw down those numbers.

These accounts are particularly rich and detailed because General Galvin was a meticulous note-taker, correspondent, and documentarian who kept 3x5 cards by the thousands—written in the moment or shortly after, capturing the essence of nearly every significant dialogue: the characters and nuances, including observations about and responses to an array of military and world leaders. These and a lifelong exchange of letters with his father and others close to him punctuate and color these stories, giving them both richness and immediacy.

Fighting the Cold War gives us in incredible detail the tense give-and-take exchanges with General Manuel Noriega not long before the U.S. invasion of Panama; an impassioned defense of the need for a nonviolent response from President Duarte of El Salvador after the murder of four U.S. Marines; a one-on-one with Augusto Pinochet of Chile "keening over his loss of importance"; delicate debates with Prime Minister Margaret Thatcher over the pace of NATO's and Britain's arms reductions; and a meeting in the Kremlin with Mikhail Gorbachev, not far from the coup that would topple him, still bristling from a fresh rebuke in the Chamber of Deputies.

We chart in this memoir the advent of nuclear weapons and the "nonchalance" with which the U.S. Army sought to integrate short-range nuclear weapons into the nation's arsenal ("like artillery, only bigger"). Incredulous about an early exercise with gasoline barrels simulating nuclear explosions and a safe withdrawal conveniently sized to the small rented training area, Jack Galvin goes on to describe the continuing, decades-long tension surrounding command and control procedures governing the use of these weapons—taking up the question of "whether the Alliance strategy of threatening to use nuclear weapons was viable." The tone is frank, open, and direct; and the revelations are often surprising, as I suspect they will be even to the most assiduous students of history.

This memoir is above all, however, a study in leadership, recalling how General Galvin learned to deal with bureaucracy and staff procedure as he energetically threw himself into the practice of team building, as he considered the qualities of the best (and worst) of leaders, and as he sought to develop his own leadership abilities in the midst of combat and the Cold War.

Perhaps most interesting, especially in light of current events, is General Galvin's foresight, over the five decades of the Cold War, in anticipating a very different military context—one that would require the very skills he was building (diplomacy, articulation, negotiation, global-mindedness, and a power to influence) and adapting to new forms of warfare, combining high- and low-intensity combat, requiring the use of mobile reserves and light infantry, yet with an emphasis on being able to fight a war of maneuver. Writing on the role of the Special Forces in the early 1970s, General Galvin argued that "all military operations in this epoch of total war must consider more than ever the effect of the fighting on the local population," and he pointed to "the mistake of thinking that a ten-to-one ratio of military to insurgents will overcome them." (Years later, when I oversaw the drafting of the Army/Marine Corps Counterinsurgency Field Manual, our team spent considerable time on this topic, eventually writing that a twenty- to twenty-five-to-one ratio was necessary.)

Events of the past decade have shown that the lessons General Galvin distilled over the years are as vital today as they were during his own time in uniform. He thus shares his life story as both a record of an earlier era and a provocation to consider what is needed in this one: what kinds of leaders can rise to the challenges of today's uncertainties and unknowns, what kinds of teams will be needed to face down present-day adversaries, and what kinds of minds will be wanted to tackle those problems and opportunities.

Fortunately for all of us, General Galvin's influence continues to be felt throughout the ranks of not just the American military but of the many others he touched around the world as well. This book will expand that influence further.

Fighting the Cold War delivers, in sum, the stories of a born storyteller, the deliberations of an active and inquiring mind, and the studied attention of a brilliant observer of the most fundamental of considerations: family, friends, and teams—and contributions to missions larger than self.

I hope that you find General Galvin's memoirs as instructive and as inspirational as the man who wrote them has been to me and so many others over the years.

General David H. Petraeus,
USA (Ret.)

Preface

Everything changed at the end of World War II, with the fall of Berlin and the destruction of Hiroshima and Nagasaki. The Russians determined to stay, and the Soviet Union occupied the conquered territory of the Eastern Bloc, pressuring nations to take up the red flag. Tensions gave way to conflicts around the globe; and a tired world entered the long and fragile stalemate we came to know as the Cold War.

My parents lived through the First World War—the War to End All Wars—and close on its heels the Great Depression. I came of age as the world entered an even bigger war, building to a crescendo that shaped my earliest experiences and my thinking long after.

In high school, my fellow students and I asked homecoming veterans whether peace was possible; and our celebrations at the war's end were soon tempered by uncertainty. Through the years I would have a continuing wariness about the Soviet Union and a growing unease about the question of nuclear weapons—their strategy and tactics, and their administration, if one can call it that.

This memoir is a series of stories exploring these challenges, the way events unfolded, and their meaning. Against this backdrop, I offer a sense of what I came to believe are essential elements of leadership, yet ones I was not always successful in practicing: self-awareness, teamwork, communication, and sensitivity to change.

PART 1

Pleasant Street

1

The Flashing Eyes

"Do you mind if I say hello?"

Jo Rogers. My father saw her for the first time in the New England autumn of the year 1926, down by the shore of Lake Quannapowitt in Wakefield, Massachusetts, on the eve of Thanksgiving, at the annual carnival. Drawn there by the lights, the music, and the lazy smoke from small wood fires, he and some friends joined the crowd of townsfolk and visitors, a thousand people maybe, filling the lakeside common from the bandstand at one end to Cubberley's Boathouse and Dance Hall on the other. Jack was twenty-three. He walked among the hanging kerosene lanterns in the tented carnival stalls in a crush of people and a whirl of chatter, laughter, and dancing to tunes from Mike Sibelli's Brass Band. It was what New Englanders call beautiful fall weather: the sky was clear, the wind light, the temperature above freezing.

In cracked and curled brown photos from that time, he is wearing a wool cap cocked back to show a heavy shock of black hair, parted almost but not quite in the middle. His light blue eyes were framed by doubled lashes so heavy that they looked mascaraed. His jaw was angular, and he had a slight, but noticeable, limp. Early in his life, the family doctor had advised Jack's mother to wait a few years, let her son develop, and then see what the specialists would say. This she did, and in 1915, when he was twelve (and weighing sixty-five pounds), he was taken to Children's Hospital in Boston for treatment. Diagnosed as infantile paralysis, the affliction had caused atrophy in his left calf and foot and also in his right shoulder. He underwent surgery to reroute the tendons of his foot so as to give him more mobility, but otherwise there was nothing that could be done.

My father's case was interesting enough to cause an experience he would never forget. The surgeon who attended him decided to use him as an illustration in a lecture—an "in session," it was called—to a group of other doctors. He arranged for my father to stand on a small table and remove his hospital robe, leaving him naked. The surgeon and the others then examined and compared the healthy and diseased areas. My father was mortified.

In 1922, weighing 145 pounds, my father played left tackle on his high school football team, beating out the team captain for the position. "Most plays only take three steps," he said. "If it had to be more, there was a problem."

Some forty years later, he said in one of his letters to me: "I found out today that Gen. Henry Knox affected a silk handkerchief to hide his hand that had been marred in an early hunting accident. Sort of reminded me of myself as a young man. I used to wear a cloth-made muscle strapped to the back of my leg so my trousers would fill out the same. I spent a lot of time shaping it before a mirror before I put on my football and baseball suits, too."

Jo was twenty-one. She kept her black hair short and bobbed. Her smile was accompanied by deep dimples and light blue eyes. Her sister always said she was an outrageous flirt. The flash of her eyes made you instantly aware if she glanced at you, even across a roomful of people. On this evening she moved with her companions along the line of tents, laughing, tossing her head, happy to be the center of attention, hardly looking at the games or at the wares for sale. Jack could not help watching her appear in the lighted gaps, then disappear into the dark again. At some point she looked directly at him for an instant and then turned away. That look stopped him, he once told me, as if he'd hit a wall, and I fully understood why. She and her group continued on into the crowd.

So the girl with the flashing eyes was Jo Rogers. He must have heard her voice before, because she was one of Wakefield's telephone switchboard operators. He learned that she was dating Francis Bowman, a medical student at Harvard. "Jo and Bo," they were called.

He also learned that she was an excellent ice skater who spent her free time on the lake whenever there was good ice. Skating was not for Jack, but he began to take walks along the lakeshore when Quannapowitt froze over. He still had not met her, and he didn't see her again until sometime into the new year, 1927, but by then she knew of him through his assiduous cultivation of her girlfriends. (At the last second at the carnival, Jack had recognized one of her companions.) Finally, on a gusty and short afternoon, nearing a winter sunset, he spied her far out on the lake, alone, flying along, hands in the pockets of a heavy, high-collared knit sweater. She stayed far out, until at dusk she was among the last skaters. When she did come to shore, it was at a place he didn't anticipate, near the looming ramshackle ice houses, but by the time she had changed from skates to boots, he was nearing the bench where she sat. He always remembered that he said, "Do you mind if I say hello?" She looked at him with that look, and after a pause that he remembered as about an hour long, she said, "Hello."

They talked. He walked her home, and along the way, up Elm Street, he mentioned a current motion picture, *The Big Parade*, and eventually asked if he could take her to Boston to see it. She said yes, and thus gave him his chance to compete with Bo Bowman. When the day came, he waited for her at the railroad station, the Center Depot, about a mile from her house. As train time grew near, he became less and less convinced that she would hold to her promise. He counted all the reasons why she might not really want to spend the better part of a day with him—but then he saw her, far up on North Avenue, striding along, just in time to make the train.

Sometime later, when Jo told her mother, Elizabeth, that she needed to look up her birth certificate, her mother said, "First, I have a story to tell you." The story was this: Elizabeth King had married a man whose name I know only as Logan. They were both Irish immigrants; they had three children. Then one day Logan disappeared. It turned out that Logan was already married to a woman back in Ireland. Some time later, Elizabeth married Thaddeus Rogers, also an Irish immigrant. They had two children. I can only imagine how Elizabeth told this story to her daughter Jo, her second child by Logan. This was at a time when no one ever spoke of such things. All I know is that my mother adamantly refused to believe that Logan ever existed and, with only one exception, never spoke his name, and never considered that her father was anyone but Tad Rogers. The one exception was when she told her husband-to-be, who said it had nothing to do with his love for her, and only told me about it many years later, when I came on some yellowed documents.

As Jo and Jack left Saint Joseph's Church on their wedding day, Jack gave his last five dollars to Father Halloran and then drove his new bride back to Elm Square for the reception. He had a car; he had a rented apartment in town; and he had zero funds. As the reception was ending, he looked out the kitchen window and saw his brother

Henry tying tin cans to his car—so he and Jo slipped out the front door and stole Henry's car, drove the six miles to Wilmington, stopped and took photographs, and returned to their Wakefield apartment. That is the story of their honeymoon, and that is why my middle name is Rogers.

2

Shadows on the Ceiling

"A downward spiral"

My first remembrance of my father was as a mountain. The best thing in the world for me was to climb into his bed and nestle my back against his broad back and just stay there, safe and happy. He was always the encourager and protector. When I got on the bad side of the fourth-grade bully, who condemned me to a life of bumps and pushes and threats, I turned to my father and asked him what to do. He said, "Just remember that you're not made of ice cream." I did that—and, miraculously, it worked. I discovered much later that he and the bully had had a conversation about leaving me alone.

For me, the Great Depression was a wonderful time to be a kid. I learned only later what it was all about. The men were home with nothing to do, and for a good part of the day you could hear the light clink and clang of horseshoes against the iron stakes, the ringers and the leaners, the muttering and measuring. From an open window, sporadic intonations emanated from the bulking Zenith radio with its tiny dial face, telling the never-ending story of the beloved Boston Red Sox: "One and two the count. Looks for the sign. Nods. Winds up. Looks over at first. Looks back. Pitch. High outside. Ball two. Two and two." My grandmother would say, "Two and two, three and three, four and four—don't any of you ever get tired of all those numbers?" My uncles, Willy and Jimmy and Greg, would be there, and my Dad, and my Grampa Rogers, and Mr. Hall from next door, and various men and older boys from down the street. If they weren't playing horseshoes, they played an easygoing game of catch or they hit fly balls in the field behind the house, maneuvering in the knee-deep grass of the outfield. Before I was old enough for school they had taught me to bat left-handed (even though I am right-handed)—because, they said, with great conviction, "A lefty swing puts you one step toward first base."

My father worked for a plasterer named Scott until he quit his apprenticeship and went out on his own, with no truck and practically no equipment beyond his white tool bag. At first he moved his planks and other equipment by wheelbarrow in several loads, usually at night so that people would not notice that he didn't have a truck. Later the local bank loaned him enough money to buy a secondhand Dodge Brothers pickup truck. They would help him many times in the years to come, when it became hard to meet a payroll.

As time went on, I could see that the most important happenings in the world had to do with the arrival of the plasterers in the early morning to load the truck. Every day I begged to go with them. On most days, though, I had to stay home, causing my mother to search desperately for ways to keep me busy. She found one that gave her some comfort: she convinced me that my father needed a daily report on the doings of the neighborhood. She took writing paper and, with a ruler, divided each sheet into small blocks. My job was to sit at the windows and fill the blocks with sketches of everything that I saw happen. I soon found that my mother was right—there was much to be recorded— and on many days I filled sheet after sheet, chronicling with an increasing level of detail. My sketches took in the several neighborhood cats: one for each house, including ours (Lindy, born on the night Lindbergh landed in Paris). They and the many dogs proceeded on their choreographed daily tours, and I developed over time an abbreviated sketch of each of them that could be drawn with a few pencil scratches—real time-savers for a busy artist.

There was the scissor grinder with his three-wheeled pushcart that could be unfolded into a workbench with a stone grinding wheel. There were pick-and-shovel men who came to dig trenches in the street, neighbors tending their vegetable gardens, once even an autogiro, carefully preserved on my page like a prize butterfly. In the 1930s it was not only the milkman who had a horse and wagon, but the rag collector calling out his presence, the iceman, the grocer. Automobiles came by, but lots of people walked to the stores and to the railroad station and the trolley line, heading for the shoe factory, the knitting mill, the rattan furniture factory. Others pedaled their bicycles or pushed their baby carriages. Very few people walked just for exercise. There was enough necessary walking to take care of that.

And of course there were the trains. The railroad track was only a garden away, and every day the Boston-to-Portland express, the Flying Yankee, made its run north in the morning and south in the afternoon. Its passing was always accorded a prominent part of my checkerboard sketch. Close to our house the roadbed made a climbing turn to cut through the layers of rock and gravel next to Lake Quannapowitt. That's where you could hear the heavy pant of the steam locomotive, laboring hard to keep up speed in the cut, and if you were near, you could see the gray smoke darken to black. Even in the daytime the flashing yellow flames in the open firebox would silhouette the shoveler swinging coal deep into the flames, the huffing now a throaty "hoo-hoo-hoo-hoo." Later in the day, the special sound of the express was unmistakable out in the distance as the locomotive engineer was not driving anymore but driven, tilting into the downgrade, the great engine now serving as a brake against the thrust of the dozen cars behind it, all that steel running free, ringing, "langa-langa-langa-langa." I was always the first to hear it—then off on the run through the hayfield to the fence. When it thundered past, pure white smoke streaming back across the roof of the cab, I was there, halfway up on the fence, exultant, waving a salute to Jerry Muffin, the engineer, who always lifted his cuffed gray glove off the iron sill of his open window just enough to acknowledge our connection: I the boy on the swaying fence, imagining that I was he, the boy at the throttle, serene, reining back that magnificent galloping monster.

The older I grew, the more I wanted to be accepted as part of the plastering team. Born in 1929, by the mid-1930s I was able to be of some little help on the job, and I gladly took on any and every task. I filled the drinking water bucket and jumped to ladle a portion whenever anyone asked—and even when they didn't ask. I ran to get small items from the truck. I learned how to clean trowels, hawks, pointers, pails, straightedges, slickers, brushes, hods. I cleaned the rough floors of houses under construction, first scraping off the lumps of plaster, and I tried to do it as well as the grown men, no matter how long it took, always fearful that the other team members might decide they didn't need me.

Plastering is pretty much a forgotten trade now. It is a tough, exacting mix of techniques that can create smooth white walls and ceilings and arches, but it bent and crippled the lives of many of the journeymen who worked the trade. The mortar that plasterers used was a mix of gypsum and sand, and it was heavy. Compared with drywall construction, plastering is more complex, requires much more skill, takes more time, and costs more—and it is very hard work. You had to be fast, besides being good at slinging mud, as they called it.

To work the ceiling and the upper part of a room, plasterers moved back and forth on a staging made of planks set on adjustable jacks. The planks were arranged so that the gaps between them were equal to the stride of the plasterers, who would be looking upward, not at the planks under their feet—so if a plank moved out of place, they could stumble and fall. If the planks were arranged side by side, leaving no gaps, the weight of the constantly moving workers and their table—called the board and stand, where the hod carrier dumped the plaster—would cause the planks to bend unevenly and trip the men. As it was, the planks of the staging flexed and shook as the men moved around, often walking backward. Before they used a new staging, the plasterers would walk it forward, backward, and crosswise, testing it out. When the upper part of a room was finished, the laborers dismantled the staging and moved it to the next room, while the plasterers continued with the bottom half.

Teams usually consisted of three men, each team having its own set of planks and jacks. Each wall and ceiling saw the team four times. Inside the building, a rough choreography unfolded. Scratch coat, brown coat, skim (or finish) coat. Long strokes overhead and up and down; straightening and smoothing with a darby and a slicker. You reserved your highest-level skills for the skim coat: a wet, white mix of lime and plaster of Paris and sometimes a retarder, to keep it from setting too quickly. You wet-brushed and troweled hard on the lime, working it as smooth as glass: no scratches, no "holidays" that let the brown coat show through. This was your last chance to correct the slightest irregularities that may have crept into the earlier coats.

Troweling, troweling, brushing; troweling again, brushing again. This was the dangerous time: if the lime got in your eyes, it would burn, and the damage could be permanent unless you got it out fast, splashing your eyes with water from the drinking pail, which sat in the corner with its steel ladle. Even the best journeymen caught an eyeful now and then. Plasterers were always looking along the white surfaces, their eyes only a few inches away from the ceilings and walls, ensuring that things were straight and level and plumb and smooth. Their cheeks and temples had deep bird's-foot wrinkles. Their hands were cracked. Plasterers wore their white gloves sometimes, but not on the finish coat. Gloves are too clumsy; you don't get the feel. So the lime dried their skin—especially on the hands, where there was always a deep crack between the thumb and forefinger.

I think of those years as a wonderful experience of teamwork. I didn't know until later that there were times in the late thirties, the worst part of the Depression years, when my father stood in a long line at the hiring table of the very few buildings that were under construction in Boston, waiting for noon, when half of the plasterers working inside—the slower half—would be fired and replaced by selections from the group standing outside. Your credentials were your plastering tools—hawk and trowel, pointer and brush—in your white canvas bag.

It was in 1936, seven years after the crash, when things actually became worse, and hard work did not cure the problems. Builders who owed my father money went bankrupt. I still have his notebook filled with debts to Deering Lumber, New England Brick, Red Top Mortar. Then a new competitor arrived to make things even harder. Drywall was growing ever more popular as a substitute, to my father's great disdain, and he refused to have anything to do with it. There would always be patching and repair jobs, always purists who wanted good plastering in a new house—and there were still a few builders or architects who wanted stucco as an exterior surface.

Competition made my father a driver of his crew. He became a man who would come home dead tired and fall on the living room couch in his white plastering overalls. At supper he would cut into the butter and spread it on his cracked hands. Mary was a year old, Jim was almost four, Barbara was six, and I was eight. Working himself and his men at night, my father built a brick barn for his equipment. He bought a new and heftier Dodge truck. His crew had grown to seventeen, and he was taking on big plastering jobs—a church in Cliftondale, a school in Salem, a street of houses in Cohasset, a mansion in Tamworth—going after jobs all the way from southern New Hampshire to Cape Cod. He had a payroll to meet each week, and he was constantly on the road, visiting builders who owed him money and who paid him a little at a time because they were strapped also. He still believed that hard work was the answer—not aware that the Age of Paperwork had arrived. The tax people came to see him and went away confounded by his mathematical hieroglyphics.

My mother left behind one letter, dated in 1936: a short note to my father, who had his team in Tamworth, New Hampshire, plastering a mansion there. Reading that letter, I see why I have memories of her tension in those months. The letter is about stress, about instability and worry, about the uncontrollable crowding of events and the need for help, to the degree that she daydreams about a bigger house and a live-in servant. Her words mark the beginning of a downward spiral that was well under way when baby Mary grew ill and died of what might have been pneumonia. I know Mary now only as images recorded by our faithful Brownie camera in a ragged black photo album. She is there in her wicker carriage, bonneted, with pinchable cheeks and an uncomprehending smile.

My mother began to have some kind of physical trouble. She went to see Dr. Duggan, who said there was nothing she needed more than a good rest, maybe a change of scene, a vacation. She also saw Dr. Burke, who said she needed surgery, a hysterectomy. She decided to go to Father Halloran, pastor of Saint Joseph's Church, a stern leader whom she trusted. He supported Dr. Duggan: "Don't let them take a part of your body unless it is a matter of life and death."

It was Kate, my father's oldest sister, who came to help. Kate rented a cottage at the Todd Camps by Newfound Lake. A registered nurse, she argued for a rest, and invited Jo to go with her and other family members who had planned a two-week stay at the cottage. I insisted on going. In the midst of my heroic fuss, I heard Kate say, "Don't let him come. You'll get no rest at all. Don't do it. Come on. He'll be fine here. You need to get away." But at the last minute my mother said, "I want to take him." She got out of the car and came back into the house to get me. I was overjoyed. I didn't mind that Aunt Kate pursed her lips and stared at me. At the lake I was a dynamo, overloaded with energy, an explorer of every nook and cranny. It was more wonderful than in my dreams. I rode with Mr. Todd in a Model T Ford pickup truck to deliver ice to the campers, and went along with his teenage son in the dory with the Palmer one-cylinder engine, the "one lunger," to get groceries at the south end of the lake. I fished for minnows off the docks and sold them to fishermen for two cents each—minimum wage. I learned to row. I memorized the license plate of a truck that caused a minor accident (New Hampshire B-1294), and reported it to everyone in the camp. I found and held a floating log and sallied forth into deep water, then had to fight the ant colony that inhabited the log. (I had not yet learned to swim.)

I can't believe that I have so many vivid images of those two weeks. Captive green rowboats nudging the dock, their floorboards floating in rain water. Motionless pickerel far down below among the boulders at the bottom of the clear lake. A boy and a girl sitting side by side on the tiny beach, teasing, and the girl's soft comment: "You like to hurt me, don't you?" I thought, "He wasn't hurting her." This was still the time of mysteries and secrets—of limitless unknowns.

In the fall and winter of 1937 my mother's health did not improve. Dr. Burke became more insistent, and she more willing to listen. She decided to have surgery.

For all of us there are certain days that we look back on: days when time stopped at a particular place and left us with an image—like a photograph, only more than a photograph could ever be. There is a window in that house, one of those stairway windows that were popular in the early 1900s when that house was built. It had a two-square-foot pane of clear glass, surrounded by smaller stained-glass panes of different colors. One day my mother was halfway down the stairs and I was following, when she turned to tell me some things to do while she was away, and the light through the colored panes dappled her face in bright hues as she talked to me. That moment is a treasure that comes back often to me. I did all the things she told me to do that day as she said good-bye. They took her to the hospital and she had an operation. And then, two days later, a second operation.

In my father's notes I find:

Dr. Cahill	$250
Dr. Duggan	$147
Dr. Murphy	$ 6
Dr. Kenney	$ 3
Mr. Gately	$531

Mr. Gately was the undertaker. The cause of death was listed as peritonitis. My father told me, some years later, that just before she died the girl who had given him a bright "hello" beside the frozen lake now looked at him and mouthed the words, "I love you." She was thirty-three. After a while he left the Malden Hospital and walked home, forgetting that he had left his truck in the parking lot. His brother Henry retrieved the truck for him.

We three children were not at home; we had been hustled into a car and driven across town in the dark to the home of an uncle and aunt. When we arrived, we were hurried up the front steps and into the house. A lady was there, but no uncle and no aunt. There was some calm, quiet talk that I couldn't quite make out, and then the others went back to the car and left. The lady, stout, serious, kind, gave us a late supper in the kitchen, where I remember the little black places in the worn linoleum. She listened to us chatter at the table, but she didn't say anything until we were heading upstairs to bed. Then she said, "Do you know why you are here tonight?" It didn't sound like a question. She just said it. I said no. She said, "Oh, God." She stopped and looked at us, and then followed us upstairs. After she showed us where we would sleep and turned down the covers, she said to me, "Didn't they tell you anything?" She seemed scared, and I was getting scared, too.

And then she said, "Your mother is dead. I have to tell you. She is dead. That's why you're here."

The poor woman. Simple, blunt, good-hearted, well-meaning, inarticulate, she set things right. We had to know. That was her duty to us. She kept talking to us until she felt that we—or at least I—understood. I know we cried. I think she did, too, and then there was panic in our little group. With a great deal of pain she put us to bed, and later she came up and said we had to stop crying now and to control ourselves. We tried to do what we were told. We asked if we could leave our doors open a little so some light would come in, and she said yes. We were in separate rooms off the narrow hall. In my room there were shadows moving across the ceiling, even when I shut my eyes. There were layers of darkness spreading slowly across the room from different directions. On a side table a self-important mantel clock ticked away, its sound deepened by its wooden shoulders. It seemed to grow louder as the night wore on. Even today I don't sleep well in a room with a ticking clock.

There is a gap in my memory until someone came for us a day or two later and took us home. There was a black wreath on the front door. The next few minutes I recall only too well. There was no place to park, so we got out and walked up the driveway, squeezing between the cars, eventually reaching the back steps and then the crowded kitchen. There was no room for anyone. An avuncular hand came gently but firmly down on my shoulder and moved me up against people until they stopped talking and looked down and gave me a little room to pass. It was hot in this now strange place, our house, and there was an overwhelming, cloying, choking odor of flowers that made me want to throw up. I was pushed along through the crowded dining room and into the parlor, both packed full of people all dressed up. The furniture was missing. I stumbled on inch by inch as directed by various hands, all polite. And then someone bent and whispered, "Kneel down here," and I just stood there and looked. I felt a stab of complete horror, and everything wobbled, like a top spinning down. My mother was framed in clouds of white silk and flowers. Her lips were closed firmly and, for whatever ungodly reasons, her nostrils were filled with a smooth pink wax and there was a thin line of wax along the meeting of her upper and lower lips. Why? I was panicked by the thought that she couldn't breathe. Her rosary beads were in her hands, but she wasn't really holding them. Someone, some grown-up, said, "She's not gone, Jackie, she is still with you and she will watch over you for the rest of your life." Now and then an aunt or uncle would ask gently, "Do you remember her?" I would say yes, I remember.

I was unnerved by a sense that something was terribly out of control—and it was connected to silk and wax and especially flowers. Until then I had paid about as much attention to flowers as any nine-year-old boy. Now their smell became repulsive, like some kind of gas. I regret that flowers have such a powerful effect on the ability to recall.

Over the next two years my father's business collapsed. One by one the team broke up. His brother Henry joined the town police force. Jimmy Rogers opened a hardware store. Willy Rogers became a building inspector. Elesey Jean, the lather, moved easily into drywall work. Harry Starrett and Johnny Walker retired. Hal McWhinnie, the longtime laborer, stayed on. My father and Joe Brehaut formed a partnership that took small plastering jobs, some bricklaying, and stonework. They called their firm "The Syndicate."

Sensing the trouble my father was facing, Aunt Kate let us all move in with her. Kate's acceptance of us was a beautifully generous act that took me some years to recognize. Kate and Ed Cronin had six children of their own, all living at home, in one side of an 1880s mansard-roofed duplex in a bad state of disrepair. There was one toilet, a loose metal bathtub, and no heat in most of the bedrooms. Our arrival increased the total inhabitants on that side of the house—which was called "the shack" by the neighbors—to twelve. The gray exterior paint, which could have been the original, had become desiccated into thousands and thousands of tiny squares. The two tall front doors, each with skinny twin windows, overlooked a decorative, useless porch about three feet wide and gave the house the look of a perched, fat owl. There was room for a driveway on the right and on the left. The narrow ribbon of front lawn had been trampled to death long ago.

I was getting independent, if not rebellious. More than once Kate said to me, in sheer exasperation, "You'll drive me to Danvers [an insane asylum], but before I go I'll send you to Shirley [a reform school]."

I was sent to live with another aunt just down the street: Alice, a lovely and patient woman, never to be forgotten. "The eider-duck," she was called, from an incident when she was a little girl. She had climbed up the pantry shelves, and calling out, "I'm the eider-duck!" she jumped, to a broken arm. Many years later, when she was bedridden and I visited her, she held up a wrinkled hand and, smiling, said, "I'm still the eider-duck." I could not hold back my tears.

3

The Pleasant Street Army

"What was that voice saying?"

In 1941, my father bought Kate's house for $1,200, which was what Kate had paid to replace the mansard roof after a fire. The Cronin family moved into a newly built place in another part of town. With our family together again, we shifted from one part of the duplex to another while my father converted the building into four apartments. Whenever a section was ready for rental, we relocated to an unfinished part and rented the remodeled section. In four years, we were receiving rent from three tenants and were enjoying a new apartment for ourselves.

All the while, I'd been fascinated by the developing story of the stolid Russian fight for survival against the onslaught of the Germans in 1941. As a newsboy I delivered the *Boston Globe* and the *Wakefield Daily Item,* and I made sure to read the headlines and maps and columns on the daily events of the war. At the Saturday matinee there was always the Pathé News, with its stunning graphic reporting. The Wehrmacht turned east against Poland and Russia in October 1941; in the fall of that year I recruited my kid brother Jim and all of the neighborhood boys—the Shanahans, D'Alessandro, Brown, Meuse, Curran—and formed the Pleasant Street Army. We built a bunker, found a map of Wakefield, and laid out the defense of the town, or at least of our end of it. We made silhouettes of Stukas and other enemy aircraft and practiced reporting. When we started to build a two-story air watchtower in my backyard, however, the neighbors thought we had gone far enough and vetoed the project, leaving a worrisome gap in the defense of Wakefield. After a few months I dismissed the troops and we moved on to other wartime service, which included collecting scrap metal and bundles of newspapers. On Sundays my father piled the family into our Plymouth Club coupe and took us for a ritual ride, usually to visit relatives.

On one of those trips, on 7 December 1941, we drove into Boston to the Fenway. This was a pre-Christmas visit to Aunt Floss, who lived in a small apartment at 65 Park Drive. I had a feeling that the day would be long and dull. Floss and my father liked to talk, and that day they did, throughout the afternoon. Then Floss turned on the small yellow Art Deco radio, which came to life slowly—with talk, not music—as they talked. Floss moved the dial needle toward another station, but then paused and reversed it. What was that voice saying?

"Pearl Harbor, Hawaii. Japanese airplanes. Heavy damage to the U.S. fleet."

Driving through Medford on the way home, my father pounded on the steering wheel. "Those foolish Japs! The gall! Imagine! We'll destroy them in three months! I give them three months!"

That sounded right to me. The Japanese attack came as a complete surprise, but Japan's expansionist efforts, mostly against China, had been rumbling since the end of the First World War. We had seen the blitz—the enormously successful German attacks that caused the fall of Poland, Norway, Belgium, Holland, and even France—and we had our heroes from the ongoing war in Europe, like Paddy Finucane, flying for the British Royal Air Force over the Channel in his shot-up Spitfire, calmly radioing that he was unable to open his damaged canopy and would therefore have to bid farewell. Hundreds of times I framed and reframed my own terse remarks as I went down in flames.

By December 1941, when the United States entered the fray, there had been plenty of war. We had seen Dunkirk, and we had cheered the RAF in its battle for the skies over England. The German army was at the gates of Moscow and Leningrad—and, it seemed, everywhere. The explosion of Japanese assaults after Pearl Harbor was unbeliev-able: right away we lost Guam and Wake Island, and then down went Hong Kong, Malaya, Java, Thailand, Borneo, Burma, Netherland East Indies, and more of China (that is, more than the Japanese already had). We struck back hard with aircraft carrier task groups in the Coral Sea and even harder near Midway Island, but we lost the fight in the Phil-ippines, because we elected to stop Hitler first and Hirohito next. After six months we felt able to say that we were beginning to turn the tide in the Pacific, but there was a cost that we still did not yet fully appreciate.

I admired John ("Huck") Cronin, Aunt Kate's son, and his high school friends, who hung around the Wakefield Diner on the west side of Main Street and the pool room across the street, wearing zoot suits and broad fedoras, long jackets, and the irreplaceable hallmark, pegged pants—wide at the knee and tight at the ankle, a watch chain hanging from a side pocket and falling almost to the ground and back up to the suspenders. In these outfits, Huck and his friends, just out of high school and working at places like the Dine Shoe Factory, went to out-of-town road clubs where they sipped beer and danced the jitterbug with the girls, who came as groups and sat in the booths. The jukeboxes played Tommy Dorsey, Glenn Miller, the Andrews Sisters. They were a more or less respectable gang. They had names for each other: Little Man, Spider, Count Backwards, the Duke, the Deacon. They had a language of their own: "to wheel" was to drive; "the woman" was the girlfriend; "pleats" were trousers.

Their lives changed abruptly on 7 December. Huck and his high school friends stayed around for Christmas, and after a day of discussions joined the Marines and arrived at Parris Island in South Carolina for training in the first week of January. A few months later, home on leave before shipping out for the Pacific, Huck joked, "When the sergeant with a southern accent said, 'Anyone here know anything about motors?' I thought, 'Motors? I get to ride!' I held up my hand, and now I'm carrying a sixty-millimeter mortar base plate everywhere I go."

Beginning in August 1942, the six-month slogging fight that was the Solomons showed us the long and hard road ahead in the Pacific. Huck was part of 1st Marine Division on Guadalcanal, where our town's National Guard company, part of the American Division, later joined the fight. My cousin Dan survived the sinking of the cruiser *Quincy* off of Guadalcanal by swimming alone throughout the night.

This faraway little island that was Guadalcanal loomed large in Wakefield, where the tone became gloomy and watchful but hopeful—and scared. I was a paperboy with a route through the western part of town, where I saw the growing number of pennants that told of family members in the service: blue stars for those serving, gold for the dead. On Saturday afternoon the movie theater (where I worked as an usher) was surrendered to the kids, who would shake the building in a wild and happy rage when the Pathé News report would inevitably roll out releases showing Adolf Hitler frothing through a speech. The young boys would then do their best—or worst—to imitate and exaggerate the guttural, choking delivery of the Führer.

When we are schoolchildren, and maybe afterward, a kind of hero worship heightens our regard for the people who are a few years ahead of us in age. The Wakefield Diner on Main Street became the meeting place for soldiers and sailors home on leave. Soon its walls were overflowing with photographs marked with the names of battlefields the world over. Many of us youngsters slipped in to sit at the stools of the long, marble-topped bar and drink coffee in thick, chipped mugs as we looked at the overlapping photos (with new ones always arriving). We paid homage, listening to the comments of veterans at home on leave and visualizing ourselves under those battered palm trees or in those winter foxholes, helmets and hats inevitably cocked to one side, faces smiling behind ragged flags displaying rising suns or swastikas.

German submarines were destroying shipping right off our coast, in view of neighboring towns: Lynn, Salem, Swampscott, Marblehead, Newburyport. In our town we kept our curtains down to reduce the nighttime glow that silhouetted our ships and made them better targets. We painted over the top half of all automobile headlights. On some Sundays I walked the beach at Wingaersheek, completely absorbed in a squinting search out across the North Atlantic sea lanes, hoping to be the first to sight a conning tower or the wake of a periscope. I belonged to my own imaginary organization, transmitting imaginary reports: "Cape Ann Sea Patrol Unit One reporting U-boat—estimate six miles due east of Rockport light—on the surface—bearing south—over." I would be as calm as the actor Alan Ladd, as in my mind I'd hear a crackling "Roger, stand by, on the way."

One moonlit winter night, a Grumman Avenger torpedo plane, its engine failing, coughed over our hilltop at a hundred feet or less, crash-landing on frozen, snow-covered Lake Quannapowitt a few blocks away. In my imagination I often piloted that sputtering aircraft to its belly landing and its magnificent slide across the lake. All safe. Later, a P-51 Mustang fighter crashed just to our east, in Saugus. In my thoughts I flew that one too, jettisoning my canopy and climbing out into the slipstream to bail out at the very last moment.

Camp Curtis Guild, on the northern edge of town, was then and is now a small National Guard post, just large enough to hold a motor pool, a few buildings, and a rifle range. In 1942 it filled up to overflowing and became part of Boston's role as a major port of embarkation for troops outbound for England and North Africa. Wakefield Square filled with soldiers getting ready to bid the USA good-bye. The town itself was dry, so many of the troops who could get away from camp crowded the nearby roadhouses on Route 1, the Newburyport Turnpike.

When I entered Wakefield High School in September 1943, Wakefield's radio stations, newspapers, movies, and everything else that made up the collective conversation of the town were full of fact and fiction on the war. The high school kept its distance—a remarkable ivory tower, sending each year's graduates off into the conflict. The Russians were pummeled and overrun by the German blitz. They retreated and made new stands, only to be defeated again. Repeatedly thrown back, they surrendered by the tens of thousands and were driven deeper and deeper to the east. Then, out of nowhere, came altogether new armies, speeding through the snowstorms in the Saturday newsreels, singing their victory songs, smashing their way westward. The Germans blamed the ice and snow and mud, but the weather was the same for both sides. I admired the Russians, but shivered a bit: there was something worrisome about our juggernaut friends. In the 1930s they were the Communists that my father said were stirring up the unions and ruining small business. Now they were our relentless, charging allies. The Russians had not yet become the Soviet Threat.

Meanwhile, in the Pacific after Guadalcanal came a series of Navy carrier task force victories at sea and ground assaults into islands to secure airfields ever closer to mainland Japan: New Guinea, Tarawa, Iwo Jima, Leyte and Luzon in the Philippines, Okinawa, Saipan. All costly victories that led to the ultimate task—the invasion of the Japanese homeland.

In November 1942 U.S. forces took part in Allied landings in North Africa and continued on to Sicily and Italy and southern France. Then came the Normandy landing and the drive across France to meet the Russians in Germany in May of 1945. That still left Japan to deal with. The war-weary town of Wakefield, having lost seventy of its citizens to the war, watched the barracks and tents of Camp Curtis Guild overflow once again, this time with soldiers headed westward by railroad train to points of embarkation for the Pacific theater. The feeling in the town was one of deep apprehension.

After Saipan, our B-29 long-range bombers began a systematic pounding of Japan itself, leveling sixty-six cities, while the U.S. fleet roved up and down the Japanese home islands, close in, blasting away. The whole string of islands seemed like a ship on fire—yet the Japanese hung on with all the power they could muster. They dug in and dug in and waited for the inevitable invasion. After the cost of Okinawa, and the many other clashes, we had learned some hard lessons: everybody I knew agreed that there was little hope that our enemy would do anything but fight for their homeland, inch by inch, death by death. Surrender was unthinkable, and in the islands they had proved it.

I was sixteen at the time of the gigantic explosion over Hiroshima, and another over Nagasaki, followed almost immediately by the capitulation of Japan. The response in my hometown was stunned surprise, followed by relief and contagious celebrations. There would be no fighting inch by inch into the Japanese homeland. No more war. Our troops passing through the staging area on the edge of Wakefield halted. Later, people would say that the atomic bomb was the first indication that our inventions could lead to our doom. At the time, though, we didn't think of that. We celebrated. Church bells chimed. We couldn't have been happier. We had won.

4

If God Was Mad

"Now there are three of us."

My father was a bricklayer as well as a plasterer. Our job one Saturday was to take the weather-beaten chimney down from the top of a tall, three-story Victorian house tucked between the hill and the railroad tracks near Greenwood Station, clean the brick, and build the chimney back up again. We were going to try to get it done in one day—and we did.

A day of mixing brick mortar was far easier than a day of mixing plaster. The mortar was heavier, but bricklayers used it up slowly, while plasterers went through hodful after hodful very fast. We didn't have a power mixer of any kind. I took the mortar tub up to the staging, then came down and mixed the first batch in the mortar bed. I carried a pailful up to my father, and for the trip down I loaded broken brick and pieces of old mortar. Then it was back up again.

I liked to watch my father, although on this day there wasn't too much time for that. The climb was high and the day was hot, hot on the ground and hotter on the roof—and there was no breeze. We didn't drink much water. Just makes you sweat more, we always said. My father could lay brick fast, and I tried to stay ahead of him, to anticipate what he needed next and get it to him before he asked. He would comment about the mortar, saying "Too stiff," which meant that it was dry, or "It's setting up" or "Fatten it," which meant add more mortar cement and less sand. At lunchtime, when we came down and sat on the shady side of the house and ate our sandwiches, the chimney was down to the roof, the new flashing was on, and he had a few courses up on the stack. "We'll make it today," he said. "A good day's work."

When you work hard for hours in the sun—mixing mortar with a hoe, climbing ladders, shouldering pails of mortar and hods of brick,

23

changing scaffolding, cleaning roofs, taking down trash—your shirt becomes soaked with sweat, which evaporates and leaves a white high-water mark. Then you get a second wind and work up another soaking sweat, after which you take a break for lunch, so you feel dry and rested as you go into the afternoon. You're soon soggy again, reentering the cycles of wet and dry, and white stripes of the salt frontiers decorate your shirt and overalls. Lifted by an athlete's kind of euphoria, you reach the end of the workday but keep going. Just a bit more and we can finish, get a jump on tomorrow. But then there is the takedown of stagings and ladders, all to be loaded on the truck.

Then my father says, "Let's take this over to the job in Melrose Highlands, so we won't have to load on Monday morning." You're burnt out, but so is he, and he's forty-three, an old man to you, so you say, "OK, let's go." You splash water from the drinking pail onto your face to rinse off the red and white dust, jump into the cab of the truck after one last check of the ladder tie-downs, and you're off to the new job.

The July sun had not yet set at six-thirty when we unloaded in the Highlands, but at that point in the workday you feel as if you are back at the beginning of the morning—ready to start over. Rattling home in the now load-free truck, high and perky on its springs, hot, humid air blowing in through the vents and the open windows, we dried out. The combination of dust, dirt, and salt stiffened our shirts. I had reached the point of light-headedness that sometimes follows a day like that—of hard-driving teamwork, side by side, giving all you have, a good piece of journeyman work. Yielding a topped-out chimney that will stand there for a long, long time. In fact, it's still there—and I don't ever drive by without glancing up at it.

We are completely spent, and it is, I can see, a shared sense of satisfaction. Everything accomplished, just as planned, and more. The next job is set up and ready, we are ahead of the game, and we could go on forever. We turn the corner of Pleasant Street, one block from home. Up ahead, cars are parked on both sides of the street—which is not allowed. Some of the vehicles are police cars. There is only a small space to squeeze through. There is an ambulance. People are standing along both sidewalks, in front of our house—mostly people we know, neighbors, some from blocks away. No one says a word.

Our front door was open. A police car in our driveway moved out to give us room, and we pulled in and got out of the truck. I recognized just about everybody—but nobody spoke. My father's brother Henry, a policeman, appeared in our doorway along with some other police officers in their blue uniforms, but they walked away and left Uncle Henry standing alone, waiting for us. So then we knew it was family.

We walked up the porch stairs, and my father looked at his brother. "Which one?" he said. It had to be my sister or my brother. My uncle had tears running down his sunburned, creased jowls. He said, "Barbara," and they embraced and his dark blue hat fell off and he cried hard on my father's shoulder. He then led us up the narrow front hall stairs. I picked up his hat.

At the top there was a landing. Barbara was there, on her back, covered by a blanket. Only her feet showed, with her brown-and-white saddle shoes; and I saw that her ankles were crossed, which made her look as if she were just resting, taking it easy. Years later I would see those crossed ankles on soldiers . . . when they were turned over.

My father said nothing, did nothing, simply looked at Uncle Henry, who was breathing heavily. He said in a hoarse way, "She and Ruthie next door were playing in the attic . . . with your .22 . . .

"And?"

"It went off. That's all we know as of now."

"That's it?"

"Jack, that's it." Uncle Henry looked down.

"Gone, then."

Uncle Henry said nothing. Nobody moved. We just stood there on the second-floor landing. Some other policemen came up the stairs. I had no idea what to do. I gave my uncle his hat. He didn't put it on. After a while he said softly to my father, "Jack, we're going to need an undertaker."

We waited. My father didn't respond. I don't think he had heard. A long time passed. Then he walked through the second-floor rooms, and I followed him. When he got to the bathroom he looked in the open door for a minute, and then went in. At the sink he lifted one of his T-shirts up out of the soapy water, and then he saw our small scrubbing board.

"She was washing my undershirts," he said, and he put the shirt gently back. He walked into his bedroom and stood there and said, over and over, "Now there are three of us."

When I used to be a paperboy for the *Boston Globe* and the *Wakefield Daily Item*, part of my route was Albion Street, and one of my customers was John T. Stringer, the undertaker, who was well known in town. His office was up over a store, so I had to leave my bicycle on the sidewalk and go up the stairs to give him his paper. He got the *Item*, which cost three cents—or eighteen cents for six days of deliveries, which left two cents for me. Most people would give me two dimes or a quarter and let me keep the change. At the end of my first week on the job, Mr. Stringer gave me two dimes and I thanked him and turned away. He said sternly, "Young man, since when did the *Item* go up in price?" After that I was careful to give him the correct change. He was the only undertaker I knew. I went back to Uncle Henry and said, "Mister Stringer will be OK." He nodded and put his arm around my shoulders and tried to say something. Then he put his hat on and went downstairs to talk with the other policemen.

The next day was Sunday. Family and friends from everywhere were coming and going, not at our house but at my grandparents' place next door. Our house was empty. I went upstairs and saw that there was much left to take care of. Even though some good people had been there ahead of me, I found, and did away with, many signs of what had happened, from the rooms in the attic down to the landing on the second floor. I focused on a single goal: everything I made disappear would never be seen by my father.

Then I went outside and sat down. I thought of a game we used to play, Barbara and Jim and I. We had found a cutoff piece of a ladder, only a few rungs in length. To this we nailed the seat and back of an old kitchen chair, making the kind of sedan chair that a princess could be carried on. Barbara was the princess. This bit of chicanery was our way of wheedling Barbara out of her allowance. From her twenty-five cents she would pay Jim and me five cents for each ride, and we were always available. We carried her down the hill, over the railroad tracks, and into the swamp. There were small paths in the swamp that were perhaps a foot higher than the rest and ran between little islands of bushes and even trees, standing out from the reeds and cat-o'-nine tails of the rest of the watery meadows. On one of the islands we had built a hideaway where, unobserved, we could watch the world. And once we had watched the world, we took her back and she paid us.

I thought about that, and then I went back inside. I was glad that I did. I'd missed seeing the tiny marks where Barbara coughed against the wall coming down the attic stairway. My father would certainly have found them at some point later on. With a powerful sense of relief I wiped them away, and then I went over every inch again.

The Monday *Daily Item* carried the story. It reported that Barbara and her best friend were playing in the attic at five o'clock Saturday afternoon and found a .22 caliber rifle and loaded it, then tried to unload it. The bullet went through her left forearm and into her chest. She was able to make it down one flight of stairs.

Barbara was a brave little girl. I thought about another day back in 1937 when she was in the first grade at Saint Mary's Grammar School, run by the nuns. I was in the third grade. We always walked to school together, because you had to cross Main Street down by Friends Bakery, and there was heavy traffic. At school the sisters taught her about sins venial and mortal, then guided her through the procedures of her first confession and communion. All went well. Then, when it was time to confess again, I went with her. In the church we sat together and waited outside the confessional, a dark little house with a narrow wooden door for the priest to go in and a door on each side, covered by green curtains, for the sinners. The pews gradually filled up around us. We were the closest, so we would be the first to go into the confessional, on the left-hand side.

Father Dowd arrived, and with a smile and a nod in our direction, went to the center door. Before going inside, he took a small white sign he was carrying and put it in a slot in the door. The sign said "FR DOWD."

I whispered to Barbara, "You should go ahead now." We had already discussed the side we were supposed to use, the one closest to us, and we had gone over again what she should do. I said, "Don't forget to cross yourself," and she whispered, "OK." Then she got up slowly and slowly walked the few steps to the curtain and gingerly pushed it aside and entered. When she came out she looked a little confused, so I waved her over, told her to wait for me, and made my confession. Then we said our prayers and left to go home.

Outside the church, in the daylight, I saw that she was pale and sweating. I asked her if anything was the matter, and she said nothing was the matter. On the way home, though, she asked, "What did that sign on the door say?"

"Father Dowd," I told her.

As we walked, she said, "I thought it said 'Fall Down.'"

"Fall down?"

"Yes. I thought there must be a hole in there, and if God was mad about my sins, then I would fall in the hole."

"There is no hole in there for you to fall into," I said. "That doesn't ever happen."

"OK," she said.

We walked on, and then she pulled my sleeve and stopped me. "Don't tell," she said firmly.

"OK," I said. And I didn't tell.

Until now.

5

My Nine Lives

"A sharp lesson in the purpose of the chain of command"

I'd continued to draw and sketch since the "window sketches" of the neighborhood that my mother had inspired, and eventually I became a cartoonist for my high-school-sponsored newspaper, *The Lookout*, and later for a renegade student paper with the misspelled name *The New Chronical*. One of my cartoons was published by *Scholastic Roto* magazine, and I was awarded a $25 war bond. This convinced me that I could make a living as a cartoonist. I opened an office in the basement of my uncle's appliance repair store and, still in school, went into business. I designed posters and business cards, and drew cartoons for trade magazines. I got some work, along with lots of rejections. Calculating my earnings after the first year, I found that gross profits amounted to about ten cents per hour. I decided to go into a new business.

With a cousin I collected old treadle sewing machines and sold them for the heads, which were used in new portable electric versions. We also bought "job lots" of toilet paper at the rail yards in Everett. Job lots were large cardboard boxes of paper that had been rejected at the mills (either for being badly cut, or for being too small or too large). We culled them, saving paper that was in fairly reasonable shape, and sold boxes of it wherever we could. And there was no lack of buyers.

It was inevitable that I would pick up the plasterer's hawk and trowel, which are somewhat like an artist's pallet and trowel. The men on my father's team were amused, and let me work ahead of them (so that they could correct all my errors). One day soon after, however, my father watched me for a while, and at home that evening he said to me, "I want you to leave the tools alone. You're not going to be a plasterer. You're going to college." I argued with him. I said I liked working with him and with the team, and learning a trade wouldn't stop me from going to college. He was adamant. I must not touch the tools. I said, "Well, *you* touched them."

That's when he said, "Sit down."

He talked and I listened, for about a half-hour. He reminded me that he had dropped out of high school for two years before returning and finishing. After graduation he went on to a clerkship in a Boston office. But, he noted, "I had already learned the plastering trade working with my Uncle Mike. There was a building under construction right outside the window where I worked," he said. "I kept thinking I'd be more at home in a building under construction than in the one I was in. I didn't make a choice then; I had made the choice back before, when I first picked up the tools."

We talked some more. I said I loved the team. He acknowledged that. He told me he'd always want me on the job—but as a laborer, not an apprentice. I could work summers and other vacations. But I had to remember, he said, that he would be very disappointed if I didn't go to college. I agreed to go. When the time came, I got my driver's license and drove the truck, set up stagings, and did all that laborers do, but not without one more confrontation with my father.

A short time later, when we were stuccoing the outside of a small building on Albion Street, I picked up a hawk and trowel and helped. No one said anything. We were putting the first (or scratch) coat on Clinton wire, and I felt a thrilling sense of accomplishment when I saw that I could do what I had so carefully watched for years. Flipping both wrists as trowel and hawk met, with the trowel picking up just the right amount of mortar; then the swing of arm and shoulder that spread an arc of gray mortar across the network of wire; then the next, and the next. A flip, and an arc. A flip, and an arc. A rhythm, a creation. The taste of a physical skill. I could have been good at it, I said to myself.

My father came along and saw me, and called me off the staging. "We made a deal," he said. "What happened to it?"

"Nothing," was all I could think of to say.

"OK, nothing. Remember that."

"OK."

That is the way he was. Quiet. I stopped for good.

Graduating from high school was like walking out of a movie theater after a matinee, squinting and stumbling from the darkness into the bright sunlight of the real world; leaving the illusions behind with nothing to replace them. I entered Boston University in the fall of 1947. After attending crowded freshman classes, some held in auditoriums where I could hardly see the professor (who dealt with us via student assistants in any case), I dropped out and entered Merrimack College, which was in its opening year.

One evening in the spring of 1948, my father and I had one of our many talks at the kitchen table. I told him that I didn't want to continue at Merrimack; instead, I wanted to study art and keep working with cartoons. There was, I told him, a school for illustrators, the School of Practical Art on Newbury Street in Boston, where I felt I could learn more about the techniques of sketching. He was disappointed, to say the least. For the second time, I was a dropout. I studied art and worked part-time as a laborer.

Most of the boys in my high school class felt there was little choice as far as their future was concerned. Even though the war was over, induction into the armed forces continued. You could wait to be called, or you could join up. If you waited, it would be hard to get a job, because employers knew you would be vulnerable to the draft. Better to join up, get it over with, and then start a career.

When Huck Cronin returned from World War II, he joined the National Guard as a lieutenant. One evening a week I would visit him, just to talk while we drank a beer and watched the *Ed Sullivan Show* on his tiny blue TV screen. He always insisted that he was not in the business of providing advice, that, if anything, he needed advice himself. That was not so, and we both knew it. And one of our conversations at his house in fact turned my life in a new direction. I asked Huck what I should do about the draft. Should I wait for my number to come up, or should I join right away? This led first to a talk about what I wanted to do with my life. I had told him before that I would like to be a cat, with nine lives, and he reminded me of that. We roamed through the fields of opportunity that would be open to us if we were afforded nine lives instead of just one. We both knew we were digressing and might not get back to the original question for some time, which just made the evening all the more memorable. All of our talks were that way.

Huck's own plan was to get the schooling, become a teacher, prove that farming is still possible in New Hampshire (with time for fishing), and build houses. My plan was: be an architect, be a political cartoonist, be a magazine editor, be a traveling journalist, teach, write, be a bush pilot, and travel the country in a van, writing stories about people.

"You could think about joining our National Guard unit," he

told me. "That way, you can finish your schooling and you won't get drafted. If we do have another war, and there's a pretty good chance of that, at least you'll be with people you know, friends, folks from around here." National Guard Company E from Wakefield was part of the 182nd Infantry Regimental Combat Team, which had landed in Guadalcanal to reinforce the 1st Marine Division, Huck's unit; and he told me one of his very few war stories, about a chance he had to visit with hometown friends. "We had a pocket of Japs cornered on a little peninsula. One by one they tried to swim out to sea, and one by one we picked them off. You couldn't miss. After a while I started throwing up. I backed off from behind a log and someone took my place. Right after that I managed to get over to E Company (the Wakefield unit), and just being able to talk to people I knew was very helpful."

On 23 June 1948, I took Huck's advice and joined the 182nd Infantry, just in time to take part in summer training. At that time, the Soviets, blockading Berlin, announced that they had managed to create an atom bomb—and proved it with a detonation. At the same time, they brought the Warsaw Pact into being. The atmosphere was grim, and it grew worse when Russian tanks rolled into Prague and shut down the Czech government.

When the recruiter found the term "pre-medical/dental" in my Merrimack College records, he assigned me as a medic. The Medical Detachment almost immediately left for summer training—and the Detachment First Sergeant, James A. Smith, decided to make me an expert at inoculation. Throughout that summer, he had me perfect my skills with a glass syringe by means of incessant stabbing of grapefruit, oranges, and eventually human beings. The method of hypodermic injection, in conjunction with the crude level of the equipment, meant that my lessons were in sharp contrast with his desire for perfection and made my sessions with him somewhat trying, to put it mildly.

The syringe came in three parts—the glass cylinder, the solid glass piston, and the needle—and could be used over and over again as long as it was dipped for twenty minutes in boiling water. Boiling water was defined as water from which steam arose, and twenty minutes became a matter for subjective judgment when the needles were cycling through the flat pan and a long line of soldiers waited. For each shot, after I assembled and prepared the syringe, I put my left hand under the soldier's armpit, squeezed his arm, and with my right hand inserted the needle into his upper arm at an angle of about thirty degrees. My first human patient became dizzy, and as we lowered him into a chair I heard the sound of a helmet bouncing on the floor. One of the other soldiers, far from the front of the line, had passed out.

This happened more than once, so I came up with a method to neutralize the problem. I carried a half-dollar coin, and made a bet with the first soldier in line: I laid down the coin and said, "You can have it if you can tell me exactly when this needle goes in. You say, 'Now!'" And then I set up as usual and tapped my prisoner with my knuckle instead of the needle. Invariably the soldier would say, "Now!" and I would respond, "Wrong!" and insert the needle. The recipient, and often others waiting, accepted the action with good humor, and we got along well.

My medical training was based on three fundamental rules: stop the bleeding, protect the wound, and prevent shock. Everything else was a list of homilies. The pressure points. Don't give water to a stomach wound. How to give blood plasma: if it keeps leaking out, just put more in. "When does that have to stop?" I asked one night.

"I don't know" was the answer. "Never, as long as he's still alive, as far as I'm concerned. On Guadalcanal I put twelve bags into one guy, and he was still OK when he left me."

I liked associating with World War II veterans, who made up more than half of our detachment. I soaked up their reminiscences, and I agreed when they looked on with some cynicism as U.S. forces streamed out of Europe, leaving crises in Greece, Czechoslovakia, Poland, and Hungary. They took heart, and so did I, when in April 1948 America responded with a gigantic airlift to blockaded Berlin.

In July of the following year, when the troops of the 182nd again headed for Camp Edwards on Cape Cod for training, I drove an ambulance following one of the convoys. The two weeks at Camp Edwards were our opportunity to put into practice the lessons we had learned in our Thursday evening sessions throughout the year. We were attached to the various units to provide first aid if needed. I was much better prepared than when I'd started as a medic, but I had no idea how many blisters, scrapes, bruises, sprains, coughs, and even broken bones and instances of heat exhaustion might be encountered in a regiment of soldiers out in the field. Bustling about with my medical kit bag, I took great satisfaction, in addition to a feeling of importance, from patching people up, passing out aspirin, and giving sage medical advice. I didn't know much at all about marching or marksmanship, but as "Doc" I was much in demand and always ready to diagnose. I expended bottle after bottle of iodine, bandaged and splinted left and right, and forced salt tablets on everyone I could find (including the colonel). I found that the medic is like the chaplain: someone for soldiers to go to to talk, and escape.

There was much I had to learn. One hot day, on one of the regimental marches, I was following along in the rear, driving an ambulance, when an officer waved me to a stop and said, "The troops are running out of water. Canteens are empty and there's no water source. Go back to the barracks area and get some water, enough for all of us." I zipped back, filled several five-gallon cans, and returned—but then, instead of reporting to the officer who sent me, I drove up to a hillock, opened the ambulance doors, and yelled, "Water here!"

My signal caused the marchers to break ranks and dash over to my cans in what almost amounted to a riot, with cans spilled as the men tried to fill their canteens. Pretty quickly a couple of sergeants brought order to the situation, and I received a sharp lesson in the purpose of the chain of command.

In the fall of 1949 a fire broke out in the Harold Parker State Forest in Andover. Governor Paul Dever called out elements of the 182nd Infantry to help put it out—which for me meant a combination of bandaging and digging. And lots of coughing. If you are not a professional firefighter, the sight of a line of flames in the smoke is unsettling. For two days I had no idea where I was, where the fire was, or how things were going. I scraped and shoveled on line with the others and made shallow, trench-like paths in all directions. I rode through the smoke in the back of canvas-covered trucks, dismounted, and dug where I was told to dig, until it was time to go somewhere else in the forest. I have always remembered this experience with the satisfaction of someone who has done something important.

Later that fall, on a Thursday drill night, Sergeant Jim Smith told me to stay after the session. A few months earlier, he had sent me for an interview at the Massachusetts Military Academy, the training school for National Guard officer candidates; I was not selected. Now he told me that a message had come from the adjutant general's office in Boston. Exam time was coming up for National Guard candidates for West Point. He wanted me to apply to take the test.

"Sarge," I said, "You know they didn't take me at the Academy."

"That was then."

"I don't want to try that again."

We looked at each other for a few long seconds, and then he said something close to this: "We're not talking about what you want. It's what *I* want. If you don't try for this, there is going to be a lot of shit coming your way for all the time you are in this outfit."

On the evening before the two-day examination, which had both physical and academic components, I rode the train in to North Station in Boston and walked in the rain to the gate of Boston Army Base. I saw a string of guys my age. A sergeant on guard wished us luck and directed us to a warehouse-like building that had a large room, filled on that night with an array of seventy-two cots for the candidates. Each cot had an empty coffee can beside it for use as an ashtray and wastebasket. It was a thoughtful addition, but as candidates kept arriving and the lights were turned down, every last one of us managed to kick our bedside can at least once, punctuating the ambient noise and making sleep erratic. That was the part of the exam I remember best.

What followed the next day was a jumble of questions and answers in math, science, and English. I recall my session with the psychiatrist, who I think was bored with a day of asking routine questions. With a faraway look, he asked me whether I ever found life difficult, and he was already marking "No" when I said, "Yes." He straightened up, looking delighted to find something to brighten his day.

"Well, well," he said. "Please tell me about it. Go right ahead."

I explained to him that I was often bothered with a self-conscious feeling about my hair: that it was hard to keep in place, always tousled, uncontrollable. He looked downcast and went back to his list, and I was soon out of his office.

The academic part of the test left me with the conviction that I had flunked. I passed, however, and received an official letter that directed me to report on a certain date to the 182nd Infantry Regimental Combat Team commander, Colonel Otis Whitney, who was much respected and feared and was sure to be aware of my failed MMA interview. As I climbed the stairway to his office in the Boston Armory, I stopped to look at a display of military uniforms, including the stiff-collared dark-blue dress coat from the Army of 1918. Having thumbed through *West Point: Key to America*, a recent book, I thought to myself, "That's the kind of collar I would have to wear. I wonder how hard it would be to get used to that?"

When I reached his office Colonel Whitney came out from behind his desk and shook my hand, gripping it hard and moving it quickly up one inch, then down one inch. That done, he said, "I trust that you will show we made the right decision."

That said, he escorted me to the door. Colonel Whitney was not known to be loquacious.

Part 2

Army Life

6

West Point: A Time for Testing

"I want to be right where I am."

In the early evening of the Fourth of July 1950 some of my high school friends accompanied me to Boston's South Station, where over a beer or two they saw me off to New York. In a splurge I had acquired a Pullman car cabin. My plan was to reach West Point fresh from a good night's sleep, but instead I arrived in New York having slept not a moment. I made my way to the Weehawken ferry, which took me and a handful of other candidates across the Hudson to another train, which carried us up alongside the river to West Point. All the way I thought of myself as a round peg heading for a square hole, and in many ways that was an accurate description of my situation.

The West Point railroad station, tucked beneath the stone cliffs and the gray towers of the Academy, did not provide me with a sense of hearty welcome. Along with the other arrivals I made my way up the steep hill to the grim awaiting senior cadets and put myself in their hands, as Jonah might have approached the whale. A year later I wrote an article for the magazine *National Guardsman* that described the first moments of my arrival at the Academy. It began like this:

A voice said, "Through that door over there." I was tying to my belt-loop a card bearing my name and height—I looked up to see our guide, the sergeant who had brought us up from the railroad station, pointing to a large door at the end of the room. In shirtsleeves now, with my trousers rolled up at the bottom and my little tag fluttering, I stumbled outside, immediately blinded by the brilliant sunlight on the wide cement quadrangle. I hesitated.

"Well, good *morning*, mister," said a voice filled with authority and topped off with sarcasm, "Come over here!" The harshness of this command momentarily cleared confusion away, and I hurried over to a cadet meticulously dressed in gray and white. I spoke my first words as a cadet: "Yes, sir." These two words became my complete vocabulary for quite some time.

All I wanted to do was comply, but that turned out to be impossible. Even some rather well-known facts—including my name—were not immediately available to my confused mind. The room assigned to me and two other new cadets was on the third floor of South Area, and I scooted up and down the stairs to and from that perch so often that day that I acquired leg cramps. Nevertheless I moved everywhere on the double, at the urging of eagle-eyed upperclassmen who, it seemed to me, had fixed their entire attention on me alone.

The plebe system is a time of testing, which puts new cadets under pressure by demanding a level of performance that is almost impossible to achieve, while maintaining an impersonal distance. That impersonality, along with the insistence on excellence in performance, allows a view of the new cadet under pressure. Being held to the highest standards and to the smallest detail creates a "mission impossible" experience. The issues may be mundane, but the pressure is intense. What new arrivals need to show is coolness under fire, manifested in an ability to stay organized and keep thinking. It's all about self-discipline.

My letters home show that even in the early days of exhaustion, confusion, and what seemed to me my utter incapacity to meet the demands of the situation, I was awestruck and deeply impressed with the senior cadets, including the ones who were the cause of my troubles. A week after one of my two roommates resigned, in a letter to my father I tried to be philosophical: "You asked if I think I'll like it here. I am getting to like it more and more each day, and I realize more and more what a great school this is. But there are some tough times. The upperclassmen are tough, but under that toughness I'm beginning to see that there was never a better collection of damn nice guys anywhere."

This letter began a series of letters back and forth with JJG that lasted thirty-seven years.

One event at the end of my first month at West Point became a turning point.

By the end of that month, I was still on an emotional roller coaster, and my squad leader, Cadet Ransom Barber, felt that he had had enough of me. On top of an aggregation of mishaps, I did something that caused him to explode. I no longer remember what it was that elicited his ire, but I do remember what he had to say about it. "You're a disaster," he growled at me through gritted teeth. "Do you ever get anything right? Why on earth did you come to the United States Military Academy?" Before I could answer, he continued, "Look, do you have any idea of what the Fourth Class System is all about?"

"Yes, sir."

"You do?"

"Yes, sir."

"All right. I'll tell you what. You have twenty-four hours to prove it. By this time tomorrow I want a paper from you that shows me some glimmer of understanding of what you've gotten yourself into. You will provide me an essay on the meaning of the Fourth Class System. In your own words. Don't quote anything. I want to hear it from you. And it better be good. That's it. Post!"

"Post" is short for "Take your post," an order commonly heard at parade. In the cadet lingo of my time, it meant, with emphasis, "Get out of my sight." I got out of his sight, and as soon as I reached the sanctuary of my room, I hustled to write down on scrap paper some stray thoughts that passed through my jangled consciousness. I didn't have twenty-four hours; I had until reveille the next morning, because the rest of the day would be taken up with training, and it was already early evening.

Recalling that night, I have often concluded that putting my thoughts on paper about plebe life may have enabled my survival as a cadet. I had studied the wording of the Fourth Class System in my booklet entitled "Bugle Notes," but now I thought, What truly is it all about? What do I really think of it, and of all this? I'm miserable, yes, but do I want to leave? No. Well, then . . . think, about *why* I don't.

I threw away probably half a dozen wooden and insipid drafts. Sitting on the hall floor under a dim ceiling light, I lapsed into sleep, woke up with a start—and listened. It was all quiet. I put aside what I had written and thought it over. Simply writing down aphorisms, each with some elaboration, would not do. Also, as I grew more tired, I think the distinctions among the detailed bylaws of the Fourth Class System became blurred, as did the overall meaning of the West Point experience. I wrote and rewrote into the early morning hours and slipped into my bunk not long before reveille.

That paper is lost, but it went something like this:

The first day, from the moment that you walk through that archway, is very hard. You are doing your best, but today, and for many days, that will not seem to be quite enough. For they have done what you are about to do, and they know very well that in the back of your mind is a question: Can I make it? Though they will from the first moment seem so inhumanly cold, you need only try your level best and they are with you. You must always remember that you are one of them.

You had expected that this would be a test of how much you could stand, but it is not long before you realize that it is not that at all. It is worse than that, for that would involve a single challenge: to accept the pressure and wait until it passed. The problem is that this type of buffeting never comes, but something much more difficult comes in its place. When you realize that they are actually pulling for you, it is very bad, because the giant obstacle that you must conquer is yourself.

Next morning I gave my paper to Barber. Later that day he told me that my response was sufficient. Then he mumbled, "More than sufficient," as he turned away.

On 26 August 1950 I wrote to my father: "You know that theme I wrote on Fourth Class Customs? I was in my squad leader's room and I saw it on his desk with a memo stapled to it saying, 'Check this!' He must be going to send it to someone."

Late that afternoon I took my place in formation five minutes ahead of time, as all plebes must do. As the upperclassmen joined the ranks, we adjusted to correct the spacing on the line. The ranks filled, and we were called to parade rest for the first part of the bugle call for retreat, then to attention as retreat sounded in the distance.

I said to myself, "Regardless of the pressure, I want to be right where I am at this moment."

Al Sousa, my Wakefield High School classmate, was serving as a soldier in the Army support unit stationed at West Point, where he could observe cadet activities. "They drive you till you drop," he told me. "They never let up." I thought, I know how to work hard. I may drop, but not before the others do. Maybe they'll give me a shovel and tell me to dig to China. OK, I'll dig to China.

When the time came, however, they didn't ask me to dig; they asked me to march. And to memorize, to work mathematical problems, to look sharp, to keep my bunk and locker immaculate, to run cross-country, to salute (I saluted the U.S. mail carrier more than once)—and to do everything on time and with precision. I don't remember doing any digging, but at times I might have welcomed it.

16 September 1950—to my father:

> Boy, that first week [academics] was Hell—I did everything wrong. I missed a class—7 demerits. I had to write an explanation why I missed it. In late—2 demerits. I wore the wrong uniform to gym—3 demerits. I was division inspection (assistant), and I inspected the rooms in the wrong order—3 demerits. I left my tie in my desk—1 demerit. Shoes not properly shined—1 demerit. I got 19 the first week. I have now gone through two Saturday inspections and a full week without a single quill [demerit], but if I get two more in the next 15 days I'll be walking the area [for punishment].

As it turned out, eight more demerits came my way, and I spent seven hours marching up and down the concrete of Central Area, listening to the distant cheers of cadets watching the Army-Harvard football game at Michie Stadium.

When I saw some stonemasons working on a swinging staging up along the side of one of the school buildings, hammering away at cracked mortar and lowering the rubble down in a battered bucket, I had to fight off the urge to scramble up the ladder and join them in their happy—and free—existence.

Academically my first year was a very hard one—at least in math, which was a constant struggle. I went over and over the math every weekend; I spent all my weekend free time on it. I worked and worked and worked at it. I was "Deficient" going into the last exam at Christmas—and I would always be in trouble, because the larger part of West Point academics was based on mathematics. In December I wrote my father, "I know you are confident in me, and your confidence has brought me through all the other tough spots, so here we go for the big one."

I passed. In the other subjects I managed to do all right, finishing in the middle of the class.

In a paper on Shakespeare's *Richard II*, I asserted that had Richard not believed in the divine right of kings, he would have been a great ruler. "Richard's childish belief that God will help a man who makes no move to help himself," I argued, "strips Richard of his greatness, and

not even a gallant death can restore his loss." My professor's response—
he was Ike's son, Captain John Eisenhower—was: "Good point, but the-
sis sentence is overstated." At one point he lost a paper I had turned in
to him, so he gave me my average, which was 6.0, the maximum.

In the first weeks after our class entered the Academy, elements of the
24th Infantry Division on the other side of the world saw their first
heavy contact with North Korean Army forces at Osan, twenty-five
miles south of Seoul. The Americans of Task Force Smith were outnumbered and overrun. General Bill Dean, commanding 24th Division,
pushed his units forward as they arrived from Japan in a desperate
delaying action, fighting for time while other U.S. forces, hastily assembled, made their way northward on the Korean peninsula. Dean's
troops made five defensive stands in fifty miles and were holding Tae-
jon, a crossroads city. In the action there, General Dean himself was
listed as missing while trying to stop North Korean tanks.

General Dean's son, Bill, was my classmate and would soon be
assigned as my roommate. Throughout his first year at West Point, Bill
would not know the fate of his father. He was faced with rumors that
his father was dead, or was a prisoner, or was somehow still evading
capture. A helmet was found that seemed to be his—with a bullet hole
in it. Other American prisoners found ways to report that he was still
alive. Bill's suffering was clear to us all—the one hundred cadets in H-1
Company, his instructors, and indeed the whole Corps.

I wrote home at various times about the crosscurrents of Bill's life,
as when I wrote my father on 2 January 1951 to let him know that Bill
was going to Washington (on 9 January) to get his dad's Congressional
Medal of Honor.

Later that year Major General Dean's name was set in bronze in
Cullum Hall at West Point. I was selected to go along with Bill junior, as
an escort in the ceremony.

Just before Bill left the Academy, he and I had a good talk. He was
his old self, quiet, just a great guy. He was "turned back"—that is,
required to repeat the year for having failed one subject: math. "Someday they'll check into my head and find it was full of sawdust all along,"
Bill remarked. "Then they'll say, 'Well, he came a long way, considering
what he had to work with.'"

Our tactical officer, Colonel Joe Conmy, once said to me, after listening to my grousing, "You see the cracks in the ceiling, but you don't

see the strength of the building itself and the service it does, and the people who keep things running. You're right: the cracks need fixing. Maybe now, maybe later. Everything in its time. I'll tell you what. Keep a notebook, and when you see something wrong, put down the details, the cracks, and write how you feel about it all. Then do what you can to fix it, what it takes to keep that show on the road. Then over time you can come back to your notes and see if you still feel the same way." I thought about it. He was telling me that I needed to have a sense of perspective. And he was the best of the soldiers. He had to be right. I started a notebook and am still at it.

Conmy also told me, "An infantry officer can do anything." I was planning to try for infantry, and his advice convinced me—and was indeed correct.

A couple of days after Inauguration Day in 1953, on 22 January, I wrote my father about my experience traveling with the Corps of Cadets from West Point to Washington, D.C., to participate in the parade:

> We left here at 9:30 Monday night by Pullman, and arrived in the freight yards at D.C. about 6:00 a.m. In the yards they had dining cars set up and we had breakfast, shined equipment, had dinner, and marched uptown.
>
> President Eisenhower had marched in the inauguration ceremony for President Woodrow Wilson in 1909 (the participation of West Point Cadets goes back to President Grant's second inaugural in 1873). We had practiced without music . . . did a series of battalion half left turns, rank after rank, the whole Corps down where Pennsylvania Avenue turns smooth across trolley tracks. Stars and stripes flying, yellow company guidons high, cadence perfect even with several bands echoing off the buildings. Hope you saw it. Past the reviewing stand at eyes left, and I looked to see if Ike was wearing his West Point ring. Answer, no. So be it.
>
> A few sidelights: While we were at a halt, a girl in a yellow sweater opened a window in the House Office Building. The Corps had been cooped up for quite some time, and I never saw anyone open a window quite that way before—at any rate, the whole Corps broke into a cheer, so she did it again. We almost shook the building down.
>
> I went out to a tea-dance at Trinity College, met a girl from

Pennsylvania there, and we went to the Iron Gate to eat, then to the Inaugural Ball. I was very lucky in being one of the last cadets to leave the city. Our trains left in sections, and mine was the last section to leave (11:59), so I was one of the only cadets at the Ball, with the exception of the Glee Club. I went to the one at the Armory (tickets $24; she paid), and I saw Ike et al. Got back to the train and climbed in my bunk while the inspecting officer was two bunks away (typical cadet evening!). The girl was very pretty and photographers took her picture, saying she had a good profile. I agreed. In the usual West Point way, I crammed about four years into one day. Classes the next day, too—we got back just in time for them.

Another letter to my father, 12 April 1953:

Gen. Montgomery was up here this week to speak to us—he is a good speaker, but I had the feeling he was talking down to us (such things as pointing out North Africa on the map, so we would know where it was, and explaining the European East-West situation in kindergarten terms). He seems to have an exaggerated sense of importance for himself and the United Kingdom, but I guess that he can be patriotic, too.

8 July 1953. Dick Shea, a fine cartoonist as well as star track runner, was killed in Korea as a twenty-six-year-old first lieutenant and company commander on Pork Chop Hill, winning a posthumous Medal of Honor. A year earlier, on 18 July 1952, Dick McCullough, also a cartoonist, had been killed in action in Korea at age twenty-five and had won the Distinguished Service Cross. He and I drew cartoons for the cadet magazine, *The Pointer*, and I much enjoyed his work. Two marvelous friends, both better artists than I was. I admired them both.

As a budding cartoonist, I was very interested in Bill Mauldin, the famous World War II cartoonist, and one Saturday, while we were preparing our rooms for Saturday inspection, Colonel Conmy knocked on the door. When we opened it, we were surprised to see that he had Bill Mauldin with him! He said, "Bill, I'd like you to meet our cartoonist here for *The Pointer*, Cadet Galvin." Mauldin said, "Well, gee whiz, I'm really happy to see you. Can I see some of your stuff?" That was the kind of guy Joe Conmy was: he knew how much meeting Bill Mauldin would mean to me. For a fantastic half-hour Mauldin and I talked about his work and mine, a chat that still sparkles in my memory.

While I was a cadet I went to see John Kennedy, who was one of our Massachusetts senators, because my brother Jim was trying to get into Annapolis. As I remember it, Kennedy had an interesting way of operating. It was like a dentist. He had two offices. You would be ushered into one office and then they'd say, "The senator will be here soon." He'd be in the other office, talking. Then they would go to the other office and say, "Senator, we really have to pull you away now for something else." So he could leave somebody in there and say, "Gee, I've got to leave, but stay a while and finish your coffee." Then he'd go back to office number one and say, "Hi, how are you?"

I, however, wasn't allowed to be in either office, but instead waited in between them. So when Kennedy walked from one office to the other, I got to talk to him. It was a pleasant few seconds. But Jim was impatient and didn't wait to hear about Annapolis. He joined the Navy as a sailor.

As my Class of 1954 counted the days of March, April, and May, eager for graduation, the French fought the battle of Dien Bien Phu, which finally fell on 7 May.

One day in that spring of my last year, cadet members of an engineering class (including me) attended a talk by Dr. Wernher von Braun, the German scientist who figured significantly in the Wehrmacht programs that developed the V-1 and V-2 missiles near the end of World War II. He was known for his expertise regarding missile development; and we, sitting in the small, steep auditorium of the West Academic Building, were not surprised to hear his technical analysis of the latest developments in delivery systems and capabilities. Then, near the end of his talk, he turned to future possibilities and said to us, "I assure you that within your lifetimes, man will walk on the moon."

His words generated soft ripples of suppressed laughter as we tried hard to keep from being impolite. I was embarrassed at our manners, but also stunned that a scientist of high reputation would make such a daring prediction, and disappointed to think that a person of his stature would be such a showman. As the little auditorium emptied out, the cynical cadet comments that I remember were along the lines of "What will he tell us next?"

7

Fort Benning: Just Like Artillery, Only Bigger

"The arrival of nuclear weapons on the battlefield"

I signed in at Fort Benning on Monday, 9 August 1954, on a typical hot, muggy summer day in Georgia. As we began the fifteen-week Basic Infantry Officer Course, I spent the Labor Day holiday weekend driving to Atlanta to see the Civil War battlefields. I wrote to my father, "I think we ought to try to make a book of battlefields. This one [Kennesaw Battlefield] was very interesting. I did not have enough time to explore the whole distance to Kennesaw Mountain, but I did look over very closely the spot on Cheatham's Hill where the 4th Vol. Inf. attacked—commanded at that point by a sergeant."

At Benning I received my serving of the basics of infantry tactics: how to lead at the level of rifles and machine guns and mortars. Missing, I felt, was the personal experience of combat, the understanding in some detail of what actually happened to others who faced leadership challenges of the kind we lieutenants might encounter. The solutions to the problems we were presented with were uninspiring: we were given a hypothetical situation—"If this happened, what would you do?" After we answered, we were told, "Well, here's the best solution; this is what Fort Benning says you should do." I asked an officer on the faculty, Captain Philip Bardos, a veteran of Korea and a member of the Weapons Department of the school, about this. Was there any book, any collection of examples of squad and platoon combat from the war now just finished or from earlier times? It seemed to me that a loose-leaf book would be good for a study of small-unit tactics: one side would show a sketch map, and the other side would present a historically accurate factual situation—for example, the story of an ambush: "I was attacked by such and such from this direction and also from this other direction. My men were pinned down and I had a man wounded; however, I did have contact with the artillery." This was the situation. Now, after you have studied the map, what would you do? "OK, in this case I would do this and I would do that and that." Then you turn the page, where you find not the school solution, but what the person actually did, for better or for worse. It might be better than your plan, it might not be; it might have been successful, and it might not have been—but at least now you have thought about this historical situation enough to have become really involved in it, and now you understand what the officer involved actually did. Maybe he made a mistake or maybe he pulled it off pretty well; but at least this isn't somebody's school solution. The value would be in the authenticity of the stories. The book would start out as a pamphlet and grow as we were able to find contributors.

Captain Bardos and I drew up a letter explaining what we wanted to do. Captain Bardos knew many infantry lieutenants and sergeants who had fought in small-unit engagements in Korea, and we wrote to them. We said we wanted to publish a pocket edition of combat situations, titled "A Platoon Leader's Decisions." We recognized that in any war the small unit, the platoon, the squad is the driving force, and its leader the inspiration. In a rather stilted way, we tried to coax responses to a questionnaire that we sent to a long list of veteran leaders, along with a letter signed by Bardos. We wanted to come as close as possible to the reality of combat—to a true experience—rather than offering a theoretical problem with its school-approved solution. We told each other that leaders should learn not from the perfect example but rather in the way that most things are learned—by trial and error. Our format, we decided, would allow new pages of text and maps to be inserted, so that each leader's notebook eventually could be distinct in its content.

But time ran out. Getting combat stories was slow and hard. The events were too recent, and officers were reluctant to assert a personal version that might be seen by others involved as subjective. The style of our letter was not entirely helpful. We asked not for simple yes or no answers, but for detailed descriptions of the action, including dates, places, and unit identification, followed by analysis and conclusions. The conclusions we sought were not "what to do," but "what I did."

This approach proved naïve, as we learned from the replies we received to our letter. Captain Bardos and I went on to new assignments, and our attempt to create the book by mail grew unwieldy. Many wished us well and expressed interest in reading the product, but practically no one wanted to contribute. Some were reluctant to talk about successful actions, worried that their tale would be seen as self-promotion—"a war story." One officer replied that he was better at making the right tactical moves than he would be at writing about them. And when it came to failed operations, we had no volunteers at all.

The largest group of recipients was comprised of those who simply didn't answer. We thought our potential authors would be bursting to tell their stories. But as it turned out, not many lieutenants wanted to "go public" on tactical situations that could be seen from several very different angles. We had expected too much.

I didn't stop, however.

I bought an English translation of *The Most Important Principles for the Conduct of War to Complete My Course of Instruction of His Royal Highness the Crown Prince,* written by General Carl von Clausewitz, revered by many as the greatest of all military thinkers. The Crown Prince was Russian czar Alexander I, who was moving his army against Napoleon in 1812. "These principles," wrote Clausewitz, ". . . will stimulate and serve as a guide for your reflections."

Second Lieutenant Galvin thereupon added to the margins his own reflections, among them that he found Clausewitz somewhat cloudy in his assertions. For example, Clausewitz had written:

> In our plan of battle we must set this great aim: the attack on a large enemy column and its complete destruction. If our aim is low, while that of the enemy is high, we will naturally get the worst of it.

To that I appended:

> Plan well, but don't try to make all the enemy's decisions for him.
>   Put yourself in his shoes, but remember that he is still wearing them.

On tactics, considering the employment of divisions and corps in the attack, Clausewitz writes:

> The true method consists in giving each commander . . . the

main direction of his march, pointing out the enemy as the objective and victory as the goal.

My bold reply reads:

> This whole paragraph is no good. Control is too vague, respon-sibilities not clear. It is hard to see how this could have applied even then.

While I was criticizing Clausewitz, Fort Benning and the rest of the Army were trying to figure out how to deal with a gigantic increase in our enemies' destructive power, and had decided that for the time being our response would stress nonchalance. When I graduated from West Point I entered the Pentomic army, wherein we came to under-stand—we thought—how to deal with the arrival of nuclear weapons on the battlefield. It was all a matter of dispersion and the use of greater firepower, and we certainly could handle that. We would spread out on the battlefield, in units too small to be much of a target, and when the enemy massed their ground forces for an attack on us, we would fire our nuclear artillery and destroy them.

At Fort Benning we learned how to do this from confident instruc-tors. We were told that atomic weapons were just like artillery, only bigger—nothing new, just the latest in a long history of improvements in the support of infantry. There were, admittedly, a few novelties that we needed to take into account. One was fallout. This was explained by means of a series of diagrammatic exercises. We calculated the radius of probable error. We laid out wind vectors and the height of burst. We had beautifully simple map exercises wherein we plotted the impact point of a nuclear strike and planned our maneuver to overrun a stunned enemy. Simple enough. From this we were to gain confidence that we were moving from the unknown to the known in logical steps.

The atomic weapon of choice in 1954 was the short-range tacti-cal nuclear missile. This was to be a battlefield warhead with limited accuracy but a powerful delivery of lethal radiation. Templates showed how we would size up our enemy, choose our targets for maximum advantage, and fire to destroy the amassing forces. Wearing gas masks if necessary, we would advance into the target area or bypass it, and then—what? A success would mean we now controlled a hot area, whereupon all the responsibilities of an occupation would fall to us. Somehow or other, this would constitute a victory.

After these events and others in the Basic Infantry course, I joined the officers going to the Airborne School just down the road, for more advanced infantry training. This consisted of three weeks of physical exercise and jumps from skeleton-stripped and grounded cargo planes, followed by jumps from a thirty-four-foot-tall steel tower.

My roommate and lifelong pal was Spanish Army lieutenant Joaquin Caridad Arias. We made our first jump in early February 1955. I expected to find myself falling directly down, as if I were jumping off a cliff, but I had not counted on the speed of the 119 Boxcar plane when I lunged out into the slipstream. I whipped rearward like a cigarette that had been tossed out of a speeding car window. Following the training I'd received from the jump sergeants, I counted: "One thousand, two thousand, three thousand, four thousand" and waited for the opening shock, but nothing happened: I had counted too fast. My immediate reaction was to holler, "Four thousand!!" to my parachute, as if we had agreed on something and it was not following through. It promptly opened. Gratified, I sailed away toward the rest of my life.

At about this time in the course the school announced a few openings for second lieutenants in the 65th Infantry Regiment, stationed in Puerto Rico. Spanish speakers were preferred. A few of my classmates accepted, but most maintained their assignments to coveted positions with units in Germany. With my two years of Spanish in high school and two more at West Point, I felt ready to put the language to work. So I gave up my assignment to Germany and signed up for the 65th.

The prevailing wisdom was to go where the action was; and the action was in Europe. Nevertheless, I saw this as a chance to stand out, to take a path less traveled—and it turned out to be a good choice.

Our class made the required four more jumps, gained the wings of Army parachutists, and departed to duty around the world. I stayed, and with several of my classmates set off for Ranger School, on another part of Fort Benning. There, a new Ranger class was forming under the leadership of Captain Robert C. Kingston, a tough veteran of the Korean War who had the reputation of having spent more time behind enemy lines than on our side. It so happened that the first week of this Ranger course was deemed a refresher for student officers who were already trained and up-to-date on orienteering and some other skills. I was told I was free for the first week. That sounded strange to me, so I decided to go out to the school anyway, to see whether I should elect to take the first week or not. I quickly found the answer when I reported to Captain Kingston at the Ranger barracks. He informed me, and not too politely, that I had damned well better get my rump into the barracks prior to sundown—an invitation that I hastily accepted, which proved wise.

The Ranger School emphasized teaming, with the use of a buddy system, to such a degree that the success or failure of either member of the two-man team would apply to both.

One night in late February I found myself in freezing rain up in the mountains of Toccoa, Georgia. At midnight, the moon was only a skinny crescent, yet bright enough to make it fairly easy to navigate. Our mission: night reconnaissance. Our patrol of six lieutenants had orders to find the location and type of enemy activity at a point about a mile to our front. In other words, go out and reconnoiter a certain road and come back and report the activity on that road. I was the leader, and my Ranger buddy, Ed Cutolo, was my second in command. Faces blackened, wearing caps instead of helmets, we set off in a file about ten feet apart. Our instructor, camouflaged to the degree that we were, took a place in the middle, saying nothing. In that formation we moved downhill into a jungle of tall brush and trees. We followed a map and compass course to a stream about knee-deep and started uphill, when we heard a truck motor ahead on the azimuth we were following. I moved the patrol closer to the sound. When I judged us to be about a hundred yards from the truck, I halted the patrol and got together with Cutolo to confirm the plan we had worked out earlier: I would go up and take a look while he brought our troops together, ready to support me if I needed it. Cutolo would take over the mission if necessary. I made my way up the hill toward the sound of the truck. The faculty observer followed quietly about five yards behind.

When I neared the truck, I saw that it was moving slowly along a trail, passing back and forth in front of two or three artillery pieces. It was a representation, a very simple one, of a truck resupplying artillery. So what to do? I had a burp gun with me, with blank ammo in it. The truck came rolling close by and I stayed out of sight. It turned around a hundred or two hundred yards up the dirt road and came back very slowly. At this point I made my first of several mistakes. I caught up with the truck and jumped up on the running board on the driver's side of the cabin. I stuck the gun in the driver's face and said, "Just keep driving." He said, "OK." The trail opened on a small field, and I could see a howitzer and crew. As we passed the artillery pieces, I fired away with my burp gun. This was a reconnaissance patrol, and instead

I was playing John Wayne. In the meantime, my observing instructor had blown a gasket. By the time we were back in camp, he gave me a lecture I have never forgotten.

In another phase of my Ranger training we moved to the swamps of north Florida. This time Ed and I took the lead, riding a black patrol boat to a night landing on the Gulf side of the Santa Rosa strip of islands, moving inland with our team through the swamps, finding and rescuing some prisoners, and returning. Fortunately, this time we were successful in our mission.

Of all the schools in the Army and elsewhere, Ranger School was the one that taught me the most about leadership.

8

Puerto Rico: Schooling

"The word 'impossible'"

After Ranger School, I drove to the Brooklyn Navy Yard, turned in my car for shipment to Puerto Rico, and on the last day of March 1955 found myself looking up in awe as our troopship eased into the narrow channel between Isla de Cabras and the looming walls of the fortress San Felipe del Morro. The ever-pounding waves out of the north pushed us along through the slot and into San Juan Harbor, where we docked at Fort Buchanan.

My orders sent me to the 65th Infantry Regimental Combat Team. I arrived at Ponce as a platoon leader just in time to go on a field maneuver. I scrambled into my fatigues and boots, then dashed for the line of trucks. The lead vehicles were already on the move, and by the time I ran down to the truck bearing the I Company guidon I was barely able to find the platoon and jump for the tailgate before we moved out. My platoon sergeant gave me a hand and pulled me in. I told him that I was the new platoon leader and said, "You've probably heard about that." He replied, rather mournfully, "Yes."

As we bounced along under the canvas with the dust pouring in over the tailgate, I went down the line of seats and shook hands with the squad leaders and troops. It was awkward: stepping over packs and weapons and ration boxes; trying to talk over the noise of the truck's engine and the flip-flap of loose canvas. Sergeant First Class Vidró had been the acting platoon leader for quite a while, and he was still the platoon leader as far as he was concerned. He made room for me, though, and we shook hands, and amid quizzical looks I squeezed in between him and the tailgate. As we drove along, first through the cane fields and then up into the hills of the National Forest, I quizzed him on what we could anticipate on arrival, and on how we could expect the day to go.

Sergeant Vidró was taciturn, his responses hesitant. He looked off into the dust behind us and said something close to, "It will be just like always. An order from the captain and we move out." It was hard to extract much more detail. After we got out to the forest, Vidró and I had our first of several talks about how we would work this out: what his job was now as platoon sergeant once again and what mine was as platoon leader. It was the first big challenge that I faced in my professional life: to keep him motivated and happy, to keep the platoon itself feeling that the right thing had been done, and to insert myself into the proper leadership position. All this took place over several weeks.

Our field maneuvers in Puerto Rico with the 65th followed a certain pattern, in accordance with the colonel's goal, which was to improve our ability to fight a nuclear war. We would move out to some area that we had rented, seize the best ground, dig our foxholes deep, and await the aggressors. Our plan was to defend as long as we could, then pull back quickly (at night), leaving a small covering force and falling back ten kilometers. Before first light, we would fire a nuclear weapon equivalent to thousands of tons of conventional explosives, which the umpires out in front of us would simulate by detonating a barrel of a gasoline mix. Then—watching carefully in order to avoid our own fallout pattern—we would charge forward and mop up, attacking and defeating the remaining enemy. On a warm, gentle, breezy night in Puerto Rico, with our hill position surrounded by distant fires as the harvested sugar cane fields were burnt off, the sweet smell drifting over us—along with the smell, as in a library, of oxidizing paper—and the sudden flash of fire on the top of a hill gave me a sense of vertigo. One time I said to the company commander, "We're only backing up a mile or so. The radius from ground zero would be far more than that." With a pained look he explained, "If we back up any more we'll be outside the training area that we rented."

Every soldier in my platoon was Puerto Rican, but among the first things I learned was the prohibition against speaking Spanish on duty. No Spanish whatsoever, not even a friendly word or two in passing. I decided to quietly modify the rule by using Spanish to aid and abet the improvement of my soldiers' English. No one seriously challenged that, and indeed the rule was mostly ignored in practice.

Soon I was beginning to feel comfortable, if far from fluent, in the language. Still a bachelor, I moved quickly into the life of Puerto Rico, often to the bolero music of Rafael Muñoz—"Caminos de Ayer," "Niebla de Riachuelo," "Olvidame"—and the merengue at the Club

Deportivo de Ponce. In my 1952 Ford I traveled over the mountains from Ponce to Mayagüez and to places like Adjuntas along roads on which every driver had fastened a rotating knob to the steering wheel to help spin it on the hairpin curves that had names like Curva de Hasta Luego (Curve of So Long) and Curva de Dios Me Bendiga (Curve of God Bless Me).

After I had been platoon leader for a while, in August 1955, I was charged with creating and running the Expert Infantry Badge test for the regiment. I wrote the test and had seven officers and several enlisted men under me administer the test to three hundred men and twenty-five officers of the 65th. Fifteen officers and two enlisted men passed the test. "*Hard,*" I wrote to my father. "*Colonel was mad.*" It was a situation in which there were not enough resources to make it the right kind of test. It was thrown together with support from units in different places and I, as a brand-new lieutenant, was trying to run it.

After all of the work that goes into staffing and running students through, and after the efforts of the students themselves, mealtime needs to provide a little boost to morale and some decent food. Several times during the testing I had gone into the mess hall, which was just a tent out in a field, where I found the food poorly cooked. One night I went in and noticed that the only person sitting there eating was my clerk, PFC Pfaff. I went over to join him and noticed he was trying to eat rock-hard potatoes—and I got upset. I walked up to the serving table and called for the mess sergeant. I picked up three or four of the potatoes and said, "This is bad stuff to be feeding the troops." He said, "What's the matter with it?" And I said, "Let me show you." I began throwing the potatoes around the tent, bouncing them off the stoves and everywhere else, like golf balls. In the meantime, the duty officer had walked into the back of the tent. He asked me what was going on, and I told him. The word got around and the troops were happy, but the colonel was infuriated.

It was just then that the regiment was opening a school for non-commissioned officers (NCOs) based on the Fort Benning Ranger School model, teaching leadership by the use of patrols. The school commander was to be Captain Ralph Puckett. I got word that Captain Puckett was looking for me, so I set out along the dirt runway looking for him. It was only two months since I'd arrived in the regiment, and my job was about to change.

I already knew and admired Puckett as possessing unbelievable physical stamina even with his several combat wounds, and as a calm, straightforward, effective leader under all conditions, a man whose motto was well known: "The word 'impossible' does not exist."

Back in 1952, the U.S. Eighth Army was up on the South Korea–China border. It was much stretched and weakened, and its commander was scraping up every unit he could find to add to his force. Someone on the staff found that the 25th Infantry Division had been authorized to receive a company of Rangers, but no Rangers had ever been added to the division. Lieutenant General Walton H. Walker called for Puckett and said, "Find the troops somewhere, give them a leader, train them, and send them up here right away."

Puckett commandeered soldiers from U.S. rear units in South Korea and Japan and arrived up on the front lines in time to lead the point units as the corps was being driven back by Chinese forces. In these actions he was wounded three times and earned the Distinguished Service Cross. (Later, in Vietnam, he was awarded a second DSC and two Silver Stars while being twice more wounded.) He had recommended me for the position of operations officer at the NCO School, and he continued to help and encourage me throughout my life. I will remember Ralph Puckett, like Joe Conmy, as a quintessential combat soldier.

Puckett expected miracles. One day he nonchalantly commented, "We need a grandstand over there for the people visiting tomorrow." I said, "Yes, sir," and made an entry in my notebook, adding to the long list of requests he had already given—enough, probably, for a couple of weeks of work. As usual, our team huddled together afterward to sort out the tasks.

Puckett talked leadership and tactics and very little else. We members of the school staff all agreed that this was to be a crash course for us, the team, as well as for the students.

I wrote to my father, "We are trying to push enough men through this mill to make this a combat-ready outfit, and they are coming along fine"—and then a month later we got news that the Army was taking our regiment off the active rolls.

Moving back from the NCO School to I Company in Ponce in October 1955, I became commander of my truncated, fading company. Being "Acting Company Commander" felt good. I had a home, but not for long. Sergeant Vidró and I were the ones who locked the barracks doors and said good-bye to the regiment a few months later, while Captain Puckett left to help establish a Ranger School in Colombia. I was sent up to Antilles Command Headquarters in San Juan as the Assistant Training Officer for the post. (The Training Officer was on the pistol team, taking part in the Army's annual marksmanship competition at

Camp Perry in Ohio.) I met Master Sergeant Wallace, the training sergeant, and asked him to help me figure out what I was supposed to
be doing. He showed me, and I started studying the list of my duties,
where I came upon this intriguing reference: "This headquarters will go
on an annual bivouac."

This was 1956, and Antilles Command was left over from World
War II, when the United States had built airfields all the way down to
the Galapágos to meet the great fear that Japan was going to attack us
at the Panama Canal. The Command headquarters at Antilles had two
L-19 scout planes at the airfield, and eight maintenance sergeants for
these two airplanes.

I had right in front of me the standing orders that we were supposed to go on an annual bivouac to a place called Punta Salinas, which
was about twenty miles away. I issued an order. The Headquarters
would go to the field. Then one day I got word that the Antilles Command Operations Officer wanted to see me about the bivouac. I hurried
to the massive headquarters building, expecting some sort of praise. As
soon as I had reported to him he barked, "Shut the door!" So I shut the
door. He said, "Who in the hell do you think you are?" I said, "Sir?" He
said, "How could you possibly have come up with this bivouac without even addressing it with me?" He bellowed, "Do you realize—do
you know that the last time this headquarters went on a bivouac we
not only lost tents and tables, we lost desks, we lost everything, we lost
millions of dollars' worth of stuff? This staff couldn't go on a bivouac
if it would save their lives. How did you ever come up with this? Why
didn't you talk to me first? You get back to that office of yours and don't
ever let me see you again!" I think he said much more than that, too.

In the end, we did go on the bivouac, a series of field exercises in
which our success was mixed. Master Sergeant Wallace and I pulled
together a seven-man team of clerks to join us as the opposing force,
with our group's mission defined as: harass the headquarters, feigning
attacks against the outposts by day and by night, with me in the lead.
This we did well until the last night, when a headquarters defender
threw an artillery simulator that bounced up against my leg and
exploded. I spent the next three days in the hospital, where the two
girls that I liked most visited me at the same time. These were not my
best moments.

At the foot of the walls of San Felipe del Morro was a door leading out
to a gun position just above water level. There my boss had constructed

a pistol range where he practiced for meets. He was an Army champion, and I fired along with him and learned much.

In January 1956 I was assigned living quarters in the wall of San Felipe del Morro. The wall facing the sea is miles long—so extensive that it is an integral part of the old city, made up not only of watchtowers but also of forts, big and small. I lived in San Sebastian Bastion: a romantic place now, with beautiful masses of stone, but grim in the days of imperial war and banditry—an odd mix of dreamy, paradisaical aspects versus the cold historical facts of how the native Boriquas were exploited and eventually eliminated in the process of building these giant stone fortresses, used to defend against the attacks of fellow Europeans.

Close by, the Property Disposal Yard was full of books on sale for pennies—mostly secondhand, worn library books. I shipped home three or four footlockers full of books, essentially the beginning of my library; I still go back to them. Among them I came across a booklet that seemed very close to the kind of studies that Philip Bardos and I had attempted at Fort Benning: "Small Unit Actions during the German Campaign in Russia." This was part of a series of pamphlets published in the 1950s by the U.S. Army, based on manuscripts created by its European Command Historical Division. I read the whole series, which concentrates on small-unit tactical experiences and evaluations. To me these pamphlets were a gold mine of information about Soviet military leaders at my professional level.

The series contains a short appraisal of airborne operations. It is a gem, containing contributions by nearly all the key figures in the development and leadership of German parachute forces: General Field Marshal Albert Kesselring, General Eugen Meindl, Colonel General Kurt Student, Major General Werner Ehrig, and Oberst Friedrich August Freiherr von der Heydte. The last I later came to know, and he helped me substantially with my own writings in the field. Kesselring makes extensive remarks in the study, which is introduced by Franz Halder, chief of staff of the German Army from 1938 to 1942.

In these booklets the surviving leaders of the Wehrmacht give their reasons for failure. The bad weather, the mud, the cold. The crazy orders of Hitler, which took away their initiative. The logistics of fighting on two fronts. Several of the former German generals, commanders who fought on the eastern front, were commissioned to recount their experiences. Thus, in "Operations of Encircled Forces" (#23-230) we read:

The [Russian] soldier seemed to need nothing and to withstand everything. His fatalistic attitude enables the Russian to bear extreme hardship and privation. He can suffer without succumbing. . . . The frugality of the Russian soldier was beyond German comprehension. . . . At times he subsisted on wild berries or the bark of trees. His personal equipment consisted of a small field bag, an overcoat, and occasionally one blanket, which had to suffice even in severe winter. Since he traveled so light he was extremely mobile and did not depend on the arrival of rations and personal equipment during the course of operations. (p. 3)

And this:

In the twinkling of an eye, the terrain in front of the German line teemed with Russian soldiers. They seemed to grow out of the earth, and nothing would stop their advance for a while. Gaps closed automatically and the mass surged on until the supply of men was used up and the wave, substantially thinned, receded again. The Germans often witnessed this picture of a typical Russian attack. It is impressive and astounding, on the other hand, how frequently the mass failed to recede, but rolled on and on, nothing able to stop it. . . . Only the true soldier, the experienced individual fighter, could in the long run stand up under the strain; only a multitude of them could stop these masses. (p. 26)

Or this:

The Russians were superior to all peoples in Central and Western Europe in enduring rigors of weather and climate. Casualties from the cold were an exception in the Red Army. Soldiers with frostbite were severely punished. Even in the harsh winter of 1941–1942 the Russians were able to spend many days in the snow, protected only by simple windbreaks. (p. 39)

As I read these pamphlets in the old Spanish fortress at the entrance to the San Juan harbor, the sweep of the massive Soviet counterattack westward, a thousand miles from Moscow and Stalingrad to Berlin, had one central meaning: even under the conditions of 1942, when it had been smashed and overrun to the degree that many in the West saw its defeat as palpably imminent, the Soviet Union had the power to stagger to its feet—under fire—and roll back a formidable enemy. In the language of infantry small units, these were tough fighters: resourceful, tenacious, unyielding even under the worst of conditions.

One of the strategic messages carried a particular significance. On the level of grand strategy, Hitler, like Napoleon, had grossly underestimated the strength and resiliency of the Russians.

9

Lanceros: *Continuen*

"I realized I was thinking all of this out in Spanish."

In October 1956, a query came to the Antilles Command headquarters from Infantry Branch: "Is Lieutenant Galvin available for transfer to the U.S. Army Mission to Colombia?" Captain Ralph Puckett had recommended me as his replacement at the Colombian Lancero School. I was elated—I felt like a lost swimmer who sees the rescue boat headed his way. It's quite possible that some of the San Juan headquarters people felt the same sense of relief after the fiasco of the "annual" bivouac.

Within three weeks I was in Bogotá. The Lancero School, named in honor of a small group of heroic lancers who fought with Simón Bolívar, is very much like the U.S. Army's Ranger School: it uses tactical patrolling as a means of small-unit leadership training. With barracks atop a four-hundred-foot mesa in the Sumapaz River Valley, a three-hour drive southwest of Bogotá, the student lieutenants and sergeants go through a grueling two months of mountain and jungle operations at platoon level, opposed by a Colombian infantry company that plays the role of the enemy. Preparatory training includes rock climbing and rappelling, which happened to be in progress on the day I arrived. The site, called La Roca, was one of the abrupt cliffs that mark the edge of the mesa and provide magnificent views of the Sumapaz and the mountains on the opposite side. At the rope training point, the cliff makes a sheer drop of thirty-five feet to a narrow ledge, then drops another thirty feet to the river below.

From my notes:

> Monday, 22 October 1956—Arrived at the Lancero School with Lt. Col. Sadler. Went out to the rappelling site to watch

the class. Lt. Patino in charge, teaching the hasty rappel with hand-over-hand climb to return to the top. Lt. Fernandez, demonstrating the technique, went down and started back up. He neared the top, just a foot or two away. I watched him falter, lose his hold on the rope, and begin to slide against the wall. I felt as if I were falling myself. My arm muscles tightened. There was nothing to do but join in the yells of the group, urging him to hold on. He managed to maintain his grip on the ¾ inch manila rope during part of the fall, which caused severe burns on both hands but probably saved his life. About fifteen feet from the bottom he struck an out-jutting piece of rock and tumbled from there to the ledge, where he landed between the wall and a large stone that kept him from rolling off and falling the rest of the way to the river below.

My first entry in my log that night was, "F. finally brought up on a Swiss seat with much trouble and taken to Tolemaida infirmary and sewed up."

Lieutenant Roberto Fernandez Guzman, a graduate of the U.S. Army's Ranger School, was assigned to help develop the Lancero School because he had proven to be a successful leader in combat against some of the most dangerous of the guerrilla groups of that time. He was short, fiery, erect, and handsome. He had a boxer's body, powerful of neck and back, and a quick hand. He also hated flies, and there were many to hate. It was his habit to catch them on the wing and nonchalantly dash them to their deaths against the floor, this without interrupting the flow of his conversation.

Fernandez was a cavalry officer, an extraordinary rider, who kept a half-wild horse at the Escuela de Caballería in Bogotá. I rode at the school with him just one time; he selected for me a horse much tamer than his, but still a monster who at the first good opportunity brushed me off against the paddock wall. It was a kind of initiation, the thing that fighter pilots like to do with unsuspecting neophytes when they take them up for a ride. Fernandez became my closest friend among the many officers that I got to know in Colombia. He was also the very best of the lieutenants who served as instructors and students at the Lancero School.

One night on a patrol, Fernandez and I slept in an abandoned mud-and-wattle little wreck of a house with a roof of straw bundles. At dawn I woke up to see that the ridge pole was moving just slightly. I shook my partner and said, "I think the roof is moving." He rubbed his eyes and said, "So it is." The boa moved a little more, which showed his length and girth, and we agreed it would be better if we left.

Settling into my new responsibilities as advisor to the school, I assumed that full support and understanding from my boss in Bogotá, Colonel Murray Cheston, would be forthcoming. That didn't quite happen, however—and I must admit I could have done much more to *make* it happen. Two days into the job, I got a telephone call from Lieutenant Colonel Sadler, who told me that Colonel Cheston wanted my views on how young officers could be retained in higher percentages in the U.S. Army. There was some kind of questionnaire he had to answer. The only experience I had in Army units, however, was my time with the (dissolving) 65th Infantry and the (antiquated) Antilles Command Headquarters. Ruminating over the lack of inspiration in those experiences, I concluded that, with the exception of the time I served under Captain Puckett, there was not much to say about the joys of being a lieutenant. This was my chance to speak out. I took a deep breath and sounded off. As I look at my log now, it is painful to see what I wrote:

> 1. Many junior officers have already decided on a civilian career before entering the service. 2. Present economic situation in civilian life is good. 3. Army work is hard, long hours. 4. Operations within service sometimes disgust young officers. 5. Prestige of officers not as high as that of doctors, lawyers, engineers. 6. Young officer is not too affected by retirement plans and security. Suggest more pay, more prestige, better post standards.

I had no idea how much friction my first communication with headquarters would cause. It was certainly not the right way to start out with Colonel Cheston. Three months later, at his first opportunity to submit an opinion of me, he wrote: "Not self-contained . . . opinionated . . . stubborn . . . immature judgment."

Discouraged, I wrote to Captain Puckett and asked for his advice, telling him that the colonel had never visited the school, so he must be depending on what I wrote him. Puckett wrote back to share with me some thoughts on communication. He asked, "Have you invited the Colonel to visit the camp? Are you giving him full information in your reports? *Stay in touch.* See him at every chance you get."

In the meantime, Colonel A. A. Greene, an officer I saw only once in my life, came to visit the Lancero School. I knew he was from headquarters in the Panama Canal Zone, but it did not occur to me that he might be the reviewer of my efficiency report. I showed him around the camp, told him what I was trying to do, and tried to answer his many questions—which were right on target, and which impressed me almost as much as his fluent Spanish. Later I found that he had recommended to West Point that I be sent there to teach Spanish. What I did not discover for more than thirty years was his grasp of my simplistic and tactless ways, and his determination to change Colonel Cheston's view of his lieutenant at the Lancero School. Going through records years later, I found that he had convinced my boss to reverse, almost word for word, his next couple of reports. When I came to know this, I sought to look him up; but by then Colonel Greene, an artillery battalion commander in World War II, had passed away. God bless him. I didn't deserve the care and concern he gave to my situation and his patience with my tendency toward abrupt responses. He and Captain Puckett helped pull me out of a deep rut. It would take much more time, however, before I learned about tact.

Most of the Colombian instructor officers stayed at the school during the week and returned home on weekends. We lived two to a room in a barracks next to a plain but beautifully classic two-story old plantation house with a broad veranda on all four sides, about a mile across the mesa from the school. The house, then called Tolemaida, was our officers' club. There was nowhere else to go, so we spent our free time sitting around a couple of large Formica-topped tables, smoking powerful Pielroja cigarettes and exchanging stories. Several of us were there late one afternoon when a soldier hurried in to report a drowning in a pond close by. We rushed to the spot, where we saw people standing in a circle around a body on the ground. They had pulled the soldier from the water, but no one seemed to know what to do next. I couldn't remember how to say "artificial respiration" in Spanish, so I asked if anyone had given first aid. Next, to quote from my notes:

> No comprehension, and no time to do anything but begin myself. I used the old style. Soldier prone, head turned, arm under head, pressure on the lower back and then release. The crowd of onlookers grew and grew. Some said he had been under for only three or four minutes. It was hot, and the soldier felt warm and limber. More and more people gathered, but

not a one knew how to do artificial respiration, so they urged me on, confident that I could bring him back. I worked on him for three hours, because I couldn't bring myself to give up. I stopped when blood came from his mouth. I had been kneeling over him for so long that I couldn't get up for a minute or two. I had to be helped home, because my legs got cramped.

We added first aid to our list of classes.

Monday, 19 November 1956. The talk among officers was all about the Prague rebellion: the depth of the resistance—5,000 Czech citizens and 3,500 Soviets; the executions. General Rojas Pinilla, president of Colombia, arrived, on a visit to observe the ongoing construction of our training center. This was not long before he would be forced out of the presidency he had gained in a coup that promised to end the Violencia (he would remain a strong force in Colombian politics). The Lancero students and the troops of the Battalion Colombia, led by veterans of Korea, were armed with American M-1 (Garand) rifles. To achieve a level of realism in tactical training maneuvers of small units against each other, we needed blank ammunition, along with small explosives to simulate hand grenades. We had none of this training ammunition in the school, so we made our own by hand. We modified live rounds by removing the steel bullet from the cartridge, taking out some of the powder, then substituting a hand-carved wooden plug of roughly the same shape as the steel bullet. This allowed the plug to "chamber" (enter into the barrel) easily, but there were disadvantages: when we fired the cartridge, the wood plug would disintegrate and the flaming pieces would travel in short, erratic streaks, which at night sometimes looked like tracers.

As a rule, the soldiers on maneuvers also carried clips of live ammunition in some of the pockets of their cartridge belts, because the Lancero School patrols passed through areas in which guerrillas sometimes operated. The troops kept white medical tape over the live rounds, but the tape didn't always survive the vicissitudes of operations in the mountains and the tension and haste of an action, so now and then we would hear the crack of a live round. This led to some uneasy moments, but no soldier in Colombia wanted to be without live ammunition.

There was another problem related to realistic training: we had no means of simulating the automatic fire of a machine gun. Instead, we fired live rounds from U.S. M-1 carbines into the air.

Makeshift approaches like these afforded a certain level of experience to the trainees, but the risk of accident was high. And there was a third arrangement that added to the risk. We also felt it was necessary to simulate the sound of grenades and artillery. Our solution was to use ordinary dynamite sticks, which we would cut into halves or quarters, then pack fuses into the pieces. During training patrols we would light the fuse and toss the stick off to one side.

A day earlier, on Sunday, 18 November 1956, Lieutenant Villegas had been in charge of the opposing force, comprising about thirty soldiers, while most of the school's officers joined the student patrols as observers. I decided to go out a few hours ahead with Villegas to help him position the "enemy" in locations where they were likely to make contact with the students. On that night, though, the fighting became *too* realistic, as both sides stumbled into each other. Tempers flared and a melee developed, which Villegas quickly brought under control. Later, with a different patrol at a bridge over the Sumapaz River, the same thing happened. Members of the student patrol, all lieutenants, clearly felt that the "enemy"—all soldiers—were pressing them too hard. My log reads:

> Watched this attack from behind a mud house. Poor treatment of the "aggressor" soldiers. Use of rifle butt and bayonet. Bawled out one Lancero student in English. Soldiers afraid of the officers. Took a rifle and led an attack which caught the patrol resting on a road near the objective. I was so mad and loud that they did not try to capture me. They didn't want to have to listen to me.

Villegas and I moved the soldiers into an ambush position along the likely line of return of another of the student patrols. Near Las Ceibas we deployed the troops on high ground behind a long, low stone wall within a hundred yards of a trail that curved below. Our plan was to let the patrol move into our ambush site, throw some dynamite sticks (not too close to the patrol), and open fire with our wooden bullets and also with live rounds from two carbines on "automatic," aimed at the sky.

The first part of this exercise came off as planned: we caught the patrol in our trap and began to fire our blanks and toss our dynamite. We had cut the sticks in half with bayonets. Some of the red, greasy sticks had settled during storage and were flat-sided. As a result, they were not easy to cut; they tended to become shapeless. As the fight began, there was a bright flash and an earsplitting explosion among the troops on my right along the wall. I saw a soldier stand up and walk away to the rear, cradling his right hand. I trotted over to him. He knelt down, and then sat down. It was Soldado Pulido. His hand was simply bones and tatters, still attached to him by a flap of skin. I did what I'd been taught to do as a medic. I started to cut off his sleeve. But it was taking too much time, so I made a tourniquet from my belt and my knife scabbard, put it halfway up his forearm, and wrapped some gauze, all we had, around his hand. Soldiers one by one held out their bandanas, and I added three or four of those. Pulido was show-ing no signs of shock, but he was hurt in a lot of ways. We covered him up with parts of our uniforms. He had been in the act of throwing a half-stick of dynamite, which exploded just as it left his hand. His right arm and chest were torn by bone splinters from his hand, and splinters made the right side of his face into a half-mask of bristles. His right eye looked bad, but he said he could see pretty well.

Injuries to the other soldiers were minor. Lieutenant Villegas met with Lieutenant Restrepo, who was with the student patrol, and they called a halt to all action. We found that Pulido could walk, which was a great relief because we had no vehicles. It was almost 3:00 a.m. We turned over command to the student patrol leader and to the senior sergeant of the troops, and we started for the road to Girardot, about a half-mile down the slope. We had enough help along with us in case we needed to carry Pulido, but he was strong and quiet and walked well. We guided him. My feeling was that he could see less and less, so I asked him again and he said, "It's getting bright now. I can see better." But it was still dark. It was bright only for him.

Someone went ahead and stopped a pickup truck heading to mar-ket. We all climbed aboard for a bouncing, dusty ride to the clinic at Girardot. It was tough on Pulido. When I asked him how he felt, he thought it over for a while and said, so softly that I could barely hear him, "Only God knows how much this hurts." I had been releasing the tourniquet often, taking it off every five minutes or so, as I had been taught, to allow blood to flow down into his forearm as far as possible.

The clinic was a miserable place. We arrived before dawn and waited two hours for the doctor. In the meantime, Pulido remained composed and silent as we smoked our Pielrojas. I hadn't realized how dirty Pulido was. His face was hard to look at. So much caked blood, dust, mud, shards of bone (which I did not dare to remove), and dried gashes. A lump of bandanas at the end of his arm. His chest peppered with small, oozing cuts.

The room had a long, steel-legged table with a white enamel top, chipped and scratched in a hundred places, parts of it rusty and parts spot-painted off-white. Well-used aprons hanging on the wall were the only decoration. When the doctor entered I told him about the bright light; I was more worried about that than about his hand. The doctor had us help Pulido onto the table, while he put on his (used) apron. Looking more closely at the hand, he said, "Yes, yes, that of course will come off. As for the eye, who knows?" Major Hernando Bernal, the Lancero camp commander, appeared at seven o'clock. We all left soon after. Pulido lost both his right hand and his right eye.

Soon after, rambling around the Lancero supply room, I found a World War II U.S. training grenade—which was just like a combat grenade, except that it was empty of powder and had a hole in the base to show that it was inert. I took one of our "live" grenades, unscrewed the pin mechanism, and lifted out the handle, pin, and detonator, which is all one assembly. I then transferred the mechanism to the inert grenade. If this could serve as a simulator, I thought, we could stop using volatile, unpredictable pieces of dynamite for that task. We could still train realistically in grenade throwing, since the mechanism would work the same way, and the shape and weight of the grenade were practically the same. So: pull the pin, let the handle spring off, throw it, and in about eight seconds the detonator would explode inside the hollow steel shell, giving off noise and smoke through the hole in the bottom. Then the outer casing would be reusable, with a new ring, pin, handle, and detonator. Why didn't we think of this before?

Time to move to the next test. I screwed a detonator mechanism into the empty training grenade, took it outside the barracks, closed the door behind me, removed the pin, let the handle fly, and tossed the grenade about ten feet into the yard. In a few seconds, the grenade exploded with a much louder bang than I expected, sending fragments in all directions. My ears were ringing. The force of the detonator inside the confined space of the training grenade had burst the shell of the thing into about twenty pieces, along the striation lines of the grenade; I found some embedded in the door behind me. My comrades came out of the buildings to see what was going on. I replied nonchalantly that it was nothing, just an experiment that didn't work out too well.

I had other bad days. On 5 December 1956 I returned from a patrol in the mountains and wrote these words in my pocket notebook: "Convinced by this problem that school (as it now functions) comes close to being worthless. Smoking, whistles, calls, no care of rifles, no security, no spirit, no cooperation, no stamina, no knowledge of maps, no ability to use compass, no comprehension of situation, no camouflage, no disposal of wastes, no light discipline, no noise discipline—no discipline."

I don't like this wrinkled page from half a century ago. This was pure venting. I had forgotten my own stupid mistakes in the U.S. Ranger School. What is missing from my notes is a teacher's understanding of the dynamics of learning.

January 1957. Brigadier General Navas Pardo reviewed the new Lancero class on a Monday, after passing overhead in his helicopter and noticing the formation. The review was spontaneous, as were his remarks on the poor uniform discipline of the officers. The general again expressed his interest in the school and exhorted all to study hard and train well. He said he would personally push for solutions of any problems that came up at the school. I of course referred immediately to the lack of training ammunition, and told him the story of Soldado Pulido. A week later, the general invited me to lunch in Bogotá, where I gave him a list of our shortages.

By then I had decided what to do about my frustrations. I wanted to be on the team, not an outsider. If I became a visible help to the team, a coequal, my advice would be more acceptable: they would be hearing it from one of their own. I talked this over with Fernandez and Negret, another of the instructors, who agreed that the school could use another hand at the oars, and that my suggestions would be easier to put across if I were one of the workers. I went to Major Bernal and told him that I thought I could do more for the school than simply make suggestions, especially since he was shorthanded. I could be another instructor, teaching classes and acting as an observer on training patrols. As for assessment and advice, I could provide those in spare moments here and there. The main thing the school needed, I said, was another officer to help carry the load. Two days later, Major Bernal assigned me to teach classes on hand grenades, rifle grenades, demolitions, and map reading. He also added my name to the list of officers assigned to accompany and monitor patrols.

I was, meanwhile, the butt of an ever-growing number of jokes about my errors in Spanish, which was part of a growing camaraderie that I liked very much. My name went from John Rogers Galvin to Juan Rojelio Galvez, echoing a surname popular with the local farmers. Several of my worst malapropisms, with accompanying mispronunciations, became part of the vocabulary of my fellow lieutenants. Bustamonte's name became "Boxtimonte"; hand grenades became "garinadie de manu." The teasing was strong motivation to improve, though even as I got better, my companions resolutely hung on to the original choppy dialect of Juan Rojelio Galvez, giving rise to an exotic species of mimicry. They professed to be learning my dialect.

One evening at the Tolemaida house, trying to juggle some additions to my vocabulary, I realized I could pencil new words on the Formica tabletop and then simply erase them, with no damage done. One by one we all drew up to the table and held our first Spanish-English class, writing and sketching to explain our conversations. This became our main entertainment for the evenings when we were not on patrol or other duties.

It was not a class in the usual sense, however—not by any means. It was more what in English might be called a roast: everybody made fun of everybody else, interruptions were the rule, and oafish assertions were met with equally oafish counterpoints. These evenings of penciling, however lighthearted and jocular, were nonetheless pragmatic; although the talk ranged far and wide and uncontrolled, we all acknowledged, in various ways, that the underlying subjects were two: language and small-unit tactics. One night hilarity ran high, as we all pitched in to help Lieutenant Muñoz, one of our fellow instructors, through several rough drafts of a letter in English to the love of his life at that moment, Hollywood actress Jayne Mansfield, asking for a photo. Muñoz, after much thought and encouragement from the rest of us, selected the most gentlemanly version and sent it off. (Ms. Mansfield replied with her picture, endorsed by a nice note.)

This was an extraordinary time in my life. I had become part of the team, sharing the work of the school, and I was gradually being seen (almost) as Colombian. On those evenings, especially, my contemporaries would forget the difference. In one of our longest sessions, Filiberto Medina Puerto sketched out for us the details of a raid that he had led against a guerrilla headquarters. While he drew on the table and answered questions, all of us helped him translate the story into English. An excerpt will give some idea of those evenings at the plantation house, and of the kind of combat situations for which we trained our students. This was a night attack:

> The farm was surrounded by 8 foxholes at the edge of the patio,
> all of which were occupied immediately by the enemy, and 2 or

3 snipers climbed into trees and began to fire from these positions. Tree snipers were cleared out almost before they were able to get into action. Medina advanced in the center, using his .45 Colt and throwing all the grenades. Rojas, unable to move, continued to fire on the position from 250 yards out. One guerrilla became exasperated with a rifle which would not fire and threw it down, running out to attack M's Sgt with a knife, and was killed. Fight lasted 2 hours. M was able to get grenades into the house. M called to Rojas and told him that he was ready to close on the house. Rojas ceased fire and Medina moved in with a final rush. All guerrillas were killed with the exception of one 80-year-old who was found inside the house. 17 dead in all. 12 Remington rifles cal .22, some shot guns, a 25-pound box of .22 ammunition, field manuals, and personal information on each man. Clean-up patrols sent out on order of Capt Marin after he had been informed of the situation, netted 2 more killed and one prisoner, a boy of 13 carrying 2 revolvers, a belt of ammunition, a hunting knife. No losses were suffered by Medina and his troops.

Medina's report resembled the kind of book that Captain Bardos and I tried to create at Fort Benning.

I was too involved in the discussions that followed, so there are no notes about the rest of the night. We swatted mosquitoes, wiped away sweat, and argued with Medina about the fight and his conclusions. We would talk tactics and small-unit battles, but would invariably get around to asking one question: What would it take to win this war against the guerrilla forces? As lieutenants, we came up with answers that had to do with more troops, better equipment, better training; but we inevitably got around to the underlying issues. There was "La Violencia"—guerrilla and paramilitary civil war violence in Colombia arising from conflicts between the Conservative and Liberal parties. People writing about La Violencia often speak of it as beginning in the 1960s, but in the 1950s it was in full swing, and although many things have changed, it is still strong even as I write this. The Colombian people are resilient and valiant—but so are the guerrillas. The military campaign to suppress La Violencia was then called "Orden Publico." The six brigades of the army were spread across the country with the enormous but vague mission of keeping public order—seeing to it that the local government was able to function, roads were open, and daily life and business were uninterrupted. We referred to the guerrillas as *ban-doleros*—bandits who took advantage of a weak governmental struc-ture and a tepid economy. We wondered if there was an atmosphere of lawlessness that supported violence. We saw a threat from Commu-nist cells helped by the Soviets via Cuba. We were worried about an expanding drug trade. (I had no idea then that in the half-century to follow, the traffic in drugs would tear the country to shreds even as it tried, time after time and crisis after crisis, to re-create itself.)

I talked often with Father Jerome, chaplain for the school, a small and gentle Catholic priest. In this windy, dusty, hot place, wearing his rumpled and no longer white vestments, he was always available for a chat, and deeply concerned about the hard life and sufferings of the indigenous people. Their restlessness, he felt, derived from the com-bined pressure of local caciques (bosses) and the lack of governmental authority, but that was no excuse for their sins. He gave me a book, *Lo que Dios no Perdona* (That Which God Does Not Forgive), and with my dictionary at my side I read the words of another priest, who insisted that the violence had reached a level of ferocity that God would not forgive.

Log entries:

> Saturday 10 November 1956: Changed Sumapaz River patrol to farther downstream to avoid the rapids and variation in height. There have been some close calls with men and equipment.
>
> All five boats underway by 0315. F and myself in the last boat. Lots of obstacles in the river. Used flashlight.
>
> 0330 Rubber boat hits a group of logs in the river and is punctured. After freeing the boat we continue, using one man to keep his hand over the hole. Boat hits two more obstacles and we lose control both times in the fast river. On the fourth obstacle the boat is again punctured by a log or rock. We con-tinue, using two men to cover the holes. Fired on by the aggres-sors from the bridge position. Romero and I separate from the patrol and join the aggressors at the bridge. Attack on the bridge is spirited but too close to out of control. Use of live rounds is a little dangerous but there are no blanks available. Last bunker holds out for thirty minutes, perhaps because all the students know that the firing from the bunker is live rounds. . . . called

off at 0700 as everyone is getting rough. 0730 Confidence test: jumping from bridge, height 24 ft.

"Gringo al agua!" is the call, so I jump too.

For long, dry months the Sumapaz is a sluggish, placid, dull, meandering thing covered in its eddies with blossoms floating on slime, home to billions of living beings that fly, swim, and crawl; but it becomes a different river in its rainy season. The change can come slowly, with a gradual rise in water level, or tumultuously in torrential rains, smashing straight ahead even where the bed of the river turns, gathering trees by the dozens and converting them into battering rams, driving them toward the Magdalena with a force that I had seen only in the ocean. In early November I scratched into my notebook, "Sumapaz rose high last night and took out the pumps." Rainfall in that month was not unusual in amount, but it was steady. The seductive river rose and fell. The farmers can back away, and they do, but the Colombian soldier has to deal with rivers in all their seasons and incarnations, and the Lancers have to set an example: confident and undeterred by the river.

There was a cave-in on the river banks; a soldier fell into the brown roiling Sumapaz and was carried away. When I heard this, I hurried to the barracks and asked to join the search party, but the word had already come that there would be no search.

No search? I remember my astonishment. Negret said he'd been in touch with the major, who said no: the river was too dangerous; we would keep an eye out and wait for the vultures to find him. From the mesa we could see only a few miles of the river. The vultures, from their altitude, could see everything; they would be our guide. Their circling would tell us. It was the way such things were resolved. So Sunday passed, and Monday. On Tuesday the soldier's father and brother came to the post and asked for help in finding him. They were told the same thing: we could not spare troops for such dangerous and probably fruitless work. So they went out to follow the river themselves, the two of them mounted on a farm tractor and towing a trailer. The next day, the waiting was too much for me. Early on Wednesday morning, 28 November, I borrowed Negret's jeep; Sergeant Bermudez, who knew the river, rode with me. We took the road west toward Girardot, following the river downstream, watching the sky, turning down muddy farm trails to get closer to the river, where we could see a few vultures flying aimlessly but nothing more, for several hours. Then, in mid-afternoon, we spotted over the treetops a flock of about twenty vultures gliding and flapping in a broad circle. We drove along pathways through fields, following barbed-wire fences to their crude gates, fording little streams, trying to keep the jeep's nose pointed toward the black, circling birds. We were completely mud-spattered by the time we arrived at the river bank where the birds were gathered. They were feasting on the carcass of a cow.

The local police located the soldier's body at about noon that day and called the military post. When Sergeant Bermudez and I returned, we found that a truck had been sent to recover the body, but it was attacked and damaged on the way by a large bull. That night a second truck brought the soldier's body back to camp and to his exhausted father and brother.

About this time I decided to take a look at the arms room, where weapons and ammunition were stored in racks and on shelves. The regulations of all armies pay great attention to arms rooms, for reasons of accountability and readiness. Everything in the arms room radiates a reverence for orderliness—as did this one, with one startling exception: One corner was piled high with boxes marked "Dynamite 92%," a total of a thousand pounds of sticks. Alongside these boxes were others containing rifle and pistol ammunition. A red liquid had stained the bottoms of the dynamite boxes and was oozing out on the floor. I decided to end my inspection at that point.

I got in touch with Colonel Sadler in Bogotá, who referred me to the engineer advisor, Colonel Guerdum, who observed that dynamite is nitroglycerin mixed with sawdust; it might be that in the heat of the arms room the nitro had liquefied and was leaking out. The boxes, he advised, needed to be turned over with some frequency to keep this from happening. But then again, he continued, maybe you should just get rid of the dynamite. I took up the matter with Fernandez and Negret. Maybe, we thought, we could lay the sticks out in the sun and let them dry. We tried this, but when I consulted Colonel Guerdum, he maintained that the weather could cause further damage. We were determined, however, to keep the dynamite, so we moved the boxes into an unfinished and empty building that was later to become our mess hall.

In early February 1957, Colonel Guerdum paid a visit to the school, and Fernandez and I took him to see the dynamite. We had opened a box or two to show him the condition of the explosives. He stood and looked, silently.

"First," he said, "we're going to back softly out of here. Let's do that." When we got outside, he said he would like to keep walking to get clear of the building, which we did. We stopped fifty yards away, and he grew pensive. He said that the red liquid on the floor was indeed partly nitroglycerin. We needed to remove all the boxes from the building and destroy all the dynamite. He added, with a smile, "Please do it after I leave, and oh . . . don't wear shoes in there." Beyond those comments, as far as I remember, he had no advice about how to get rid of the dynamite. We—Fernandez, Negret, and I—considered what to do. We had no good answer, and in the end we took most of it in several jeep loads down to the river and threw it in.

On 18 February 1957, the Melgar Recruit Training Center opened, with General Rojas present for the dedication ceremony. All the Colombian department governors attended.

Two months later, in April 1957, I was ordered to "assist and advise the Recruit Training Center in the planning and coordination of all matters pertaining to conduct of instruction, programming, scheduling, preparation of subject matter, recruit training doctrine, training inspections, and recruit training tests," while at the same time keeping my original assignment. I was also assigned an extra duty as advisor to the Battalion Colombia, the most modern unit in the Colombian Army, which was being moved from Bogotá to the Melgar Center to take advantage of the larger training areas. And as a fourth job, I was sent to assist with the summer field training of the cadets in the military school in Bogotá.

Of the twelve officers in the U.S. Army Mission, eleven lived in Bogotá and all had Army sedans. Most of the road up through the mountains past Fusagasuga to the capital was unpaved, and I didn't mind rides with Colombian army jeeps and trucks. The colonel did at one point mention to me that my personal appearance on arrival at Mission Headquarters could be better. It was on a day that I had ridden in the back of a Colombian Army ammunition truck, though I normally was able to share a jeep ride with someone from the school. I promptly made a request for one of the Chevrolet pickup trucks, and after some initial reluctance, the sergeant major was forthcoming and I had my truck, but only for a short couple of months. Then it was the truck's appearance that was deemed not up to standard, and I had to give it back to the motor pool, where it could be better cared for.

Letter to my father, 6 April 1957:

Just a short note. The mail is going up now to Bogotá. Have had a lot of success in the last few weeks' training. Battalion "Colombia" is now getting ready to move into Melgar, and I am to be advisor to them. They will be in constant field training. My job gets bigger all the time. The Lanceros have been grouped together for combat at Ibague and have had (this and last week) fantastic success—really a boost for the school. The plan is now to organize a group of assault platoons with Lancero officers and noncoms. Next week I am going to Ibague to see about the organization.

Another letter to my father, 7 May 1957:

On Monday the commanding generals of the six brigades of the army are coming to the Lancero School for a 4-hour orientation, so this Saturday and Sunday are very busy days— like the Rangers, we have to "sell ourselves" to the rest of the army, who don't understand exactly what the school is for, how much it is worth, results, etc. (and who are also a little jealous of the attention we get). On Tuesday I go to Bogotá to talk to the Commander of the Army, General Navas Pardo, to explain what is needed at the school. We are in a bad way—not much ammunition and supply, and a lot of other problems. He is a fine leader, and I hope he'll help us out. He is one of the only officers who really understands the school.

In effect, I was moving Colonel Cheston out of the way and taking over his role. I don't know how I survived this, except for what came next.

Log, Tuesday, 7 May 1957:

Riots in Bogotá and Cali. Vehicles passing here with branches in front of the front wheels to brush tacks out of their path. Lots of rumors and talk of moving units to the large cities.

Log, Wednesday, 8 May 1957:

Students still causing a lot of trouble in Bogotá. 2 killed in riots against the President. Orders that one recruit battalion will go to Bogotá, but no one knows when. Ammo issued and battal-

ion prepared to move. Lot of speeches, etc. being made. President looks very much in control of things, and comments are
that this disorder will soon be quelled. Papers very quiet, since
all are controlled by the government.

Letter to my father, 10 May 1957:

At 0600 it was announced that the President had "resigned"
and that a junta had taken over the country. Everything became
very confused—armed units sent to the house of the camp
commander, all companies of the two battalions receiving arms
and ammunition, plans and preparations to move immediately
to any one of many different cities: Melgar, Bogotá, Girardot—
doubt as to what the Presidential Guard would do next, radio-
grams every 5 minutes, practices for the defense of the post,
issuing of field jackets for cold weather use, such as in Bogotá.
In the afternoon things began to clear up. The junta was formed
by several generals including Navas Pardo, Paris, and others.
They have outlined 15 major points which are their general
aims, including freedom of the press, free passage [along] the
highways, [and] new governors for some of the departments.

Another letter to my father, 11 May 1957:

Announcements and speeches are being made to the people
saying that the Junta Militar will turn the government over to
the people within the year—[so there will be] elections—and
[identifying] the terminating date of the junta, which is 7 October 1958. Many of the major politicians of the two parties spoke
on radio and television this afternoon, calming the people and
saying that they are in agreement with the junta. Our last patrol
came in at 1100, and we are confined to the post, so Dulcey and
I made a recon for a problem at the airstrip in order to have
work for the students tomorrow.

During the month of May, the students at the military school in
Bogotá moved into the mountains above the city for combat training. I
went along.

September 1957, on the outskirts of Sumapaz—the hills so steep
that at least half the time the trail becomes a stairway with thick stone

steps, their treads eroded by centuries of the shuffling climb of humans and animals and from the pounding mountain rains, when the steps become a sluice that can knock you or your mule down. (The soldiers called the altitudes "orange, then coffee, then rocks.") The school was in the patrolling phase of class number six, and I was in charge of the opposing force. I took a platoon from Battalion Colombia across the Sumapaz and up the slopes to rebuild some of the bunkers we used as the targets of Lancero reconnaissance and attack patrols. As we climbed the slopes, I was also looking for more good locations where we might ambush the students. During the long climb I sometimes moved off on my own to study the lay of the land and make some notes on my map, then caught up later when the troops stopped to work on bunkers or simply to rest.

At one point I walked out on a jutting ledge and stood for a few minutes looking back across the valley to the walls of the mesa, formed into a vast triangle by the work of three rivers: the volatile Sumapaz, the Paguey, and the small, quiet, persistent Chelenchele on the right. I could make out Tolemaida in the center of the mesa, my home for more than a year now, and las Ceibas, the trees that characterized the place. Directly below me, still in the shade of early morning, I watched the brown Sumapaz twist around the town of Melgar. Far beyond, fifty miles farther to the east, were the massive mountains, where the red ball of the sun edging up over El Tolima gave warning of a blistering day to come.

I was comforted by the idea that I had managed to fit in well in this faraway place, this corner known to few. But I had work to do. I unfolded my map, which was getting more and more ragged, and turned it to match my view down the slope of our patrol routes. I made out the *taberinto*, the crude cable car in which I had crossed the Sumapaz, and spied it in the dusk below. With that as a reference point, I searched up and down the river with field glasses, looking for new possible crossing places.

I was talking to myself. If the patrols had to cross at the sharp bend I'd spotted in the river, they would be on a point of land hard to traverse and favorable for an ambush site. They would be tempted to use the taberinto to cross the Sumapaz rather than take the time to build rafts. This would concentrate them in a place well known to us. If they did not get through, there were only three or four routes that would allow them to climb the skirts of the valley, which would make their choices more predictable: probably to use a good trail rather than follow a compass azimuth and stay far from the trails, as we had taught them. Our ambushes would be simple to carry out, using high ground that dominated the trails.

I realized I was thinking all of this out in Spanish—which was wonderful to me, one of my happiest moments ever. I had promised myself to learn the language to a degree that would let me break free from the requirements of mental translation. Now, this one time, it had happened, which meant I could indeed reach that level: it was possible. Later I would meet many people who remembered the precise time and place where they had enjoyed this same experience in learning a language.

There are all kinds of teaming. Learning the language, working hard on it in all forms—poetry, songs, mottos, toasts—is also a reaching out, showing that you want to be a team member for the long term. Memorizing Pablo Neruda: "Ya no la quiero, es cierto, pero tal vez la quiero. Es tan corto el amor, y es tan largo el olvido" ("I no longer love her, that's certain, but maybe I love her. Love is so short, forgetting is so long").

I started up the trail and found that it took a sharp turn. One moment I had looked at the far horizons, and at the next I was in a dark canyon of stone and roots and foliage, a place where there had been a small mudslide. From the world of the condor to that of the pack mule, I thought. I heard the sounds that horses make, picking their way down over the stone steps. Several horses and riders. It didn't sound like a pack train. I stepped out of the way, almost in the underbrush, as the first horse came around a twist in the trail just a few feet away. The rider stopped, and then I could see some others. They had rifles and shotguns slung over their shoulders, and machetes in fringed scabbards at their belts. Broad-rimmed floppy hats. Some pistols. They looked surprised to see me, to see the uniform. I was carrying a carbine. We stared at each other for a few seconds. Short beards. Heavy mustaches. Kerchiefs. Good horses. Good saddlery.

I stayed where I was, on the side of a crooked step, and said, "*Continuen.*"

I said it firmly, militarily. It is what a Colombian officer would say to mean "Keep on with what you're doing." It was, in effect, an order—or I hoped it was. They looked at each other and went on, looking around them but not at me, their stirrups passing within a few inches of me. It took only a minute or two for them to be out of sight, if not out of hearing, and I slipped into the tangle of green and moved away from the trail as quickly as I could without making too much noise. At about a hundred yards, I waited and listened. Nothing. My guess is that they couldn't imagine my being there by myself; they must have thought my soldiers must be all around them, or at least close by. I went on, found the patrol, and by early morning we were back in camp. I described to Fernandez and Negret, two of my fellow instructors, what happened and asked what they thought. Fernandez said, "Was he skinny, like Negret?" Negret smiled. "That was Varela [a legendary guerrilla fighter in these parts]. No doubt about it."

4 October 1957. News arrived that the Russians had launched Sputnik. Fernandez, goading: "So what are you going to do about that?" Me, sanguine: "I don't know. I'm thinking about it. Give me time. I'll find a solution."

Letter to my father, 20 January 1958:

> I find myself thinking constantly of my Russian counterpart, and wondering what he is doing. That keeps me working hard—that, among other things. I know that they are better soldiers than most of us are at this date, and any sensible officer will tell you the same. Many times I use my Spanish to speak to Germans who also speak Spanish, some of them recently escaped from satellite countries, and I ask questions about the Russians. I have heard, for instance, that no Russian officer is left too long in East Germany, because he gets "soft." Well, anyway, I have enough small training problems to keep me from worrying about such things.
>
> Another thing is: We should be helping South America a lot more than we do. In a sense, "peaceful interests abroad" are about the same for the Russians as they are for us. We should be trying to have our nose in everything, as they do.
>
> It was a shock to us all when General [James M.] Gavin retired, and I noticed that, talking of our attitude toward world problems today, he said, "You can't be just against Communism; you've got to be for something." That's what is the matter with some of us.

Coming out of West Point, my classmates and I aimed to position ourselves for the most coveted assignments: those of company commanders—specifically in the Airborne. My choice to go to Latin America instead of Europe and my luck in being tapped for the Lanceros program now paid dividends as I received my next orders, to go to the 101st Airborne Division.

By the time I left Colombia, my Spanish was much better. In fact, I had spoken English only about once a month. A salesman for the H-13 helicopter was down in the area, showing the helicopter around, and came to our base. I heard he was from Rochester, New York, so I went over to meet him and to ask if he was indeed a New Yorker. He said yes, and we started to talk for a while. I said, "It's great to be able to use my English again." He said, "You ought to keep it up, because you have practically no accent whatsoever." I said, "Wait a minute, I'm from Boston!" He said, "Really?"

10

101st Airborne Division

"Khrushchev, Red China, Jordan, Lebanon, threats and counterthreats. . . . When I hear all that, I don't mind studying my tactics."

In May 1958 I reported to Fort Campbell and was assigned as a platoon leader in A Company, 501st Airborne Battle Group, 101st Airborne Division. When I arrived, everyone was still talking about the mass parachute jump at Campbell a few days earlier, in which several soldiers were killed. A strong gust of wind had slammed the jumpers to the ground and dragged them, some unconscious, over a rough field. Only the first airplanes dropped their troops; the rest, on seeing the danger, returned to the airfield, where the commanding general, William Westmoreland, waited for the wind to die down, then continued the operation, jumping first himself from the lead plane. "Typical of him," they said. "He's always in the middle of things."

About a week later, I and half a dozen other new lieutenants were called to the general's office, where we had almost an hour of discussion. We expected a one-way lecture, but to our surprise it didn't turn out that way; we talked more than he did. A few weeks later, General Westmoreland walked into the post barbershop while I was in one of the chairs, covered by a barber's cloth. He remembered my name, sat in the chair next to me, and continued one of the themes of the earlier talk—the role of the junior officer in keeping the division ready to deploy. I was impressed. The barber told me later it happened all the time.

The 101st was one of the "Pentomic" divisions, designed to fight under the conditions of nuclear war. In place of the old three-regiment structure, there were five smaller battle groups, each with five maneuver companies. The result was a somewhat smaller division, with amplified communications and higher mobility. The Army was faced with the job of considering how to employ nuclear weapons and how to defend against them. It seemed logical to configure a unit able to disperse quickly if an atomic weapons attack was seen to be imminent, and then to regather nimbly for an attack of its own.

In a Pentomic division, the general and his colonels could communicate and make quick decisions to outmaneuver the enemy. Companies and platoons had more small ground vehicles—jeeps and "mules" to carry weapons, ammunition, and supplies—than before, and the troops were always ready for movement by air. The battle groups were trimmed, with small staffs and light equipment. The four-engine turboprop C-130 was arriving in numbers to replace the C-119 Flying Boxcar and the C-123, both small, two-engine, piston-driven aircraft. (The old C-47 was already out to pasture, although about two thousand of them were still flying throughout the world.)

A week after our barbershop conversation, General Westmoreland inspected my company at training. As usual, his visit was unannounced. That afternoon he left word at A Company asking me to play squash with him, which I was delighted to do. I planned to take it easy on my forty-four-year-old opponent, but there was no need for that: he beat me soundly.

In the conversation during our game he said he'd like to hear more specifics regarding the life of a lieutenant on Fort Campbell. Brashly enough, I took the opportunity to bring up the lack of good housing for bachelor officers like me. Army tradition held that bachelor officers were well off enough, with each given two rooms in cinder-block barracks with two officers sharing a connecting bathroom; they needn't have quarters like those of married officers—single family and duplex-style homes instead of barracks. I still don't know why I chose this to complain about. I had lived in a barracks room for almost all of my Army time, and what I had at Campbell was spacious by comparison. I certainly didn't realize that my words would meet with a receptive audience; Westmoreland had been a bachelor for the first several years of his own Army career. In July, word came that family quarters on post would be open to all officers, and in August I was given a two-story row house.

Letter to my father, 19 May 1958:

I played squash with Gen. Westmoreland Thursday, and he beat me. What stamina he has! Took over as the executive officer of A Company on 18 May (Saturday). Tomorrow, Ground Safety Officer for a jump. Jumped 119s on Armed Forces Day. I found myself on top of Lt. Shuff's chute, but we got away from each other.

Have been working long days learning loading charts, specifications, aircraft details, alert plans for all types of operations. The 130s left for Lebanon carrying interesting supplies.

In the event that I have to leave here in a hurry, you would have to come down to pick up my car and personal things. I will put everything in the trunk of the car, and place the car in a parking lot. The registration is 4C 9680 NY. It will be marked with my name and list you as recipient. All you'd have to do is ask the MPs where it is, and identify yourself.

About two weeks into my new assignment, I was sent out in a jeep to Zon Drop Zone, a place that took its name from a town in Holland where the 101st fought the German 59th Division in September 1944. The drop zone was a relatively small, brushy field in the woodlands of Fort Campbell. I was the drop zone safety officer, and my duty was simple enough: if the wind was higher than fifteen knots, set off a red smoke grenade, signaling to half a dozen incoming C-130 Hercules aircraft that the jump was off. Otherwise, let the white smoke keep billowing up, which showed wind direction and also cleared the jump as a "go." Platoon Sergeant Guzman said he would go along with me, and I was happy to have his extensive experience. The wind was out of the east. We set up the fabric panels in the form of a T, the symbol for the drop point. I held the wind-speed indicator by its handle and watched the little red ball float inside a clear plastic tube, driven by the force of air pressing through an opening near the bottom. On this gusty morning the red ball was restless; it wavered between the five- and fifteen-knot markers and couldn't resist jumping up to twenty knots every now and then.

I looked over at the other side of the T-shaped marker on the ground and saw that Sergeant Guzman was readying a red smoke grenade along with the white ones. The planes, which had been gray specks down close to the western horizon, were now recognizable black silhouettes about five miles out over the treetops. Sergeant Guzman and I gave each other a thumbs-up. The red ball was still bouncing up and down. We ignited the white smoke grenades, and the C-130s came on in two Vs at fifteen hundred feet, into the wind. I pocketed the wind-speed indicator, which was useless at that point. The jump went well, all chutes OK, no incidents. I had sweated out my first decision as a member of the 101st Airborne Division. It could be dismissed as a routine moment, I suppose, but I often recall it when there is a tough call to be made: I see those planes coming in over the trees, heading for white smoke. As for the wind-speed indicator, I saw that it was manufactured by the F. W. Dwyer Company of Michigan City, Indiana. Probably the low bidder, I thought. I made a note to buy a better one of my own.

About this time I decided to learn how to fly airplanes—I wanted to get to know more about the vehicles I would be riding in if my future was to be in parachute units. Outlaw Field was a small airport not far from the front gate of Fort Campbell. On a warm Sunday in late May 1958, I drove over to see the field. It was a small and quiet meadow, with a runway marked off by two parallel rows of old automobile tires painted white. It must have been a farm at some earlier time. There was no tower and no hangars; not much more than an operations shack, a dusty gray windsock, and a few airplanes parked wingtip to wingtip. The only scheduled commercial traffic in and out of the field was a single daily DC-3. Several times I watched it drift down on its approach, propellers idling quietly, the silver plane looking too large for the tree-lined sod runway.

I met J. B. Krost, a lanky and laconic man who became my flight instructor and thereafter an indelible figure in my life and memory. My time with Krost showed me why pilots always refer to their flight instructors as something other than ordinary mortals. J. B. was the prototypical instructor: tanned, craggy, slow-talking, unemotional, correct, tactful, and somewhat wary. Not removed, not negative—just wary.

I told him I'd like to take some lessons, and he said, "OK, let's go look at the airplane." We walked over through the grass to the parked planes—two or three yellow Cubs and a couple of others. From any angle, the Cub is a beautiful thing to see, a yellow tail-dragger that I still feel comes very close to the ideal of form following function; it is the picture of simplicity. These Cubs had a bit more power than the original Cub and were better balanced, so that a pilot riding alone in the tandem two-seater could sit in front, rather than in the rear seat. They have fat, low-pressure tires, good for running on sod fields. Only the engine housing is metal-covered; the rest of the plane, including the wings and fuselage, is made of fabric over a tubular frame. This model, the PA-18

Super Cub, had a fixed-pitch steel propeller; no brakes, no flaps, no starter, no intercom, no radio. It just flew, that's all.

Krost talked me through a preflight check of the plane; then he dropped the half-door down and pushed the Plexiglas window up against the underside of the wing, and I climbed into the front seat. The instrument panel had an ignition key, an airspeed indicator, a turn-and-bank indicator, and a fuel gauge. The power control was on the left, under the window. Krost looked around, walked up front, shouted "Contact," spun the prop, started the engine—a 125-horsepower Lycoming—and then climbed into the rear seat and took over his set of controls, as we taxied out alongside the automobile tires. It was not difficult to see over the nose of the cub, but Krost taught me the curving taxi run used by all tail-draggers—how to work the rudder pedals left and right in order to see for certain what might be directly ahead. On taxiing, the springy tail wheel bounced and rattled, the prop fanned, the cross-braced shock absorbers twanged, and the overall vibration of the fabric gave off a drumming sound—altogether, an enjoyable cacophony.

With Krost in control, we climbed out to the west toward Fort Campbell, then turned back east over farm country. He gave me the controls and helped me learn how to watch the horizon and keep the plane flying straight and level. After that we made some gentle turns, coordinating the rudder pedals and stick. Then Krost said, "Now, if we wanted to go back to the field, where is it from here?" I said something like, "Well, um, now that you mention it . . ." He chided me about navigation and about knowing wind direction, and for half an hour he let me get accustomed to flying level and making easy turns. Over the next few weeks I flew with Krost for a total of twelve hours—takeoffs, landings, slow flight, stalls, spirals, and emergency landings (where you needed to know wind direction and pick out a field).

On one of those days with Krost, a balmy summer afternoon, we were doing touch-and-go landings, flying downwind: pull back on power, roll left onto base, left again onto final, engine idling, descend to just above the grassy strip, level out, sink gently until the wheels touch and settle, put a little forward pressure on the stick to hold the tail up, push power on, right rudder to balance the torque, pick up speed, and then fly again. Climb to five hundred feet, roll left ninety degrees and then left onto the downwind leg once again, and the cycle begins to repeat itself. Pleasant, and deeply satisfying. I felt I could fly the pattern forever and never get tired of it: climbing into the sky, watching patches of forest and field as the horizon widens, then banking back to the grassy haven below.

Then Krost told me it was time to take it on my own. Actually, he just said, "OK, land"; and when I did, he said, "Let me out here." He climbed out of the back seat and said in his quiet way, "It's yours."

I went back down the runway, turned around, and pushed the power forward with my left hand; and as the plane picked up speed I pushed the stick forward to bring the tail up—all moves that were not yet automatic for me—and the Cub lifted off the ground. I eased back on the stick and started climbing. I felt like singing. Maybe I did sing. At any rate the Lycoming engine sang, because when I leveled off I kept the power full on, which came to my attention when the Plexiglas windshield flexed slightly. I pulled the power back to cruising airspeed, but of course Krost had heard the four or five extra seconds of song.

After a few trips around the field, I aligned myself on downwind leg, watched the field out my left window, flew parallel to the runway, rolled onto base leg, cut power, and started down. I turned left on final approach and dropped to just above idle, and as I neared the touch-down point I saw I was high, so I slipped and straightened out to glide along and roll down the center of the runway.

After the wheels touched I kept the tail up, kept the Cub horizontal, and pushed the lever slowly forward into full power again, and we lifted off. This time I cut back to cruise as I leveled out, and as I came around for another touch-and-go I could see Krost walking along the side of the runway toward the office. That meant he wanted me to keep up the touch-and-go practice. All was OK.

It was half an hour of pure joy. I kept glancing around at the plane's interior; it was hard to believe I was up there all alone, nobody but me. After some more touch-and-go's I landed, taxied to the parking tie-downs, and cut the engine. Krost came over, and we closed up the Cub and tied it down. "Good solo," he said. "For the most part." The next day we flew "dual" for thirty minutes, and then I flew solo for another thirty.

Two days later, there was a shake-up in A Company, and I became the interim company commander, the only lieutenant to command a company in the battle group. I walked into the company commander's office—my office—on the first day, and with no lack of enthusiasm dug into the pile of paperwork waiting for me. I went through all of the documents with speed and flourish, stabbing my initials into the upper-right-hand corner, acknowledging the flow of information, set-tling issues, and making decisions. Then off to the field to be with the troops. When I returned at noon, refreshed with what I'd seen and with the deference I had been accorded all morning, First Sergeant Vierck came into my office and pointed out the little "distribution" stamp, a kind of grid in that upper corner, where my "JRG" was splayed across all the boxes, leaving little room for anyone else. "We only get one copy of most of this stuff," he said quietly but firmly. "Quite a few folks have to see these things, and I need to know they've been informed. You're not leaving them much room. See this little block here? That's the one we have for you. You do get it first, of course." This incident marked the beginning of my realization that your mentors are not necessarily your bosses.

Six days after that, the company was placed on two-hour alert for a possible move to Lebanon. Ours, we were told, would be the first unit to depart. Our orders were to be ready to go in two hours.

Letter to my father, 26 July 1958:

> We stored our extra personal gear, closed the barracks, and moved to the airfield, where we set up our pup tents not far from the C-124 Globemaster planes which were standing by on a taxiway. I inspected the troops, weapons, and equipment, feeling the weight of responsibility, but proud of hearing myself called "The Old Man" by sergeants quite a lot older than me.
>
> The day has been spent in studies of the Middle East, listen-ing to lectures given by recently returned officers. We have been inspected by everyone, but nothing has been found wrong. Even the pictures have been taken off the walls, and the cur-tains are down in the mess hall. The field kitchen is loaded. The flight manifests are drawn up. Packs are rolled, and I held a formation to see how they look. Gen. W. was here again today. He said that the Bekaa Valley has excellent drop zones, and he gave us information on other stuff.

We stayed on two-hour alert for two weeks and then were relieved by another rifle company. Instead of returning to barracks, we loaded into aircraft and made a jump at Fort Campbell. I reported to my father: "I drove home in a jeep, leading a column of trucks through the forests. The sweet coolness of the grass and trees and the quietness and rab-bits hopping along the road were wonderful after the blast of four jet-driven propellers and the heat and gasoline. I saw all the quiet streams wandering off into the woods and looked at myself all sweat and grease and dust and I thought: 'Galvin, you are a nut.' This may be very true, too."

My father replied, "I'll admit you're a 'nut.' . . . But what a sweet time you have being one."

On 4 August 1958 I wrote to my father: "And all is not glory. I have given 'hard labor' or 'extra duty' to 16 men in 3 weeks, and have 'busted' 2 sergeants, 3 corporals, and 2 PFCs, all for fighting, AWOL, stealing, etc., etc., etc. You have to be an SOB to run an Airborne rifle company, and that is just what I am. This is no exaggeration."

And then, a week later: "Even in my free time, if I hear a convoy of trucks, I think about the alert and a long checklist runs through my brain."

I added that the radio that day talked of "Khrushchev, Red China, Jordan, Lebanon, threats and counterthreats. . . . When I hear all that, I don't mind studying my tactics a few extra hours." I told him that we could very well end up in Quemoy or Matsu (islands off the coast of China, claimed by Taiwan and being shelled by Communist Chinese forces), and he wrote back, "I think our State Dept. handed Eisenhower a hot potato, and I hope he can get us out of this mess. I don't see the importance of Quemoy, especially, when the 'Commys' can blast every inch of it. We may lose face, but on the other hand, it would be militarily idiotic to defend it. It isn't a disgrace to admit this, even to the world."

There was only one tank platoon at Fort Campbell. It was not part of the division, and it was not up to strength. I was told that its job was to provide "orientation" for the rest of us, so one day in August I went over to visit the tank company commander to see if we could get together on a training exercise. He was delighted with the idea, but he cautioned that there was no approved route for his platoon of five tanks to move to the maneuver areas. There was no tank trail; the tanks had never been out to the field. We quickly agreed to find the best way to get out there and see if Division would approve it. We took a jeep and searched the garrison area for crossings that would not over-load bridges, damage road surfaces, or knock down trees, signs, or tele-phone poles.

Fort Campbell was half dust and half mud, but the roads had been built with good drainage. The division engineers accepted our pro-posed tank trail, and Division Headquarters then approved it. Not long after that, A Company, 501st Airborne Battle Group, met in the field with First Platoon, D Company, 66th Tank Battalion, led by Master Sergeant E. J. Duncan. First Sergeant Vierck called our paratroopers into a cluster around one of the tanks, and I climbed aboard, Westmoreland-style, to talk to everyone about teamwork. A few minutes into my speech, though, I realized I had everything backwards. I thought I was on the front deck of the tank, because that's where the gun was pointing, but the turret was reversed and the gun was in "travel lock," as it is when it is out of combat and simply being driven or transported from one place to another. I didn't know anything about travel locks, and that turned out to be only one of hundreds of things I didn't know about tanks. We worked our way through a good exercise, and after that I set out to learn more about armored units and tactics. Early in the process, I found that there were more infantry officers in an armored division than there were armor officers. I could only hope that those infantrymen knew more than I did.

Meantime, I was slipping over to Outlaw Field whenever I could get free, which was not very often. By 18 August, I had only two hours and thirty-five minutes of solo flying time in thirty-six days, along with an hour and forty minutes of dual time with Krost. But I was confident. I saw myself as a man of many interests and many skills. On Sunday, 7 September, when I could have been flying, I spent the day instead searching out the countryside around General Ulysses S. Grant's first substantial victory, in 1862: the taking of Forts Henry on the Tennessee River and Donaldson on the Cumberland, both close to the west side of Fort Campbell. I wrote home:

> The area [Donaldson] has not been "improved" and remains essentially the same as on the battle days. On the same day I drove on to Fort Henry. I arrived at Kentucky Lake, a man-made development on the Tennessee River, and followed winding dirt roads (and broke a shock absorber) deep into the woods. I finally arrived at lake's edge, and the road dead-ended at a farm owned by B. Phillips. The owner came out— old and grizzled—and when I asked directions to Fort Henry he said, "You're standing on it, son." It has disappeared completely in the new lake, except for a few almost indistinguishable traces of barricades on the Phillips farm.

This was not lost time, by any means. I put a few scratches and a lot of mud on my new Ford Fairlane convertible while learning what it would have been like to be General Grant, moving twenty-five thousand troops through about fifteen miles of bad roads while coordinating with the Navy.

A month later, on 14 September 1958, my father wrote again of his concern about the Far East: "The China situation is certainly a mess. The President has been handed a tough kettle of fish. How to get out of it is a problem. We have to lose face (maybe). The Chinese have a perfect setup and no matter how we move we are going to stir up a mess of stew. The next few weeks will tell the tale."

The pressure of staying ready for Quemoy was heavy, but on one of the days when we were not earmarked to go on the early echelons, on 10 October, I managed to get a free day. I drove to Shiloh and went over every inch of the ground there. At one place on the battlefield I read a historic sign that said that the location of a battery of Union artillery at that point in the battle was now marked by a line of guns to the north of my position. I looked to the north and there they were: lined up, about eight of them, less than a hundred yards away, aimed at me. For a half-second I found myself in the battle of Shiloh.

There were other opportunities to fly, but it was sixty-three more days until I got around to it. I was nonchalant about it; after all, I thought, flying is simple enough. On 18 October I flew another hour with Krost, and then on 20 October I signed out the PA-18, planning to do some solo takeoffs and landings. As I taxied out, the interior of the Cub was very hot, so I slid back the left side window. At the end of the runway, given the green light from the shack, I started my takeoff roll. As I lifted off and began to climb, the left window rattled and I reached up to slide it closed. As I did that, somehow I caught the sleeve of my shirt in the power lever and thereby returned the engine to idle.

The next moments were awkward. I didn't know what had happened, except that the Cub was beginning to mush ahead at an up angle. I was at about four hundred, maybe five hundred, feet. I pushed the stick to get the nose down and saw a patch of pines come up ahead. It took me three or four seconds to figure out what I had done and push the power back to full. Then I waited, nose down, for airspeed to build, while the trees kept getting bigger. I didn't think I had enough room, but I was afraid a turn would drop me even lower. I did not even try to look at the instrument panel, or at anything other than those tall, tall pines. I had the stick centered and was listening to the engine wind up;

when I couldn't face the upcoming pines any longer I pulled back, having no idea whether the Cub could get me out of this mess.

It could, and did, of course. I leveled off and flew around aimlessly for a few minutes, thinking about what had happened. My responses had been slow to the point of ponderous. I should have been on the power lever instinctively, but instead I had mentally thumbed through the possibilities while the plane wallowed. Not good. I got back in the pattern and did touch-and-go's for twenty minutes until I called it a day, landed, and taxied to the tie-downs near the operations shack.

Krost had arrived and was standing by the shack. He walked over and helped me tie down the plane, check it over, and lock up. Then he said, "What was that out there?" He listened to my story and said nothing for some time. Finally he looked off into the sky and muttered, "It's a very forgiving airplane, but you *do* have to fly it."

That fall we were back on alert, with Quemoy and Matsu in mind. There is a two-month gap in my log book, after which I flew twice more with Krost and another half-hour solo. In November, after we had been out together doing stalls, slow flights, and slips, Krost said, "That was OK, but we're not going to get a cross-country in until you find time to fly some more." He was right, I knew: I had to fly more often or not at all. That week, however, was the beginning of the competition for the best rifle squad out of the more than two hundred squads in the division.

Following the rules of the contest, I held a competition within the company to pick out the best squad. Each competitor had to be a bona fide "come as you are" squad, not one put together from the best riflemen in the company—everyone studied the personnel records to ensure that this rule was followed. This process produced a clear winner, which the company then supported in its preparations for the test at battle-group level. Knowing that the psychological aspect has much to do with winning or losing in such endeavors, we coined the name "Supersquad" for our winning squad and created our own style of camouflage uniform, which we called "snakesuits." Everyone in the company regarded the Supersquad as *our* squad, and all of us worked for them. The preparatory work provided training for the rest of us as well. We sensed we had a winner, at least for the next stage, and spirits were high as NCOs from other squads helped with their expertise—with radio communications and reconnaissance, with physical training, and with maintenance.

All of this training we fitted into a demanding schedule of airborne jumps and preparations, readying ourselves for rapid deployment. From my notes, 23 November 1958:

> Cold November night—our C-119 "boxcar," shadowed in the weak floodlights of the field, showing its battered ribs like an old sea-beaten Navy destroyer. Most airplanes look something like a bird, which I find comfortable. The Flying Boxcar, adequately named, is different, in my opinion. Anything shaped like a box is not entirely credible as an air vehicle. The reserve pilots are no youngsters either but all nice guys, old-timers, civilians now, always full of wisecracks. "I know this plane is OK—I flew it during WWII." The pilot, giving instructions on emergency procedures, told us to hook up and jump when he rang the emergency bell. "If you feel someone shoving from behind," he said, "it'll be me." This went on all during preparations for flight. At last the pilot said, "I'm going to radio the tower and inform them to stand by while I try to take off."

The slow swing of the heavy, four-bladed propeller. The long, agonizing series of bronchial coughs as various of its radial pistons awoke with surprise and fired away with a red smoky flash, at first ragged and struggling but then showing more of a sequence, the blend of its smoky exhaust enveloping the engine, then streaming back through the cowlings, changing from white to brown to yellow and then an angry and assertive red, followed finally by what we wanted to see: a self-confident blue, a tenor voice, and then a howling, rocking, full-throttle test of the two engines at the starting end of the runway, with the old freight car heaving and straining like a fire horse at the sound of the alarm.

On 7 December 1958, Captain Sinclair Melner arrived to take command of A Company. I knew it would happen eventually; I knew I was only the temporary commander; but stepping back to be the executive officer was heart-wrenching. After a couple of weeks assisting the new commander, I asked for a leave and drove home to Massachusetts for the Christmas holidays, then headed back to Fort Campbell. I drove straight through, as usual, and on arriving back at Campbell I wrote a note to myself: "1 January 1959. Left Wakefield just at sunrise, with one star in the sky, lake frozen and white. Out through PA 1st night and down Ohio Valley, the Ford black with coal dust from the West Va. roads. At sunset turned south, Cincinnati, Louisville, thru Bowling Green at 0430. From there on, the roads were full of rabbits on the move. Killed 2, couldn't see them well enough in ground fog but didn't want to slow down. Felt guilty, sad, lonesome."

Captain Melner went on to three stars. When I was with him, Melner would look about three weeks ahead and would say to me, "We have training area Alpha, assigned to us for that week. Give me a training plan for that. What are we going to do? Let's go to the field on Monday evening and come back on Thursday afternoon." From then on I had responsibility for laying out the exercise, which was wonderful. I would get a jeep, drive out to the area, look at it from all sides, and make up a plan—which Melner very rarely changed. He might say, "Let's do attack, withdrawal, defense." Or "Let's do something that gets us some ground maneuver." So I had pretty much free rein to set up the area, get other units involved, get some artillery to support us if we were going to do any live fire, and work everything out with the artillery people. I learned, among other things, that you always had to have an ambulance on call. Each time I set up one of these training exercises I learned something new. Altogether, it was a great learning experience for me.

Another learning experience for me had to do with the rifle squad competition. Knowing that the tasks of the competition would come down to a series of tactical surprises, we emphasized responsiveness to swift change: "Be ready for anything, everything, all the time." If we were to succeed against intense competition from equally well-trained and highly motivated squads (224 of them in the division), every member of the squad had to view every change, big or small, as an opportunity to function as a team. Machinelike performance was not enough; in the face of any and every challenge, the first thought-word had to be: *team.*

Our squad won the contest at battle-group level and then went on to be named best rifle squad in the 101st Airborne Division. The men in the squad were rewarded with due ceremony and a special trip to New York. Sadly, however, before the end of the competition, the original squad leader, Sergeant First Class Barrett, was killed in an auto accident. One of the two fire team leaders, Sergeant Ochotorena, took over and led the squad to its win.

Letter to my father, 26 January 1959:

Just got back from Fort Breckenridge, where we jumped in (jump #17 for me) on an assault. It was very cold on Friday, the day of the jump—we took off from Campbell at 0630—dark and about 5–10 degrees at the field. I jumped as "Pathfinder" for A Co, 15 minutes before the rest of the 501st, in a lone plane carrying the reconnaissance platoon, pathfinders from the other companies (3 each), and Col. Ashworth. Sgts. Smith and Perschka from "A" jumped with me.

As soon as I was out of the plane I saw the fields laid out just as in the maps and aerial photos, and I picked out our assembly area. The ground was hard-frozen and covered with a light powder snow. The wind was light, but getting stronger. I hit hard enough to dent the cans of rations in my pack, but was not hurt. The planes, piloted by reserve pilots from the N.Y. area (all Pan Am and Eastern pilots—$15,000–$30,000-a-year men) were badly scattered and off target, and our men swerved into trees and rivers, etc.—we lost 10 hospitalized immediately, and most of our vehicles either never got in or broke up in the high trees. From then on we knew it was not going to be easy. My C.O. [commanding officer] didn't show up, so I moved out in the assault on three hills as soon as I could gather enough troopers to take them. Gen. Westmoreland appeared out of nowhere and called me by name, as usual, and asked about the situation. He was pleased to see me carrying an M-1 rifle instead of a carbine; also liked the action of A Co.

I got jump #23, a good training jump. We took off in an L-20 "Beaver" single engine aircraft just before midnight in a light rain. The wind was pretty high, but Major Millett was jumpmaster of another L-20 and when he is along the decision is always "drop 'em" regardless of wind or weather.

As we neared the objective I swung my legs outside the door and sat in the doorway with my feet on the step. The rain soon soaked my legs. On the ground below a shallow fog drifted over the fields, and the treetops stuck through. In open spots I could see the roads and occasionally a light. Looking back, I could see the glow of Hopkinsville, Kentucky. Four of us were jumping, and my friend Larry Zittrain, "Big Train," was the pilot. From time to time we would talk. It's a slow plane, no real rush of wind, soft growl of a single radial engine. Then Larry adjusted his headset and talked to the pathfinders on the ground ahead and gave me the sign "one minute." I checked my men and got ready to go. I told Sergeant Perschka, "See you on the ground, Pershk," and he said, "OK, sir," and I got the sign from the co-pilot to Go.

I pushed off and fell away, and I could feel my chute coming off my back, more slowly than the way it rips off in the slipstream of the Hercules. When I got the opening shock, I checked the canopy, and it was fully deployed and looking fine. The landmarks were hard to see on the ground because of the rain, fog, and darkness. At about 400 feet I saw the fog blow away, and nothing below but big trees sticking through. I saw a small field and I started to pull down on my left risers and slip into it, but the wind was also blowing to the left and I began to drop fast. I kept trying, but at last I knew I could not make it, and I would soon be in the trees. My muscles started to tense but I made myself relax, and just before I hit I thought how beautiful the whole scene was, with the blowing fog and dark wet trees flying past. I tumbled and bounced through the branches and finally came to a stop hanging just above the ground with my chute caught in the top of a tree about 50 feet high. I worked my way loose and went to meet the others. I didn't get even scratched.

I have had some talks with Gen. Westmoreland and Col. Ashworth and Maj. Millett about some patrol ideas that have been in my head for a while. Gen. W. has ordered the Major to try this new patrol out and see how it works, and I have given him some written notes on the concept. He agreed with every detail, which was a surprise to me, and this whole thing is being pushed by the General.

Westmoreland used to like to come up to where the soldiers were training and stop and say to the commander, "Bring the troops up. Have the troops fall out and come over here by my jeep." Then he would get up on the hood of his jeep and make an impromptu speech to them. He would say, "Here's what's going on in the division now. Here's what we're aiming for. These are the things that I think we need to work on. I'm glad to see you doing these things today." Then, almost always— and I saw this happen more than once—he would look out and spot a soldier and say, "Sergeant Snead, you were in C Company of the 187th in Korea, weren't you, when I was commanding?" Sergeant Snead, of course, said, "Yes, sir." And Westmoreland would reply, "I remember that you did such and such." He had what to me was a phenomenal recall: an ability to relate specific memories to soldiers, calling them by name.

Later on, in 1962, after I left Fort Campbell for Fort Knox, my wife and I traveled to Columbia University and then up to West Point, where I was to teach, and where Westmoreland was then superintendent. The first time I went through a receiving line there, at some kind of Christmas function, Westmoreland met me and my wife, Ginny. Then he said to me, "You weren't married in the 101st, so you must have been married between then and now." I replied, "Yes, we have been married for a year." The following year there was another reception, and as Ginny came through he said to her, "Well, this must be pretty close to your second anniversary."

Westmoreland wore the shoulder patch of the 101st, which was an eagle, and he looked like an eagle himself. A handsome man with bushy eyebrows, he had an almost dueling-like scar across his face. He was tall and always erect and soldierly, well turned out, changing his uniform often. That was common among officers at that time, changing uniforms twice a day to stay creased and starched.

In early June 1959, after a year in A Company, I was transferred to battlegroup headquarters and put in charge of the administration center. Someone had made the decision that, "for greater efficiency," all the company clerks in our battle group, totaling fourteen, should be gathered together under a staff sergeant. This was to be my new command. I was stunned. "Don't ask me how it happened," I wrote home, "just one of those inexplicable decisions up at Group Headquarters. I am completely disgusted with my new job and I lack experience. I feel like looking for a new home. I have a big desk and about 20 clerks typing all around me. I can't describe how much I regret leaving the company for such an idiot's paradise as this. My old friend Ray Allen had this job, but he had a nervous breakdown last Friday. Maybe I am due for the same."

There was no available space in barracks for this orphan outfit, so the admin center was housed in two large tents that the Army calls "general purpose, medium." When fitted out with field desks, folding metal chairs, file cabinets, and clerks, the tents were small and crowded.

The duty of the clerks was to keep the records of the company, including a daily report of the comings and goings of the people in each unit—anything that needed to be typed. But the clerks, God bless them, couldn't type well at all. Some of them were so slow that, in order to sound like rapid-fire experts, they had developed the nervous habit of pounding on the "shift" keys with left and right hands, which would bounce the carriage without advancing the typing: *click-click-click—bang-bang—click-bang-bang-click-click-click*. It sounded like progress, but nothing was happening.

The tents, with their small plastic windows, were dark inside. The sides could be rolled up, but when that was done the flies came in. There were flexible screens that could be rolled down, but that made the tents hot. So the clerks sweated and squinted and slapped flies and typed. It reminded me of a Mediterranean galley. Clearly, this was not the place to be in July at Fort Campbell, but there we were. The clerks, lost souls, banged away at the shift keys, completely miserable. I joined them in their misery, determined to alleviate it. But how?

My knowledge of company administration was . . . modest. I had a disdain for paperwork, and now it was my stock in trade. Right away I found that everybody—even my own friends, fellow lieutenants—brought their administrative problems to me. At first my response was "How in hell should I know what to do about that?" but that didn't work. They would say, "Hey, you're the admin guy."

I studied day and night the enormous, overwhelming manuals on administration, which made me even more miserable. It would take me years, a lifetime, to find my way through all I needed to know. In a week's time I gained an undying respect for people who know administration—especially my deputy, the patient and long-suffering Sergeant First Class Edwin J. Russell. Early on, I took a long walk with SFC Russell and asked him to tell me everything I needed to know about the admin center: about his background in this work and his dealings with all the company commanders and first sergeants, and also about his life, his family, his friends—plus anything that could help me out.

Russell was a good, honest, likable man, accomplished in the details of his job, patient with the troops (and with me), unassuming, unassertive, inarticulate, one of the finest individuals I have been lucky enough to know.

Russell told me that things were going along about as well as could be expected, given that nobody—and this definitely went for the officers—considered the admin center to be at anywhere near the top of the totem pole. (I have to admit that I had been part of that kind of thinking.) It was hard to get much support, he said. The company first sergeants and platoon sergeants all outranked him and were quick to criticize and slow to listen. All we had to do was look at the workplace.

We were the only part of the battle group not in a permanent building. In fact, we were not in any kind of building.

With Russell's calm and straightforward comments in mind, I went around to visit all the company commanders and first sergeants, catching them wherever I could. I also buttonholed quite a few of my lieutenant friends and the several senior NCOs that I had come to know pretty well. After this interviewing experience, I thought of this whole group—especially the first sergeants—as the Chorus. Apparently nothing was right or good about the admin center, except that it served as a dartboard that everyone targeted with their multiple frustrations. My green pocket notebook was soon stuffed with the gripes of the Chorus. The clerks should never have been taken away from the companies, they all said. The old face-to-face communication was gone, they complained. Errors multiplied. The clerks took the typewriters with them, but the companies, supposedly relieved of all typing, found that there was still typing to be done, outside of the clerks' domain. The clerks had lost a sense of what goes on in the companies and were like strangers who slept in the barracks but never got the word about anything. These "light duty" outcasts were having an easy time and were not getting proper training besides. They were ipso facto not part of the team.

With these pleasant thoughts in mind, I shuffled home to the tents. I needed to have more talks with my fellow outcast, SFC Russell. We agreed to invite our admin clerks, one by one, to a chat. I told each one that, as the rookie on the job, I needed suggestions on how to improve the work we were doing. The lieutenant was asking the PFCs, rather than the reverse—and the answers were straightforward and specific. We discussed the need for more electric fans, better waterproofing, more efficient drainage, ways to cut down the amount of dust, and much else—nothing Russell and I had not talked over, except for a couple of comments that also kept coming up: the men saw their work as probably necessary but nonetheless unimportant, or at best unappreciated. They were just clerks, nobodies, as far as anyone was concerned, and they looked on themselves as the wimps of the rear echelon. Now I was catching on. For the first time, I joined their side and became their leader in heart as well as in title.

The battle group deputy was Lieutenant Colonel Bill McKean, of Braintree, Massachusetts, one of the best officers I ever knew—in the long run. At that time, though, I became his nemesis. I stalked him and badgered him incessantly about getting building space for my troops. I asked him to come and inspect our area, which he did, finishing his walk-through with an admission that quality of life was indeed low in the tents and assurances that remedying the problem was high on his priority list. Leveraging this visit, I requested that in the meantime the clerks be allowed to work in T-shirts while inside the tents. This might sound like a modest proposal, but it was not: it required broad coordination, intense discussion, and acquiescence at the general-officer level. Eventually, however, permission came down. The admin troops—and everyone else—saw this as recognition and support from the top. Inevitably, it set a precedent that caused Colonel McKean to be pummeled with similar requests from all kinds of units. He held out against any other relaxation of the regulations, however, whereupon admin center morale went up another several notches. We were now the select few.

SFC Russell and I then drafted a "report card"—in reality, a list of the manifold tasks that the clerks were responsible for carrying out in support of their companies. We passed the report card around first to the clerks, who took pride in the length of the list, and then to all company first sergeants, who made changes, mostly additions, to the tasks we laid out. The process had the extra advantage of bringing attention to the clerks and to the amount of work they did in furtherance of their duties. We made sure that copies of the final checklist went to everyone who could possibly be interested in us—and with respect to that category we were generous. We asked the first sergeants to fill out our report card at the end of each month, checking off any failures or inadequacies on our part, and we promised to visit all units personally—I and SFC Russell and the clerk involved—to see what needed to be improved.

The first sergeants were pleased with our efforts, but they were always pressed for time, and practically none of them replied after the first month—so I stopped by to visit with them anyway, and found that there weren't any problems big enough to warrant discussion. They all promised me they would let me know if anything came up—and then promptly got in touch with SFC Russell to instruct him, with first sergeant directness, to see to it that I didn't come around anymore, at least not on the subject of that checklist. I was not surprised. The two years I had spent working my way up to private first class were, and still are, precious to me. It was in those days that I learned how to look up to noncommissioned officers. I knew how much they affect a soldier's life—and I knew how first sergeants feel about somebody else's checklist. I happily moved on to other issues.

The 101st Airborne Division was a part of XVIII Airborne Corps, also known as the Strategic Army Corps, or STRAC. The acronym developed a second meaning: Strong, Tough, Ready Around the Clock. Further evolution produced an adjective, "strac," as in "strac trooper," meaning someone who's got it all together—as in, for example, "Now you're lookin' strac!" Needless to say, the clerks of the admin center were not seen as strac troopers, and this hurt their feelings. My next task, as I saw it, was to transform the admin center from non-strac to strac.

Peacetime paperwork called for one file cabinet per clerk, but a file cabinet simply cannot be strac. Even a folding field desk has a hard time being strac. A truck can look reasonably strac coming down from the sky by parachute—but a file cabinet? A desk? No. SFC Russell and I went to work on this dilemma. We converted a footlocker into a combination file cabinet and desk. Without going into too much description, let me just say that it worked: the lid unfolded into a desktop, and everything else, legs and all, could be stored in it, along with a typewriter and the files. Every clerk got a footlocker-desk that could ride to earth as part of a pallet.

We installed the strac desks and hung new signs over the doors of our two tents, telling the world that we were: "501st Admin Center—STRAC."

When anyone challenged our self-promotion, we invited them to come in and see our new strac equipment, which we explained via a detailed tutorial that discouraged any further remarks about our credentials. I also requested that the center be allowed to take part in field exercises. (Up to then, we were always left behind.) With Colonel McKean's permission we moved our tents to the airfield for a division-level deployment exercise that was to be visited by the Army chief of staff, General Lyman Lemnitzer. On that occasion, ninety-six transport aircraft carried almost two thousand troops to the Caribbean in a test of our ability to be, as we said, strac.

Letter to my father, 24 July 1959:

The 501st is on maneuvers in Puerto Rico this week. It is hard to see all the troops boarding aircraft, all dressed in battle gear and their faces blackened—and have the job of controlling the departure and taking care that the ammo and rations are loaded on the correct aircraft etc., etc., etc. But I think that I have learned a great deal since I took over as assistant adjutant. Patience, if no more.

I am beginning to appreciate my new job as an opportunity to learn more. I also realize that, just as a pitcher must change his style to become more crafty after losing his speed, I must also adjust and begin to use my head more than before. It is a very similar situation.

SFC Russell and I were given, at our request, permission to show General Lemnitzer our admin center in action at the airfield, and the Associated Press carried a photo datelined Ramey Air Force Base, Puerto Rico, showing the two of us explaining to the general the inner workings of the addressograph machine, one of the clumsy mechanical forerunners to the computer. After this, we were definitely and conclusively strac.

Twenty-nine years later, I would show that photo to retired General Lemnitzer and listen to his advice again as I got ready to take over his old job four times removed, supreme allied commander in Europe. Then, as earlier, it was the same: "Recognize that you will have to be stubborn and full of repetition in obtaining what you know you have to have"—words that reinforced what I was already up to.

Each company in the battle group had a volleyball team. I talked the league coaches into letting the admin center clerks put up a team. We bought T-shirts adorned with our symbol—a tiger's head superimposed on a large airborne badge. We practiced hard, got ourselves in better shape, and started winning a few games. I failed to make the team, but I became a loyal fan.

The other teams didn't know how to take us. How could admin be tigers? We said, "Why not?" and laughed along with everyone else, while in the meantime we won a few games. We also started going to work not just in T-shirts, but in *tiger* T-shirts. Eventually, acceptance on the volleyball courts transferred to the admin center and to the battle group. We were not only a tiger team; we were members in good standing of the strac team.

My father wanted to hear about the details of every parachute jump I made. On 29 September, as part of my weekly letter, I wrote:

> We flew out over the Cumberland and made a turn back toward the fort as we crossed the junction of the Tennessee and Cumberland. My plane was on the right wing of the V. The sun was setting and we headed away from it as it sat on the horizon—red in the haze. The many small ponds glittered in its reflected rays. I watched the smokehouses on the farms below

to get an idea of the wind, and it seemed strong. We passed a factory and the smoke was blowing hard away to the north. On our first pass over the field, Major Benty (a new major) and another man jumped to test the wind. I watched them go from the wing—they were in the lead "boxcar," about 200 feet ahead and to our left. It certainly is an exhilarating feeling to see them tumble out and go shooting past, "down the slot" at 120 miles per hour.

I put Martinez in the door behind me because he is being transferred to Europe and this was his last jump. I told him, "Nos vemos alla abajo" (I'll see you down below), and he said with a smile, "Eso tiene dos sentidos." (That has two meanings.) Then we watched the landmarks ahead, and the crew chief leaned over and yelled in my ear, "One minute out— wind 3 knots on the ground." The men had been worried at the predicted "18–20 knots, gusting to 35" that the Air Force had put out at 3 o'clock, and I thought that the crew chief was telling a white lie, but I passed it along to the men and watched their stares of disbelief as the word went from man to man— they all had seen the windblown smoke, too.

When we jumped the wind was strong at 1,000 feet, but the ground wind was . . . three knots, just as he said. 187 DZ [Drop Zone] is ploughed now and looks different in the air and on the ground. Many of the trees have been cut down this month and it surprised me at first sight, but I was too busy avoiding other men in the air to bother much. The landing was as nice as a ploughed field can be—very sweet. It was dark twilight when we hit.

In October I wrote with other news:

My leave was cancelled by Col. Ashworth, and I have a new job: I am commanding Company B. Captain Clemons, the hero of that movie *Pork Chop Hill*, is turning the command over to me tomorrow, and if I can fit in his footsteps I'll be doing all right. You can imagine how happy I am. The Colonel says he expects me to give him a winner as I did last year with A Company—a rifle squad to take 1st place in division tests. Capt. Clemons is moving up to staff. We leave for field training on Monday, 217 strong, and I am walking on a cloud. I picked my own "top kick," master sergeant Clifton Reavy, an old veteran, and also got my choice of officers, including Lts. Swanson and Brunkow. We are training the squads to work as a team—eleven men divided into two fire teams, each team anchored on the fire of a Browning Automatic Rifle. Drill, drill, drill it is going to be, until, like a ball team, each man knows what the other will do next. Then on to platoon drills, and then the whole company.

But to start with, on my first day as commander I announced that I had canceled the trucks that were going to take us to the field (cheers), and the company would march out (muffled groans) and back (loud groans). An hour later we started on the march to our assigned training area, about twenty miles away. It was a hot day, and we marched on dusty roads to the end of the reservation. Four hours later, as we reached the turnaround point, an H-13 light helicopter, a little bubble, circled us a couple of times, then landed nearby. We halted, and I walked over to see what this meant. The pilot told me that he had orders to find me and bring me back. "The CG [commanding general] wants to see you."

I can't remember what the reason was now, but here I was, going to get in a helicopter and fly away. Worse still, as we started to fly away, I wanted to salute the company as I left. But sitting in there, because of the bubble and the way it was turned, I kind of waved my hand down low out the bottom of the door of the helicopter. I later learned of a nickname the troops were using for me, which was "Ramar," pronounced Ray-Mar. I'd never seen the television serial, but there was a cartoon for kids called *Ramar of the Jungle*. Ramar was a Tarzan-like character. The combination of the march plus the Ranger School and the Lanceros jungle operations combined to make me known as Ramar. I found out my nickname when I noticed that when I would walk into the mess hall, some of the troops would lean over and wave their hands down by the floor, meaning, "Here comes Ramar."

In late November 1959, as the 1960s approached, the Army changed its structure for the second time in five years, moving away from the Pentomic concept and toward a more versatile organization in which each division would contain three brigades, each of which would in turn control a mix of battalions depending on the combat mission. Even though this change was less than a year away, the Infantry School at Fort Benning planned to continue to teach the Pentomic concept right up until the change took place. The Armor School at Fort Knox had never made the change to Pentomic in the first place. Armored divisions had a built-in flexibility that allowed them to mix units to respond to changes on the battlefield. What is more, the Armor School's training in communications, map reading, maintenance, and gunnery was better than that offered by the programs at the Infantry School. (Other subjects were the same at both schools.) I had phoned staff officers who managed infantry assignments to see about the possibility of my attending the Armor School instead of going to Fort Benning's advanced course. The answer was, "Possibility? Zero. Absolutely zero."

In early December 1959 I explained to my father my next moves: "Word came down from Dept. of Army (Infantry) that I would go to Fort Benning in August for the Advanced Infantry course. Brig. Gen. Tucker happened to be on a visit to Fort Campbell [he was head of assignments in Infantry], and I restated my desire to go to Fort Knox instead of Fort Benning. He said he'd look into it on his return to D.C., but I know him from before and he is forgetful. So I'll more than likely go to Benning in August."

I was wrong. On 22 December 1959, I received a letter from the general:

> Dear Lieutenant Galvin:
>
> This is in reference to our recent conversation at Fort Campbell.
>
> The way things now stand, you are programmed for attendance at the Armor Officer Advanced Course in August 1960. This is a fine school and will add to your professional qualifications.
>
> If there is anything further we can do for you, please let us know.
> Sincerely,
> R. H. Tucker
> Brigadier General, USA
> Chief, Infantry Branch

It was during this time that my rifle squad, with Sergeant Williford as squad leader, tied for first place with a squad from E Company. There was to be a runoff for both squads the following week. If we won, we would represent the 501st in division competition, which we had won the year before in A Company.

On 6 February 1960 our Supersquad won first place in the division, and four days later another letter came in to me from General Tucker.

Dear Lieutenant Galvin:
Congratulations on your selection to attend the Armor Officer Advanced Course at Fort Knox. I know you especially desired this course and, fortunately, we were able to get a space for you. You will be the only Infantry officer in this class.
Several factors were considered in permitting you to attend the course at Knox; however, among the most important are that you stood high on the list for attendance at the Infantry Officer Advanced Course and your record indicates that you will be an outstanding Infantry representative. Your record and background indicate you will make valuable contributions to the class and will present the Infantry point of view clearly and diplomatically.
The basic purpose of this letter is to impress on you the importance I place on the attitude of the Infantry student toward this assignment. You are fortunate to attend this course, and the impression you make on the officers of other combat arms will be extremely far-reaching.
I am sure you will find your coming year challenging and enjoyable. The associations you form during your stay will prove profitable in your later career.
Again, congratulations. I will be delighted for you to visit the Branch and discuss this assignment at any time you may find it convenient.
Sincerely,
R. H. Tucker
Brigadier General, USA
Chief, Infantry Branch, OAD

Then Colonel Ashworth wrote from Korea:

Det "A" KMAG
APO 301 San Francisco
28 February '60
Dear Jack,
I just read in the *Army Times* that your squad was judged

the best in the division. I shall never forget that a year ago you also trained Sgts. Barrett and Ocho into a winning combination. This is no small accomplishment and one in which you can be justly proud.

There are all kinds of competitions in the 101st, but to me the rifle squad is the one that counts. Please give my best wishes to S/Sgt. Williford, Sgts. Jacobs and Terrance, and Kane, Ritter, Kennedy, Smith, Lowe, Fritz, Nemith and Pollard. I would bet my shirt they are the finest squad in the Army!

Most sincerely,

Robert L. Ashworth

For myself, I believed that the achievement of "best squad" in two different squads (in a division of 224 squads) in successive annual competitions was definitely the result of teamwork—not only with respect to the squads competing but also in terms of the teaming spirit of the rest of the supporting company.

In April 1960 I was sent to Vieques Island, off Puerto Rico, as an observer of a Marine Corps amphibious landing exercise. On a dirt road near the top of a line of sand dunes, I was talking to a Marine lieutenant as we stood on the edge of the road, chatting nonchalantly, he with his arms folded, as a column of tanks rolled past a few feet away. The dust was so heavy we could hardly see each other—he looked like a brown shadow. It wasn't comfortable, but we liked it. Among the lieutenants it was important, a sign of the true professional, to ignore the "iron" pounding along next to us, shaking the ground, forty tons of M-48 medium tanks heaving up over the hillock and ploughing down the other side. Tanks passed, one after the other, spaced about twenty-five yards apart. My partner in conversation started to say something. Just then the dust blew in, and in an instant he disappeared. I was stunned. I looked down the road and saw him being dragged along, ever closer to the tank, as if he were a fish being reeled in. I ran after him through the dust. Unknowingly my friend had been standing in a loop of telephone wire left behind by troops, and the wire was caught up in an end connector between the track pads of the tank; it lassoed him around the ankles and dragged him down the road. Just as the revolving track began to lift him up, the wire snapped and he fell back. I caught up to him and pulled him off the road as the next tank came up.

He was unhurt. Not a scratch, nothing even where the wire had circled his combat boots. We walked away from the road and sat down. He whacked listlessly at dust and dirt on his fatigues, and I did the same.

"Well," he said, after a while, "so much for setting an example."

A month later, on 13 May 1960, I wrote to my father with more news: "I know you'll be glad to hear that 1st platoon of B Co. was picked as best platoon in the 101st Airborne Division today. We have worked hard for this and we won, which makes us the first unit to ever win both awards in the same year (Division Best Squad, Division Best Platoon). You are one of the few people who will know how happy and proud I am tonight. The platoon leader was Dick Brunkow. His platoon sergeant was Manzi."

We relished the victory, but quickly shifted our focus back to jumps and preparations, training and readiness.

B Co 501 McCoy. We are heading in for Camp McCoy, Wisconsin, and the red light comes on. We have ten minutes—maybe. Stand up . . . hook up. . . . We work mechanically through the memorized checks of parachutes and equipment. I am watching out the open door of the aircraft for some sign of the ground fifteen hundred feet below, but I can see nothing as I squint into the whiteness of the clouds, nothing but our shadow flitting along right below us. Not the best weather.

There is a flash of green forest below, then another, and I sense our speed as these holes in the clouds snap by us. Then we break into a larger pocket with nothing I can recognize, and then we are into the brilliant white again. I have no idea where we are. On the door frame we have a steady red light. I give the crew chief a questioning look and stick up a thumb, and he talks into his hand mike. He presses in on his big rubber earphones to blot out the engine and wind sounds, then returns my "thumbs up" gesture. So the pilot, our airline pilot, says we're on track and good for the jump. OK. I give an unnecessary thumbs up to the troops, who want nothing more than to go charging out the door.

Part of the purpose of this jump is to acclimatize our troops to the long flight that might precede a jump into someplace like Quemoy, and at this moment most of us are showing signs that we need more of this type of training. The last half-hour of this ride has been bumpy. I am standing in the right door, watching the C-123 cruising along on

our right and a little back. It is the right wing of our tight V-forma-
tion. Since we are slowing to 120 or 110 knots, it is hard for the pilots
to match each other's airspeed. Our plane is handsome and fairly new,
at that moment dramatically suspended, appearing and fading as the
scud flashes by, easing up a little, down a little, as if hunting us; closer
in, then drifting away. I am mesmerized in those few unforgettable seconds, headed in at 1,500 feet across the Wisconsin forests and meadows, with the ex-paratrooper at my side, yelling over the noise, "How
in the hell did you convince me to do this?"

My first sergeant, Clifton Reavy, was ten years and two wars older
than I, and his face showed it: lines of wear and tear, lines of determination, sun-squint lines, deep worry lines, scars, webs across his face,
cracks like in an ancient Roman bust of Cicero. He was old school,
quiet, deferential. He had carried a copy of Kipling through World War
II, growling stray lines of Kipling to fit the moment.

On that flight to the fields of Camp McCoy in C-123s, we ran
through our ragged repetitions of Kipling's poetry as we had at Camp
Breckenridge. Reavy would break out over the steel song of the twin
engines and the angry, whining beat of the propellers, and I would follow. In our spontaneous recitations of our favorites, we sympathized
with Jack Barrett's B Company transfer to Quetta, we agreed with the
harsh view of the woman who didn't care, and we bewailed the forgotten old veterans of the Light Brigade.

As a lieutenant and a platoon leader, I was concerned with what we
called "TA-50," the soldier's own equipment: his harness, cartridge belt,
canteen, and pack. We had recently been issued a new TA-50, which I
felt had a lot of things wrong with it. The older TA-50 was clipped onto
the cartridge belt. This new TA-50 had an open hook that went through
the soldier's belt but didn't close itself; and there were all kinds of small
buckles as well. The new issue had been designed for quick release, so
that in an ambush, when you needed to be lighter, you could pull these
quick releases and your cargo pack would fall off. But the real need for
TA-50 equipment is when you wake up in the frozen mud and you're
trying to put the stuff on, not take it off—anybody can take it off—
and it's all frozen and clotted up. Then the hooks would rotate around,
and pretty soon you'd look like a barber pole. I found something like
ninety-five things I felt were wrong with it and wrote a letter to General
Westmoreland about the problem. It got to him, and Westmoreland told
somebody on the staff, "Send Galvin up to Natick and tell him to show
those people what's wrong with this stuff." So I went on my first TDY

(temporary duty) to Natick, Massachusetts, as a lieutenant. I arranged a dummy with the equipment and then gave a briefing to the experts at Natick—majors and lieutenant colonels—just a few miles from my hometown. They were surprised ("We've heard nothing but praise for this stuff we've created"), but they did accept some of the changes.

The visit to Natick was my parting assignment with the 501st. It coincided with the timing of my departure, as General Westmoreland was aware in sending me. I went straight on from there to my next round of officer training.

11

Fort Knox and Ginny

"We took up the study of tactical nuclear weapons."

In early 1960, I was at the Armor School at Fort Knox, among the young leaders of heavy forces. I learned about tank gunnery on the old M-48. I still have sketches of tanks on the range. I took a great interest in the armor course, which was focused on armor's roles and tactics, with a good bit of emphasis on maintenance and gunnery. Map reading at thirty miles per hour, rather than infantry's three miles per hour; and assembling task forces to meet situations and react quickly—this perspective really contributed, I thought, to my development as a soldier.

We started out with a long map maneuver, in which armored forces were met with one challenge after another. Every time the tankers came to something they really didn't want to deal with, they said, "We'll leave that for the infantry to mop up"—which meant let the infantry take care of things that might slow the armor down. After a while, I raised my hand and said, "By my count, we've used about five times as much infantry as we could ever expect to have on any kind of maneuver like this." It got a laugh, but they continued on. Of course I enjoyed fielding all of the infantry questions and just being different; at that time it was strange for an officer to be walking around Fort Knox with crossed rifles on his lapels.

The only infantry officer stationed at the school was "the infantry rep," the liaison officer on the staff, who gave a talk now and then or answered the occasional question about his branch, or perhaps translated a line from some dusty field manual or made excuses for people who dug trenches for a living. As a result of his position in exile, far from the home of infantry, the rep tended to be humorless and wry; he was not the kind of man from whom you would expect a bear hug.

At one point, about the middle of the year, I was in a class, maybe on tactics, and someone came in and spoke to the instructor. The instructor then turned and said, "Captain Galvin, you are wanted up in the infantry rep's office." So I went out into the hall and quickly put on my green jacket, heading up to see the rep.

As I hurried down the hallway, I brushed past a late-arriving classmate, who, ignorant of what turned out to be a plot by his fellow armor classmates, called me back and said, "Jack! What are you doing in armor brass? I had no idea you would do this!" Unwittingly he had saved me from an embarrassing moment, trying to explain to the infantry rep just why I was sporting armor brass. In the flash of a second I realized what they'd done in swapping my insignia, and I had to join in—sort of—with the co-conspirators as they howled in laughter, one and all: colonel, staff, teacher, classmates. To this day I still console myself with the realization that the plan was overly complex—a weakness of armor tacticians.

The bachelors in the class were in the minority at that time. I was sitting one night with several other bachelor officers, all captains in the course. (I had by then been promoted.) Together we were bewailing the fact that none of us had a date that night, because all the really charming women already had boyfriends. Here we were, learning all about tactics, and we didn't know enough tactics to figure out how to get a date. We agreed to get serious in applying our tactical training to the problem. The Army *Five Paragraph Field Order* was just right for us. It taught that the first thing to do, always, was to size up the situation. Our situation was that any woman at Fort Knox that we would like to date was already dating someone else. We decided that what we had to do was somehow separate these girls from their dates. But how? We had to somehow attract them, while repelling their male companions. From a chorus of ideas we came up with a plan: we would pick a Saturday afternoon when a major football game was scheduled, then announce an afternoon tea dance—figuring that the name of the event alone would definitely not appeal to any self-respecting tank officer. Then we formulated an advertising and publicity campaign on the local radio stations and in the newspapers, targeted not only at Fort Knox but at all the surrounding cities and towns. We plastered up posters in stores and restaurants. Everywhere we noted that tickets were free for women and costly for men. On the Saturday of the dance, very few men—besides ourselves—were in attendance.

Ginny Brennan was one of the women who came. She had a boyfriend, but he had opted for the football game. I saw her sitting at a table with a girlfriend or two, and I hurried over and asked her to dance. We danced several times, as I signaled my fellow officers to stay away. At some point I asked her if I could drive her home after the dance. She said no, that her boyfriend was going to arrive soon. I said, "Soon? What time?" She said, "Five o'clock." It was then about 4:15. So we danced some more, while I waited until five o'clock came around. At about one minute after five I asked innocently, "Did your friend come yet?" She said, "No, but he'll be along." I waited about fifteen minutes and asked her again. "No," he wasn't here. Then at 5:30 I said to her, "You're a fascinating woman. One of the things about you that really impresses me is your patience. It is getting towards six, and you don't seem to be bothered by it at all." I could see her getting angry. I kept this up quietly but relentlessly. Finally she said, "You can take me home," and I knew then that I had a chance. On the way to her house—she lived on Fort Knox, to my surprise—I asked her if she would go to breakfast with me the following morning. I suggested the Doe Run Inn, which for me at that moment was one of the most wonderful restaurants in Kentucky. She said yes.

On Sunday morning, I picked her up and we drove over through the little valley where the Doe Run Inn is located. We pulled up outside, and I realized right away that something was wrong: there were no other cars in the parking lot. So I said, "Wait here, Ginny." I went up to a woman at the door and said, "You're open for breakfast, I hope." And she said, "We're closed on Sundays. I'm sorry." I said, "Ma'am, you can't be closed on Sundays. If you are, I've got the biggest problem of my life. Last night I met the most wonderful girl that you can imagine, and I invited her to come here for breakfast today. And here we are." She said, "I'm very sorry for you, but we are closed. The kitchen is closed. There is no staff here." I looked in and noticed that the fireplace was burning. I said, "Couldn't you just toast some bread over that fire? Or do something like that?" She laughed and said, "Come on in." So we went in. Of course, by this time Ginny realized that the place was closed, and she was quite impressed that we were going to have breakfast there anyway, that I could open a closed restaurant for her. For six months I courted Ginny as I finished the school year.

In May we took up the study of tactical nuclear weapons. As I noted to my father in a letter of 1 May 1961, "We are studying nuclear weapons employment problems—all theory, since no one knows what will really happen when they are used. The world situation is the topic of constant conjecture here. Some day my Ranger-jungle work will stand me in good stead. [President] Kennedy is discovering that the world is a very complicated place, but it is hard to say what should be done."

Later that month I and a fellow student, Captain Dan Mizell, wrote a study on the use of the Davy Crockett. This nuclear-tipped missile could be launched from a jeep and was so simple that a lieutenant might be in charge of it. We concluded that a battalion commander could "withhold a smaller reserve, maintain closer contact in withdrawals, disperse his forces in the proximity of enemy strength, and in general be less conservative on tactical employment because of the 'backup' provided by the Davy Crockett weapon."

That year, I was happy to be selected to teach English at West Point. Told I could pick among various graduate schools at which to obtain a master's degree, I chose Columbia, and Columbia accepted me. On the day of my graduation from the Armor School, Ginny and I were married at the Fort Knox chapel, and we went to live in Manhattan on 120th Street and Amsterdam Avenue for a year, where I continued my schooling and Ginny soon became pregnant with our first child.

To be allowed to study for a master's in English at Columbia, I had to show ability in either French or German. Using a little French and a bit more Spanish, and exploiting the fact that the test called for a translation from French to English (a passage on Hawthorne, from the memoirs of François Mauriac) and not vice versa, I took the test, and a week later, Ginny and I went to see how I had done. This was a Saturday.

The building was marked "Philosophy." I said to Ginny, "Well, English must be here." We went inside. Only one other person was there. I said, "Excuse me, ma'am, do you know where the grades for languages tests are posted?" I thought I was talking to a cleaning lady; in fact, I was addressing Marjorie Hope Nicolson, chair of the Department of English and Comparative Literature. I thanked God that I had been courteous. She pointed down the corridor, and said, "You'll see the list on that last door on this side. I pinned it there myself." We thanked her and hurried along through the emptiness to the aforementioned door and found that I had received a passing grade.

I somehow got the impression that Nicolson's class on Milton in the fall of 1961 would be a pleasant experience, and on this I was wrong about her for the second time. In class she was as curt, precise, and demanding as a drill sergeant. "I expect a lot" were her first words to us.

On the other hand, she taught Milton with nonchalance and was given to drifting away into distant realms of thought, and as a result I still cherish my notes from that class. She seemed to know everything about everything, and I liked her style of delivery, even when she lost me in a tangle of allusions, whereupon I would scurry to write down a few phrases in the margins of my Merritt Hughes edition.

The class itself was all about Milton and his critics (Ralph Waldo Emerson, Matthew Arnold, Samuel Johnson), and comparisons of Milton with Dante—this was a graduate class. We didn't stop to parse any lines, much less examine diction and style or ruminate on the power of poetry and the like. What saved me was Milton's military imagery: Satan as warrior, Michael, Abdiel. Nicolson called our attention to the influence exerted on Milton by Edmund Spencer, who himself emulated Chaucer in his choice of archaic words.

I thought, if I'm going to teach poetry, I ought to try writing it.

Accordingly, I wrote "Elegy for Daniel Townsend" in early 1962. The rhythm is a four-beat, like the cadence of marching, and it is also written in an early style (as in *Beowulf*). I wanted it to convey the emotion of before-dawn rallying, with an intimation of building, pulsating danger. Daniel Townsend of Lynnfield, Massachusetts, gave his life at the Battle of Menotomy, of which he had become a symbol. This simple and resolute man had led his small force directly, unerringly, from the far outskirts of the battle area straight into the center. My father had chiseled the stone for his monument in Lynnfield.

In a letter to my father, I reflected on the challenge of writing about Daniel Townsend: "I suffered with my poem, in the writing, more than in any other work ever done by me, and I learned a lot about self-expression as an art. To be able to write you have to know more than the facts: You have to know the reader and how to make him see it all. That is where the real skill lies. Even if the poem is rejected I have benefitted from it. (Your support was appreciated—we poets are very touchy.)"

Marjorie Nicolson liked my attempt at writing poetry.

In the course of my year at Columbia, Robert Frost read to us and Ayn Rand told us how we should think. Meanwhile, a more contemporary hero intervened. As I noted in a letter to my father on 23 February 1962: "We all watched anxiously for the results of Col. Glenn's flight, and were overjoyed and jubilant here. Ticker tape parade is planned next week down Broadway, and I intend to be there with Ginny. Want to be able to tell our kids how we saw the new Lindy."

Just a week later, my letter to my father told of another memorable event:

> I worked on Townsend all day today (Sunday), except for a walk with Ginny on Riverside Drive. As we were walking, a boy about 18 was struck by a car while bicycling and was dragged about 30 feet, caught in the undercarriage. I ran over and helped him out while four or five men lifted the car, then I assisted in making him comfortable until it was obvious that he would be OK. He was badly scraped and bloody all over, but seemed to be in no danger of shock. His bicycle was ground into a ball. He was lucky.
>
> I could see an ambulance arriving, so I walked over to a water fountain to wash and I noticed that my clothes were spattered also. Then I saw that Gin was still holding . . . two ice cream cones, and in an act of bravado I asked for mine, and as we walked along I finished it. Gin was impressed. I was nonchalant. "After all," I told her in a stuffy way, "I am a medic. Such things are common and to be expected."

Three months later, on 18 June, Gin and I were in our small apartment. It was close to midnight as I quit my homework and opened a can of beer. After a couple of gulps, I said, "One beer and I'm drunk." A minute later, Ginny said, "There's water going down my legs." I said, "I'm sober." I ran downstairs and outside to flag a taxi. The Army hospital was on Governor's Island, and my worry was that a cabbie might not want to make the long run to the ferry with a woman in the beginnings of labor, but the first one I asked said, "OK, let's go."

We made it to the ferry and waited on the wooden benches for the boat to cross to our side. I called the hospital to send for an ambulance, and what they sent was a jeep. Ginny, now in pains, said, "How am I going to climb into that thing?" With the help of the medic driver, we struggled aboard and drove to the hospital. The medical crew sent me to wait on some benches until they finally let me in to see our first baby, Mary Jo.

In the meantime, however, Ginny had hemorrhaged, and the nurse, in a businesslike way, asked me to help change the sheets. As I began to work with the nurse, the room turned dark and the nurse seemed to walk up the wall. Then she turned, put a firm arm on my shoulder, and said, "Sit down."

We sat down in the hall stairway. I bent over and rested my fore-head on my knees, and the nurse broke a small vial and held it to my nose. The gyroscopes in my ears settled down, the nurse shook off my apologies, and after a short walk in the corridor she let me return to Ginny's room. So the medic-Ranger sat and sniffed ammonia while extra nurses took care of Ginny.

In the late winter not long before Mary Jo was born, I had decided to invite myself to an office visit with Colonel Russell Alspach, head of the English Department up the Hudson Valley at West Point, who in response invited me to dinner at his house. The colonel was one of a kind. With respect to the uniform, for example, he conceded to the higher authorities in the Academy's chain of command, but with a few exceptions: he wore the jacket to work, but on arrival at his office he donned a sport coat, and instead of the shiny brown official shoes he preferred a crepe-sole pair that he wore on most occasions.

On a wintry day I drove up the Hudson Valley to West Point—and to one of the most enjoyable and memorable conversations I have ever had. The joy of excellent conversation is one of life's true plea-sures, especially when it involves a mutual search for answers. Colonel Alspach understood that, and moved our talk along with captivating skill—even if (or because) his acerbic wit could sound like abruptness, and he often conveyed his lack of interest in what he considered petty chat.

Our conversation that night would have been satisfying in any case, but something he told me that evening changed my life. We were talking about his research on William Butler Yeats. He remembered my poems on West Point eight years earlier and told me that they were why he had recommended me for the West Point faculty. But he con-fided that he much regretted the many intensive moments of concen-tration during his research, when he brushed away random thoughts that might have been productive in future work. "When I was working hard on the Yeats material," he said, "I was often annoyed with myself and dismayed to find my mind roving to other subjects. I saw this as a lack of self-discipline, and I forced myself to suppress these stray ideas and stick to the work at hand."

I was like the colonel in suppressing my mind's wandering. We are constructed such that we can absorb and transmit to our brains thou-sands of sensations every minute. Almost all of them have to do with the routines of life, and we have become expert at dismissing them and focusing on an immediate task. Our minds filter and block out far more than they let in. Yet, even when I'm reading with great attention some book or paper that is truly absorbing, I still find that my mind will wander off—and often the wandering can be quite productive. Alspach's comments started me thinking about ways to *capture* my thoughts and feelings, ways that would fit my own style of thinking.

From then on I began to take notes during the day on scraps of paper and put them away in shoe boxes. When I could afford 3x5 cards I kept them always in my shirt pocket for daily writings, scribbled at odd moments during other activities. At times I collected my thoughts at the end of the day, but normally the days were long and full, and by nighttime I was ready to sleep rather than to write, especially as the next day would begin at reveille. Also, the sense of mission was a hard driver. Besides, exhaustion was a pleasurable feeling, and I could not feel satisfied with myself unless I had expended all of my mental and physical energy. The thought that I could do no more let me sleep easier.

To this day I use my 3x5 cards to capture thoughts in the moment, categorize them, analyze them later, and store them if they seem valuable or discard them if they don't. This helps to keep my thinking productive, by enabling me to hold on to things that come to mind as departures or distractions from the main effort of the moment. Also, I find that by jotting down these stray thoughts I can get more quickly back to the subject at hand. These notes have found their way into articles, letters, speeches, and books—and in a substantial miscellany of files accumulated over the years.

I also discovered fairly early that returning in my mind too often to a certain event in the past caused a fading of details and an anecdotal oversimplification—leading to distortions that I called a "wearing out" of the recalled experience. This was part of my motivation in writing notes to myself. Going through these notes tended to intensify all of them, which heightened them rather than allowing them to lose their meaning. Thus their number increased, as did my enjoyment of the process.

Turning over and over what Colonel Alspach said, I began to view life as a series of thousands of overlapping stories—and the more of them you can hold on to, the better. The habit of taking notes can also have various and interesting effects. Commenting on your own responses to events tends to heighten and intensify your experiences. There is the moment itself; then the capturing of that moment in a note;

then reference to the note as time passes, which is another and different matter. This is of course what we all do, what our minds are doing all the time. And when a thought is released from storage and then returned, it is also changed.

Colonel Alspach wanted everyone coming into the English Department for the first time to take a summer course at Columbia called Advanced Grammar. Peter T. Ward taught the course and had been teaching it for years. He was an anachronism, a holdover from an earlier time. Everyone knew this, and so did he. He was flexible, progressive, responsive, understanding, and easygoing—thin, ragged, not stuffy, always smiling, astute, and entirely likable—but still a man from the nineteenth century. His heroes were George Lyman Kittredge and Frank Edgar Farley, authors of a fine but old grammar book.

I was convinced that grammar was boring and regimented, an ancient and irrelevant set of rules, and I had heard that Professor Ward was already semi-retired. I was full of energy and momentum, and excited by the courses offered that summer and the opportunities they represented. I thought that anyone who would teach grammar for a lifetime had to be a pedant, someone holding on tenaciously to an eroding language, defending old laws that were arbitrary in the first place. I also felt defensive about my lack of interest in grammar, and I was afraid of being shown how little I knew and how much I had forgotten—how I depended on "usage" and didn't know precisely why something "felt right." I tried to obliterate grammar.

Yet here was Ward teaching that "usage makes the rules." Whoever heard of an easygoing grammarian? Ward was ready to accept idiomatic constructions like "What are you up to?" He taught me grammar—but he also taught me tolerance, common sense, and a feeling of warmth with regard to our changing language. He was a mentor, and a good one.

In the summer of 1961, as I prepared for my time at Columbia, in addition to Peter Ward's course, I signed up for an introductory class on literary criticism taught by Professor Davis—which proved to be an experience akin to living through a hurricane. The first class began with the distribution of a dreadful four-page list, which I still have in my files. On the top of the first page were these chilling words: "There is no list of minimum readings. You are responsible for the field of literature. This list and its two supplements, far from setting limits, offer suggestions. You will find an adequate collection in Butler Library."

Back in our shabby apartment on 120th and Amsterdam, Ginny

and I looked in dismay at the list of authors and their works. The readings that I could cross off at the start were a pitiful thirty-two, or one book for every year of my life. Not a laudable number. Professor Davis was right, I thought. I shouldn't be here unless I had read the books on that list. I went to the library and checked out the first half-dozen I hadn't read, and got started.

It worked for a while, for about a month or so, until one morning on the way up the slight slope to Butler Hall, I stopped and asked Ginny to carry my books for me.

"Why?" she said.

"I'm too tired," I stuttered.

She insisted that I go to the medical clinic at the university to talk to a doctor. The next time she heard from me was after they had sent me, by ambulance, to Governor's Island, just below the southern tip of Manhattan, where I was admitted as a patient at the military hospital there. I had pneumonia.

At West Point I taught a variety of courses, beginning with composition and continuing to American and British literature. At the same time I was commuting to the University of Pennsylvania, where I worked toward a doctorate in English, on the early poetry of William Butler Yeats. I had planned to extend my time at West Point to enable me to finish those studies, but I changed those plans when my mentor, Colonel Bill McKean, advised me to go to the Command and Staff College at Leavenworth and thence to Vietnam. I took his advice, stopping my Yeats studies and turning to my notes on the battle of Lexington and Concord. At Leavenworth I learned how to be a division staff officer. I learned very little about Vietnam; in fact, I joined an informal study group that met irregularly to discuss counterguerrilla tactics with veterans of the fighting there. Leavenworth's master's degree in military arts and science required an essay. The manuscript I submitted was later published under the title *The Minute Men: The First Fight: Myths and Realities of the American Revolution* as I was headed for Vietnam, and won the American Revolution Round Table Book of the Year Award for 1966. Near the end of the school year, Ms. Betty Bohannon, head of interlibrary loans at Leavenworth, said to me, "You have used one-half of my budget. Your classmates used the other half."

Part 3

War

12

First Vietnam

"It's not working out."

10 July 1966. Early morning. I gave my bag to the driver at Vails Gate and climbed into a Greyhound bus headed for New York City. Never again would I pass through that crossroads without feeling a sense of loneliness. The driver cranked the door closed and we pulled away. Standing in the aisle, I looked out a window and got a glimpse of Ginny in the Plymouth. She had put on her large reddish sunglasses and was staring straight ahead.

After our year at the staff college, and with me now off to Vietnam, Ginny wanted to return to West Point. "I'm an Army brat," she said. "I want to stay in the Army—that's the life I know. I want to be with the other military families. We still have lots of friends at the Academy, and I know the doctors and nurses at the hospital and the people at the commissary and the school and the child care center." We had found a small apartment in nearby Cornwall-on-Hudson, where she would spend a year folding diapers, fretting over bills, trying in vain to keep a $350 reserve at the Marine Midland Bank, and writing a letter to me every evening. Her routine would include an early reveille to prepare the kids for the drive over the mountain road to West Point, where she left Mary Jo (age four) and Beth (age one) at the post nursery while she went to her courses at Ladycliff College or her volunteer work at the West Point museum. Then came shopping and a drive home with the children; then her studies and the household chores. Her letters kept me in her world and made it all seem interesting, as she laughed at the mini-disasters and was amused when a neighbor made an unsophisticated pass. Reading her letters again now, I see a young woman fighting loneliness and uncertainty, worn from the constant realization that she has no one to share problems with or spell her when she could use a rest, harried by the news of combat in Vietnam, lovingly annoyed with what little kids do and don't do, and pressured by the endless bills to pay. I see also a woman determined, able, realistic, who attended thirteen different schools in twelve years as the Army moved her father through World War II, the Japan occupation, Korea, France, Germany, and various posts in the United States.

Later that day, my flight out of McGuire Air Force Base followed a route over Pittsburgh, where I tried unsuccessfully to pick out Hazelwood, where Ginny was born. Three hours later, above Fort Leavenworth, I saw clearly from thirty thousand feet the tiny house we had just left, on the bluff over the Missouri River. Then over scattered thunderheads at Topeka and patches of snow in the High Rockies, and into Travis Air Force Base for refueling. Then a night landing in Honolulu, a sunrise north of Iwo Jima, and a landing at Okinawa for more fuel. Filled up again, we headed for Vietnam in the early morning. I had taken with me to Vietnam Shakespeare's *Henry IV, Part 1* and *Part 2*. (I still have the paperbacks I read in Vietnam, reddish-colored from the laterite mud and dust.) At about midday, the four engines of the 707 became quieter, and we started down through the open sky toward the white cloud cover stretching off to the horizon on all sides, some fifteen thousand feet below us.

In a few minutes, we were coasting along over the tops of the whiteness. Then we dipped in. Some columns of white flicked by; then the slope of our approach steepened and we passed through layer after layer of gray, darker and darker, almost black. Then the splatter of heavy rain, the whine of flaps deploying, and the groans of wheels coming down. We flattened out, saw lights flash by, and dropped hard onto a watery runway. The engines roared in reverse, the brakes took hold, and then things grew quiet as we turned onto the taxiway.

The rain stayed heavy at Camp Alpha, the replacement center for the 1st Infantry Division. It was rotation time, the completion of the 1st Division's initial year in Vietnam. It was also a year of buildup of U.S. forces. Veterans leaving in droves were outnumbered by replacements like me pouring in, along with new units. I lugged my belongings through the water to a tent with a plywood floor, slippery with mud. I found a cot, dropped my equipment on it, sat down, and fell asleep. After what seemed like a minute, a sergeant tapped me on the shoulder and said, "They're here for you, sir." He told me that a helicopter was waiting to take me to 1st Brigade of the division, which at that time was at Phuoc Vinh. I would be replacing the S3, the operations officer. I had expected to go out to an infantry battalion staff, but instead I was flattered and happy to be selected as a brigade operations officer. For an infantry major there could not be a better assignment.

The Phuoc Vinh base camp had been a French fort, then a Vietnamese army post, then a cantonment for U.S. Special Forces, and then a brigade headquarters. It was a sprawling place, far bigger than I had imagined. I pictured foxholes, trenches, pup tents, and makeshift poncho lean-tos, all camouflaged and hidden, but what I saw ahead in the blue-green jungle was a giant red mud triangular fort, three-quarters of a mile long on each side, crisscrossed by roads and dotted with a jumble of tents, barracks, nondescript huts, and steel shipping containers. There was an airstrip with revetments for helicopters, and there were circular artillery firing positions that looked like forts in themselves. All of this was adorned with miles of concertina wire and thousands of sandbags.

We circled down. There were troops everywhere. A small provincial town seemed to grow out from one side of the perimeter, and a Vietnamese Army garrison clung to another side. I thought, how could this be a brigade headquarters? What are all these troops doing here? The sight of this fortress told me that there was much I needed to rethink, and as this day wore on I realized that the base camp was home to scores of different units, large and small, that had to have someplace to put everything belonging to them but not needed in the jungle. The main command post for the brigade was also the rear area for the infantry and artillery and engineer battalions. We landed at one of the many red clay helicopter pads, this one called appropriately "Downtown." I found a jeep and went first to see the brigade commander, Colonel Sidney Berry. Somebody pointed out his office in a colony of huts, and there I reported to him as he sat behind his desk, erect in his chair, shoulders squared back, head lifted. He was wearing well-starched garrison fatigues, not the jungle variety. He had a courtly air and an unreadable smile. I would be his right-hand man.

"Well," he said, "Can you handle the job?" To him, that was a straightforward question, a way to help me get started on his team. He was looking for enthusiasm, but I didn't want to sound like a cheerleader. I said, with what I thought was an air of confidence, "I think so, sir."

"You think so?" He didn't like that. I saw that this was to be a ritualistic exchange, and I replied with more firmness, "I can handle the job, sir."

We shook hands.

Colonel Berry was being pushed hard. At the end of his one-year tour as an advisor to the Vietnamese forces, he had volunteered to stay on and take command of the brigade. Recently, just as he arrived, there had been some heavy fighting, and now things were quiet. Too quiet. The outgoing operations officer showed me around, introducing me to the staff officers and NCOs. I sensed an unease that became more evident as the first hours went by. The turnover had had its disrupting effect, but there was more to it than that. The new division commander, Major General William E. DePuy, had been a prominent member of General William Westmoreland's staff in Saigon, and from that vantage point he had become convinced that the 1st Infantry Division needed resuscitation. To him this division was sedentary in its fortified bases like Phuoc Vinh—"flat on its ass," to quote him; more of a target than a force to be reckoned with. And now the division's most voluble critic was its commander.

The leaders in the chain of command were anxious to please him, and were jumpy in his presence. The Westmoreland approach to fighting the war, as interpreted and influenced by General DePuy, had an aspect to it that I understood only later. Both generals felt that the Vietnam jungle war was pulling us away from our main mission. The readiness of the Army was always to be foremost, and the way to maintain that level of readiness was to fight this war with the same structure that would be needed for the defense of America against any major threat. To the extent possible, priorities were to be established in support of this goal. Officers were assigned command positions for six months only, which maintained a generation of the right kind of combat veterans, trained within the traditional infrastructure. General Westmoreland was determined to do his part in preserving the ability of the U.S. Army to fight a big, intense, complex war. We held the best cards, he would say. We had overwhelming firepower, and all we needed to do was bring it to bear, focusing it on defined targets. In large part it was a management issue: we would find the enemy, pin him down, and destroy him with an orchestrated combination of ground fire, artillery, helicopter gunships, air strikes, naval gunfire, and high-altitude bombing. It took precise coordination, and it would require not only the platoon, company, and battalion structure, but also division and corps command organization. All of this power was ready and available. What was needed were leaders with the skill to trap the enemy and create the inferno, time after time. When this jungle war was over, the 1st Division would still be ready for heavy duty in high-intensity warfare.

General DePuy often summed it up at classes for his officers: fire-power demonstrations, simultaneous delivery of all weapons on a few acres of jungle, "servicing the targets," as he sometimes called it. We would do what we did best—the heavy fighting, locked in jungle and mountain battle. "But instead, what?" he would say. "You're sitting around. Get off your duffs."

Our brigade area of operations was a ten-mile square to the north-west of Saigon. Route 16 ran north up through the middle to the Cambodian border, and the little town of Phuoc Vinh sat in the center of the square, astraddle some of the main routes and trails into Saigon from the north and west. For all of us, the spring was wound tight. We concentrated on action, on seizing the initiative, but the brigade also had to keep its three battalions supplied with ammunition, fuel, and food, along with everything from barbed wire to toilet paper to spare parts for helicopters, bulldozers, and generators. Mail, medicine, and light miscellaneous supplies arrived regularly by helicopter, but most support came from the rear, by truck, during four-day periods carved out of each month, when the road would be cleared and defended for a shuttle of truck convoys. The cycle was, of course, predictable, and local Viet Cong units would do their best to exact a toll for our use of the road, but their response was also like clockwork, giving us a chance to engage them, concentrating our infantry and cavalry and fire support units along the road. As I arrived, one of these supply operations was under way, with three hundred trucks shuttling on the route from Phuoc Vinh to supply dumps in the division rear at Di An, on the outskirts of Saigon.

The next day, 15 July, as the monsoon season deepened, I took over the position as brigade S3. Colonel Berry was a man of action; he wanted me to be with him so that I could see firsthand what he expected the brigade to do. In the command helicopter we moved restlessly among our battalions, where we discussed the mission, the current situation, problems, plans, and possible future changes. En route we watched the progress of the convoys and kept in touch with the brigade staff by radio. The experience of following the action every day helped me get to know our potential battlefields; at the same time I tried to keep abreast of my brigade operations assistants, the intelligence section, and the division headquarters staff in Lai Khe. By the time we returned from hours in the Huey, I had compiled a formidable list of things to be done before we took off on the following day—and the captains and sergeants were waiting with their lists for me.

We would work into the night, dealing with issues of the day while watching over the night operations of the battalions; and every morning before seven we crowded into one of the wooden huts and sat in rows on metal folding chairs, waiting for a call to order. In the front row sat the lieutenant colonel commanding the battalion defending the Phuoc Vinh base, plus the artillery commander, the brigade staff officers and some of their assistants, the Air Force liaison officer, the engineer company commander, the battalion and division liaison officers, and representatives from tenant units stationed on the base, along with visiting senior commanders, media people, and others. We would all stand for the arrival of the brigade commander. Then the briefing, led by me, would commence. Gecko lizards climbed the screens and chirped as we went over the details of the past twenty-four hours and the next.

The base defense commander at that time happened to be Lieutenant Colonel Paul Gorman, always a fighter, who detested being pulled off the line with his battalion to protect the brigade headquarters and other elements at Phuoc Vinh. I could expect a withering criticism of any detail of my reporting that disagreed with his views. After a particular morning (22 July) when he had battered me and the rest of the brigade staff, I went to see him and said, "Sir, what do you expect the relationship between your staff and Brigade to be?" He answered, "Tension," and tension it was. The competition for resources pitted staff officers and even commanders against each other over all kinds of issues—replacements, helicopters, bulldozers, demolitions, even mission assignments. Part of this was due to pressure from above. Part of it could be attributed to the unusual amount of turnover of leaders at all levels. Part was no doubt the fog of war. Part may have been my imagination.

Colonel Berry hated to be cooped up in a fortified camp. He declared that the briefing hut was too bare. He wanted enlarged regimental insignia painted on wooden plaques, representing all the units of the division, to hang under the low rafters. He ordered Leroy ink on the ever-changing briefing maps. (The grease pencil was too sloppy.) He called for the ceiling of the hut to be covered with parachute silk and a brigade sign to be hung over the doorway, and demanded a red-and-white pointer for the use of briefers. He wanted these trappings, but he also disliked them. It was *War and Peace*, a collision of the controlled and orderly world with the pragmatic untidiness of battle. He much preferred a field command post—but if it had to be garrison, then it also had to be spit-shined boots and starched fatigues.

We found parachutes and plywood and ink. The missing pointer became a test case. Somewhere we found paint to achieve the red-and-white striping of the pointer, but the paint was stiff and we had no paint thinner, so we used gasoline instead, which caused the paint to remain sticky. Wet or dry, we had to go with it, and the pointer's debut was another minor fiasco, with the air liaison officer, Air Force Major Jim Lancaster, making his report with a pointer stuck to his open hand. Nobody laughed.

While we ran the convoys, we planned an attack into a place we called the Heart-Shaped Woods. When the resupply was finished, we airlifted four U.S. battalions and one battalion of the Vietnamese 5th Infantry Division into that area. On our way in we encountered heavy rain, with fog rising out of the jungle canopy. We dodged among fat blue columns of descending water and carried the battalions into small open areas in a practically featureless forest, drew them into a tight circle, and had some skirmishes, but the enemy chose to get out of the area rather than fight, and the result was not what we had hoped. In a letter to my father I said that the plan "sounds pretty simple, but on helicopter-borne operations involving multiple battalions, the whole thing can become rather complicated and (once the fight starts) can turn into chaos in a moment if you're not careful. When action begins I do a lot of odd jobs but mostly maintain communication with everyone and just try to hang on and keep them all going the same way. . . . Came back with a flight of UH1B choppers through a monsoon rain—each chopper leaving a long trail (or wake) in the heavy, foggy rain. Looked like a speedboat race."

At the end of the letter I wrote, "Hope to do a lot better."

General DePuy obviously hoped so, too. He was not a happy man. Convinced that the enemy must be farther northwest, he took all but one of our battalions away to reinforce another brigade, telling us to make plans to move north to Quan Loi and Loc Ninh, closer to the Cambodian border. Meantime, a Viet Cong battalion was gathering south of us. That day I flew with our Air Force liaison officer in a light aircraft to look at some of the routes used by the Viet Cong to move supplies. I knew little about the enemy's infrastructure, including the trail system and how it was used. With my three weeks of experience, I concluded that instead of searching through the jungle, we should give more importance to blocking and ambushing along the trails that were getting the most activity. The Viet Cong had to keep their own supplies moving, and it was clear that whoever moved in the jungle became vulnerable. I said we should act like a "dog in the manger," a phrase that was not apt. It didn't sound like something General DePuy would want. Colonel Berry considered it and said, "We can't wait for them; we have to go get them. If they want to come after us, fine. As long as we get contact."

In early August, General Harold K. Johnson, chief of staff of the Army, came to see General Westmoreland and to visit some of the U.S. units, including our brigade with our one battalion. Colonel Berry told me to prepare a briefing for the general. He said, "Let me hear it from beginning to end, just the way you're going to brief it." I made ready and we went to the briefing hut. He sat where General Johnson would sit and said, "OK, begin."

I started out with, "Good morning, General . . ."

"No," he said. "No good mornings."

And it went downhill from there. It was a skeet shoot. That night, while I put the shattered pieces of the briefing together in the form Colonel Berry wanted, I felt that a door was beginning to close, or that it had not yet opened.

Next day, however, the briefing went all right. General Johnson said very little. Our battalions came back to us on 8 August and we moved immediately into an attack near Chon Thanh, about ten miles northwest of Phuoc Vinh, where our patrols had been skirmishing with what looked like enemy scouts from a larger unit. We were given forty-two helicopter sorties from various locations, and I guided the battalions to the fight. We made contact, and both sides took casualties in a running battle as the enemy again slipped away. This activity around us meant something was up, but without much specific knowledge of our enemy's moves we tended to react to a tip from a single captured soldier or to a hunch on the part of one of our commanders, or to an intercepted radio message or a fleeting glimpse from a helicopter. We were proud of our mobility through the air, which allowed us to move relatively long distances over rough terrain in a short time—though we had to concede that an ad hoc lift with Hueys carrying a few soldiers each amounted to a slow buildup. Firepower we had, and plenty of it. Our consistent weakness was our lack of intelligence at the tactical level.

Colonel Berry decided to move us onto the major rice trails. On 13 August at 10:30 a.m., we had just finished giving the brigade order for an operation to be called "Gallop," aimed at shutting down the trails at one of the places where they seemed to come together, a ganglion in the network. But the operation never took place. I described what did happen in a letter to Ginny:

> General DePuy called for Colonel Berry and me to meet him east of Thu Dau Mot for a briefing on something new that had come up. We took off in a Huey and arrived there about 10:55 in a driving rain. . . . [The division] had picked up a "rallier" (defector) who put the finger on his battalion—along the Saigon River just above Cu Chi. . . . The upshot was that 1st Brigade was to get three battalions—1/16 Inf, 1/26 Inf, and 2/28 Inf to go after the VC—only one of those Bns was actually with us at PV [Phuoc Vinh]—1/26, Col. Gorman. We ordered it airborne to Phu Loi immediately (in the heaviest rain I've seen so far) and Col. B. took the VC and went with him out to recon, leaving me to coordinate the arrival of the Bns. The VC were in close to the river in wood lines along the rice paddies, also fortified underground on 3 hills.
>
> We got 1/26 on the ground and attacking by 1430. 1/16 (Col. Wallace) in there by 1700, from Lai Khe, and 2/28 also coming in thru the rain at darkness, starting 1800 and in by 2000 (from Lai Khe). The helicopter Co. Commander was wounded in the foot on 1st lift—flew all day without telling anyone. Very heavy fire with everyone taking hits—Gen. DePuy's ship took 2, Col. Wallace's shotgunner [door gunner] wounded about 1200, Wallace called in about 1300—hit again and going down—another pilot called 5 min. later to say Wallace's pilot managed to make Phu Loi, a relief to all of us—the air was full of fighters, artillery very heavy—but after darkness the VC broke contact and slipped away thru tunnels, etc.
>
> Next morning, after a bad night in the paddies, Brigade attacked to the river—I stayed at the forward command post in a fort (ARVN) near Cu Chi. . . . In the afternoon I got up to take charge when Col. Berry went in for fuel and for the first time (a very few minutes) I controlled a battle—the air full of helicopters lifting troops and fighters on strafing, napalm, and bomb runs.

But we didn't have much to show for it all, and General DePuy was unhappy. Small body count. The rallier was probably telling the truth, and a good portion of the VC battalion was in the bunker system when the operation started. This base area was only one of dozens in the radius of a few miles. All of them had been painstakingly constructed over the years. The tunnel systems were extensive and well constructed, primitive as they were.

General DePuy had been monitoring our radio net. At one point he landed next to the little bedraggled fort and walked over to watch me work the radios. In a quiet few minutes, we talked. He was almost amiable; but his comment, the one I remember most, was, "Jack, your trouble is, you don't know how to be a prick." With that he walked away, and I went back to the radios.

19 August 1966, 1900 p.m., Phuoc Vinh—to Gin:

Hello Sweetheart—

The cycle begins to repeat itself. Tonight we are getting ready to run a convoy down to Di An to resupply ourselves at Phuoc Vinh. We have to do this about once a month, and it means a 4–5-day operation, clearing the road so that the trucks can move. Tomorrow we send troops all along the road from PV down to Bien Hoa. The VC are beginning to concentrate here around our own area, because the monsoon rains and swollen rivers have forced them to come down out of the mountains. We had planned to go up there after them, but the fights may well take place down here, fairly close to the Saigon area.

My visit to 10th [Vietnamese Army] Division paid dividends. Today the 10th Division Commander and staff came over here to PV to coordinate with us on plans to make some attacks south of PV.

One of our jobs is to push the VC away from the Song Be—one of their aims is to cross the Song Be and gain control of the land up above Saigon. The Song Be also marks the boundary between ourselves and 10th ARVN Division, and we are trying to operate in conjunction with them. We work along with the 5th ARVN Division at Phu Loi and the 10th ARVN Division at Xuan Loc.

We (1st Brigade) sit right between C Zone and D Zone, along the VC routes between their two "safe" areas. We're trying to catch them passing between these areas. They have

to move a lot of rice and supplies, and we try to keep them
from doing it.

I am pretty well settled down now, and more or less
confident that I can hang on to my job, though not at all
happy with results so far. All I can say is that I'm doing
the best I know how—the job many times every day seems
more than I can handle, and I am forever behind the 8-ball,
but just giving it my best and hoping that all will turn out
well.

Perhaps my greatest impression of beauty is the jungle,
when it stretches out below like a green, misty carpet under
me. It is so lovely and yet so full of death and destruction that
there comes a fascination hard to describe. I have come to
know certain areas of it pretty well—just like my hometown,
and perhaps even better—but I still have a lot to learn. If I
only had more time to reflect on all of this! Perhaps later,
when I am more sure of what I'm doing.

I miss you more than I can ever say. This year away from
you will make me love you more than I ever thought possible.
All I want is to be with you once again, when we can live our
lives and love each other.

Today again, no rain. Thank goodness. The monsoons are
now half over. They will be finished by the end of September
or the middle of October. By then I'll be here three months.
I hope by then I'll have a little more control of this job and a
little more experience.

Sometimes I think of home and you and the kids, but to
tell the truth it is very hard to dwell on such things for long.
Just don't dare to think too much. The jungle closes in. But my
morale and my faith in myself is still strong and will continue
to be. Nothing is too hard, and if others have done it, so can
I. In the end I will be proud of this service to my country—
as proud as I have ever been of anything. I can show them,
as many have done before me, the quality of the West Point
product when the chips are down (and, of course, the quality
of the Boston Irish!).

I hope this is not depressing—actually I'm as content as
anyone here could be, looking forward to a year of action and
service—and then to my wife, my family, and my home. I

could never express how much I miss you especially, but also
the kids, Cornwall, Coo & Larry, and all the rest.
Love forever, Jack

It was now time to conduct once again our resupply operations, the
four-day cycle of truck convoys to the rear areas and back. I recommended that this time we keep the brigade command post at Phuoc
Vinh, where communication was good in all directions, aviation was
available, and defense was well established. It was a place we had to
defend anyway, I noted, and if we came under attack at a hastily established location in the field, or at a spot between locations, it would
detract from our ability to run the convoys and still be ready for anything else that might happen. "That's been the problem with this outfit," Berry observed. "We're stuck in Phuoc Vinh." He wanted a tactical
command post out along the road. I added into the brigade order that
we would locate a part of our brigade headquarters in one of the artillery battery positions about halfway along the convoy route to Di An.

On 24 August the battalions moved to the road, each with a troop of
cavalry. The following morning at 7:40, a sixteen-man patrol from one
of the battalions reported itself heavily engaged by automatic weapons
and mortar fire within a large enemy bunker area. A little later, the sergeant leading the patrol reported that his two machine guns were out of
action and that the patrol was in danger of being overrun. He retreated
to an empty enemy bunker and called for artillery fire on his own position; the shells broke up the enemy attack, but communication with
him stopped. The acting battalion commander, Major Richard Clark,
sent eighty-five men, including a platoon of cavalry under Captain William Mullen to reinforce the patrol. Mullen headed southwest toward
the patrol's last known location and was soon in thick terrain, pushing
along with a tank in the lead, followed by a few tracked armored carriers, smashing a path toward the patrol, about three jungle miles away.
Major Clark alerted the rest of his battalion to get ready to move.

Colonel Berry and I were up over the fight, along with Air Force
Liaison Officer Major Lancaster and Lieutenant Colonel Rodgers, the
artillery battalion commander. Berry ordered Lieutenant Colonel Gorman, whose battalion was on the southeast side of the fight, to come in
on the south, and fast. Gorman commandeered several engineer dump
trucks and loaded his troops aboard, and at 8:43 he started up the road
to meet with some cavalry tanks and armored carriers and drive north
into the jungle. At 9:10, Major Clark had the rest of his battalion on the

north and east sides moving toward the fight, along with the part of the armored cavalry under his control, and at the same time his lead company commander, Captain Mullen, gave us his location and said he was in a firefight. At 10:00, one of Gorman's companies, commanded by Captain Madden, arrived on the south side and moved into dense jungle toward Mullen. At 11:10, General DePuy gave us another battalion, under Lieutenant Colonel Wallace, and we ordered it in from the west.

Colonel Wallace reported his battalion in a heavy firefight on the west side at 1:05 p.m. At this point, Major Clark was struggling to get the three other companies of his battalion into action and link up with his captain, Madden, who had worked out a hasty plan with Mullen. Those two companies pushed on into the bunkers under heavy fire. Then Madden reported to Colonel Gorman that he had a prisoner who said that his unit was moving out of the fight toward the west. Gorman, who had been moving the rest of his battalion along the south side, called Berry and got permission to cut off this move, and with part of his battalion he started for Bong Trang, westward. At 1:45 an Air Force medevac helicopter was shot down in the middle of the fight. Division also notified us that a fourth battalion, under Lieutenant Colonel Elmer Pendleton, was given to us, and we told Pendleton to come in from the northwest, blocking the last open corner of the square.

We were at that point about five hours into the action. There had been no word from the lost patrol, but we assumed (correctly) that it was in the center of our square. We began to make the square smaller. Clark's companies were split up on the north and east sides, and intermingled with one of Gorman's companies (the one led by Madden). The cavalry was trying to fill gaps in the square, and had two tanks out of action. Clark had been guiding his commanders from the air in a small H-13 observation helicopter, which was constantly under fire. Colonel Berry told him to get on the ground and take charge of his battalion from there—whereupon Clark landed in a small clearing close to the heaviest part of the fighting, dismounted, and sent his helicopter away. I noted the place, and a little later Colonel Berry said he wanted to go in and talk to Clark face to face, to get a clear picture of how things looked on the ground and instruct Clark and the others on what to do next. We landed in brush near a wood line, more or less in the spot where Clark had landed; Berry climbed out and went into the woods to search for him. I lifted off and got back up over the fight again, working the radio nets.

In the square there were a few small areas of high and low brush, grass, and scattered high trees. Throughout most of the square, though, there was nothing but thick green canopy blocking out everything. In the air we maneuvered so that we flew over the fight from different angles each time. I was able to differentiate the clumps of higher trees as their shapes grew familiar. One very high tree stood out from all the rest ("Green Giant," I said to myself); another had broken limbs showing orange slashes ("Orange Tree"). A group of three tall clumps formed a straight north-south line ("The Line-Up"). These mini-landmarks kept me oriented on my map. I called for smoke from the companies, one by one, and used my reference points to mark their map positions. Nobody liked giving positions away with smoke grenades, but they knew we had to maneuver arriving units into the ongoing fight at the right places.

My map was covered with decoding scribbles and unit symbols, enemy positions, air strike targets, and possible landing zones for reinforcement. As distances between units became shorter, the danger of fratricide increased, and radio calls from battalions and even companies asking for their own precise map coordinates became the highest priority for ground troops, air force support, artillery, attack helicopters, medevac helicopters, and commanders at every level.

At 3:00, Colonel Berry radioed from the ground on Clark's frequency. Amid the sharp crack of bullets, he told me that Clark had just been killed, that he, Berry, would take charge on the ground, and that I should continue to work the reinforcements and supporting fires. Berry then radioed Gorman, who with part of his battalion was still looking for enemy out to the west, and called him back to the fight. As Gorman reported later, "We were searching around Ap Bong Trang when I got an urgent order from Berry to 'get up here as soon as possible,' and I could tell from his voice that he meant it."

The Phu Loi battalion began jamming our command radio nets. We could work through the jamming, but this slowed our communications, which at this time were crowded with what amounted to a roll call of commanders across the division, and I didn't want to stop receiving information that I might need. At that point the issue was net control. Our brigade forward command post was still relocating, having left Phuoc Vinh by road convoy when the road opened in the morning while the brigade main command post remained open at Phuoc Vinh; but the fighting units were so close to each other that I had to have the last word on coordination—and I held to that, though there were questions aplenty about who was in charge of what.

In those moments the entire division was a mix of ad hoc teams. The mission had become "rescue the lost patrol, reinforce the units in contact, and surround and destroy the enemy." We juggled all three missions. Sitting next to me, Major Lancaster controlled the Air Force fighter-bombers and Lieutenant Colonel Rodgers worked the artillery, each of us on multiple radio frequencies. Everyone wanted exact locations of friendly forces. Whenever I was unsure, I called the unit, requesting "pop smoke," and at times the enemy, listening in on the radio frequency, showed smoke too. This VC battalion was one of their best; they knew us well. At times they even matched the color of our smoke. But in either case they signaled their own position, which I also noted. At times ammunition was critical. At other times it was medevac.

On the frequencies at various times were the division commander, the division staff, the forward command post (still arriving and setting up), and the convoys (with trucks still moving). Colonel Berry, still on the ground, was doing his best to organize the small-unit leaders and coordinate their efforts, using radios wherever he could find them. He saw to it that the wounded were put into armored carriers for the run to the clearings, where they could be picked up by helicopters. At one point a medevac pilot called in, asking for the location for picking up the wounded. I gave it to him quickly, and General DePuy broke in and ordered, "Guide him in yourself." We dropped down and skimmed the trees there and I threw out a smoke grenade; then we climbed back up and resumed the ongoing communications.

At about 4:00 p.m., Lieutenant Colonel Gorman arrived and took over the ground fight from Colonel Berry, who then called for me to pick him up. I landed at the spot where I had left Berry, and he came out of the wood line and scrub a few yards away, carrying an M-16 rifle he had found. We resumed flying the area. At dusk there was a clang as we took a round through the helicopter's underbelly that left a hole between Jim Lancaster's feet and continued out the top, passing through a fuel tank on the way. We called for a replacement, and when it was ready we landed and made the exchange. By the time we got back over the fight it was dark, and contact had been reduced to sporadic firing.

At 8:40 p.m. we landed at our forward command post. From there we kept up a quick succession of messages to and from units as they reorganized, adjusted their positions, and were resupplied with ammunition of all kinds and with rations and water—and brought out their remaining dead and wounded. At Berry's side I marked the edges of my map with dozens of encoded reports, using letters for numbers and vice versa, where a pencil point's difference could mean lives lost or saved.

At 6:15 a.m. on the 26th, it was light enough to see when we lifted off in the brigade command helicopter. The patrol was still missing. At 7:21, Gorman reported heavy small arms fire from bunkers to his front, and requested an east-west air strike fifty meters north of his position. Within fifteen minutes, fighter-bombers came in with napalm. Gorman asked for more strikes in the same place. One canister hit into the high treetops very close to Gorman himself, and part of the fiery napalm splashed down on him and his command group; it burned the map he was holding and knocked out his radio. He got hold of a workable radio and asked for another strike, same place, and again it hit friendly as well as enemy positions. At this point Colonel Berry called off further air support. From then on our effort became one of mopping up, with the remainder of the VC battalion fighting as individuals and moving away toward the northwest along a variety of different routes. We were elated when nine men from the patrol, who had been hiding in an enemy bunker throughout the action, walked into our lines. A little later, Lieutenant Colonel Wallace reported finding the remaining six, all dead. They had elected to fight their way out and were overwhelmed.

At 8:30 a.m. Berry dropped me off at the command post, so I could work on the casualty reports. I was sitting at a table in an open field, taking radio reports during a lull in the fighting, when Brigadier General Hollingsworth, the assistant division commander, circled in his helicopter and landed close by. He listened over my shoulder and differed with me on my count of enemy dead. We could not reach agreement, so I gave him my radio handset and said, "Sir." He took it and reported his view of the numbers. As for our own casualties, my notes at 3:50 p.m. on 26 August read: "Killed in action 30, wounded in action 183." My father sent me a clipping from the *Boston Traveler* of 27 August 1966 that reads: "U.S. officials gave correspondents exact figures on Americans killed and wounded in the napalm accident but asked that they not be used in dispatches."

Early that evening, Colonel Berry and I were in a small tent, and I was shaving off a two-day stubble. He came over and said he wanted to tell me something, and when I looked around, he said, "This is not working out."

"Sir?"

"You and I," he said. "It's not working out. The chemistry is not there. We're not a good combination." A pause. Then he added, "I'm going to replace you."

I don't remember what else got said. It was a quiet conversation—the first time I felt that we had made a close connection. I think he explained it as well as he could, given the gap between us. The teaming wasn't there—the chemistry, as he called it—and that was true. It wasn't just this two-day fight. I never made the Berry-DePuy team.

I was not simply relieved of my position as brigade operations officer; I was to be sent out of the brigade altogether, out of the 1st Infantry Division, and back to Saigon, where a job would be found for me somewhere in the rear. My recollection of the next hours is only a vertigo compounded of exhaustion, aloneness, and something far deeper than regret. Later, I helped Major Roger Culbertson, my friend and Leavenworth classmate, settle in and take over my responsibilities. I then signed the brigade daily report for the last time. I had hit rock bottom.

The next morning, Monday, 28 August, I rode back to brigade main headquarters at Phuoc Vinh on a helicopter that was carrying bags marked "U.S. Mail." When we arrived, I went to the operations center and said good-bye to the brigade staff officers and NCOs there, then gathered my belongings into a duffel bag and headed back to the helicopter. What followed was an incongruous moment. I discovered that in the mailbag were rumpled packages from Ginny: cookies. I stuffed them into my already full duffel bag and we took off for Di An, the rear area. The door gunner smiled and said, "Are we going to share?" It was the only light moment in the several days before and after. I broke open a box of crushed but homemade chocolate chip cookies, and as we flew along in the rain, just under low gray scud hanging in festoons, we munched on cookie fragments. Forty days. Four fights. I later wrote to Ginny: "My mind was both full of thousands of thoughts and also a blank. I even stopped at the new chapel there and knelt down for a while to see if I could get myself an organized picture of the past and future, but I almost fell asleep instead."

Two days after the action along the convoy route to Di An, I walked over through a heavy rain to Third Field Hospital in Long Binh to see some of the troops that had been in the fight, including a lieutenant named Tom Galvin, one of Gorman's platoon leaders.

Part of the hospital was a run-down brick building surrounded by ankle-deep muddy water in all directions. I sloshed up onto a porch and through a doorway—with no door—and went down a hall that had two inches of water on the floor. A bedraggled and preoccupied nurse wearing flip-flops was coming the other way. She stopped, as if she had forgotten something. She was stoop-shouldered with exhaustion. I said, "Wet day," and she nodded, "Wet day." I asked her if she knew whether Tom Galvin was somewhere in there, and she looked at my name tag and then again at me. I said, "No relation." She gave me directions. On the way to Tom Galvin's ward, I saw a bedraggled rat plop into the water and paddle away. I got lost, wandering around the wards. A little later I spoke to a doctor, a major, and she pointed me again toward the ward where Tom was. She said Tom had damage to the left side of his head and his left eye. His right eye seemed OK, but she wasn't sure. He had cuts on his legs and on his left ear, left cheekbone, forehead, and shoulders. His right arm was fractured. That's all she could remember at the moment. The Third Field was no place for conversations on that day.

Finally I saw the name "Galvin" at the foot of a bed. There was no other way to know Tom. His head and face were completely bandaged, leaving only his mouth, which itself wasn't much to look at: a hole in the bandages, cracked and battered. One arm was bandaged and the other was in a cast, both of them across his chest. He could talk, though, and he wanted to tell me, in a voice that was weak and hoarse, that he was OK and was getting good care. His main concern was for his wife, Carol, and his folks. I took down Carol's telephone number and told him I'd have Ginny call her and pass on the news that he was doing fine. Then I asked him if he'd like to dictate a letter that I could send to her, and together we wrote letters to Carol and to Tom's mother and father. Just before I left, Tom said, "We really kicked the shit out of them, didn't we?"

I said, "We sure did."

That night, with the help of a ham shortwave radio operator who contacted a friendly ham in California, I made a good telephone connection to Ginny in New York and gave her Carol's phone number in Palisades Park, New Jersey. "Tell her that he's OK and will be home soon," I told Ginny.

Tom recovered.

The U.S. Army headquarters in Saigon was housed in a couple of boxlike cinderblock buildings alongside Tan Son Nhut airfield. After a couple of weeks of doing nothing, I was assigned to the logistics section. Among my administrative duties, I was made staff action officer for the turnover of the Caribou aircraft from the Army to the Air Force. The

Army said the planes were in excellent condition; the Air Force said they were flying junkyards. Negotiations had reached a standstill. I recommended that the Air Force senior crew chiefs begin flying alongside their Army counterparts. This was accomplished, and one by one the crew chiefs of both services found ways to reach agreement on the exchange. Once again, I thought to myself, the tutelage I had received from Staff Sergeant Smith in my National Guard days had provided me with the answer: give hands-on NCOs a crack at the problem.

My new duties as a logistics staffer were more or less an eight-to-five routine, with an occasional long day. In the evenings I walked to my quarters, ate some snack food, and stumbled along on a small portable typewriter, teaching myself to touch-type (with the help of the Rowe College Typing manual). I also spent some time thinking how I could convince my boss, Lieutenant Colonel Sheffey, and his boss, Colonel Alvin C. Isaacs, and *his* boss, Brigadier General Earl F. Cole, to let me go out to a combat unit. Thus went my days in Saigon.

Often when the staff work was light I went to the operations shop and read the files of combat reports over the past year. The 1st Cavalry Division reports were so interesting that I decided to write another book, this one on the change in warfare with the arrival of the helicopter, which made the ground war three-dimensional: the flat-surface map became a cube, although not every tactician was willing to accept this. In the library I found a set of the series that we call the Green Books, a history of the U.S. Army in World War II. These I knew were well written, and I dove into them to get a rough idea of each of the American airborne operations of the war. This gave me a start on my next book, *Air Assault*. In spare moments I also continued to search through the Vietnam after-action reports of the 1st Cavalry Division and the other divisions, focusing on the parts having to do with helicopter operations. I knew that these would give me a good background if I managed to get back to a combat unit. They would also help with my research to see what had been written about parachute and glider operations since their beginnings in World War II.

Ginny and I had turned in the manuscript of *The Minute Men* a week before I left for Vietnam. My contract with the publisher, Hawthorn, called for a bountiful advance of $750 to be paid at that point—and now, four months later and unaware of how leisurely publishers view the handling of financial matters like royalties and such, we expected that the contract would have resulted in a check. Instead, we were still waiting for this considerable sum of money to boost our bank account up to a safe level. Our subsequent exchange of letters made me think of our parents, hers and mine, who were never able to stay very far ahead of the grocer.

We had promised each other to write letters that were not sugar-coated, and for the most part we kept to that oath, but October 1966 was not a good month for us, as we tried to get used to a conversation that had a delay of about two weeks between question and answer. On 29 September Ginny wrote a letter that I received on 9 October. In it she said, "I have three quarters in my purse to do till payday—Monday, I hope. And two of those will go to wash diapers on Saturday. I guess I will study and sew the weekend away." I answered her that evening, noting that our September pay would arrive soon to keep the wolves from her door, and cheerily reminding her that the Hawthorn money would help out, "if I have to shoot someone to get it."

The weekend passed, and on Monday, 3 October, Ginny wrote,

Today was a day to remember. I have to try to keep a sense of humor about it because I don't know what else I'd do! After class I planned on going to the commissary since I didn't even have baby food and milk. But I thought I'd better stop by the bank to check on my pay. Well, the girl said, "Oh yes, I can check your balance—would you know if [your check is] in?" I assured her there would be some indication in my balance. It was crowded in the bank and there were people all around me waiting for help. When the girl came back and said, "Mrs. Galvin, there is 62 cents in your account," I couldn't decide whether to laugh or cry. So I asked her to please check and see if the check might not have come in the mail. She called the auditing dept., and then I found out that not only was my check not in, and 62 cents in the bank, but they had an overdrawn check they were holding for me, awaiting the pay. Needless to say, I left as fast as I could get thru the crowd there.

In the car I sat and thought for five minutes. What would I do? I had to have food and milk for the kids—and I had $1.02 in my wallet. At home I had no vegetables, meat, bread, oleo, or milk and two baby food jars (for lunch today). So, I took 10 deep breaths, started the car, and headed for the commissary. There I got the bare necessities—for $8—and wrote a check, praying as I wrote it that the pay would be in—and left for home.

Actually the situation is so ridiculous that I have to be able to laugh—I'll be so happy when that damned $750 for the book comes in and I'll have something to rely on in situations like this. I get so fed up with the government not getting our pay out by payday; there is no excuse to go to the 5th of the month (like last month) before it arrives. If the situation continues, I'll picket in front of CBS in NYC saying something like "U.S. Gov't. unfair to Vietnam Wives."

And so, as the sun (or moon, rather) sets in the West—and a rash climbs slowly up my itchy arm—I will close for tonight. I hope tomorrow's letter isn't this adventurous!

Really, I'm holding up well—but I know you'll worry about me now. I knew you'd want to know everything, since you keep asking how things are going, but I was tempted not to say anything about today (but also, I knew you'd wonder a bit if my return address changes to "NY State Reformatory for Women" (if they catch me!!!).

In the next letter, she said:

Oh, am I a mess today! My whole face and neck are covered with a red itching rash. There are patches of it all over me, too. My lips all are covered with bumps too. I really look as if I'd gotten a good case of measles.

I waited till 9:30 a.m. and then called to check on the allotment. Not in yet. Boy, that was just about the straw that broke the camel's back—I feel that there is no reason on earth why we should exist on no money at all, just because the Army can't pay us on time. This happens every month, where we go thru the first week before our $ arrives. By the time the money does come in & I sit down and write the bills out, I usually have second notices.

On that day I wrote: "Dear Itchy, I just got your letter of 4 October, and you still had not gotten the pay. There is no need for that, and I am going to look into it from this end, to see what is the matter. It should have arrived—the difference of eight or nine days to hear something from you and then get an answer back to you is frustrating! I hope to get a letter tonight telling me that you are back in the black again."

5 October 1966—from Gin:

When I got up at 8 this morning my hives were running rampant. My nose was so swollen and sore—so were my ears. They
were spreading on top of my arms and up and down my legs.
I kept waking up last nite, I itched so much. So, I knew I had to
go to the Dr. for something!

I got us all dressed, then called the bank—again they said:
Nothing in my account. I hung up and called Finance & said I
wanted to speak only to the Finance Officer. Well, he was very
kind and understanding and sensed my being very upset; he
talked to me for about 10 minutes, and in the conversation
told me that my not getting my check till the 4th or 5th was
not good—he couldn't understand it because the Finance
Center is now sending out to the bank simply a list of the
allotments . . . and then sends one huge check to cover everyone on the list. He told me this always arrives at the bank
by the second of the month. Also he told me he's been to the
Marine Midland before, because what is happening is that the
bank gets the list, but it takes them three to four days to credit
all the accounts. The Colonel said he told them at the bank
that it's not fair for me (the depositor) to suffer for the slow-
ness. He said he'd call finance center and check on when the
list went out—and then if he finds what he suspects, will get
on the bank again.

I felt better after talking to him—he sounded sincere and
willing to help. So off to the nursery and on to the hospital.

While I sat at the hospital, I thought about what the Colonel
said about the bank—having the money but not in my account.
I made a decision. After the hospital I went directly to the bank
and requested to see the Vice Pres. (Start almost at the top!!!)
I told him what the situation was—and that the finance officer told me about the list and the big check. I told him I could
not go on getting second overdue notices on bills (three last
month by the way), and that my bills were due on the first and
I wanted to pay them then. He agreed and went back to the
bookkeeper to "check out the situation"—when he got back, he
confirmed my name on the list (for $750 . . . but not yet in my
account). He then told me that I should write my bills, etc., on
the first—the bank has a policy where it holds them until the

pay comes in, at no charge to me. He was trying to be nice—
and smooth things over—so I simply smiled and said, "Well,
sir, you'd better make sure that the rest of the bank knows this,
because I intend to do just that—pay all my bills & everything
by the first—and I'd better not get calls that I am $400 over-
drawn." While I sat there he talked to the bookkeeper, and they
assured him, this was their policy. So I thanked him and cashed
a check for $50 right then! Ah, money—I'd been since Friday
with $1.32 (a record?).

The rash slowly disappeared, the publisher's advance came along, and
Ginny's letters returned to humor and understanding and love. I continued to do odd jobs. I worked on the details of the arrival of a large number of mobile home trailers to be used as offices and storage and quarters.
I served as a guide for visiting senior leaders in the logistics field. I
attended coordination meetings galore, and took notes for my bosses. I
helped out with the plans for reducing the number of U.S. military units
and facilities in the city of Saigon. I was content with my assignments,
because they could easily be shifted to someone else if I did manage to
escape Saigon. But things looked dim, as I wrote to Ginny:

> Today I was called in by Col. Sheffey, the boss between me and
> Col. Isaacs. He told me that he had been talking to Col. Isaacs
> and that they had arranged big things for me. I was suspicious
> from the start. He mentioned a challenging new assignment
> with a trip to Hawaii included, and the gist of the whole thing
> was that they were not going to release me as planned, that I
> would stay in Saigon for the rest of the time.
>
> You have to understand how horrible I have felt in this rot-
> ten place to see my point on this. I told him I wanted to see Col.
> Isaacs right away, and we had a long and rather violent talk.
> Sheffey's point was that he needs me in the job and can't afford
> to lose me. He says that I will be a staff officer no matter where
> I go, either here or out in the field, and that it's all the same, so
> why move? I told him that this place is the bottom end of the
> whole system, that I don't want to work here, and that I had
> been promised a field assignment and I wanted to go back out. I
> said I would submit a request for transfer, and he said he would
> disapprove it. His last words on the subject were, "You'll leave
> here over my dead body." That put it rather succinctly.

Sheffey was insulted and infuriated, and rightly so. I was desperate, which is no excuse. On 10 November, I signed a formal request to be reassigned to a combat unit. Two days later I wrote a letter to Ginny that was also a letter to myself. In it I said:

> I have been trying to exist in two worlds, actually, in the world of the thinking man and the world of the action man. Nick [my roommate in Saigon] feels that you can never be successful in both of these, that you have to choose one, and that the Army is obviously the world of the action man. I hate to admit he is right, and I have not up to now. But it seems that the work at Columbia was not as good as it could have been because I had spent too much time in units like the 101st and too little time reading and thinking. And the work at Leavenworth suffered a bit because I was spread a little too thin with the extra stuff that I was doing. If I had been more interested all along in the nuts and bolts of the Army, who knows—I may have been able to do better out in the 1st Div.
>
> But the conviction I still have is that my true value to the Army, and to anything for that matter, is the ability I have to work in both areas. I know I can hold my own intellectually with any of the rest, and I am sure that in the field I can do as well as any of them. This is the one thing that I want to clear up before I leave here. I think that of the two areas the action area is my weakness because I tend to think too much. But I can also act. And it is something that I like and want as much as the life of thoughts. The most important way to combine these two is in writing, and that is still the final goal—and the sooner I can spend all my days doing that, the better.

13 November. My request for reassignment came back to me from Colonel Isaacs with his comment in red letters: "Giggle file"—an imaginary place to put laughable correspondence. I knew then that Colonel Isaacs would not support me in my effort to leave Saigon. The decision to let me go, then, rested with Brigadier General Cole. Among the senior officers at headquarters, he was the only one I had known before the war. As a colonel he had been the chief of staff at West Point in the spring of 1965. At the end of that school year, when my teaching responsibilities were over, I volunteered to help solve the Academy's housing problem. Starting that year, the Academy expanded, doubling the size of

the Corps of Cadets. The academic staff had to be increased also, but it would take time to build housing for the inflow of junior officers. Working out of General Cole's office, I had spent several weeks scouting the countryside of the Hudson Valley within commuting distance of the Academy, visiting homes for rent or for sale and compiling descriptions of them, then taking newly appointed staff members and their families out to see them. Cole remembered this, and he took an interest in getting me out to combat units. This is another of the many times in my life that I asked for help and people listened.

I wrote to Ginny on 16 November:

I hope that you understand why I have to go out to a unit again. It is a feeling so strong in me that there is no question about it. . . . Going out to a unit is part of being the man that I am, a feeling deep in my heart, and not just the idea that it might be good for my career or anything like that. I'm sure that you understand this, Gin. This is a rotten war and I don't know how I really feel about it. The government here seems to be so corrupt and so dedicated to their own ends that the reforms necessary will never come, even with all our help, and if we win the war and then leave here, they will still be the same and it will start all over again. But that is only one side of it. As much as I have criticized the army and the academy, my values are their values, and I want to serve my country well, and as an Infantryman.

On 26 November I took a long chance. I telephoned Colonel Herbert E. Wolff, chief of staff of the 1st Cavalry Division, at An Khe. I had never met him. I told him I had been fired from the 1st Infantry Division and asked him for a job, any job, and promised him I would do it well. He of course was not ready to deal with my request, which was something out of the blue, but he wanted to know more. It turned out that he was going on R&R leave in a few days and would be flying out of Tan Son Nhut on 30 November. If I met him at the plane, he said, we could talk about it.

Two days later, I hurried along the edge of Tan Son Nhut airport, which at that time was an overcrowded, run-down, sandbagged merry-go-round, a shambles soaked with rain—with runways that looked like rivers and C-130s making takeoffs in roostertails and landings with reverse pitch blowing like whales. I found Colonel Wolff's plane and waited there. Eventually he came sloshing along, and I caught his eye and saluted him. I knew I would have a minute or two, no more, but it was much easier to talk to him face to face than it had been over the military radiotelephone, competing with the static and the microwave cross-traffic. I delivered my soliloquy. For a few long seconds he squinted at me in the rain. "OK," he said. "I'll think about it and let you know when I get back. Gimme your number." I tore a page out of my green pocket notebook and wrote it out for him. He climbed the ladder into the aircraft. And Colonel Wolff turned out to be a savior: he made the decision to allow me to come up to 1st Cav, where I wanted so much to be.

The next couple of weeks consisted of stubborn days that dragged their feet and refused to go by. Lieutenant Colonel Sheffey, who for all our arguments was a good friend, admitted that I was an extra, meaning that the hold on me was not strong. In a good-natured way, Colonel Isaacs said to me, "I'm convinced you're crazy. You have a good job here, but all right. I'll let you go. I guess I was wrong. I thought you had some brains." But he was smiling.

Sheffey, Isaacs, Cole, and Wolff had turned my life around. I had another chance.

On Christmas Eve 1966 I arrived at 1st Cavalry Division Headquarters at An Khe. The place was wet, cold, muddy, and beautiful. My classmate and good friend Andre Broumas, who was commanding the Engineers and was later killed in Vietnam, was waiting to welcome me. We trotted through the rain to a mess tent for some food and talk. He then took me over a pathway of duckboards to the tent of Lieutenant Colonel James Root, the division operations officer, G3. There he dropped me off. After that, Andre and I were often together until fate took him.

The 1st Cavalry Division was commanded by Major General John Norton, whose background and personality made him the right leader. He had jumped into Normandy on the night before D-Day with the 82nd Airborne Division; he was a qualified pilot of helicopters and airplanes; he had served on the Howze Board, which designed the airmobile division; and he was for three years the Chief of Army Aviation. Norton was an innovator and a man of action, the kind of leader I wanted to be. As the year 1967 began, he was given a new mission: "Protect and develop the Binh Dinh Plains." He would devote every asset to this task, everything we had, in cooperation with the South

Vietnamese armed forces and with the Republic of Korea Capital Mechanized Infantry Division, our neighbor on the plain. We could expect to meet strong resistance from the VC and from North Vietnamese forces, which were thick in Binh Dinh Province.

Norton's deputy was Brigadier General George Blanchard, who like me had begun his career as a private in the National Guard. Blanchard was also a brilliant leader who had served as a platoon leader and company commander in France and Germany in World War II. Colonel George Casey was a brigade commander in the division, also much involved in planning as well as operations. I was assigned as an extra in the G3 plans section, working for Major Hal Iverson on the new plan as the division moved from the mountains to the plains.

The 1st Cavalry Division had helicopters—435 of them. The division cleared a "golf course" and began to work the uplands in the same way as the French had. They soon found that helicopters (Hueys) could get you into action at 80 knots, but once on the ground, friend and foe faced off in the same jungle, the same rain forest, the same mountains, the same fields of bamboo, the same highland paddies—and the same driving monsoon rain.

The cavalry forces ran a series of battalion-size fights to drive the North Vietnamese back westward toward the border and take pressure off the 22nd ARVN Division and the Capital South Korean Division in the Binh Dinh plains and hills, and to acquaint themselves with the terrain and the enemy.

I wrote to my father:

> Here is our situation now. We are up against the 3rd North Vietnamese Division in its own home area, centered on the river town of Bong Son near the coast, about 80 km above Qui Nhon. The division has 3 regiments (18th, 22nd, and "2nd VC"—the last is North Vietnamese like the others, but initially was a VC regiment and still retains the name). In addition there are 3–4 VC battalions in this area, but they are pretty well shot up.
>
> They also have had time—years—to organize the area (the VC have done this—we are fighting the NVA first, then the VC infrastructure). They also have other reinforcements which they can bring in if they want to.
>
> The battle moves fast, back and forth over the same areas. We are spread thin one minute and shoulder to shoulder the next.

Under Colonel Root and Major Iverson, I took over the drafting of a new plan, called "Pershing II," the second time on the plains. I laid out a rough plan: a kind of checkerboard operation in which the entire area that we had was divided up into subareas we would progressively clear and protect—jumping around from one to the other, all in the same general space. General Norton liked it. From then on I talked with Norton just about every night—and it kept getting better. Norton was a big, loud man, a demanding leader, full of ideas, and in love with argument. He was the first senior commander to try to adapt a powerful division—with plenty of helicopters, many of them strong enough to lift heavy artillery—into a counterinsurgency role, combining high- and low-intensity warfare. As an operation, Pershing II, rather than the typical three or four days or couple of weeks, lasted six months, almost my entire time there.

The division had conducted large sweeps to clear the North Vietnamese units out of the coastal plains, but the enemy moved into the hills to wait us out. We needed to know more about our opponents, our allies, the population, and the terrain—"the arena." Our new plan envisioned a careful preparation of the likely battlefields where future fights would take place, within the rice-growing plains that stretch 80 kilometers north from Qui Nhon to the Quang Nai border and 40 kilometers from the sea across the plains and into the first line of mountains. The mountains on three sides were our palisades, with the South China Sea closing off the fourth side.

Preparation of the battle arena made it more difficult for the enemy to have access to the population and helped us make contact with the enemy in areas selected by us, where they would be at a disadvantage. We made a rough matrix of our area of operations—a patchwork of varying sizes and shapes, depending on the characteristics of the terrain. We began to fill it in with everything we knew about each of those patches, including the history of fights that had taken place, the signs and sightings of enemy presence, and the trails, base camps, and bunker complexes. We patterned our responses not just to meet a presence of enemy forces, but to attain a situational grasp of what a battle would be like in each particular area. This battlefield preparation also involved categorizing all available landing zones (with a constant updating); selecting and preparing fire bases to support a variety of schemes of maneuver within and adjacent to the divisional operational area; clearing and by "barrier zones" denying access to the outlying valleys and open areas through which enemy units had to pass to enter populated areas; destroying enemy fortifications throughout the area; and maintaining day and night surveillance over the trail network by a variety of means, producing pinpoint low-level aerial photographs of every hamlet and important terrain feature. We began to "own" the arena at least as much as the enemy did.

On 15 February 1967 I wrote happily to Gin: "2400. Gen Norton just left, and the whole thing went very well. He liked the plans and gave us the go-ahead on them, and in his usual fashion thought of a half dozen other things for us to do. So off we go again. The group I have here in plans is functioning like a real team, and this may turn out to be one of the best jobs I have ever had. Let's hope that all goes along as well as it has so far, which would be just great."

Working for Norton was no picnic, though. He drove himself and everyone else. He punctuated all meetings with his monologues, but he would stop and encourage us all to talk back to his specific, stabbing questions, and he did listen, a characteristic not too often found in commanders; in fact, he loved discursive analysis of our operations. He would call for a nighttime gathering of the available senior officers of the command post for what became known as "the séances." These could go on for hours. He would want to know: What did we accomplish today, yesterday, this month, this year? What are the strengths and weaknesses of our planning? How can we squeeze our resources, get more out of them? To the intelligence officer: What do you think of our use of airlift? To the logistician: How is intelligence serving you? To the operations officer: What do you see as our prime problem in the personnel area? To the planner: How is our maintenance program working, overall? To the adjutant: Give me your views of current operations. Back to the logistics officer: What do you think of what you just heard about intelligence and operations? Thus the hours would pass.

18 February 1967—to Gin, the day after a visit by General Westmoreland: an infantry major critiques a four-star general:

He seemed to me to have many of the old characteristics that I used to admire, but in addition he has grown more aware of the kind of world this war is and the many interests of the people that he deals with. As I see him now, this war has matured him more than the experiences he had as a division and corps commander. Some of this may have started up there at West Point, where he was exposed to the many different minds that visited there and to the academic interests that were represented. Whatever it was, he now listens not only with an ear cocked to pick up the essential facts, but with a wide knowledge of people and what he can expect of them. His questions, always so precise, are now evidencing a broad knowledge of the problems and the people here, including our own people. If I were a reporter, I would write a study of how this job has changed him—and I think for the better, in a greater sense than I thought. The change really struck me, as you can see.

To Gin, the same day: the same major considers the long-range strategic outlook:

On the article about the political possibilities in Vietnam at the present time, I feel that the problem continues to be a lack of power at the grass roots. It is in the hamlets that the VC get their strength. I am beginning to see, especially in the results of interrogations of prisoners of war, that the communist ideology is not the thing that drives most of the VC that we pick up. They are fighting for a rather vague idea of a better life for the average guy, and to get a responsive government at the lowest levels. There is no doubt that the machine itself is set up by the communists, but there is practically no rabid political orientation [in] the prisoners of war we get. This proves all the more how bad . . . the present and past governments of this place have been. Anyone who promised to try to take care of the people here, and meant it, would be able to do what the VC have done, given a little time. The problem of the government is that they don't mean it, and this is clear to the man on the receiving end. The VC really try hard and are as idealistic as hell. We are always finding their school notebooks and other stuff that show, at least at the low levels, a strong ring of sincerity. The revolutionary development program, if it is backed by the same kind of sincerity, sacrifice, and sense that the VC are willing to expend, can go a long way. The RD cadre going out to the hamlets in the program that is going on here in the Phu My area—our biggest program—seem very well motivated. I wonder, though, if the same motivation can be mirrored at the higher levels. If so, and if we can provide a shield of military power to keep the main force VC and NVA units off their backs, the whole thing might have a chance. I won't say that I am pes-

simistic about it, but I will say that the effort involved is one
that will take about 20 years at the absolute minimum. And
the same effort must be made in so many other countries that
unless we are able to inspire a large percentage of the young
folks of the world, we will not be able to provide the kind of
resources that could do this kind of development in, say, fifteen
or twenty countries around the globe.

Letter to my father, 19 February 1967:

For every five or six plans I make, we use one, and that is
quickly changed to suit the battle as it develops—but the dis-
carded plans have served their purposes, generating plenty
of discussion—my tent is the scene of much talk—the general
[Norton] here almost every night, often past midnight, smoking his cigar and listening, until all have had their say—and
then getting up to talk, first as a kind of chat, then more and
more precise until he bangs down the "go ahead" and walks
out, leaving us to put the modified plan together and write the
final order, to go out by air courier to all units before morning.

To Gin, 15 March 1967, Bong Son—back to Westmoreland:

Today Westy came, and I briefed him on the long-range plans.
He remembered me at once, in his usual manner, and just as
I was about to start talking he said, "Hi, Jack! How've you
been?" and turned to Norton and said, "Jack has worked for
me a couple of times—we were in Korea together." He missed
the place, but had the rest right. It rattled me, and instead of
talking of the 1st Air Cav, I called the division "the 101st"—
then corrected myself and told him that my mind slipped back
to other days. The briefing went very well and the chief of staff
was quite happy afterwards, so the slip was forgotten. Westy
again was impressive with the (for me) change from the rather
simple and single-minded man he used to be. He is not in the
least worn down by the heavy workload, the way many of the
officers are—he seems to thrive on it and grow with it.

1 April 1967, Bong Son. Gin had sent me an Easter basket that contained a mechanical duck that popped up among the candy eggs to

quack when the basket was opened. I stopped by the hut of a large Vietnamese farm family, the dirt around the hut beaten hard and smooth by bare feet, and ceremoniously presented the basket to a frightened mother and her many children, who all stood bewildered, seeming to say, "What on earth can this mean?" I thought the children would be fascinated as I showed them how it worked, but they froze, dumbfounded, and then ran away. Mechanical ducks and candy eggs for a family that has seen hell over and over again. Well, I said to myself, I have to go. No time to chase kids with a basket. When they recover from the surprise they will eat the candy eggs. I went past the hut many times later, but there was never any sign of the mother and her children. After my tour was up I would go home with the same feeling I had walking away from this ragged, fatherless family: we're trying, but it is not working.

On 7 April 1967 I chatted with Major Woody Martin. He and I had been attending classes together at the University of Pennsylvania, working toward our PhDs. A week later he was killed trying to coax VC soldiers and families out of a complex of caves.

25 April 1967, Bong Son—to Gin:

My jungle fatigues are beginning to wear out. What a marvelous sign.

Today thousands of yellow butterflies flew across the camp here, across the dirt airstrip. For hours they kept coming, flying at about 90 degrees to the wind, like a sailboat trying to make the most of the wind, all in the same direction. Where they were coming from or going I don't know, but I watched for a long time. They all went east. The ocean is only a few miles off in that direction.

Going home. I left An Khe on an empty Caribou that flew east to the port of Binh Dinh and then south along the coast to Saigon. I sat near the open rear ramp as we cruised at about three thousand feet, just below the cloud ceiling. The conical mountains, covered with green rain forest, plunge so steeply into the sea down through there that I felt the sensation of tipping and falling through space. In between the mountains are the narrow, flat valleys that bottom out in chains of rice paddies, decked out at this time of year in every variation of green. We banked around tall blue-gray columns of rain falling from the dark ceiling to form a gigantic temple, as peaceful and beautiful as any place on earth. I thought how wonderful it would be to come back to this place someday when the war is gone. My last months had been gratifying, but my work had been planning, not commanding—not putting plans into action, as the battalion commanders were doing. My ability in that sense was something that in my own mind remained unproven.

Ginny met me in San Francisco. She was, believe me, the best-looking woman in that town. She was twenty-six. Her dark hair was teased and curled inward. She had full bangs cut straight just at her eyebrows. Above her long eyelashes was a little tinge of light blue, and her lips were pink, almost white. We rented a brand-new maroon '67 Mustang and drove down the coast road to Monterey. The hit song that played over and over began, "You're just too good to be true." In that valley under the Sierra de Salinas we found, as so many before and after us found, a few days of paradise.

13

Pentagon: The Papers

"Some highly classified work"

Ginny had rented a house for us, a split-level on a hillside road in Spring-field, Virginia. The place was just right, although I didn't see much of it. While we—which is to say, Ginny—moved in and put the girls into schools, I reported to the Pentagon, where I had been assigned to the staff of the Chief of Information, Major General Keith Ware. There I met my boss, Colonel Phil Stevens, head of the current news section. I was to be Phil's assistant. We teamed together well. He was a good editor, a precise writer, and a kind and thoughtful man. He knew the Pentagon in all its glories as well as its aches and pains. On the wall next to his desk he had long lists of scribbled telephone numbers of people who had served in the building years before, which functioned as a kind of code: to call someone, you had to know the chain of staffers that person had replaced. It was generational.

After the shop closed down in the evening, we had long, good talks about the world of the media, and about newswriting as a skill. A goodly proportion of the Army leadership felt that infantry officers who had master's degrees in English had spent too much time in the wrong places. Moreover, I had served in Puerto Rico and Colombia instead of Germany, and had gone to the Armor School instead of stay-ing with the infantry; *and* I had taught at West Point—in the English Department. What kind of developmental track was that?

The Army had thus sent me to the Pentagon, to the Office of the Chief of Information—thinking perhaps, who knows, that I could be put to better use there than in most other places. What I found there was that our view of "the press" was to keep them at bay, because for "the press" bad news is good, and good news is not. I had studied psy-chology and leadership under Major General Ware when he was teaching at the Military Academy; as a cadet in September 1951, I had written home about him, saying:

> My psychology professor had always impressed me as a quiet type of guy. He is Lieutenant Colonel Ware—very well-groomed, soft spoken—he looks like a typical certified public accountant. Yesterday he wore his dress uniform to class because he had to go somewhere afterwards, and he had on all his medals. The first thing I saw when I came in the room was that light blue ribbon with the white stars—the Medal of Honor. Besides this he has the Silver Star, Bronze Star with two clusters, D.S.C. [Distinguished Service Cross], and the Soldier's Medal.
>
> He gave us a lecture that day on fear in battle, and how to stop it. He told us that Audie Murphy was one of his platoon leaders, and he said that Audie was even better than they say.

That day as we stood at attention by our desks, I felt a swelling wave of admiration, as we all did. Ware was, not surprisingly, a firm leader. He was quiet, withdrawn, taciturn, and relatively inarticulate—not someone you would think of as the spokesman for the Army and the principal media advisor to the now chief of staff, General Westmoreland.

Every Wednesday morning, the secretary of the Army, Stanley Resor, would bring together the senior Army generals for a coordination meeting. Fifteen minutes of this meeting were reserved for General Ware, who would sum up the previous week's media commentary of interest to the Army. My new job was to prepare the draft statement for General Ware. His guidance: "I want to give them analysis, rather than simple reporting. Call 'em as we see 'em." He wanted a wider range of commentary, the thinking of leaders far and wide: the arguments, the priorities, and who stands where. To this last category I added what I called the Versus List—a compilation of arguments culled from a variety of vitriolic quotations by holders of opposing points of view, pro and con, across a wide spread of subjects of interest to the Army. Beginning right after one of these meetings and throughout the ensuing week, I would gather and study the daily clips of audio, audiovisual, and print that the Army collected. I did other work, but this was my main effort, and I liked it: how to put a week's worth of the world's opinion of the United States Army into fifteen minutes and get it right. But I didn't get it right.

After three or four weeks, General Ware called me into his office. He wanted to talk about the overall thrust of the media briefing. The Army leadership, he said, was engaged in fighting the Vietnam War, an enormous burden, and we did not need to add to that burden with too much negative comment by the press or by anyone else. This was the way he saw it. The Wednesday meetings were tough enough without bad tidings. He felt this strongly and sincerely. He wanted to know if I understood, and I said, "Yes, sir, I understand." I went back to work and also began to look for another Army job. Phil Stevens understood, and when I did find work he went to General Ware and said they ought to let me go. I once again became a free agent.

The job on the Chief of Information's staff turned out to be the first of several assignments—sometimes unofficial assignments—that I had as a writer. I learned, and kept on learning, that skill in writing was only part of the job. The other parts were understanding the hierarchy, the circumstances, and the bureaucratic influences that would come into play; the informal teaming that underlies the hierarchy; the worldview that that hierarchy endorses; and the way that reality is not always easy to see, given conflicting loyalties, the prerogatives of command, and the flow of information.

At home, at the rolltop desk inherited from my great-uncle Mike, I was putting together the final draft of my new book, *Air Assault*, and the work was moving slowly. I wrote late at night, which made it a struggle to throw off the blankets and roll out of bed on dark mornings, even when hurried along by the deep grumble of traffic building up on the beltway nearby. In accordance with my "transition plan" to get ready for a new career, I had also found a moonlighting job with the University of Virginia, teaching English in their continuing education program. Twice a week, in the evening, I taught a course called "English III: Modern British Writers." I had applied to teach at the university and was quickly accepted. Perhaps part of the reason I got the job was that the course had been advertised and was due to start the following week, but the lecturer had somehow disappeared. I signed up on a Thursday, put a new course together over the weekend, and held my first class on Tuesday of that next week.

When my first class met, at a local high school, I found an inspiring group of people, with worldly experience, but hemmed in by their working lives and responsibilities; their repetitious and unfulfilling days, marked by quotidian schedules and a decided lack of variety; and, in general, the agendas that ruled their existence. For my students the course became not English III, but a struggle to get out of a rut and open up life's possibilities. These were working people, pulling themselves up by their own bootstraps, coming back to school with a wage earner's nose-to-the-grindstone respect for the classroom as an almost sacred place, and with a trust in me as the teacher, the source of wisdom and of another chance.

I had to use the time well, and I couldn't let them down. I worked around the clock to write a syllabus, come up with a reading list, and prepare a sequence of classes that made sense. I decided that when the students wrote a theme, I would write one too, and we would make an exchange: I would grade their papers, and they would grade mine. Grades would be more like the comments of an editor, in pencil, using standard editing symbols. We would read the papers in groups. A paper could be rewritten and resubmitted for a higher grade. You could not change a grade by disputing it, but there would be no limit on the number of rewrites.

Not everyone liked the idea. About half the class very much preferred to do just the minimum amount of work that would result in a passing grade. They told me, "It's not what we learn. It's whether we pass." After the first class, a student summed up her view. She told me, "I don't really want to grade your paper or compare papers. I just want a good grade on my paper, and I want you to show me how to get through the course. A high grade isn't everything. What's important to me is to finish this course and get on to some of the others that I need for my degree. I've been at this now going on five years, and it will be at least two years more for the degree, which the HR people say will let me move up in my work. That's the only way I can look at it. I have a lot of other things going on in my life." I told her we could work out a way to have our cake and eat it, too: she could get her grade if she did the work that was fundamental to the class, but there would be ways to do the rest as well. We would make it work.

On 17 September 1967, the day before the Virginia course began, I was called up to the front office of the secretary of defense, Robert McNamara, where I was to meet with Paul Gorman to discuss "some highly classified work." It was near the end of the Defense Department's work on the Pentagon Papers, and Gorman was Leslie Gelb's deputy on that work. I met Gorman in an outer office, where he outlined for me the ongoing effort to pull together secret archives of the Vietnam War. A team of writers was aggregating thousands of the most important, most relevant papers and creating a kind of history by linking them in a chronological chain. The secretary, Gorman said, was afraid that the story of the birth and life of the war would be lost as the papers and their meaning drifted away. I was impressed as Gorman talked of McNamara's willingness to chronicle in deep detail the raw materials of the war: the judgments, the rationales, the decisions—right or wrong. I became a happy recruit. We would create a pristine archive, the true story of the war, which would clarify the history of the war for later eyes—even if it could not be released until some time in the future.

Gorman, I thought, was brilliant, creative, and a man of absolute integrity. We are both of the Boston Irish. He was also pugnacious, irritable, sarcastic, intolerant, and able to smell something stupid from a long way off. All in all, I had and still have great admiration for him, and some strange feeling of kinship. Gorman said the mission was to write only enough to make sense of the surroundings of the war and to give cohesion and meaning to a motley assortment of disconnected paperwork. He added that the effort had run into problems that had driven it off schedule, which was the reason military officers were coming onto the team. The main problem, he felt, was the selfishness of the academics on the original writing group, who showed more interest in their having access to documents that increased their understanding of the war than in completing the work of organizing the papers.

I asked Gorman if he was sure he wanted me in on this effort. He said, "Yup." I said something like, "After all that happened in August of last year, why would you pick me for this group?" He said, "Because you can write." On that same evening, I taught my first class in the University of Virginia School of General Studies. I told Gorman that it would be hard to abandon that commitment, which would mean that for two evenings a week I would be unavailable. He nodded. He did not need to tell me that we would be working at least six days a week and for long hours. That was a given for anyone who worked for Paul Gorman. He took me into a large room with four windows facing out over the river entrance toward Washington. A dozen or so people were bunched in that one room, which was packed with desks and typewriters. (I was glad I had taught myself to type.) Piles of papers were everywhere. Steel cabinets with combination locks lined the wall opposite the windows. It looked like a newsroom.

With a slight bow, he pointed out the only empty desk and said, "Your new home"; then he went to his own desk and started to work on a stack of papers. Paul was the foreman on the shop floor. Les Gelb was the boss; he had a separate little office.

In my first session with Gelb, he asked me to look at a draft chapter written by one of the other members of the team. He said he wasn't happy with it; he thought it might be good if another set of eyes looked it over. "Why don't you mark it up and then let me have a look?" he said. I read the draft, with its notes and references explaining how a given document fit into the overall flow of events. It was good, but there was room for some changes, which I made. After a few days I took it back to Les; he looked through it quickly and thanked me. A day later he passed it on to another writer on the team, saying he thought it could be improved. This was his style, his method. At that time he had little personal knowledge of Vietnam, but he was a quick study. Les handed around chapters and parts of chapters in this way, pitting one team member against another and editing some parts himself. In the end it made for better work. It also meant that no one but Les could say how many hands were involved in creating the various chapters. He had me write on the early portions, the French experience, the division into two Vietnams. Soon my desk was piled high like everybody else's.

I then worked on the beginnings of American military support for Vietnam. The Joint Chiefs in April 1950 recommended aid, and President Truman approved $10 million. Marine Corps Major General Graves Erskine arrived in Saigon in mid-July 1950 to head a small group that would administer the monetary support. Within a couple of weeks, Erskine sent a report back saying that a permanent solution was beyond military action alone. The goal was to "deny Indochina to Communism," but responsibility for military action should remain with the French.

Letter to my father, 28 October 1967:

> The job with McNamara is a very satisfying one, with a lot of research and writing. The hours are long but necessarily so with the kind of work I'm doing and the need to meet deadlines. Ginny usually picks me up at the Pentagon at about 7 p.m. and the girls come along with her. When we get home, I give them each a "lesson" (reading and writing and sketching) for a total of about 40 minutes, then they're off to bed and Ginny and I sit down to supper at 8:30. I'm in bed by 11:00 because 6:30 rolls around quickly. In the morning I get up and

catch a bus about three blocks from the house, for a 45-minute ride through the heavy river of traffic into work. On Mondays and Wednesdays, the two days I have my English classes, I take the car to work, then drive to Wakefield High School for a class from 6:50 to 8:10 p.m., then home.

. . . We've got the Pentagon grounds pretty well cleaned up [after the disruption of antiwar demonstrations]. Many large branches torn off beautiful old trees—fences down—camp-fire sites and garbage—outhouse words spray-painted on the walls and walks (the spray paint can was an unfortunate invention)—I think the young soldiers were magnificent under a stream of abuse that continued for hours from a crowd that at times was out for blood.

In December 1967, as I wound down my short tenure on the Pentagon Papers effort, I wrote my father again:

Defense Dept. is querying Dept. of Army to get me up there for a permanent job working on Vietnam problems, but as of now I think I will be staying in Info, where I know my boss. Phil Stevens is very good and the job leaves me enough time to work on the book a little.

The job with McNamara was very helpful in teaching me something about international relations, showing me how researchers work (I mean the pro's), giving me some insights into the Department of Defense, and allowing me to meet some fine people. Altogether I produced one study on my own for them, and one in collaboration with another man, Mel Gurtov. I hope that I was able to give them as much as they gave me—but I think I came out better than Dept. of Defense did on the exchange.

My school-teaching will be over on 17 January, and I will not go on next year. Must get the book done. But the money has been handy in helping on the expenses of this house, and the teaching experience will stand me in good stead. I also learned a lot. Hope the students did.

I was seeing so little of my daughter Beth—who was nine months old when I left for Vietnam and was now nearing three—that she had little idea where I fitted into the family. We decided that Ginny would bring her to the Pentagon on Wednesdays for lunch to give us more time together.

Spring 1968: Contemplating resigning from the Army and feeling ready to move on, I went to get the proper forms and found that a friend of mine worked in that office. "How long do you think it will take for this to go through?" I asked. He said that it would really be only a few days, once I filled out and signed the paperwork.

A few days. When I left the office and walked outside into the late afternoon, I noticed a flock of small birds fluttering, talking to each other and changing places in the trees by the door. Driving home in our VW Bug I went over my plans. I would find a small college in New England that would let me teach English. I would write. I would finish my studies of Yeats under Professor Herbert Howarth at Pennsylvania. I would have tenure. Everything would be immutable. We would settle into a place that would always be our home, and the kids would grow up with friends and teachers and doctors and neighbors they would know all their lives. We would plant maples and apple trees and be there to live under their shade and admire and praise their colors every fall. Forever.

I never filled out the papers. That night, I told Ginny that I needed to go back to Vietnam. I was now a lieutenant colonel of infantry, a graduate of West Point, and there was a war on. I knew how to command a battalion.

In May 1968, I met my father in New York at Fraunces Tavern, where I received the American Revolution Round Table award for the best book on the Revolution in the year 1967. We agreed that it was one of our highest moments. When called on to speak, I repeated words from the book's opening pages: "This book was first suggested and encouraged by my father, John J. Galvin, a local historian of eastern Massachusetts with an abiding interest in the soldiers of that area and all the wars they have fought."

My father smiled as I told of his part in the book, the maps and scenes he sketched while walking the battle road and its many connectors, his insights on individual encounters, and his notes on the earlier and later lives of the participants. Thanks to him, I kept at my writing, even during the times when there was much else going on. On this evening I talked with my publisher, Paul Fargis, about an idea for a new book, *Three Men of Boston*, and later that month I sent him an outline.

Around this time I got word from my old boss, Colonel Phil Stevens, that I was being considered to replace Lieutenant Colonel Ted Jenes as military assistant to the secretary of the Army, Stanley Resor. The secretary wanted someone who could be his speechwriter and aide-de-camp. That same day, Resor's executive officer called to tell me to come immediately to his office. As much as I wanted to work for the secretary, however, the Phu Loi fight filled my mind to the exclusion of all else. I felt I could not allow Resor to take me into his staff without knowing about it. Otherwise he might be put in an awkward position later, I thought.

I went up to the secretary's office, above the Mall entrance, and reported to Colonel Ken Cooper, who ushered me in to meet Mr. Resor. The high windows of the secretary's office face the Washington Monument and the Capitol; a large, somber portrait of Elihu Root graced the north wall. I took notice of none of this, however. The secretary was quiet and soft-spoken, but with steady, penetrating eyes behind the pleasantries. Colonel Cooper stepped out. As soon as politeness allowed, I recited the painful words that I had put together on my walk up to Resor's office. I took a deep breath, then another, and said, "Mr. Secretary, it would be an honor to work directly for you. I think I could do a good job. But you need to know that last year in Vietnam I was relieved in combat as a brigade operations officer. This could have some effect." I had planned to say more, but it wouldn't come out.

"How did it come about?"

I can't vouch for my response, but it was close to this:

"There was a two-day fight in a bunker area in close jungle. I was in charge for some of the time. We took heavy casualties, and there was some confusion. My division and brigade commanders decided that things were not working out. They felt that they needed a change. I was the change. They sent me out of the division, back to the rear, to Saigon."

"Were they right?" he said, with a smile.

"I learned some things." This was the answer I had come to accept. Any other answer would have to be a book.

The secretary said, "Well, I'm sure you did." There was more to the interview, but it has been lost to time, if indeed it ever registered. When I left the office, Colonel Cooper said, "So, how did it go?" I told him that I didn't really know.

When I got back to McNamara's office, there was a note from Phil Stevens on my desk: "Col. Cooper says you've got the job. Wants you there soonest."

Stanley Resor was a New York lawyer with Debevoise & Plimpton, LLP, where he handled contract law and was well known for his intensity of focus and his determination to know and understand every detail. It served him well during his time in the Pentagon. It's common Pentagon knowledge, I think, that the services supply their civilian leadership with a constant flow of information, in enormous proportions and on all conceivable subjects, from the highly volatile to the arcane. The primary reason for this is honorable: the secretary needs to know. The secondary explanation is control: creating a level of dependence on the military for their mastery of the details.

Mr. Resor handled both of these realities well.

Two colonels and Lieutenant Colonel Joe Bratton sat at desks in the secretary's outer office. Behind them was a row of file cabinets, each with a security lock. The three officers had memorized the location of every paper, thousands of tabbed documents, ready to be snapped up at the call of the secretary. Sometimes, as the papers moved in and out of their secure locations, the colonels couldn't keep up with the changes and the refiling as new and old papers came and went—in which case they came in on Sundays to tidy up, reestablish control, and make note of all changes.

Mr. Resor would say, "Please get me that paper on supply systems, the one with my notes on page three."

He could absorb and retain mountains of information. He seemed to know where every M-16 in the Army was supposed to be, and whether or not it was in fact there. When he went to the Hill to testify, Colonel Bratton would fill up a shopping cart with fat loose-leaf notebooks amounting to hundreds of pages of data, containing in great detail what might be discussed on that day. Joe would sit behind Secretary Resor, listening to the questions and passing him the backup pages. The secretary would say, "If we need to go into great detail, I have a paper here that can be entered into the record. . . ."

The arrival ceremony for General Westmoreland, who was returning from Vietnam to be the new Army chief of staff, was scheduled for 3 July 1968. President Johnson was to leave for a trip on that day and would not be available. Secretary Resor would hold a small informal meeting with invited guests at 8:45 a.m. in his office, and then he and the general and others would walk outside to the Mall for the formal welcome at 9:25 a.m. That was the plan. Everything was to be low-key. Immediately, scores of onlookers filled the hallways, and our telephones rang steadily with requests to be invited.

At 8:35 a.m. the White House advised that President Johnson would attend after all. At 8:40 a.m. the Secret Service said the president had left the White House. He arrived fifteen minutes later, whereupon the number of media reporters jumped from eight to thirty-three, all wanting to be in the secretary's office and at the ceremony. The inside ceremony was noisy and hurried, with lots of pushing and shoving. The outside ceremony somehow took place on time, while people not on time trotted to and fro. I was selected to explain to General Westmoreland why this mess occurred.

A couple of months later, Secretary Resor said to me, as a kind of afterthought, "Sometime or other, check and see if that replacement for the office rug is coming along OK." I looked at the rug. I hadn't noticed how seedy it was. I said, "Yes, sir." I searched the files and found a copy of the request. The date was back in history somewhere. I made a few calls, got some "Sorry, no record" replies, and narrowed the search down to the office of Pentagon building management as the point of no return. I explained the imminent need for that rug. And I waited. No news of the status of the rug. Not even a visit to look it over and take measurements.

I went down the hall to see the Army secretary of the General Staff, Major General Elias C. Townsend. "Sir," I said, "I'm getting a little embarrassed about the rug for Secretary Resor."

"And what rug would that be?"

I got a couple of sentences into the story, and he raised his hand. "Hold it. Hold it." He turned to his executive officer, who was standing there with me. "Get me everybody who has anything to do with this matter," he said. "I want them in this office now."

It was about noontime, so it took a little while, but when we assembled in the outer office, half a dozen of us, Major General Townsend called us in and said the following:

"The secretary of the Army indicated, some time ago, that he wants a new rug. We will get that rug and put it in his office. If we do not get that rug in good time, we will all go to his office and lie down on the floor so that he will have something to walk on. Am I understood?" We understood. It was a good thing for officers to hear. The rug arrived quickly.

Mr. Resor wanted to observe the big annual NATO exercise called "Reforger," which took place in the autumn of each year. He had two questions on his mind: How does the war in Vietnam affect the readiness of Army forces in Europe? How does the U.S. support of NATO affect this country's ability to fight the Vietnam War? Colonel Cooper and the rest of our office team organized a weeklong trip, starting with Brussels (NATO's political headquarters) and continuing to Mons (the military headquarters—Supreme Headquarters Allied Powers Europe, SHAPE), then on to Heidelberg (the Army Headquarters), Nuremberg (to check on the Reforger exercise), Frankfurt (to gauge our logistics capabilities), Berlin (to visit with Army units in the divided city), and Paris (Sunday, a day of rest).

The first two visits were routine. Heidelberg was special for Cooper, first because he had questions about the balance of Army forces, and second, because as a young artillery officer in World War II, he was part of the advance on Heidelberg. With the city in range, the young officer had asked permission to take a jeep under a white flag to find the mayor or someone in charge in the city and negotiate a surrender and peaceful occupation. It worked. This time we flew to a small airfield near the city and drove to Patrick Henry Village, an American housing area on the outskirts, arriving at night.

From my notes:

I can't believe this. The autobahn on this night lies covered in the deepest dark fog, and we are driving at top speed. I lean over and look at the speedometer. It is registering 140 kilometers per hour—times point six means 84 miles per hour. I can see about forty or fifty meters ahead at best. My right foot keeps trying to lift off from an accelerator that isn't there. The colonel doesn't seem to notice, and I begin to wonder if my eyes are bad—maybe the driver and the others can see the road much better somehow than I can. We fly along the road, mile after mile, always out in the left passing lane, passing long lines of heavy trucks, while I contemplate my relatively short life and am thankful for each additional second that I remain in this world. Somehow the driver sees the exit for Heidelberg and we turn off.

The streets grow narrow now, and the fog, if anything, is thicker. We are coming into Ginny's town, the place that she has always loved, the subject of so many of her reminiscences. Here her father was stationed after the war, and here she went to high school. She has talked always of the Heidelberg castle; her school graduation had taken place there each year.

When we turn off the main road into Patrick Henry Village,

the deep fog has deepened to the extent that our guide dismounts and jogs along like a shadowing rickshaw man in our headlights, until we reach the visitors' building.

With the secretary and the colonel settled in for the night, I walk outside and see a taxi at the curb. This is my chance to see the castle, and I am sure it will be my only chance, since the next day's schedule is crowded.

"Can you take me to the castle?"

"Schloss Heidelberg?" The driver is bemused. "Who would want to go there in the midnight fog?" I would.

We careen into town and up the wet cobblestone road that climbs to the Schloss. I squint through the rain-spattered side windows, trying to see the great houses of Ginny's dreams, where the American colonels and generals lived when she was a Warrant Officer's daughter here, where she loved to be invited to a birthday party so that she could marvel over the plush interiors and the intimate back courtyard gardens. This to her was the epitome of opulence. In the rain the houses loom big enough, their facades a jumble of architectural styles.

The taxi curves into a cul-de-sac at the castle gate. I ask the driver to wait. "I won't be more than ten minutes." I had expected to be on the very top of the hill, where all castles rightfully belong. Instead we are halfway up, with the top lost in the clouds somewhere above us.

The entrance was a wrought iron gate that could serve well for a garden. In the castles of my mind, this one is having a hard time finding a place. I walk through the gates. No guard, no ticket-taker, no one at all. The dark mass of the castle is silhouetted against the diffused light of the city down in the valley below. I am in some kind of courtyard, and ahead I make out a bridge. There is a gate after all. The moat is there, a dry ditch, quite deep. Here I find the ghostly portcullis, which tells me that like the outlanders of old I am denied entry. I can see the vague shape of a ruined tower and sense the massive walls.

Later, as we arrive back at the entrance of Patrick Henry, I ask the driver to stop. I pay him and watch him turn around and drive off in the still heavy fog. I have one more place to see. Earlier I had noticed that near the chapel, close to the entrance, there was a large map posted on a billboard, showing the location of all the streets and buildings of the housing area. I walk to Ginny's street, Little Big Horn Strasse, a strange juxtaposition of a name, and remember a photo of Ginny as a young girl standing with her father at the corner of a plain, boxy, three-story building sitting in a sea of mud.

The next morning we head to the headquarters of the U.S. Army in Europe for conversations with the commander, General James K. Polk. He was greatly impressed by the Soviet response to Prague Spring, the Czech revolt. In a discussion on reinforcements, he said, "Mr. Secretary, you can send me any division and call it anything you want, as long as it has 150 tanks in it."

After my first sight of grim Berlin, Paris buildings seemed to me fat and bulging, like the burghers. Take a few steps in any direction, Paris is beautiful: blocks of hotels, parks, bridges, the Orangerie, the Seine, the Left Bank, Notre Dame, the Musée D'Orsay, the Arc de Triomphe.

On 21 December 1968 I wrote to my father: "I was in a high state of excitement about the opportunity to see at last some very important, significant places in Europe. I wanted to absorb all I could, and I was intensely aware of the things around me. At the same time, with all the petty (but necessary) responsibilities for the schedule, the transport, baggage, bills, peoples' names, and so forth, I could not afford to become engrossed to the point of forgetting anything. It was a struggle between these two sides all the way."

One of the first surprising realizations I had was that in many ways I was getting "reverse impressions": Things that were typically European reminded me of Vietnam, the Far East, or Latin America—whereas things that had actually been "imported" or picked up from Europe and carried to Bogotá or Saigon seemed to me to be the opposite. The brickwork in Belgium made me think of Colombia. The plumbing reminded me of Saigon. The machine shops—large, barn-like brick buildings—that I could see from Ambassador Harlan Cleveland's windows at NATO Headquarters reminded me at once of the shops at Quan Loi when I was there with 1st Brigade, 1st Division. Even though I was aware of how I responding, the phenomenon continued all through Europe. The concrete telephone posts (like in Saigon); the French trucks (especially a type of Citroen that I had seen all over Vietnam); the walled-in yards (as in Bogotá and, in fact, almost everywhere but here); the heavily built trucks with sides that drop down like tailgates (as in Japan). It was a fascinating double-impression that was perhaps even more interesting than it might otherwise have been because I was cognizant of my mistaken reaction each time.

Back home I helped the secretary prepare for the talks he was to give at White House ceremonies awarding the Medal of Honor. These were mainly posthumous awards. The heroes who won the medal and survived were provided an audience with President Johnson. The families of those killed in action met with Mr. Resor, but in the White House. He never repeated himself in his talks with the families; he always wanted those moments to be as sincere and singular and personal as they could be. My respect for how Resor comported himself at these meetings, and his detailed and thoughtful preparation for them, made it easier to be part of those occasions. He suffered along with the families. Reserved and formal, plain-talking, an unceremonious man at any ceremony, he cared, and in those moments of honor and grief people knew how he felt. In the sedan on the way back to the Pentagon he would say nothing, ever.

From my notes, 19 January 1969:

Tonight we drove to downtown Washington to pick up parade tickets for Mr. Resor. I took Gin and the girls with me to the Statler, Nixon's headquarters. On the way there, we were held up at 12th and Constitution by a large police escort for the president, and we watched Johnson go by, heading out toward the airport—I wonder if he left for Texas tonight.

We got to the Statler after fighting very heavy traffic—especially for a Sunday, and I went up to the 5th floor to get the reviewing stand tickets. Gin stayed in the lobby with Mary Jo (I took Beth) and saw Nixon arrive, to cheers and flashbulbs, with a dozen sidecar motorcycles all shining and roaring. Very much a holiday atmosphere, and great anticipation for the parade and the doings tomorrow.

We were sobered on the way out of the city when we passed the tents erected for the Hippies (down on 14th St. near the Washington Monument). Many of the folks there were wearing white masks—caricatures of Nixon. They want some things that I think are good—their desire to see realities as they are, and their feelings of social responsibility impress me—but their callous disrespect for institutions is bad.

To me their numbers seem smaller than I expected. I don't

think they can cause much trouble tomorrow. Maybe their demonstrations will bring more good than bad—certainly if we all re-assess our "good Samaritan" responsibilities we can't go wrong. They feel they have tried all the usual ways of objecting to "things as they are" and have failed. Now they want to knock heads, to make their presence felt. There are the usual manipulators present, but I still respect the average dissenter— he is committed, and he has the gumption to come here and suffer plenty to be heard.

Despite my time in Washington, I felt a responsibility to return to combat, as I wrote to my father on 22 March 1969: "The opportunity to command a battalion is something I relish as an extremely important job, one I have prepared for over all these years. I do want to have a crack at a good command. One of the main reasons is to show (myself) that it is possible to write about such things and also to do them. This is very important to my own idea of myself. And, of course, I am an Infantry lieutenant colonel—and a battalion command position is the main reason my rank exists."

A week later, my letter to my father touched on other events: "Ike's funeral is the subject of the day at my office here, with much ado concerning the details. We kept in touch with the hospital right to the end, and my classmate and friend Lou Mologne, now a doctor and assistant chief surgeon at Walter Reed, stayed with him through it all as he slipped away."

During this time, I continued work on my book, *Air Assault*. On 25 June I wrote my father with some news on that front:

Last Saturday (14th) I spent an hour talking to Gen. Westmoreland on the book, and he gave me an endorsement to go on the dust jacket. In the course of the conversation he told me about some changes he is making at West Point, creating a history department out of the history sections of the Social Science Dept. and the Dept. of Military Art and Engineering. He said that it was a shame no military men were now known as good writers of strategy. Liddell Hart and J. F. C. Fuller, he felt, were the last and have not been replaced by anyone in the present time. For this reason, he said, discussions of strategy lack the sense of realities of time, distance, and effort that only the men who have been involved in such things can fully understand.

16 July 1969. In the basement, I sat watching an old tiny TV screen—lift-off for the moon. I thought, my father was born in 1903, the year the Wright brothers lifted off from Kitty Hawk. I was finally finishing the manuscript for *Air Assault*—late, but the editor was not complaining. In the opening of the chapter on Vyazma, I wrote:

> The Germans reached the gates of Moscow in the first week of December 1941, after a campaign recognized as the greatest sustained offensive in the annals of military history. At Minsk they had taken 290,000 Russian prisoners; at Smolensk another 100,000; at Gomel 80,000; at Kiev 665,000; and at Bryansk 658,000.
>
> It is almost unbelievable that the Soviet Army was able to suffer such an overwhelming series of defeats and still remain basically intact and ready to fight. This stubborn survival was in itself a feat equal to the sum of German victories.

In November 1969, for a second time, I left for Vietnam with a book at the publisher's.

14

Second Vietnam: All Roads Lead to Rang Rang

"I resolved never to forget."

5 November 1969. I was going back (I thought) to the 1st Cavalry Division, earmarked for command of a battalion. This time getting through the Fort Dix bureaucracy and onto an airplane was somewhat different from my experience of two years earlier. The war had changed, and my country had changed. The main gate of the Army post was just across the street from McGuire Air Force Base, our departure airfield, but the move from Dix to McGuire had a new twist. At the appointed time we walked toward our bus—which was easy enough to find, illuminated as it was by the flashing red, white, and blue lights of the New Jersey State Police cars and motorcycles, our escorts to the war. We boarded the bus and the driver started up, taking his cues from the police as they slowly edged their way through a group of restless and vocal antiwar protesters at both gates. We squeezed into McGuire without incident, except for thumps on the bus sides and comments that were not encouraging. The soldiers sat silent and expressionless, looking from side to side out the windows. I'm sure the image stayed with them, as it has with me. The gates closed behind us.

When we reached the tarmac, a 707 from Flying Tiger Airlines stood waiting for us, and a sergeant gave me the manifest and a copy of orders informing me that I was in command of all troops aboard. Before we taxied out, I asked for the flight attendant's microphone and said: "Everyone settle down for a minute. I am Lieutenant Colonel Galvin. These orders make me responsible for your conduct from here to Vietnam. I remind all officers, all noncommissioned officers, and all soldiers that you have your duties. If there is anything that you can't

handle on this trip, come up front and see me. Let's have a nice ride."
As I anticipated, no one found it necessary to refer any issues to me
throughout the trip; it was quiet all the way. Given the fuel stops we
made, I had thirty-nine hours to sleep, meditate, and read a paperback
copy of Tolkien's *The Hobbit*. During the year to come, that book would
have a hard life. It now sits on my bedside shelf, frayed, dirty, dog-
eared, thumb-marked, hunchbacked, and layered with various hues of
clay-red. It looks, in fact, like some of the soldiers I came to know that
year. The book has 287 ragged pages. In Vietnam I read them about five
at a time—often the same five, over and over.

We droned along hour after hour inside the flying tiger, and I
thought about what lay ahead—hopefully the command of a battalion of infantry, about eight hundred men if at full strength, four rifle
companies, a reconnaissance platoon, and some mortars. I felt certain
there would be no learning time beyond whatever experience I had at
that point. What would the first days be like? When I was a company
commander, what did I like about Colonels Ashworth and McKean
when they came around to see me and my company? They cared about
the troops. They shared their time with me. They knew a lot, and they
taught me some of what they knew. I felt good whenever I saw them.
They made the day look a little better.

How did they do that? They had a steadiness in any kind of flap,
and in the airborne there were always flaps. It seemed like there was
nothing they hadn't been through already. You didn't have to wonder
what they were thinking—they told you—but they also let you have
your say. You could tell that they supported you and what you stood
for, and they gave you a strong sense, reinforced every time they talked
to you, that a lot was expected of you. They were people of integrity.
They were team builders.

After our stop in Yakoda, Japan, the pilot announced the weather
conditions ahead and the distance and time to Cam Ranh Bay. Cam
Ranh? The 1st Cav was in positions northeast of Saigon, two hundred
miles to the south, which is where I had thought we were going. But no,
Cam Ranh was the end of the line. When we arrived, another sergeant
came out to meet us, carrying a clipboard full of wrinkled papers that
ruffled like a bird turned the wrong way in the wind. Sure enough, I
was listed as "unassigned." I found a telephone and, after about a half-
hour of whistling and hollering, I raised the switchboard at the Cav
and asked to be connected to the personnel officer, who turned out to
be Lieutenant Colonel Tom Shaylor, an old friend from lieutenant days

with the 65th Infantry in Puerto Rico. With luck that stretched close to the miraculous, I managed to hold on to the connection while Tom spoke with the division chief of staff, then came back to the phone and said, "We don't have you on our list, but we want you if you can get up here." That was enough for me. While I waited for the next morning's shuttle to Saigon, I scribbled a lighthearted note to Gin: "We are still the great Americans. Since tonight is Saturday night, the EM and NCO clubs (and maybe the O club) are jumping with Vietnamese rock and roll bands and much hollering. In the meantime the men on guard duty are shuffling between the bunkers. . . . The old familiar smell of burning honey buckets from the latrines—diesel oil plus crap—unforgettable mix—permeates the camp, as always."

Next day at first light I hauled my duffel and B4 bags down to the airstrip and got aboard a twin-engined Caribou cargo plane headed for Saigon. My lack of paperwork was forgiven.

At Tan Son Nhut Airfield I caught a Huey helicopter getting ready to leave for Phuoc Vinh. As we lifted off, I could see the flat-roofed four-story shoe box of a building where I had worked on the Army staff two years before. We flew out over Bien Hoa and northward. By coincidence, the Cav was located in the same area that the 1st Division had occupied in my earlier tour. I recognized the town of Tan Uyen and kept squinting ahead, trying to make out the junction where the east-west road from Lai Khe meets Highway 16 running north. I was hoping I would recognize the area where we did battle against the Phu Loi VC battalion in August 1966. Flying low, we were almost overhead before I saw the intersection—now wider, crowned with rust-colored laterite. The jungle was gone—burned, bombed, defoliated, scoured by bulldozers, fought over again and again since our encounter there. It did not seem haunted, like the dark valley of the An Lao, but just obliterated—pounded colorless, an ugly noplace, burned into my mind. Then along the road I saw the long, skinny roadside town of Binh My; then the village of Bo La and the bridge over the Song Be; and then Phuoc Vinh. It was like old times.

The town and the base were still linked side by side, but there was more of everything, and it was all dug deeper into the ground. The old Special Forces quadrangle was now dominated by a massive command bunker next to it, constructed of creosoted telephone poles lashed together and sandbagged. Steel shipping containers by the score had come to rest at Phuoc Vinh and, mounded over with sandbags, now served as dwellings and storage of all kinds. It was a Conex elephants' graveyard. The airstrip, much improved, was walled in with revetments for helicopters and fixed wing aircraft.

When we landed, I thumbed a ride to the hut belonging to the division chief of staff, Colonel Joe Kingston. The wooden shack was, I think, the same one at which I reported to Colonel Berry almost two years earlier. Colonel Kingston pushed back his chair, leaned over the desk, held out his hand, smiled—and told me I would not be a battalion commander. I'm sure I looked disappointed. "That will come later," he said. The commanding general, Elvy Roberts, had already decided that I would replace Bob Hannas, the intelligence officer—a good leader who deserved to get out to a battalion. "But don't worry," he said. "Your time will come, and we'll get you to a command. Not now, though." I wasn't going to get the job I'd hoped for, but I was happy to be back with the Cav. I had to forget about the battalion and concentrate fully, completely, on the intelligence mission. I said to myself, "I know this part of Vietnam a little bit, and I will get to know it better every day." I had never worked in intelligence, but I felt that I knew how to do research, retrieve information, analyze it, and put together a picture out of a lot of loose facts.

Divisional shoulder patches shifted from the left to the right shoulder after a combat tour of duty with the unit. This meant that veterans returning to the 1st Cav could wear the patch—which is the largest of the division patches—on both shoulders. I was happily surprised to see that there were "Cav sandwiches" everywhere I looked. In the months to follow, Generals George Casey and Robert M. Shoemaker were the assistant division commanders, later replaced by Generals Burton and Putnam, all Cav sandwiches. I would be teamed once again with George Stotser, another Cav sandwich and my companion from two years earlier in the command post at Bong Son, where we worked together as assistants for operations and plans. Now we would be teamed again, the heads of operations and intelligence, soon to be called "The Gold Dust Twins."

The military situation was tough. Throughout Vietnam, the enemy units were more numerous than before, and our outfits were leaving one by one. Becky, Vivian, Ellen, Tina, Jamie, Vickie, Ike, Tim, Chris, Sandra, Judy, Joan, Eunice—these and scores of other fire bases opened and closed and reopened as the 1st Cavalry Division shifted its weight around an area sixty miles wide and thirty miles deep on the northwest side of Saigon, facing the Cambodian border.

Right away I went to see the Vietnamese army's 5th Division commander, Major General Nguyen Van Hieu. He had commanded the 22nd Division when I worked with him in Bong Son two years earlier, coordinating the operations of the Cav with his division, or at least trying to do that. My lower rank—a major then, lieutenant colonel now—had never bothered him. I was given a very warm reception. He took me directly to the main map on the wall of his command post. I found that the renewal of our acquaintanceship had the strength to make us old friends, and I enjoyed that feeling.

Our two divisions were now astride the "rice corridors," the complex of trails from the countryside to the markets of Saigon. Hieu wanted to talk to me about the long history of the trail network, stretching back over centuries; the effect of the tea and rubber industries on its development; and the intricacies of their current use by the VC and NVA forces. Hieu's insights in this and later conversations helped me see far more clearly the connection between the trails and the way they were adapted and augmented to support not only the movement of supplies but also the tactics of enemy forces. He pointed out local trails that connected the hamlets, and main trails that bypassed the smaller markets and led into the populated areas around Saigon. He showed me how the enemy would base their movement of supplies and forces to the degree possible on the preexisting trail system, which ran over the best terrain—the driest part—and crossed rivers, streams, and unavoidable low swampy ground at the most convenient places; how, under pressure from the North Vietnamese Army, the locals disguised these narrow trails with a latticework of living vines and bushes, bending young trees to form living mantles; and how for years they had been digging bunkers, tunnels, and trenches, improving rest areas and supply dumps, and interlocking the smaller trails, the poorest of which were always made good enough for bicycles carrying anything and everything. He also explained to me how, wherever they went, the enemy had the protection of thousands of log-covered fighting positions as well as the mobility afforded by the trails.

General Hieu helped me to see that, in the provinces around Saigon, the trail infrastructure was the basis of all tactical planning and action by the North Vietnamese Army and its able assistants, the Viet Cong, the trail builders. I saw how the historical creation of the existing system and the subsequent thousands of modifications, which made the trails ever more versatile and more usable to military forces, resulted in a masterpiece of construction that took thousands of local workers to maintain. The bald truth was clear to the local farmers: you could not survive out in the hamlets unless you were willing to be part of the war, ready to help the VC whenever called upon. I don't think we ever wanted to admit to ourselves the full extent of this infrastructure.

I took over the intelligence shop. For the first few weeks I flew with General Casey, the assistant division commander, to get acquainted with the commanders, staffs, and units of our division and its neighbors. I became a circuit rider, traveling from one unit to another, thumbing rides to anyplace where I could pick up news and fit the pieces into a mosaic. Without the help of computers, we had simple ways to gather reports together, make sense of them, and then try to explain what our opponents were up to—where, who, when, and especially why. My information came from widely differing sources: reports from the combat troops, commanders' analyses, intercepted radio messages, radar and infrared surveillance, local agents, interrogation of prisoners of war, captured documents, reconnaissance reports, even rumors. I put a big effort into mapping out the trail complex. Ranging over the area assigned to us, the air cavalry searched out and located pieces of the trails, big and small. Companies and platoons noted every trail they ran across. We named the main trails after the scouts that discovered them: the Jolley Trail, the Adams Trail, the Serges Trail. All of this we marked on acetate sheets that would fit and overlap on the same map. For each kind of source, we had a separate plastic overlay showing locations, dates, activity.

We had a good team. Pete Taylor tracked enemy operations, Larry Doss converted our thoughts into messages (which we called Dossograms) and sent them to leaders who needed to know, Chuck Wilson helped the division planners on upcoming moves, and Mike Milam monitored the secret radio intercepts. Every few hours, around the clock, we put our see-through acetates together, one on top of the other, all on the same map, and there we studied them, looking for what I called the ganglions and the blobs, the places where the grease-pencil marks congregated, one on top of the other.

With each discovery of new intelligence, we prepared enlarged and detailed sketches focusing on the particular areas involved. These were about the size of a clipboard, easy to hand around. We then used these for daily update talks with senior commanders and staff. These map sketches, color-coded to distinguish our various intelligence sources, were somewhat caustically nicknamed "pretties." They were a way to focus a leader's attention and concentration on a single important issue—often sparking a recognition that would lead to a change in tactics or strategy. Everyone was always calling for better information about what was going on, and—especially—what was going to happen next. But if we're not careful, I insisted, we begin to twist and turn the intelligence to fit the war we would like to fight.

One day in mid-February 1970 I brought a new pretty over to George Stotser in the operations side of the bunker and asked him to look at it. He was in the middle of recommending the reinforcing of a brigade, putting into action a plan that had been approved by the commanding general. His reaction was—fulmination. "Where the hell did you get this idea? You know we've already sent out orders—we've got troops on the move in the opposite direction! Get out of here with that thing!" I stomped out, and a haggard George followed me and said, "OK, let me see that again."

As II Field Force commander, Lieutenant General Julian Ewell was one of General Westmoreland's immediate subordinates. He agreed with Westmoreland: the way to fight the enemy was to search them out, find them, and then use our mobility to surround and attack. To ensure that all his units were searching, Ewell put out the word that each platoon in the force would move at least fifteen hundred meters per day. We in the Cav reported to him. On the right flank of our division was War Zone D, a little-known and lightly populated area in which the only friendly troops were occasional patrols. General Ewell's command held responsibility for the broad area and sometimes sent raiding units in there. In the middle of that wilderness was a small town called Rang Rang. As we continued to improve our understanding of the trail system, we could see that many trails entered War Zone D from the north side, near the Cambodian border, and exited on the south side, near Saigon. We turned more of our attention to that right flank, and after several weeks of watching we had the details of a pattern. When the north trails showed activity, it was followed in a few days by a rise in indicators focused on Rang Rang, and then later by a rise in activity on the south exits from the zone. We made one of our pretties and sent out a Dossogram. I talked it over with George Stotser and General Casey, who told me to bring it up in a briefing scheduled that evening for Major General Elvy B. Roberts, our division commander. The general looked at the pretty, studied the main map for a few moments, and said, "Well, it's out of our area."

I like to think I was fairly insistent on the validity and importance of this intelligence, but I can't remember that part. I do remember what happened next. With some frustration, I wrote an essay-like message entitled "All Roads Lead to Rang Rang" and sent it to General Ewell's headquarters, calling attention to the earlier reports we had sent on this activity. I did not ask our generals to read it, figuring that for us the issue was over. It was not over for General Ewell, however, who ordered a strike team to head for Rang Rang. The result was a firefight, and the discovery of supply dumps galore. A stream of reports from the strike force amounted to a long list of more than 150 tons of rockets, small arms ammunition, rocket launchers from Romania, shovels from India, tires from Cambodia, rifle grenades from North Vietnam, and telephones from Czechoslovakia. Ninety-five percent of the haul, though, came from the People's Republic of China, in thirty-three separate caches.

A "Ewell Sends" message went out to all the command, congratulating his strike team on its spectacular success. Major General Roberts read the message and sent for me. George Stotser chuckled and bade me farewell. General Casey also lacked sympathy for the downtrodden: he too laughed and told me not to expect any help. He added, as I recall, "On this one you get an A for intelligence and an F for communication." I went alone to see General Roberts. He asked me why I hadn't told him about this intelligence before I told General Ewell. I said that I had told him, and he responded, "Then you didn't give it the emphasis it needed." I elected to remain silent and take my medicine. This was the Antilles Command bivouac all over again.

5 December 1969—to Gin:

> At 4:15 this morning we had a B-52 strike by six ships about 12 miles north of here. To be in the area of one of those strikes must be an experience that is out of this world. . . . Along that line we are searching for another "ghost village"—we now know of two—that moves gypsy-like through the dense jungle from one bunker system to another. Today I saw a 23-year-old woman and her brother, both crippled with rickets (apparently since early in life), who had come out of the village. They had tried to bring their mother, who was sick, but a U.S. helicopter flew over and they scattered, losing the mother in the jungle. They couldn't find her and came out without her.

Next day I sent a note: "Guess what—we found the mother in

the woods! 62 yrs old. I never thought we'd see her. She's in Song Be tonight with her son and daughter, all happy."

One midnight, walking out with Stotser, I said, "I'm glad to be getting out of this damned bunker." At that point a rocket slammed in close enough to make our ears ring. We looked at each other. I said, "I just remembered some work I wanted to do back inside."

On 8 January, I went out to Fire Base Ike, which had been hit the night before, to talk with its commander. Water and mud. Pieces of plastic sheeting. Cardboard ration boxes. Splintered logs. At the point where the sappers finally penetrated, the wire was spiraling off in knots, with engineer stakes floating on top, ammunition cans and boxes, an overturned latrine, torn and scattered sandbags, blackened ground, loose cartridges, and empty magazines. Disorder everywhere. The commander, Bob Drudik, pointed out where two cooks provided enough firepower to drive back the assaulting troops. The troops were exhausted. On the perimeter of the fire base, near a tangle of barbed wire, I saw a gray and tattered human hand floating in a puddle. I said to a tired soldier a few feet away, "Did you see that hand?" He looked up and said:

"It just means we owe 'em one of ours."

General Casey believed in jungle volleyball. He felt it was OK if we didn't get sleep, but we had to have exercise. Casey would fly in late in the afternoon and say, "Shirts off. Volleyball." There was always too much to do, no time for exercise, but Casey was not to be put off: He wanted us to be in shape. Of course, the game was volleyball in name only; in reality, it was mayhem. We played in combat boots and according to Casey's version of "jungle rules," which went something like this: No referee. No complaints allowed. No limit to team size. Players may dunk a spike, pull the net up or down while spiking, reach over or under the net, pass, lateral, or kick the ball. Rotation of positions sometimes occurred, but Casey himself always stayed in the middle of the dusty, ragged net, which was for the most part ignored. Sidelines were dismissed as overly restricting. Blocking and tackling were tolerated. Vague scores were kept, more for the sake of argument than anything else. Rank mattered not in this melee. Only the net, while it lasted, served to indicate that this might possibly be a sporting event. Casey took his lumps along with all the rest, and after the game he waited his turn for a dousing under the water bucket before we stumbled back to the operations center.

George Casey, assistant division commander, and E. C. Meyer, chief of staff, were two of the best officers I ever knew, although their styles were entirely different—indeed, worlds apart. If Casey disagreed with you, it came out in an exchange, the likes of which I captured many times in my notes. The wording here is not exact, but representative:

"So we're moving that unit out of the valley."
Casey: "Out of the valley?"
"That's what we're looking at."
Casey, after a five-second pause: "OK."
"One of the options."
Casey: "Yeah. Understand."
"We were thinking of it, considering it."
Casey: "I see."
"It does have some downsides."
Casey: "Well—"
"Maybe later."
Casey: "Your call."
"We could stay."
Casey: "OK."

With "Shy" Meyer, the same conversation would go like this:

"So we're moving that unit out of the valley."
Meyer: "Stop. It stays. Next?"

I went out and visited with battalion commanders and learned much that way. I visited Rick Ordway, who was a good friend. One day we went out to one of his companies. Earlier the company had set up a beautiful ambush and the North Vietnamese had walked right into it, but just as they drew near, one of our soldiers fired; they had a short firefight, and the NVA got away. They may have left one or two behind, but they got away. We went up to talk to the company commander. I just tagged along, while Ordway said to the commander, "So, what happened?" The commander gave it to him straight. He said, "The trooper that fired had eight more days to go in country and he got scared that he'd get himself in a firefight and get hurt. He fired early." Then Ordway said, "So what did you do about it?" He said, "We'll get them next time." Ordway said, "Good." And I thought, Ordway is going to get a straight answer every time he asks a question. This is going to happen in my battalion when I get one.

5 February 1970—to Gin:

Today I went to Song Be, to the home of the province chief of Phuoc Long, Lieutenant Colonel Yem. General Casey wanted to bring him a gift for Tet—a bottle of cognac—and I just happened to be along. Yem's pretty wife and three daughters were there (8, 6, 4) and I held the four-year-old on my knee—she's smaller than Beth, but with the same sort of bony shoulders and pixie look—black hair and big brown eyes. Yem's house is the usual open style, high tropical ceiling with slow fan, lattice work and tile floors. He has a temporary roof because the house had suffered a few hits when the VC mortared Song Be a couple of weeks ago and set off a nearby ammo dump. I thought about his sweet family, and how the VC would like to execute them, and realized the kind of tension that must be a part of his everyday life. After a few pleasantries the talk (as usual) turned to our latest problems with the enemy, and the condition of various hamlets. The war is never away from his house—not for a minute. His front yard, which at one time must have been a good lawn and garden, is a dusty parking lot for jeeps and weapons carriers.

By this time I could better understand Casey. He was disdainful of the way the Cav had become tied down—hence lumbering, elephantine. Large, well-constructed fire bases took time to build, and soaked up troops to defend them. More than once, Casey asked, "Do you know how many tons of plywood we moved down here from Khe Sanh?" He worked hard to change us back into a fast-moving, hard-hitting example of air cavalry. We were making fortresses, he said, not fire bases, and we were using up flying hours by hauling bulldozers around. This had to stop.

Casey and Roberts were getting further apart on the use of our air mobility. Our assigned area was growing bigger as we spread out to cover the departure of other U.S. ground forces. I told my father, "The jungle is going to get lonesome." With the broader area came additional reasons for greater mobility, the hallmark of air cavalry. Casey was convinced that we were far too "heavy" in all kinds of ways. He would say, somewhat wistfully: "The cavalry troopers of the west traveled light, like their opponents. Yes, they did build log palisades at important out-posts, but those were few and far between. Those troopers were in the saddle for every waking hour, and they ranged over a lot of territory. Their opponents were unpredictable, but so were they. For a whole squadron they had a couple of wagons, one for ammunition and the other for chow. And what are we doing? We're in a box, fifty by twenty-five miles. We can fly from one side to the other in half an hour. And we're building forts. We've got to get out of the construction business."

We were becoming suspended between two different tactical con-cepts. In the meantime, Ewell was pressing us to move, make contact, and create some good news. Casey wanted full exploitation of our advantages in mobility and firepower. We were a unique division that should have a unique mission. Ewell wanted results, action. When was the Cav going to show what it could do? Under this pressure, Roberts agreed with Casey. We were a cavalry division. We would outmaneu-ver the NVA forces. They're slow. They're very deliberate. They plan and plan before they actually do something. If we built hasty positions, just enough to park our artillery for a short time, we could move from one place to another, bring our firepower to bear, and be gone before they could react. Strike hard and disappear, just as they were doing, only more so.

Casey won out. In War Zone C, on our west, there were enough open high-grass fields that offered opportunities for clearing out a space large enough to accommodate a battery of six light howitzers. As we pushed up closer to the border, we built several hasty fire bases. One of these was called "Jay." Another was "Illingworth."

It was not long before North Vietnamese Army units moved against these positions. On 16 March I sent a note to Lieutenant Colonel Bob Hannas on Ike, with a diagram showing NVA units moving closer to him. People had equated seizing the initiative with mobility, but mobil-ity is not initiative—not in the jungle, where you fight at 25 meters. In fact, he who moves in the jungle is vulnerable, and he who stays still and quiet rules. Air mobility facilitates contact with the enemy, but it doesn't always prove to be a way to prevail in the jungle.

Letter to my father, 21 March 1970:

Today as I took off in my Huey, I glanced out (we leave the doors slid back) and saw a kid about four standing on a strand of a wire fence, hanging on and watching me. He had run to jump on the fence when he saw us start up. The propwash almost blew his shirt off but he hung on and waved, and I waved back and thought of Jerry Muffin. I was his Jerry Muffin. My heart went out to that ragged kid, living the way he does, in a hut down by the barbed wire on the edge of nowhere, with the war all around him. But he was tough, with a big smile. He'll make it.

28 March 1970. Although "cavalry" was now the byword, Jay and Illingworth, the hasty fire bases, stayed in place for too long. Casey was frustrated. He wanted to move the battalions, but other uses for the helicopters predominated. Hannas, with one company on Jay, kept his other three searching the area under the protection of his six 105s.

That night the NVA struck, pounding Jay with mortar fire and following with a ground attack that penetrated the concertina wire. Hannas was seriously wounded at the very beginning of the shelling, and the defending rifle company was almost overrun. Casey left for Jay before first light, taking me with him. When we got to Jay, a C-130 gunship was still circling the fire base, looking for targets. After we landed, I went down to a place on the wire where a few prisoners from the 95C Regiment were squatting next to some riddled bodies of their companions. A translator helped me ask questions, and I posed some that were important to us. I asked about the location of their base (Cambodia), the route they had used (trails we were familiar with), and the rally points after the attack (vague indications that they were to return to base along the same routes used in the attack). Bit by bit we pieced together enough to understand the general plan of withdrawal. Over secure radio, we compared notes with Brigade and Division. They were already picking up signs that matched the information we had. I talked to Casey, who wanted to move quickly against the attackers, sure that they would be in disorder. He radioed General Roberts and began to spell out the combat units most available for pickup. Roberts, however, was more concerned about the vulnerability of our own troops. When the enemy attacked Fire Base Mary Ann some weeks earlier, he reminded Casey, they had repeated the attack on the next night, and the same thing could happen to Jay. He ordered that Jay be closed down immediately, and that Hannas's battalion be moved to a more secure fire base. Casey did not want to use up the airlift in a move that would give us no advantage, but General Roberts was adamant, and we closed Jay.

A week later, Illingworth, another hasty fire base, closer to the Cambodian border, was attacked. The base was next to a road in a flat, open area except for the north side, which was wooded. On the south was a long string of bomb craters filled with water, the result of an earlier B-52 strike. The base, commanded by Lieutenant Colonel Mike Conrad, was strong in artillery, with six 105-mm howitzers, six eight-inch guns, and two 175-mm guns. There were stacks of artillery ammunition, some of which were hit early in the fight and exploded. The main communications antenna was chopped off, but luckily it fell in such a way that Conrad could still talk to brigade headquarters in Tay Ninh. The base held, although the fires turned it black. When I saw Mike the next day, he was covered in soot and talking with a croak. The toll was heavy on both sides.

At that time I was then picked to command 1st Battalion, 8th Cavalry, in the 1st Brigade. Roberts wanted to keep me as G2; Kingston argued that I was needed in the battalion. I held my breath. Mike Conrad, an excellent candidate for the intelligence job, was finishing his allotted six months in command. He was selected, and I was allowed to take five days R&R in Hawaii. Ginny was waiting in Honolulu, and in a matter of minutes we had become quintessential tourists. Everything glowed and sparkled in the realization that it would all be over only too soon.

We had four days. We flew to Kauai, then drove to the Hanalei plantation, where we had rented a cottage on one of the sharp long ridges slanting down to the sea next to Lumahai Beach. A warm rain was falling as we walked down the sloping path to our cottage, careful not to step on the dozens of frogs along the way. From inside we could see the long waterfalls tumbling down the other ridges. We watched horses cavorting on the curved stretch of beach and in the morning walked on the empty beach. We visited Waimea Canyon, sailed a catamaran off Diamond Head, danced into the morning in a ballroom high above Waikiki beach, and spent a horribly sad and sleepless final night in one of the cottages of Halekulani. For those four days we had kept to ourselves, blocking out all news of the world around us, paying no attention to television or radio or newspapers, ignoring the occasional word of troop movements along the border with Cambodia. And then we parted, Ginny to a flight home and I to a troop plane en route to Saigon, having just learned that there was a major incursion going on, an assault across the Vietnam border into the Cambodian "sanctuary" areas occupied by the command headquarters and logistical bases of the North Vietnamese forces.

When we landed at Tan Son Nhut, I made my way to a small helicopter that had been sent for me. The night was heavily overcast, with thunderstorms on all points of the compass. The wind was unpredictable. Strong gusts whipsawed us as we hovered along the taxiway, putting us crosswise to a cold rain that drove in through the open sides and stung hard. We headed north, and I got my bearings watching the illuminating artillery fire. At Division Headquarters I learned in detail our role in the operation. We were across the border along our whole front, into Cambodia. It was a massive raid, just the kind of mission for a cavalry division.

On 3 May 1970 I wrote to Gin: "I was held up from going out to the battalion in order to handle all the reports, briefings, and communications to higher headquarters. Yesterday I got all that stuff settled into a routine, more or less, and then asked again if I could leave for 1–8. . . . Part of the reason I'm being allowed to go is that they are having some problems in the battalion and they feel I can solve them."

Major Pete Taylor, who had been my assistant intelligence officer, now became my battalion executive officer, a piece of good luck for me. In the Division Headquarters I had heard that there were several soldiers in my battalion who had been sent back to the battalion rear element at Song Be charged with insubordination, and I found that there were eleven in all. Eleven blacks—no whites. On 6 May I met with each of my company commanders. (They were never all in the same place at once.) I told them that I intended to review the pending courts-martial before those actions went any further.

I flew to our battalion rear area in Song Be, and inside a big, dark, wet, rather comfortable bunker, I talked with the troops awaiting trial. I said I had not been around to witness the events that resulted in their detention, so I wanted to hear about them now. I said, "Why are you here? Tell me what happened. Let's just go around the circle." They took me up on this. One by one they spoke, with frankness, clarity, and balance and with an understanding of themselves, and I felt I was getting the truth. They talked about missed communications, unfairness, and frustration, but they also agreed that in retrospect there were better ways to resolve problems than the routes they had taken. We talked for almost two hours. Although every man had his own individual story, these soldiers were linked together in the burden of pent-up emotions they had carried for most of their twenty-year lifetimes. When they finished, we just sat there and looked at each other for a while. I told them, "If you come home from here a veteran, it's going to mean a lot, but if you have a court-martial and a bad military discharge to deal with, you'll be on the road down. Don't take that road. If you come back, it's to your same company, and we're ready to take you back. Your life will be on the line, but if you don't go, your life is wrecked. I can get you a chance, a new start, but that's all. You have to do the rest. I will keep myself informed." We shook hands around in a solemn way, and I left without demanding a response. They all came back. Tom Shaylor, who had helped me get back to the 1st Cav six months earlier, took care of the administrative details to get them back to their companies. An unorthodox solution, perhaps, but it was supported up and down the chain of command, where the case was known and understood.

On 8 May the battalion reconnaissance platoon reported a heavily bunkered base camp and then came under fire while investigating it. One Huey helicopter in support was sprayed by rifle fire, taking fifteen hits. The pilot, wounded, somehow flew back and landed on the fire base. We counted the hits in admiration. At that time there were several definitions for the faithful Huey. One was, "The Huey is a thousand spare parts flying in formation." We lifted D Company in to reinforce; then the sporadic contact during the night became a full-fledged firefight again early the following morning. The company pushed through the fortified camp, uncovering the biggest supply dump I had seen in my time as the division intelligence officer, except for Rang Rang. It took us two days to outload everything we found.

At the same time we were searching for a spot to build our new fire support base on the Cambodian border. The division wanted it inside Vietnam but as close to Cambodia as possible, so that I could provide support for the withdrawal of the rest of the division when that happened. We located a good place, a knob less than a mile from the border. I sent Captain Brian Utermahlen's A Company to seize the top of the hill and begin building the fire base, which we called "Mo"; and I put B Company (Jim Williams) and C Company (Jack Lowe) into Cambodia on the main trail system about six miles apart. We had studied the supply routes and picked out the ones that seemed to be getting the most traffic. D Company (Perkins) went in close to Mo to check the Vietnam side of the border. Within hours, all the companies were finding North Vietnamese base camps and supply dumps. It was raining heavily as we dug in, and soon we were occupying a red, muddy bald spot on the top of that dominating hill.

Brigade headquarters published a one-page news summary, a few copies of which sometimes arrived with the supply helicopter. On that day (11 May 1970), we passed the latest edition around on the hill. Folded, muddy, and tattered, it carried this news:

The Senate Foreign Relations Committee opens hearings today on a controversial measure aimed at cutting off funds for operations in Cambodia. The proposal will probably reach the Senate floor later this week but most likely next week. The proposed bill will also prohibit aerial combat over Cambodia except for bombing raids over enemy supply routes. The measure is sponsored by four members of the Committee. The bill is believed to have wider support than another proposal by Senator George McGovern. That measure would preclude support for all operations in Indochina.

National Guardsmen using tear gas and helped by heavy rain dispersed 4,000 demonstrators who were breaking windows and tossing firecrackers at the University of Wisconsin campus. . . .

On my birthday, 13 May, B Company was due for resupply. Jim Williams was brand-new, but a veteran of hard combat on an earlier tour. He had found a small opening in the jungle, and we had begun carrying in Huey loads of ammunition and rations, including hot meals in insulated cans, when the company came under small arms fire on the perimeter. We stopped resupplying and called for artillery and Cobra gunships. During the exchange of fire on the ground, Jim reported he had three people wounded, one seriously. From overhead I talked to Pete Taylor at the fire base, who was monitoring Jim's frequency, to see how long it would take at that moment to get a medevac helicopter out of Song Be. Pete advised that the estimate was twenty minutes before the bird could get there. The Cobras were only a few minutes out. I passed the word on to Jim. Jim said he understood and added, "Be advised we have started mouth-to-mouth." I said to my pilot, Warrant Officer Fender, "Twenty minutes. That's a long time. We could go in ourselves. What do you think?" He said, "Fine." Just that one word. I told him to coordinate his run with the Cobras, and radioed to Jim on the ground that we'd be coming in.

We had been in there before. It was a grassy slope on the side of a hill, with a crest running down the center. We had to land going uphill and with the wind, then hover up to the woodline at the top. When the medics on the ground were ready, we turned for the approach, with a Cobra on each side and slightly behind, firing rockets and guns to cover us. The troops on the ground and our own door gunners on each side added their fire. We flared up and sank, nose high, over the trees and into the clearing among torn trunks and stumps. The rotor blades snapped at close-in foliage and at bark and splinters sailing up from the ground. The tail banged down, and we lurched forward hard on the skids. I looked for Jim and saw him kneeling at the edge with his handset, just as his voice came through, saying, "Go out the way you came in, if you can. The other side is bad."

We hovered into the dark upper corner, close to the tree canopy, flattening the high grass while the troops struggled up to us carrying a soldier with a bandage covering most of his chest. We kicked out ammunition and pulled him in. Then, at full torque, we wallowed sideways down the slope as we came slowly around. We lifted off laboriously, blades beating, splinters flying, and started out. We began to move forward, toward the trees at the end of the clearing. I heard loud cracks, just above us. The right door gunner, leaning out and firing toward the rear, staggered back. Someone caught his harness and pulled him inside. We eased him down to the deck, and the medic moved over to him as we lumbered up over the treetops. Fender said, "I'll bend it over," which meant he'd get maximum speed out of the Huey. We were all on the Huey's deck in the rear, working to keep both men alive. When we tried to give the gunner artificial respiration, he turned his face away. We tried again and again, but no. He knew what was happening. We were doing all we could. The B Company soldier survived. The door gunner died on the way to Song Be. He had had only twelve days to go on his Vietnam tour.

That evening, when the fighting died down, I asked myself some questions. The medevac helicopter would probably have been too late, and the ground fire would still have been the same. And besides—once a medic, always a medic. I resolved never to forget that moment of recognition. I also promised myself that if men of mine were going to die in the battalion during my time as commander, I would do my best to go to them and look them in the face, and let that moment register in my mind. Then I would know more about the cost of the decisions that I made. When we took losses in combat, I felt a certain heartsickness that was not just momentary. It was there all the time: a sadness, a question of what might have been. In the next six months there would be twenty soldiers of the battalion killed and fifty-four wounded, far fewer than in that single fight at Phu Loi in 1966, but hard to bear just the same. Joshua Chamberlain, who commanded the 20th Maine Regiment at Gettysburg and later served as president of Bowdoin College, made this—the weight of responsibility—the theme of his writing, and I have gained some comfort from knowing that he and other military leaders carried such thoughts with them long after the events. I confided my thoughts to my father, who wrote back, "All I can do is pick up a brick and lay it in place. I'm doing this so that I can automatically, with each dip, slip and tap, be thinking of you, your officers and your men. May God bless and protect them all."

George Casey, now major general, had recently taken over command of the division. He brought Stanley Resor, secretary of the Army, out to Mo (he knew I had been the secretary's aide). We pointed out the locations of my companies on the high hills to our west, then walked around the fire base, talking to the troops. Secretary Resor was interested not only in the soldiers but in the condition of their weapons. He had worked hard to get the improved M-16 rifles into their hands. Casey talked to me about the additional mission of controlling a temporary airfield at Bu Gia Map, about six miles east of Mo, part of an old fire base we called "Snuffy." The division wanted to keep the runway open for logistical support of some of our forces inside Cambodia near the town of Snoul. Fire Base Snuffy would need a commander, so I assigned the responsibility to Pete Taylor. That same day I picked him up, along with his gear, and we took off for Bu Gia Map. We saw that we were flying toward a column of black smoke on the horizon—and we soon could see explosions and flames. Snuffy was under fire. I said, "Well, Pete, there's your new home." Within a few days, Pete had set up shop for troops from thirty-two different units, 329 troops in all, and had begun to make a team out of that conglomeration.

I tried to see every unit in my battalion during its resupply, which occurred every three days for each company. I would go in with the first load and come out with the last. It meant riding out on the log bird every flyable day, sometimes to more than one unit. At my fire base I would watch supplies being loaded on the log bird, waiting until the last bit of space was left, then get aboard myself and sit on the deck with my feet dangling outside. I wore a flight helmet and the crew chief would give me an extra phone jack, connecting me into the intercom. It was my chance to get out on the ground with companies and platoons, to see the commanders and discuss what we were doing, to walk around and chat while the Huey slick shuttled back and forth between the unit and the fire base. It was a time to get the feel of the unit and the place—to listen, to be supportive, and to weigh what I heard.

Out on the border area, the so-called "floor" of the rain forest was not flat; it was wrinkled into steep-walled ravines. In places there was no "jungle floor" at all—no surface. We clambered on in darkness through an undulating mass of interlaced roots and branches: no start, no end; every bit of life of every kind struggling through the gloom toward the sun or squirming down to the muck below, twisting, looping, locked together in life and death, dark rot and decay and bright green—a struggle, a competition, everything alive is fighting to stay alive. Enormous trees, dead for years, were held upright by the embrace of new growth. Sometimes looking up was the same as looking down. A foxhole out there was a kind of bunker, with jungle variations to accommodate the root system, and the fact that everything was alive and moving all the time. The dark earth swarmed. Even the logs, though torn from the earth, were still alive, still delivering insects and animals, still draining their sap and blood, still and ever changing.

Artillery rounds into the canopy gave rise to a tart, strong mix of acrid powder and the fresh-cut greenery of smashed trees. It helped to know that the artillerymen were aware that we were out there. With few ways to distinguish one location from another, we fired artillery on prearranged points, and if that didn't work, asked for a "hanger"—a 400-foot air burst of white phosphorus that was almost soundless but left a large white cloud. Then we worked it, adjusting it into the spot where we wanted it.

On 7 June I wrote to Gin: "Eventually, after Cambodia, I'll be able to get the battalion together again, but right now I have an Infantry company and an artillery battery plus 225 men from 18 different units at Bu Gia Map, and a company plus a battery plus 2–7 Cav headquarters plus my own HQ on Mo, and two companies and a recon platoon in Cambodia, plus my HQ company and the rear detachments of all my companies at Song Be. Other than that, no problem."

In late June, the division began its pullback from Cambodia. My missions were, first, to help cover the withdrawal, and second, to fend off any attempt to reestablish an NVA presence in Long Binh.

In July, after we had pulled out of Cambodia, the North Vietnamese forces were faced with the need to rebuild their structure of trails and dumps—a mission they were well prepared to carry out, but one that forced them into heavy logistical activity in wide strips along both sides of the border. For the first time in years, they had to speed up their supply work. The regular forces as well as the Viet Cong threw them-selves into this effort.

The way they chose to rebuild their system in our area was prob-ably the only way they could see to do it: they went back to the same routes and supply lines they had so meticulously put together. Some of their widespread dumps were still intact, and since the original struc-tures were well selected the first time, it was tempting to use them again. This, however, allowed us to spread the Cavalry Division over wide distances along the border, doing typical jobs for cavalry: screen-ing, harassing, filling gaps, slowing down enemy forces that were try-ing to pass through us, providing information, and making spoiling attacks that disrupted the aims of the enemy.

It was often the company receiving logistical support that also got enemy contact, since that unit had to prepare the landing zone for the log helicopters. That was a disadvantage; but our enemy was slow in planning and moving, and we were prepared. If light contact looked like it would become something more, we alerted our company on the fire support base. We called for artillery and gunships, and mortars if they were in range, and we alerted the division to a possible change in plans with respect to USAF support.

On 6 July, the edge of the rain was not far off. Our troops on the ground were chopping away, making slow progress. Cutting into a tan-gle of bamboo is a horrible task, but they had already found the thinnest spot and were throwing themselves into the work, taking turns on the few machetes they had. A machine gunner had been badly wounded, and they wanted to get him out. But we were running a bit low on fuel, and there was no place to land. We orbited some distance off, and waited to show a medevac the location for a landing spot. The C Com-pany "Ghostriders" 229th had some great pilots, and on this day I had the best of them all: Bruce James, call sign "Zorba." He summed it up: "This place is as close to nowhere as you can get."

We waited as long as we could, then decided to go in. Zorba flared over the hole, the small break in the canopy. The bamboo tops bent in a graceful swoon as the downwash blew them back, in waves that made concentric circles. Zorba eased off the collective and we started down, ten, twenty, thirty feet into the hole. The circle became narrower as the trunks, thickening, become more stubborn; at about fifteen feet, even "ground effect" wasn't enough, and with nothing to hold back the tops, the whole elevator shaft began to close in. The main rotor blade chopped through the foliage with a snap and a spray of debris, then two or three more. We pulled back out. We asked ourselves, how can we do this? Any other place where the troops below could carry him out would be too far. Zorba said, "If we had a rope, which they do but we don't, we could maybe do something. But even with a rope, that guy is in bad shape, and we'd probably hurt him even more. They've got some more of the bamboo down, so let's try it again." The rain reached us. "Bring him over to the hole," we told them, "and get everybody else out of the way." We went down again. They were holding the wounded man as high as they could, and with all the slipping and manhandling, he was in agony. The group was a flapping tangle of arms, shirts, ponchos, and bamboo debris as they lifted him into the downwash. We got hold of him, dragged him in, and worked our way out of there. The next day I wrote my father: "We found 109 rounds of 75mm recoilless rifle ammunition just outside Mo today. Yesterday I went down between the trees to get another wounded man, as rain was starting, and clipped the trees on the way out, putting 5 holes in the rotor blades. We flew the man to the hospital at Song Be, where the helicopter was checked and ruled 'not flyable.' The boy is on his way 'back to the world,' though, and he would have died if the rain had closed in on him."

Casey told me to meet him at Bu Gia Map. Hueys were taxiing—easing along just over the high grass at the north end of the strip, beating up a red dust as they sat down to drink fuel from cylindrical rubber "blivets." On the other side of the runway down at this end, there were Air Force aluminum pallets of ammunition left by C-130s, awaiting pickup by Chinook cargo helicopters to deliver them to the new fire bases in Cambodia. Bu Gia Map was to me a name that four years earlier— or even a couple of months earlier—meant the end of the world, the last stop, a far corner lost to the enemy long ago. Now its airstrip and sprawling supply dumps and refueling points were supporting two brigades in Cambodia—and it was all mine to watch over. I kept one company there, patrolling in platoons to keep enemy fire from harassing the place. We had taken some fire the night before and had lost a pallet of 105 ammunition to a hit from a 75mm recoilless rifle. Casey wanted to see what had happened, and he had some questions. Did I think the NVA could be filtering back? No, I said, it had to be locals. Were they getting help from the Montagnards (the indigenous people)? Almost certainly.

Then there passed one of those fragments of conversation that stick in the mind forever.

"Are we killing people who are trapped into helping the VC, who are really only trying to ride out the war?" General Casey asked.

"We are killing some," I replied. "It's hard to tell a carrying party from a patrol. Yes, some are getting killed." We were walking through the overgrown ruins of the old fortified camp. "They all used to come in here to market. Most of them are still around, and if we stay here any length of time, some of them will get in the way of a bullet. They're out there in small bands, the remains of hamlets, constantly on the move but never straying too far from their old gardens and paddies."

"Whatever we do," Casey replied, "whatever plans we make, whatever operations, I don't want to get those people killed. It wouldn't make sense to save the countryside and lose the people. Can you find them and get them to come out?"

"We can try, sir. We will try."

It would be my last conversation with him.

Letter to Ginny, 9 July:

I'm sure you'll have heard already that Casey is dead, and along with him my friend Al Hottel and Sergeant Major Cooper [killed 7 July 1970 in a helicopter crash in South Vietnam when their UH-1H struck a mountain near Bao Luc in poor weather as they were en route to Cam Ranh to visit wounded troops]. I am completely unable to think that I'll never see Casey again—after all the days of talking to him and working with him. Everything I've done as a battalion commander has been with Casey in mind—trying to remember all the things he taught me, and to keep them in mind and carry them out. I never thought we were doing well unless I knew he thought so. I saw him last on the day Resor came and you have the photos, with his good-natured smile. I am really broken up over this. I can hardly think about it.

And to my father the same day:

I am heartbroken that this good man I liked so much—this Irishman with an accent like mine—is gone from earth now.

I saw him a couple of days ago in the prime of his life, and he had a few good words for me and for the Eighth Cavalry. He said he was pleased with the quick way I shifted my operations to meet the moves of the enemy. I was thinking then that he had taught me most of the tactics I'm using now—and I had been trying to follow his every word.

He's gone now, and I can hardly think about it without feeling the tears come to my eyes.

10 July. A driving rain. Pete Taylor came up from the pad, slipping and sliding in the red mud. Almost on the crest and close to the command bunker, we had built a makeshift tent, without sides, covered on top with ragged canvas and a plastic sheet. From there you could see most of Fire Base Mo. Next to it was a sandbagged revetment protecting a battery of 105mm guns of Charlie Battery, 21st Artillery. Taylor and I were sitting under the plastic top, looking at a map and discussing a helicopter lift of one of the companies, to enable better coverage of the main routes through our area of operations. A fire mission came in, and our guns, including the one next to us, began to fire. We continued to talk, but the subject shifted to artillery fire coordination between Mo and Snuffy, fifteen kilometers away.

Suddenly there was a strange, dull explosion on the other side of the sandbags, inside the gun position: a concussion, large fragments flying close over our heads, heavy black smoke in the gun pit. We both said something like, "What the hell was that?" I had never heard anything quite like it. Not an incoming mortar round, not a grenade—something in between. We jumped up and looked over the top of the revetment. Some of the gun crew were on the ground, hurt. Shells were strewn everywhere. We ran to the entrance of the gun pit and a soldier stumbled past us, heading downhill. His chest was bloody. I ran after him. He fell up against the mound of sandbags covering the medic bunker, which stuck up about two feet above the ground, and rolled onto the top. He was screaming, "Medic! Medic!" I turned him over and saw the wound. He said, "Why me? My God! Why me?" and struggled to get up. I had my first aid bandage and he had his own, but the two together were not enough for such a big opening. His sternum was not there anymore. The whole center of his chest cavity was a single open, gaping wound. He put his chin on his chest and looked down. "I can see my heart!" he said.

Our battalion surgeon, a captain, motioned to us to bring him inside the bunker. The soldier cried, "Look at me, Doc! My God! Look at me!" I couldn't believe he was so conscious, so active, not at all in shock. Doc took the biggest bandage squares he had and overlapped half a dozen or more on the wound, while the soldier continued to ask, "Why me?" We kept telling him hang on, hang on, you'll make it, but I was thinking, as a medic I never talked to anyone with a hole that big in him, and I can't believe I'm doing it now. Doc pulled plasma over. "Okay, we're going to fix you up," he said.

"I'm gonna die, Doc."

"No, you're not. Take it easy. We'll fix you."

"I'm gone."

A medevac helicopter from nearby Bu Gia Map arrived in minutes, so we were able to get the soldier and another less badly wounded one on the way quickly to the field hospital. Later we learned what had happened. The crew had been working fast, getting the fire support on target—some setting fuses, some loading, some adjusting and firing, some carrying new rounds to the gun. He was carrying a round in his arms. The nose of another round struck the base of his, and the brass cartridge primer on his round exploded. The round itself did not go off, because it requires the setback of fast acceleration to arm the shell. I never heard of such a thing happening before or since. The soldier died in a hospital in Japan. He had made it that far.

Our companies were now finding large amounts of weapons, ammunition, and supplies on the Vietnamese side of the border, including around the hill where Fire Base Mo was located. On 15 July, B Company found 250 SKS Soviet rifles, brand-new, in one of the caches close to Mo. As one soldier on Mo later told a reporter: "There I was, minding my own business. I take my shovel and go out about 20 feet from the perimeter to do a little personal work, and there it is, staring me in the face—about 20 boxes of .51 cal [machine gun ammunition]. After making a quick search of the area, we found four other piles, so we naturally moved the perimeter down and secured the area."

I reported the find and got the word back from the division that I should send the rifles back for intelligence purposes. I said, "I'm sorry, they've all been handed out to the troops that found them." We held them back, storing them in a CONEX container, so the troops could take them home. The troops, of course, liked that very much. They tried to give me one of the rifles, but I wouldn't take it. We had some extras beyond those distributed to the troops that were actually involved in finding them, so we gave an SKS to each of the forward air controllers.

When we were ordered back from the border in late July, we opened a new fire base on a dominating hill ten miles to the southeast, a place we called "Betty." Again we cleared the hilltop, using explosives to knock down the biggest trees. During the work a soldier said to me, "As soon as we dig in on the hill, the rats are there, digging with us. I don't know how they get the word to move to the new place. Must be a rat network."

Another night in July. Rain further obscures the darkness, smothering all other sound. No footfall can be heard, no movement distinguished; the soldiers are uneasy. In the muffled cacophony of sounds, no matter how intently you listen, your imagination can't focus enough to create any coherent picture, and anything could be happening just a few fronds, a few leaves, a few stalks away. The imagination struggles, searching for something, creating vision after vision, scene after scene. On one of those nights, I was walking from one bunker to another along the perimeter of our new fire base. As usual, when I got ready to move from one firing position to the next, I asked who's in the next foxhole, so I can keep from surprising anyone. The password is a name. There was always an official password, but knowing a name comes in handy. This time I said softly, "Pizarro—got room in there?"

Even though the bunkers had a layer of plastic cloth between the earthen topping and the logs, the stubborn water comes down in rivulets along the clay walls. I crawled inside. I had met Pizarro before, when his company was getting resupplied. The last time I had seen him, he had mentioned how worried his mother was about him.

After the first few words, silence. Then Pizarro said, "Sir, what are you doing out here?"

"I dunno—sitting with you." (What *am* I doing out here? Trying to find out how to communicate without talking? And who is comforting whom?) Pizarro stares ahead, showing me that he knows, at least, what he is supposed to be doing. I look out there, too. When it comes to knowing what we need to know in the fifty meters around that foxhole, we certainly are equals.

Half-smile. We return to our own lives and small reveries.

"No se como calmar a mi madre," Pizarro says. "Se preocupa tanto por mi que se enferrma. Cada carta de ella es para me un castigo. La pobre mujer. Tanto padecer." (I'm not sure how to calm my mother. She's so worried about my safety. Each of her letters is a punishment for me. The poor woman. Both of us suffer.)

"You could tell the family to talk to the Red Cross, and you could get in touch with them."

"Yes sir . . . lo voy a averiguar . . ."

Major General George Putnam arrived to replace Casey. Putnam was a Cav sandwich whom I knew well from my earlier tour. Colonel Clark, my brigade commander, was promoted and replaced by Colonel Buck Buchanan (who would soon be replaced himself after being injured in a helicopter crash). Then, on 8–9 August, we were engaged in an all-night firefight about two miles from Betty. Pizarro was killed in action.

I go out to the location.

"Where is he?"

"Over there, sir. We brought him in right after it happened."

I look down at a lumpy mound under a mud- and blood-encrusted poncho. Once again the crossed legs of a body that has been rolled over, as with Barbara years ago. Two boots sticking out in an incongruently nonchalant way. Far, far from Borinquen (Puerto Rico). I find I can't pull back the poncho.

Shift to two decades later: Sunday, 15 January 1989. I am with my family in Washington, D.C., at the Vietnam War Memorial. Up until that day I had thought of the Memorial as an ugliness. You walk into a hole in the ground to read names on a gigantic black tombstone. When I saw the winning design for the Memorial, I had said, "That, on the Mall? It would be much better to see it in Arlington Cemetery, where there are other gravestones like it." Although I was often in Washington, I had not visited the site. I thought of the half-buried black wall as a protest, rather than a memorial. Underground, hidden, cold, condemning, and sad. Only the loss—nothing of the courage and the soldiering? What's the message—that all those deaths were in vain? Whose message was that? The police crush moving slowly, insistently, through the crowd of folks blocking the bus at McGuire. The parents, the high school teachers, the cop on the block, the priest—all the leader figures, saying, "Don't go—get a deferment, go to Canada and wait it out . . ."

"Pizarro Colon, 6 July 1950–11 August 1970."

The helpful volunteer looks up the name.

In the black marble I saw, first, not the inscribed names but the reflected figures of my own family and myself—a discomfiting moment, as their faces and those names alternated in my focus.

Names and dates. A massive chronology of life's ending for so many who served . . . the war told in terms of the dying. Then again, those sacrifices were the defining moments that described Vietnam to people for whom the war really mattered, for those who, no matter the historical or political outcome, truly lost the war. It is the names, the stark endless names, and the dates of so many deaths that hold any living person in thrall, those beings that reach out from the black wall. And my thoughts were drawn back to the crossed boots and the poncho . . .

Letter to my father, 16 August 1970:

> Rain most of the time. But we are still flying, treetop level in the little space between trees and clouds. Huck would appreciate my mortarmen—every time they fire in the jungle, the baseplate plasters them with mud until they look like ant hills. But they keep putting out fire. Malaria is bad—I have 9 men down with it this month so far—one of the highest rates in the division—because we're the closest to the border, where all the malaria-ridden NVA are. We're taking over more and more missions of the U.S. units.

John Saar, the Asia Bureau chief for *Life* magazine, asked to go on operations with an infantry company of 1st Cav and brought Dick Swanson along as his photographer. Division Headquarters sent them to me, and I put them with Brian Utermahlen's A Company, which was on the fire base getting ready for seventeen days of patrolling. Brian and I walked with Saar and Swanson around the hill to give them a chance to see the setup—the circle of log-covered low bunkers along the berm, the artillery and mortar positions, the medical aid station, the communications antennas, the sandbagged ammunition and supply dumps, the interconnected rolls of barbed wire that spiderwebbed in all directions—as well as the mundane: the garbage pits, the latrines and bucket showers, the ubiquitous piss tubes (no one would dream of calling them urine tubes) sticking up out of the ground at different angles of accommodation. The prevalent smell of these bases is the smoking mix of diesel oil and fecal matter that substitutes for a septic system. All of this to provide a home for six 105mm and six 155mm guns. I was impressed with Saar's willingness to get out of Saigon and come up to see firsthand the action along the border. Later, I wished I had a word-for-word version of our conversation; I have to settle for some paraphrasing.

Saar said, give me some thoughts on the war and on why you are here on this hill, commanding this battalion, instead of all the other things you might be doing with your life. (An aside: This was the same question that Casey had asked four or five of us battalion commanders that one evening less than a month before. Our responses were very much the same: there were leaders who had set the example for us.)

I told Saar, "At my rank and with the crossed rifles I wear, the main thing for me right now is to be on this hill. Anything else would frustrate my life's aims."

Saar asked, how would you describe what it is you're doing out here?

I said, when we went into Cambodia, we upset the applecart of the NVA. Our mission now is to keep them from coming across the border with the apples back in place. We block the trails with ambushes. It's not us that the NVA want to fight; they hope to bypass us and target the cities. Our job out here is to spoil their plan, to make it risky for them to move large forces into their usual operating areas. The battalion is deep in the boondocks, patrolling as companies and platoons. They are resupplied by air every three days, weather permitting. Every seventeen days, on average, they're picked up and flown back here for a few days to clean up, rest a bit, and defend the fire base if necessary. Then the cycle repeats itself. That is the general idea, subject to the vagaries of combat, which assures that the rotation never happens quite the way it's laid out.

Saar said, how can you expect to keep up the soldiers' fighting spirit and morale when they know that the war is winding down? How can you make it logical for them? How do you deal with the situation? I don't remember exactly what I said then, but here's what I say now. The men were deeply affected by the lack of meaning of it all, given the risks they were called on to accept. They were contemporaries of the soldiers I rode with on the bus to McGuire; the dissension at home concerning the war was only a part of the vertigo they felt. It is not true that the soldiers had little idea of the many facets of the conflict. They were well aware that the American forces were pulling out, and they knew why. They were tasked with seeking out fights with the enemy, fights that were not to gain ground, not to win the war and protect the homeland, but simply to soldier on until told to stop. Everyone knew we were pulling out.

The point I make with our troops is that we're here, and the fight is still on. There's no way to change that. If we don't take the fight to the enemy, they will surely take it to us. We have to be tactically smarter and better than they are. We are a team; we fight as a team; we take care of each other. Our basic unit, the most important of all, is the squad. You can never let the squad down, and that applies to everybody in the battalion, including me.

Saar wanted to know, what is a day like for the troops?

Brian and I answered along these lines. The troops hate the days of resupply and the liftouts. It is a noisy, risky business. Sometimes they have to widen the clearing by cutting away foliage. This, along with the racket of the Hueys, echoes through the forest for miles around and creates a perfect time for the enemy to move in and strike. As the squads are lifted out, the number of troops on the ground becomes ever smaller, the outposts thinner, the troops more wary.

But there is plenty else to dislike, beginning with the fire support base itself. For the troops, it is a crazy, dangerous place that goes against all their better instincts. A red scar on top of a rise in the undulating vastness of green is an ugly thing indeed. After two, or sometimes three, weeks in the jungle, the soldier comes to the fire support base glistening with filth. Fatigues ragged, salty in patterns from sweat after sweat, his towel now a rag. Sores, cracked lips, bearded, hollow-eyed, with bug bites and festering scratches and cuts. Boots laced halfway. Patches of green tape holding together torn fabric here and there.

The soldier owns nothing but a small metal ammunition box, which adds a little weight but is also indestructible and waterproof—the only item in his possession that stays dry. Here he keeps his letters, photos, toilet paper.

Once the soldier completes cleaning his weapons and himself, he is ready to go back out whenever necessary, which makes him now available for other duties: improving fighting holes and bunkers, stringing barbed wire, burning garbage and latrine waste, making short patrols, taking his turns on the perimeter, and playing catch-up on acquiring blisters, cuts, scabs, insect bites, peeling feet, scales, and sores.

There is also what could be called "team rebuilding." The composition of a team, its collective personality, is never stable. A team that entered combat together becomes, over time, a ladder, with members spread over different rungs. An accelerated change weakens the team, makes it uneasy. A newly arriving team member brings another lifetime of experience to be assimilated, but those high on the team's ladder remember the old times as best, and fear that the youngsters are moving up too fast. The shock of a fight, even a small skirmish, turns this around. Usually the old men see that the young kids are OK after all, and the new guys gradually get more of a say, especially as members with seniority realize that at some point not too far off, the team will have to go on without them.

What the troops wanted first were leaders who knew their jobs, competent NCOs and officers. Then they wanted some assurance that their leaders truly cared about them. They expressed these thoughts in many different ways, but that is their message—everything else comes after those two needs. You can see that in Saar's 23 October 1970 article in *Life* magazine, and even in Swanson's photos.

Saar wanted to know how we responded to these needs—not a question you can answer with nonchalance. We were fighting a far-ranging jungle battle where you tried to pick your fights when you held the best cards—and you worked hard in every way to *get* those cards, those advantages. We had accomplished that time after time, and we knew why. You absolutely had to have good communication up and down the line.

Saar was perceptive. The title of his article was "You Can't Just Hand Out Orders." And he was right on the mark. You let the team members see that they were part of the leadership, that they had a say, that their words had meaning. Leadership is decision making—and teaming, even in the old-fashioned sense, means sharing. It means that the troops want to know you care.

Saar quoted a sergeant who said of the soldiers, "They go out and avoid the enemy," and I said I was sure there were times when that happened. There is a range of ways to carry out a mission, but all soldiers know that you have to be accurate about reporting your position, because you may need fire support from artillery or air strikes. You could, of course, set up a position that is more a defense than an ambush, and you might be tempted to do that if you felt your troops were too green to handle an ambush. Brian Utermahlen was the kind of commander who would listen if you said, "I didn't try for a full-up ambush last night because my folks were not ready for that." In many units no one would dare say such a thing. It's the kind of moment when all you've got going for you is the truth. As a leader you can talk a lot, but you might not be communicating. A company can run like a machine with practically no words spoken, but not for long. It slowly becomes vulnerable to a tightening web of avoidance, unreality, suspicion, and a kind of unworldliness.

Brian built trust by encouraging free expression and by his willingness to accept advice. Saar, in his article, quotes him on his view of leadership as "being honest with people and doing the best job possible for people under and over me"; he concludes, "It's not a democracy, but they want to have a say." I agreed with Brian. A good team is not just a leader and some followers; it is full of leaders, and all of them can add something to the effort. It pays to remember that.

Brian was a fighter. In one firefight he scooped up a machine gun on the run, cleared a stoppage, flopped down and opened fire, then handed the machine gun back to the gunner and continued with the rest of a successful encounter. Leadership changes with the challenge—you must constantly adapt to the requirements of the moment. There are times to be understanding and times to be demanding. For Brian, every soldier was a distinct individual, not just another GI. Soldiers knew they could go to him and talk about fear, frustration, exhaustion, bad news, anything. They could second-guess him on decisions and he would listen, and there were times he realized they were right—and said so.

Saar ended his article with this evaluation of Brian: "In contrast to his men, Captain Utermahlen will probably never be happier or more fulfilled in the service of the United States Army than he is as Alpha's commander. Against the personal exultation of doing the job for which he has been educated, trained, and equipped, other factors are relatively insignificant. In the jungle, where his resources, instincts, and intelligence are tested to the utmost, he feels no crisis of conscience about the morality of the war. Yet Utermahlen is incapable of divorcing himself from his generation, and ahead lies the certainty of strained relations with the Army."

This was true. After Vietnam, Brian was assigned to the faculty of the Infantry School at Fort Benning. He went on from there to helicopter flight school and flew for the infantry units at Fort Campbell, Kentucky—but he resigned and transferred to the National Guard in 1974 as a captain and later retired as a major. He liked to fly, but he wasn't happy in the Army of the 1970s. He went to work for the DuPont chemical company and eventually retired to Texas, where he coached high school lacrosse and now does some hunting—and some writing.

In mid-August 1970, we received a shipment of sensors (acoustic movement detectors), and I went out to Hill 336 to see Jim Williams, riding the log bird as usual. We had talked often about these devices, and now that we had them in hand, I told him to seed them along the trails that were getting the most use, in the biggest stopover areas, and anywhere else he thought there might be units passing through. These sensors picked up ground vibrations and converted them to a radio frequency that sent a message back to us, where the information could be integrated into other intelligence to help us know what was going on.

When B Company finished stocking up for another day of operation, I rode out on the last lift, and Jim moved his troops off into the jungle. This was on 20 August. On the night of 24 August, two sensors sent indications of movement. The following day during resupply I brought out more sensors. I told Jim to keep going in the direction we had planned, keep laying sensors, business as usual, and we would be listening.

That night there was a chorus of sensor messages in an area about a thousand meters to his east, and we told Jim to turn into the center of the movement. We alerted the other companies to stand by to reinforce. For two days Jim moved eastward and southward, following the continuing signals. He reported sightings, then an exchange of fire with enemy troops, then a skirmish in which one of his soldiers was killed and another wounded. Both sides were maneuvering, looking for each other. On 28 August it was time to airlift supplies to the company, which is always a giveaway of location, no matter how it is masked. Usually the companies take in the supplies of ammunition and rations and then move on, disappearing into the jungle, but on this day at 12:45 p.m. Jim reported heavy contact, which quickly became a pitched battle. About 100–150 enemy conducted six assaults during the afternoon. The enemy wore khaki shirts and blue trousers, with soldiers wearing red scarves and officers blue, along with epaulets. Some wore boots, some sandals. All were carrying small bags of rice, which we later found scattered over the battlefield. From our hill we could see the fight begin, eight kilometers to the northwest of us. With our twelve artillery pieces firing, we could watch the rounds on the way and see the impact. I walked over to Utermahlen, the company commander whose troops were on the hill, to tell him that helicopters were inbound from brigade to lift him into the fight. The battalion reconnaissance platoon would go with him, and the other companies would follow.

Most of us knew Hill 336 pretty well; it was halfway between Betty and Mo. Jim was fighting on the eastern slope of the hill, facing mostly to the north; Brian went in on Jim's west side. I alerted C Company (Rektorik) to go in on the southwest side.

When I climbed aboard the Huey to go out to the action, I saw that the left door gunner had replaced his .50 caliber machine gun with a Gatling minigun that hung by a coiled spring from the top of the door. Homing in on the light smoke drifting up from the fight, I heard a call from Jim Williams to Pete Taylor: low on ammunition. I listened to what he needed—M-60 ammo, frag grenades, smoke grenades—and I knew we had some boxes of those aboard, as always. After he finished talking to Pete, I cut in and said I could help while Pete got a second helicopter loaded. By this time I was over Jim and looking for a place that was close enough to bring it in and yet stay out of the line of fire. There wasn't any such place. As we ran low level to look at a tiny forest glade—an opening in the high trees—the left door gunner pointed and said, "B-40! Can I fire?" The pilot looked left, and so did I. I saw a team of three men running bent over, with a rocket launcher, and I said, "Fire! Fire!" The minigun put a stream of fire into the glade. There were explosions and smoke, and we turned hard to the left and saw an opening next to a stand of bamboo. I said go for it. We dropped like a stone, flared at the last few seconds, and landed hard in tall grass and tangles of splintered bamboo. The left door gunner was facing away and could fire, and that he did. I got out the right door and was almost flattened by the downwash—we had come back to a hover three or four feet off the ground and the Huey was rocking. There was a strong smell of Cordite and slashed vegetation.

The gunner pushed the ammo boxes over to me, and I hollered over the noise, "Give them everything!" We unloaded all we were carrying. The dominant sounds were the continuous sharp crack of small arms fire and the slapping noise as it went through the bamboo. I climbed back in and fumbled for the handset as we lifted and banked away. Jim was on his frequency, giving orders. He called, asking, what the hell was that? As for the minigun—I realized I had been thinking about the men in black pajamas along the dike, and the napalm in the Phu Loi battalion fight, and some other things like that. Split-second decisions that linger for a lifetime.

My old boss, Lieutenant General Norton, later spoke about this battle in testimony on Capitol Hill:

I met an officer who had fought in my division in Vietnam during 1966 when he had very few [electronic sensor] devices and who, in his second tour, was putting the capabilities of the new . . . equipment to good use. In one critical action, he had been alerted by various ground sensors to the presence of an NVA battalion which had slipped across the Cambodian border. He was ready for the enemy when they attacked. The attack soon became a defeat for the enemy and they began to withdraw. The officer had retained a reserve of certain unattended sensors for just such a situation.

A helicopter was dispatched to drop the sensors on the possible withdrawal routes. Indication of the direction of withdrawal was picked up so that follow-up action could be initiated to aggressively pursue the enemy. As a consequence, an enemy attack that could have been a costly surprise several years ago was turned into a rout for the enemy.

On 29 August we flew seventy-four Huey sorties as we spread out the companies along the major trails to try to reestablish contact with the main body of enemy forces. The next day I wrote to my father: "This will be just a short note. We are having a lot of fights up along the border, and the NVA is getting stronger. This week has been like a treadmill, day and night. We have had 5 of ours killed and a lot of wounded, and have taken a pretty heavy toll of NVA, but I think they are moving through me. I've got everything committed along the trails and we're patching together operations, working around the rain."

Fighting sputtered on for four days. We took Hill 336 again with only light resistance and found it a strange place. There were areas still littered with the debris of battle from both sides—canteens, ration cans, bamboo shards, ripped and shredded tree trunks, bloody bandages, rags, towels, ammo cans, packs, pith helmets (and some of our steel pots), bandoliers, ammo, pistol belts, rice and more rice, camouflage nets, small green plastic tarpaulins, toilet paper of all kinds—and then there were oases on the hill completely untouched by the events of the past days: no sign of anything but thousands of years of normal life, no craters, no battle jetsam.

I had underestimated the size of the unit, which turned out to be a combination of NVA line troops from the 90th and 174th Regiments and local VC supply troops from the trail system.

I wrote to Ginny on 12 September: "We're not getting our replacements in, and the battalion strength has gone down from 850 to about 750. General Putnam came right out to the jungle where B Co had a big fight and passed out 2 silver stars, 5 bronze stars, and some other medals. I was scared stiff because I thought we would get mortar fire. We didn't, and it was a great morale boost. Of course, I like Putnam all the more now."

On 15 September 1970, Air Cav scouts were at work. Small scout helicopters down low, almost in the treetops, sometimes actually at a hover a few feet off the ground, trying to see under the canopy. A pair of Cobras up above, ready to lend their support if the scouts took fire from the ground. A Huey hauling a rifle squad in case skirmishers were needed.

Monitoring the scout radio frequency at the fire base, we heard the report. Many footprints in the mud around a shallow stream crossing point. Very fresh, prints still oozing water. NVA footgear. Definite signs of troop activity—movement is southward. At the command post we plotted the location and then superimposed the trail overlay and the acetate showing activity over past weeks in our area. The red dots showed other sightings, with coded details: individuals and groups moving, gunfire from the ground at aircraft, infrared indications of small cooking fires, bunkers, trenches, dead brush used as camouflage, tracks of heavily loaded bicycles. Red marks fit closely over the place the scouts were reporting. The surge of reporting that always comes when something interesting is found. Everyone is listening for the latest intelligence—and the other scouts, the line companies, and supporting units all increase their reporting of any detail that might have some association with the new find.

At that point we always tried to keep the communications and other activities from rising above routine levels, but we had to alert companies to move closer to landing zones—small open areas in the jungle. I talked with the company commander of the troops on the fire base and showed him what we had on the map. He began to ready his unit for a move. As more reports came in, we were getting a clear picture. The mosaic was starting to make sense.

The North Vietnamese Army junior commanders could select the trails, changing even at the last minute, but the weakness of their system was that many trails in our area shared the same stopover base camps. While the commander could choose among many trails, once he committed himself we could guess accurately which camps were the possible rest stops. In this case, there were only two that we knew of, and they were not very far apart, about twenty miles to the northeast of us. The rough plan we were devising at the time was this: without increasing current reconnaissance or otherwise changing our patterns, figure out the size and direction of this NVA unit; add recon in other parts of our area out toward the Cambodian border so that we don't seem to be concentrating anywhere (and also to see if this is part of a bigger operation); start lining up the airlift and other resources we will need from Division for an attack at first light in the morning. First company in will be the one we have on the fire base.

We were hurrying, but everybody knew what to do. It was getting closer to sunset. I had alerted the brigade commander that we had a good sighting that might mean action coming up, and he said he would fly up to see us right away to discuss the situation. The wheels were in motion. Much of this happened every day and we were accustomed to it, but the adrenaline was starting to rise. Most of our 435 helicopters were in the air every day, flying air assaults, hauling artillery pieces, delivering ammunition and other supplies, reconning, serving as command and control ships. The flow of activity could shift at any moment, as was happening right now. Then the scouts sent in their first report of NVA troops on the trails: six to eight soldiers, tan uniforms, light weapons, camouflage, moving south. Also more bicycle tracks.

More reports in. Nothing happening elsewhere that would indicate a larger pattern. Pete talked with Pat Patrick, the brigade operations officer, while Tom Bell passed along the information to the intelligence section and the other staffers interconnected. This stirred Division. Everyone was thinking, "How will this affect what we're doing now?" They all began to hedge, to prepare for change.

I heard the helicopter coming and walked down the hill to the landing pad to meet the brigade commander. The aircraft turned on final approach and landed, and he hopped out before it settled. I saluted and we walked up the hill together. We still had bright sun, right on the horizon. At my command post, I pushed aside the canvas curtain and we went down inside to see the map. My small staff gathered around. I had Tom point out the intelligence we had, and then Pete described our plan and the support we were arranging with his staff at brigade.

The colonel said, "Pursue."

Colonel Chester Bailey McCoid, the Normandy veteran, wanted an immediate air assault. It could be done, but the price would be high. It would mean night airlift, a maneuver in jungle terrain, the loss of surprise, and nothing to exploit our advantages. As soon as I realized what he meant, I said something like, "Sir, can we discuss this outside?" Once away from the staff officers and NCOs, I stated my reasons for making an attack the following morning at first light. The colonel insisted that it had to go immediately. I said that I did not intend to do that. There was a standoff, and he left without further insistence on a night attack.

His report on me some weeks later said: "One of the most compassionate of commanders, he always provided the best support possible to his troops, never asking that they undertake any enterprise until every aspect of the overall effort had been addressed and until he had provided for every contingency . . . as a result, his troops enjoyed virtually insured tactical success at little cost to themselves. On one occasion however, as a consequence of this practice, an unexpected opportunity wasn't exploited with sufficient vigor."

One afternoon a short time later I rode the supply bird out to see one of my companies and talk to the commander and his lieutenants, sergeants, and troops. Things were about as usual: weapons clean; soldiers wet and muddy, brushing off ants and other creatures, but especially ants; uniforms torn here and there as a result of what were called "wait-a-minute bushes"; everyone restocking rucksacks with ammunition, water, rations, and smoke grenades; some people reading letters. Just staying ready in case anything came up. There had been a sighting of a couple of enemy, probably scouts, and the artillery forward observer was adjusting some artillery fire from Betty. Now and then a round landed about four hundred yards to our west, or maybe more. Resupply day always made the troops feel awkward and vulnerable. Betty was several miles east of us, so the rounds came whistling in along a high arc over our heads. I walked over to where the company commander was standing.

I was taken aback by the captain's hollow-eyed look. He was skinny anyway, but on this day he looked skeletal. We moved off a little, out of earshot. He said, "I'm glad you're here. I've got to come out." I started to say something, but he continued, "I'm finished. I'm shook. Everything is all mixed up. My mind doesn't work. I can't figure things out."

"You're tired," I said.

"No, no, no," he said quickly. "Not that. We're all tired. I don't sleep much, but it's more than that. I'm jumpy."

I don't remember what we said after that. At one point, another 105 round came over and he winced, even though it crashed in the bamboo far beyond us.

"See?" he said. "I'm scared of my own artillery."

I told him again that he was tired out, that's all, and that I'd take him back to the fire base for "planning," where he could get twenty-four hours of sleep, and that then he'd be fine. I kept insisting that it was exhaustion, but he wouldn't accept that.

"It wouldn't do any good," he insisted. "I just fell apart, that's all."

I didn't want to take him out, but I couldn't push him any harder.

He was adamant, and I had to think about his men. I considered ordering him to come out and rest. It would simply not do to take a company commander out for a rest, then put him back in. This officer was
a fighter, and a very savvy commander. He had already served an earlier tour, as a platoon leader, and had been decorated for bravery after a
tough nightlong battle. It wasn't about courage—I knew that. I told him
that he would be staying in. He looked away. I said he'd have to realize
that the company would be jolted if he left so abruptly with no experienced captain to replace him, and that I would talk to him tomorrow
about the changeover, which would also give him a little more time to
think. He was silent for a minute or so, then replied, "OK, sir."

Flying back to Betty, I had little hope that he would change his
mind, and I concluded that, if he felt the same way on the next day, I
should let him go. I talked that night with Pete and decided that if there
was no change in this company commander's feelings, I would relieve
him and replace him temporarily with our battalion intelligence officer—which is what I did. I still have a newspaper clipping about this
captain, quoting one of his sergeants saying, "He is the best damned
CO we've ever had. If we ever lose him, it will be bad for us." The captain's own words echo that sense of a tight-knit team: "You have to
have people [who] have confidence in themselves."

On 25 September I wrote to Gin: "The winds are changing here, coming out of the northeast now, from Cambodia, and the dry season will
soon be here. This morning the fog covered the jungle below Betty's
hill, with only the highest trees on hilltops showing through. It was
pure white and stretched for miles—and my feeling on seeing it was
like being surprised in the morning by a new snowfall."

Four days later, I sent Gin another letter:

> Gussie Moran, the tennis pro, was here on a visit yesterday. I
> thought she would be muscular, athletic, and old (she's about
> 43), but she is petite and quite good looking, with a sensu-
> ous face and not at all the athletic type. Maybe that's why she
> always made such a hit. She was wearing reddish big sun-
> glasses and a mini dress she had made from material printed
> with cartoon strips. Different and cute. I was impressed, and
> talked for 20 minutes or so with her, trying to keep from being
> too obvious about looking at her low cut front. Poor me.
>
> Today I heard that we will be pulled back off the border,

relieved, and sent to Division Headquarters at Phuoc Vinh to serve as "Palace Guard," or reserve battalion. This is to take place soon, maybe in a few days. Our losses stand at 20 killed and 54 wounded. If this happens as planned, it comes at a good time. The Mustangs are high in spirit, but tired and ragged and thin.

Phuoc Vinh again—my first and last home. I felt sorry for the strange, sad hybrid of a place. Rome plows and Agent Orange had cleared the sides of all the roads. The town was swelled with displaced people. The war was the same—the Phu Loi Battalion harassing the base.

Letter to my father, 13 October 1970:

We are back at Palace Guard duties now, and I have platoons out all over the area trying to keep mortar and rocket fire off the camp. This place, as always, is a good target because of the many helicopters. We've been hit twice since we arrived, once with 8 rounds of 82mm mortar and once with 9 rounds of 75mm recoilless rifle. We have captured 3 PWs and killed 2 or 3. All VC, not NVA. I've had 4 U.S. wounded and so far none KIA. Operations are small-sized but fast. It is good training for my new lieutenants—11 out of 12 platoons have lieutenants with less than 6 weeks on the job. Not journeymen yet.

On 5 October I wrote to Gin: "Last night I stayed in the division artillery commander's trailer and had my first hot shower since Hawaii—and it did feel good. I looked at myself in a big mirror for the first time, too—and maybe I am a bit thinner than I was—with a beet-red face and pale white body—pretty funny looking . . . really out of place in somebody's nice bathroom. I slept in a bed with a mattress—also first time in 5 months—and tossed and turned all night."

A month later, on 5 November, at 1845 I took off from Saigon on my way home from Vietnam. We got daylight about 1 hour and 30 minutes out of Yokoda, heading for Alaska. On the flight back, I whiled away the eighteen hours writing a series of notes to myself, trying to sum up in my mind the year just past and find the essence of what I had lived through. "For the most part," I put down in my notes, "I did what I had hoped to do. Whatever happens from here, I am at the high point in my life, although I know, and it's painful, that we have failed in what we as a country set out to do, which was to contain communism in this part of the world, and we wrecked Vietnam in the process."

I was home on leave, painting the interior of our house in Alexandria, Virginia, when General Westmoreland's office called, saying he would like to see me. The subject was the *Life* magazine article written by John Saar. I drove in to the Pentagon and reported to him. The general was congenial but worried. He was patient; he listened. There were standards, he said. Even in the hardest fighting, things were orderly. They had to be. How could the company commander have shown the right example to his men, the general mused, when he was unshaven, disheveled, no helmet, carrying a revolver slung on his hip, wearing a rag around his neck? How could he let the soldiers argue with his orders, and win? I said what I could to answer the string of questions that he had for me. I defended Utermahlen as an officer who had the confidence of his men to an extraordinary degree, because of his tactical knowledge and his respect for his troops. We said much more and sometimes there was agreement, but we ended with something like, "I don't know that we've gotten very far on these things, but it is probably enough." I said I would like to write a memorandum for him on my view of Saar's article, and also about Utermahlen as an officer. He took me up on that, and on 12 January 1971, I gave him fourteen paragraphs, the last two of which said this:

In the same way that Saar distorted these areas of controversy, he distorted his presentation of Captain Utermahlen's techniques of leadership. Utermahlen believes in creating an environment within the unit in which men speak up without inhibitions. There is a lot of verbal exchange at all times between the captain and his men, but as Saar brought out, there is never any doubt in anyone's mind as to who commands the company. At the time of Saar's visit, Utermahlen had been in command of that unit for about six months and knew most of the men intimately. Underlying the conventional procedures within the unit was a camaraderie which had developed among the officers and NCOs in the fighting in Cambodia and along the border. It is my conviction that the discipline within the unit was strengthened by this relationship. Utermahlen was at all times willing to listen and to argue over tactics with his men. This was merely another of his successful leadership techniques.

In the last paragraph of his article, Saar notes that the main question concerning Utermahlen is whether or not the higher Army leadership presently understands and is able to assimilate young leaders of his type. Once again there is a certain distortion in Saar's manner of putting the question; but aside from all that, it is true that today's small-unit leaders face some of the most difficult personnel problems in the history of the U.S. Army. It is my personal belief that Captain Brian Utermahlen is representative of the type of sensitive, intelligent, and courageous leader that the Army needs, with the flexibility to respond well to today's challenges of combat and peacetime leadership.

Part 4

Mixed Command and Staff Assignments

15

The Fletcher School

"Things were falling into place."

Some weeks before I left the 1st Cav in Vietnam in 1970, Colonel Edward C. "Shy" Meyer, then chief of staff of the division, told me about an Army program in which battalion commanders coming back from Vietnam were selected for a move to Europe for a second tour in command of one of our battalions stationed in the European Command. He asked me if I was interested, and I jumped at the chance. He later told me that I had been accepted. As I headed home, I happily envisioned this new opportunity. Nothing could have been better, more exciting, more fulfilling than to reach that peak—the successive command of two battalions. Ah, but when I arrived home and called Infantry branch, my friend Norm Schwarzkopf, then a lieutenant colonel like me and working in the assignments branch, let me know that this was not going to happen after all. I would go to Europe, he said, but not to any particular assignment.

Ginny and I thought it over that night, and we made a new decision: we would stay where we were, in our nice little ranch house in the Stratford Landing neighborhood of Alexandria, Virginia. We were close to Fort Belvoir, headquarters of the Army's Combat Developments Command, which helped keep the Army on track into the future. It was an interesting place and an environment that I liked, especially since it was commanded by Lieutenant General John Norton. The next day I drove over to see him. He told me that I was just what he needed, and that he would find a place for me. "We have major issues, and you can help me deal with them," he said. I left his office walking on air. At home the next day I received a telephone call from Schwarzkopf. I remember it well. He said, "What have you been up to? Norton wants to change your assignment. If this happens, we will have to scramble to find a replacement for you."

I remember replying, "You don't need to replace me. I was never placed in the first place." Our conversation, just a chat between old friends, burned up the phone wires for a minute or two and then ended, and I went to Combat Developments Command. With General Norton I had the easiest and most productive relationship I ever enjoyed with a senior boss. The best moments were in his office or at Belvoir on his back porch on long Sunday mornings—or on trips, where his restless mind would rove and focus like a magnifying lens.

I didn't realize I had fallen into a habit. In order to interrupt Norton, I would seize on some aspect of his commentary and slip in edgewise by saying, "Sir, let me give you the background on that." I tried this once too often late one evening, and he said, "Now Jack, damn it, if you and I went outside right now and looked at the moon, and if I said, 'You know, the moon seems to have a spot down the lower side,' you'd say, 'Let me give you the background on that.'"

Among many innovations, we worked on the heavy-light division as the answer to questions regarding the form of future Army forces. Norton took me to the Pentagon to brief this division concept to Lieutenant General DePuy, where the predictable happened: DePuy called the heavy-light mix "otherworldly" and wondered aloud why we needed an organization like the Combat Developments Command anyway, when there were so many legitimate requirements for officers in other endeavors. Nevertheless, with Norton's approval I wrote an article, "Three Innovations: Prime Tactical Lessons of the Vietnam War," later published in the March 1972 issue of *Army* magazine, in which I noted that "as the Vietnam war winds down, the lessons of air mobility are becoming more clear. Three major tactical innovations have emerged: the widespread employment of air mobility; the rise of the attack helicopter; and the resultant reemergence of light Infantry."

Field tests were going on at Fort Hood, presided over by General DePuy, who had moved to Training and Doctrine Command. Although the test environment considered that we were more likely to experience a mid-intensity battlefield in future fighting, the conclusion of the testing was that "the Army eschewed forces that could not support its primary mission of NATO defense." The Combat Developments Command was closed down not too long after that, and the concept of mixing heavy and light forces was dropped.

During this time, a Hebrew translation of my book *Air Assault* was published in Israel. I felt that things were falling into place for me. I was asked to join Westmoreland's staff, but elected to stay with General Norton.

In my spare time I began my third book, returning to the American prerevolutionary days of 1765–1775. I wanted to uncover an answer to the question: Why did the Revolution begin in Boston? Why not New York, or Philadelphia, or Williamsburg? The power of Norton's intellect, along with his stamina, didn't allow for much spare time on my part, so *Three Men of Boston* moved along at turtle speed.

Still working for General Norton, I was told that I could enter a fairly new program, the Army Fellows, which would send me to a top-notch university if I could meet the qualifications—and that, by adding the two summers before and after, I could at the same time complete the one-year course at the Army War College in the way that reserve officers typically did, with two summers of resident study and the remainder completed by correspondence course. The aim of the Fellows program was to show the Army close-up, to broaden the background of the selected officers, and also to provide a military presence on campus, a point of contact for students and faculty. I liked the idea, which allowed a choice among several of the best universities. I asked to go to the Fletcher School of Law and Diplomacy at Tufts University and the Army said yes, if Fletcher would take me. I could offer my Columbia University master's and the Master of Military Arts and Sciences from the Staff College at Leavenworth along with my unfinished work on Yeats at the University of Pennsylvania, plus my two published books and a third under way. Fletcher said yes.

I was happy to be accepted, especially because it would put me close to the Boston Public Library, the Houghton Library at Harvard, the Massachusetts Archives at the State House, and the Massachusetts Historical Society. It would give me a chance to be close to the records of the Massachusetts towns of the period, and in the company of thinkers with global perspectives. There were military officers studying at Harvard, too, as well as at M.I.T. and Boston University. We would get together once a month to exchange ideas. And topping it off, Fletcher was in Medford, Massachusetts, where my mother went to grammar and high school, and it was only six miles from Wakefield, my hometown and that of my father and my grandfather. Ginny and I could live that year on a military installation not too far away—Fort Devens. With twins born in November 1971, we now had four young girls, and to keep us solvent we needed the rent-free home and the nearness of a hospital and a commissary.

Settling in at Fletcher, getting to know students and staff, I began working on the book I'd proposed to Paul Fargis, dealing with the gestation of the place where the Revolution began. I also spent many days at the Boston Public Library, reading the five different newspapers that were published in the city during the years leading up to the Revolution. The Special Collections room smelled of burning leaves—which is to say, of oxidation. Two hundred years old, the library's copies still had not been reproduced, and as I turned the pages, corners and edges broke off. After an hour's reading, I would find both myself and the floor adorned in paper flakes. The librarians told me that the old newspapers had not risen high enough on the budget to allow for copying, and there had been little call for them over the years. There was little interest in the political communication that lit the fires of revolution. Even though the newspapers were printed on much better stock than those of today, time was destroying them. I was saddened by their condition, but I read on through the collection.

Addressing the question of why the American Revolution began in Boston, rather than any of the key cities of the other twelve colonies, I came to believe that the answer lay in the activities of several leaders working as a team within the Sons of Liberty, the Committees of Correspondence, and the Massachusetts Bay Continental Congress. It was clear that Samuel Adams played a major role in the movement toward conflict; other key participants included John Hancock, James Warren, Elbridge Gerry, and Paul Revere, along with others harder to identify. The person hardest for me to leave off the list was John Adams: although he figures enormously in the creation of the United States, when compared with Sam Adams he was slower to become involved initially.

In the course of my research I stumbled on James Otis, a figure who I came to believe had yet to be given his true place in American political history. To my surprise, I found that Otis was by far more influential in those early years than was commonly assumed. Otis was the thinker, Samuel Adams the doer—and Thomas Hutchinson, the Loyalist governor of Massachusetts, was the foil that gave the Adams-Otis team a target that allowed the dynamic debate to take place.

Otis was erratic to the point of being judged insane by some observers. His writings are dense and his actions were irregular, but his influence was great. True, without his connection to Samuel Adams, Otis would have been ineffective. But to an important extent it works the other way around as well: behind the fighter Samuel Adams was the scholar James Otis. To this day, James Otis has not been given the place he deserves in American history, and there are several reasons for that neglect. For one thing, Otis came first, and he burned out early. In a way he is the Hamlet of the Revolution. He had a deep respect for the king's laws, while at the same time he was furious with the way these laws were flouted in London's dealing with the colonies. These conflicting emotions made him the most articulate analyst of the mistakes that King George III and the English Parliament were making. The strain on Otis became evident in his increasingly irrational behavior, though not before he had articulated a detailed and precise legal basis for revolutionary action, a foundation that Sam Adams then brought forward in the form of public challenges in the Boston press. Rising to meet those challenges was Governor Hutchinson. Thus began the fight that brought on the war.

Otis died early, while the Adams cousins, Sam and John, went on to become the giants in American history they are today. The writings of Otis are lawyerly, scholarly, exhaustive arguments, full of Johnsonian stuffiness and eighteenth-century style. An impatient reader would pass by the works of Otis, or ask for a summary; but I am stubborn enough to think that Otis will eventually find his way into the small group at the top of the American pantheon. If I were to write *Three Men of Boston* again, I would call it *Otis*, and I would concentrate on the influence of this driven man who led us to war, and to liberty, in the earliest days of our nation. As it is, coming to know Otis helped me understand the political side of military strategy.

During that year at Fletcher, I had the chance to be often with my father. Together we worked on a book that we called *Brick and Stone*, a study of such construction in New England and a book that brought me back to my early days with him. Then seventy years old, he no longer worked at his physically challenging trade—plastering, bricklaying, and stone masonry—and spent much of his time drawing sketches relating to those types of work and speaking about the trades in local schools. His subject matter soon broadened, to include early farm life, architecture, Civil War uniforms, and historic scenes. In the process he became chairman of the Wakefield Historical Society.

I also spent part of my time at Fletcher writing "Special Forces at the Crossroads" for *Army* magazine, an article that grew out of the research

I was involved in at Fort Bragg. I concluded that the United States Army Special Forces over the past few decades were oriented primarily at strike missions rather than at using their broad and multiple expertise to augment and assist Allied forces, in spite of the intended missions clearly indicated in their structure. I noted the beginning of the "third role" of Special Forces—first as guerrilla, then counterguerrilla, now rebuilder—and concluded, "The possibility now seems remote that the United States would become involved in specific future 'stability operations' or overall socio-politico-military action . . . but the Army has come to realize, more fully than ever before, that all military operations in this epoch of total war must consider more than ever the effect of the fighting on the local population."

16

Stuttgart: The Big Staffs

"No takers. Not our problem."

After the year at Fletcher, and the two summers flanking Fletcher at the Army War College at Carlisle Barracks, Pennsylvania, I was sent to the headquarters of the U.S. European Command, in Patch Barracks, Stuttgart, Germany, where I served in the front office of the chief of staff. My immediate boss was Colonel Charles Hayward, the secretary of the Joint Staff. The American forces stationed in Europe at that time (Army, Navy, and Air Force) totaled 326,414, and their mission was broad: to help defend Western Europe against attack from the Soviet Union and the Warsaw Pact countries. There was much to do: maintaining operational readiness, showing forces, training to high standards, planning for contingencies, administering our military presence, coordinating with allied forces, gathering and analyzing intelligence, and more. For this, each of our three services was commanded by a general or admiral with a staff, which reported to the European Command Headquarters (where I was), also with a staff. We at Stuttgart in turn reported to the U.S. commander-in-chief for Europe in Casteau, Belgium.

I was one of the two staff officers who reviewed all papers sent from our staff to the chief of staff and from him to the deputy commander-in-chief, then four-star U.S. Air Force General George J. Eade, who in turn reported to the commander-in-chief, who at this time was General Andrew Goodpaster. We also filtered all our own paperwork, usually joint papers that supported outgoing messages responding to the Pentagon or going down to subordinate commands. We would review these incoming papers to see if they should go to the chief in their current form or if they needed editing. With the help of Air Force Captain Dick Galloway, I also handled the distribution of incoming messages. This involved handling the twenty or so messages, out of an average of four hundred per day, whose intended recipient was not clear—in other words, who should get the messages that nobody wanted.

The first day on the job gave me a glimpse of what military bureaucracy was going to be like. It is, I learned, a state of mind in which the institution becomes more important than the mission or the task to be done. There housekeeping rules the day: the desk (the bureau) supersedes the workbench, the status quo ante becomes the motto, and change is a danger to be avoided.

I quickly found that all organizations—finance, business, or nonprofit; government or military; public or private; big or small—tend to have the same basic structure, geared to production, development of expertise, and continuity: top leaders, front office, human relations, administration, operations, sales and service, research and development, logistics, intelligence (analysis), and media and customer relations. The organization as a whole is a bureaucracy, and each area has in addition its own internal bureaucracy, calling for more staff ("assets") and less task. The housekeeping becomes more important than the mission.

About twenty incoming messages a day fell into the category "No takers. Not our problem." These were mine to negotiate, and I would set out through the staff sections. I learned more about staff procedure than I learned at Leavenworth or anywhere else by trying to "sell" those messages, because I didn't have much authority. The last resort is to threaten and bully and pull rank: "If we cannot get an agreement, all I can do is ask my boss to look into it."

I liked the pressures of research under these conditions: limited time, scattered sources, the need for quick analysis of scanty information. People think that negotiation skills are, for the most part, style, technique, and sensitivity—the "people skills." True enough, but the bulk of negotiation is homework: the making of a case, like a lawyer. Once I had my preparation, my marginal notes on a dozen or so messages, I was ready to start my circuit rider day, resolved to be articulate and convincing, always wishing I had more ammunition, beginning with "Who had it last time?" But this does not often work. Instead I found that by calling on the staff sections in London, Ramstein, and Heidelberg, I fairly soon had "connections" throughout the structure. I learned the ropes—and gained a window into the workings of a large organization that led and managed American troops deployed in Europe, the Middle East, and Africa.

Ginny and I attended a memorable event at this time, in Blankensee in 1973, sponsored by the German-American organization Atlantik-Brücke (Atlantic Bridge), which aims to foster personal connections among leaders on both sides, a teaming of two nations. In this case each American couple was assigned to a member of the institution, who then invited us to dinner. Our host was Karl Kühne, who came from the family that owned the vast enterprise that prepared and distributed vinegar, mustard, ketchup, pickles, and other condiments. We were pleasantly surprised by his modest home, which was nevertheless a marvelous place, and then astounded to be introduced to Matthew, Mark, Luke, and John—the woodcarvings by Tilman Riemenschneider that lined the stairway to the second floor. I was stunned that the carvings were not in a museum, and said so. Kühne said, "Oh, yes, they are kept by a museum, but they're mine. I borrow them back for a while now and then."

Kühne was a masterful pianist who had designed the second floor of his house to accommodate ("resonate with" might be more apt) a grand piano, which he played for us under the eaves of a sharply pitched roof. His playing held us under his spell, and we found ourselves wishing that every one of our friends could be there with us. After dinner we talked for hours as the late evening wore on, and Kühne told us of his visit to one of the factories his father had owned in East Germany.

He was drawn back to that place out of nostalgia and curiosity: a wish to see, from a professional perspective, how the factory was faring under its new owners, the Communist government apparatus. He recognized the buildings the instant he saw them because, sadly, the only change in them was deterioration: nothing had been done to maintain them, apparently, since the day the Soviets arrived. The plant was, in fact, a ruin. Many windows had been broken over time and had been covered with boards or cardboard. The yards were deep in weeds.

He went inside, although with an uneasy feeling that this was probably not permitted. The interior was dark because of the boarded-up windows, and in place of the sound of active machines was a murmur of voices. Women were seated at tables, filling bottles by hand with a double-strength vinegar (to which the customers could then add water—this saved bottles). The bottling machines were not working, and in fact most of them had been taken away long ago. There would be no use for them anyway, since all the bottles were of different sizes. Each customer was required to bring replacement bottles, and any kind of bottle would do. At the same tables, some women cut cardboard boxes into strips and then rolled the strips into makeshift stoppers for the bottles. What had been a factory was now nothing more than a space with a roof to protect hand workers.

At the time I heard Kühne recount this, my impression was more one of sympathy for a people who had been stripped of their productive capability by the Soviets, as a way to keep them permanently in subjection. Now I see it as that and more: the Soviet-style economy, with its bureaucracy and mismanagement, had left the factory and its staff in an eddy in time. How much of this, I wondered, was what industry is really like in the Soviet Union?

I had a partial answer when Ginny rode a tour bus hired by the Würzburg Women's German-American Club, heading for the Czech border at Cheb. In her words, the visit went like this:

> It was late October that we members of the German/American Women's group trip set out for Czechoslovakia, a trip we had been planning for months. Each of us had to fill out numerous forms that were sent ahead to the Czech government in order to receive a visa to enter the country. We'd been told by previous visitors that we should stay in a first-class hotel, and even that would be below standards. You had to pay extra to have a bathroom in the room, to keep from lining up in the hall to use a common bathroom.
>
> All of the American women were required to attend a meeting given by an Army Intelligence officer, where we learned such things as always assume you are being monitored. We joked about this among ourselves, but knew we would have to be very careful.
>
> The bus was to leave at 4:30 a.m., and we would plan to bring our breakfast and eat while traveling. It was a cold, rainy morning, and the fog hovered over the fields as we rode toward Cheb. The Czech government had told us that was where we would have to enter the country. We would cross there and then head on to Pilsen, where we would tour the city, then visit one of the oldest beer factories and have lunch there.
>
> On the way we had all brought thermoses of hot coffee and tea to have with our food. We chatted, napped, and watched out the windows at the gray, rainy countryside. About halfway to Cheb we were told by the driver that the toilet on the bus malfunctioned and would not work. He told us not to worry,

there would be facilities at the border. After the tea and coffee it was not a comfortable ride for many of the ladies. Especially the German ladies, most of whom were older women.

We sat quietly, waiting for the border. As we pulled up to the first gates of the border, a young soldier carrying a rifle and wearing a helmet boarded the bus and yelled, "Passports!" Another soldier stood with his rifle outside the door, waiting. There were no smiles of welcome as the soldier came through the bus and took our passports.

One of the ladies said in German, "Can we use the restrooms while we wait?" He dismissed her with a sharp reply, "You will stay on the bus and wait till we have checked your papers." There were moans among us. By this time, we were all in need of a rest stop. Time passed very slowly as we sat there. After an hour had passed, one of the German ladies went to the door and insisted that the guard had to go inside and tell them we HAD to use the restrooms. We all watched out the windows as he turned to her, rifle held across his chest, and told her to go sit down and be quiet. We would get off the bus when they decided.

By this time we were getting apprehensive. Time slowly passed . . . Two hours, three hours. No one came out, we couldn't get off the bus, and we were at their mercy. They had all of our passports. You could hear the soft crying among the ladies who were desperate for a restroom. When a soldier came out of the building we were happy, but he came to the bus door and told us that all of our bags must be taken off the bus to be inspected. This included all our personal items we had on the bus with us. One by one the driver dragged the suitcases from the belly of the bus and put them on the wet ground, and slowly, very slowly, the soldier inspected the bags, one by one, as the rain came down and dampened the contents. The happy chatter had ceased on the bus. We were nervous, wondering why we had even decided to make this trip. Time passed . . . along with the schedule for our tours and luncheon.

It was four and a half hours later that the soldier came out, handed us our passports, and told us we could use the toilet on the side of the building, one toilet and 40 women. It was smelly, primitive, and filthy, but we could not be choosy at this time.

As we drove along, there was no more of the chatty conversation of the first part of the trip. We all sat looking out at the string of dismal grey towns, one following the other.

On arrival at Pilsen, we found we could visit the beer factory and get something light to eat in their restaurant. I ventured a little way into the town. It was very quiet, hardly any activity, only a few people about. One thing that was very noticeable was the large loudspeakers spaced on light poles, along the streets. I asked our guide what they were for. Without a smile the guide replied, "To keep the people informed." We boarded the bus and left Pilsen, heading to Prague. We were too far behind schedule and had to get to the hotel. As we drove out of the city I noted the grayness of everything. There were only a few people out on the streets. Evening was approaching.

It was early evening when we arrived in Prague. We had been on the road for over 12 hours. Our hotel had one person working at a window for check-in; one by one we were asked to fill out forms and show passports. After a couple of hours of standing in line, I got my key. We were two to a room. I asked the clerk where we could exchange money so we could go out to eat and was told, "Oh, no money today. You'll have to come tomorrow at 9 a.m."

Our rooms were dismal. There were no bathrooms except the one at the end of that floor.

I went downstairs and complained. I had paid extra for a private bathroom. The clerk looked at me coldly and said, "None of the rooms have private bathrooms. I don't know who told you they did."

The room had two small cot-type beds with mattresses of foam about 3 inches thick. The bed linens were gray looking. There was a small light bulb in the ceiling, just hanging there on its cord, and another on the nightstand between the beds. There was a small sink in the corner, stained with long rust marks where leaking water over the years had etched the porcelain.

The one-per-floor toilet and separate bath was about eight doors down the dark hall from our room. There was always a long line, especially in the morning. We were horrified when we saw how dirty they both were, and we never stepped into that black slimy tub; instead we took a bath from our room sink, as did the rest of our group. The first morning as we stepped out our door in our bathrobes we were met by a line of men, all in their underwear, waiting their turn. Not a pleasant sight!

Our guide for this portion of the trip, Maria, who met up with our group on our first morning in Prague, was a state employee, as were all the official guides. She was a tall, thin, quiet woman, about 40, who always gave the party line when we asked her questions about life in Czechoslovakia. . . . She never smiled. She was never warm or friendly towards us. She was afraid, I think. Whenever we left the group and wandered out on our own, there were always a couple of men in trench coats who followed us. At first we thought it a coincidence, but then realized they were watching us. By the end of the trip we would wave to them each time we saw them. They just stared at us.

During our time in Prague our guide took us on walking tours of this beautiful city, and we visited all the historic sights and museums. On our last day we even were taken to jewelry stores which sold garnets, for which Czechoslovakia is famous, and to shops selling all the typical tourist gifts.

On the last night there, we went out by bus to a tourist restaurant. There was music, dancers, typical Czech food specialties, and lots of other nationalities [at] the tables. Next to my table was a group of older Russians. After an evening of drinking wine we are trying to communicate, smiling and waving at each other. They called "Amerikanski" to us. Our guide, Maria, also had a little too much to drink. We were concerned that she would get into trouble if someone saw her this way, so we decided we would make sure she got back to the hotel safely. We walked to the bus, about a ten minute walk, in the falling rain. There weren't many people in the street at 11 p.m., and the air had the acrid smell of the coal that people used to heat their apartments.

Along the way Maria started to dance, singing loudly, "Roll me over in the clover, Yankee soldier, do it again." We couldn't stop laughing. On the local bus she continued her song as the people stared at us. We noticed earlier that on all public transportation the people were very quiet, as if trying to not call attention to themselves. It was the first time we'd seen a person having fun.

The next day Maria was quiet and withdrawn and very formal with us. We all hoped she was not in trouble, given the trench coat people, but we never heard one way or the other.

One of the major harassments that the American women experienced was the continuing searches of our rooms. On the first day, upon returning to our room I saw that my bag was rearranged. Things were out of place. I pointed this out to my roommate, whose bag was also searched, and we jokingly made some comments (speaking into the bed lamp where we were convinced that the microphones were hidden) that they certainly did a sloppy job in their snooping. Each day after that we would return to our room and find stuff all pulled out of the suitcase, some on the floor, as they searched for who knows what.

Throughout the trip, we talked about—worried about—the return home, and the border crossing. We had been warned before the trip that we would be required to save every receipt for each thing we purchased. Seeing how hard it was to get into the country, we made sure we complied with all the rules and diligently saved each receipt. Along with the receipts we were required to keep all the paperwork received at the banks for the money exchange, and before we left the country we had to turn in the currency not spent. None of us had made any major purchases; most of the items were simple tourist things.

The morning of the return trip we ate a breakfast of bread, a bit of jam, and a small cup of coffee. As a precaution few of us drank the coffee, knowing we might regret it later at the border. The bus was quiet as we made the drive, this time just a couple of hours back to Cheb.

When we arrived the bus was again pulled over, and we were left to sit for a while, waiting for the guard to come out. Finally a soldier, with his rifle, entered the bus and told us to get off, each bringing all of our gear, including our luggage from the belly of the bus. As we stepped off, the guard took our passports again and gave them to another soldier to take inside. Outside it was another cold, grey day with a misty rain falling. We did as we were told, gathering our belongings into piles. As we stood there, more soldiers came out and proceeded to go all through the bus, including the empty baggage compartment underneath. I couldn't figure what was going on at first, then I realized they were searching for anyone trying to escape to the

West. This, I guess, was the usual procedure for vehicles leaving Czechoslovakia.

Every item was checked, one person at a time, as they dug through our bags and pulled out stuff and asked to see all the receipts. This took quite a long time, and we were happy we had not drunk much of the coffee with breakfast. One by one we were told to get back on the bus.

Tension kept us quiet on the bus, but after about three hours the guard returned our passports. As the bus slowly pulled thru the gated area and into the West German point of entry, many of us had tears running down our cheeks. We saw in our short visit what the people living under that regime faced each day of their lives, always being frightened of what could happen and never having any control over any of it. The German guards motioned us through their area, past a large sign saying "Welcome to West Germany." We all cheered and realized we were home—and some of us cried. It was good to be back and free again.

Word came down from General Goodpaster's staff in Belgium: he needed a writer. Colonel Hayward suggested me, and General Eade sent my name up. I took the long way from Stuttgart to Casteau, the little town that housed the headquarters of Allied Command Europe. As usual I wanted to stop at historic battlefields along the way, in this instance Verdun and Eindhoven. My daughter Mary Jo and I tied our bikes on the back of the Wilk camping trailer and drove to Verdun first, where we biked over that mass of destruction, still showing a moonscape of shell craters. Mary Jo kept asking why, and my repeated answer was, "I can tell you what happened, but it is hard to tell you why." Then I would attempt to explain it in terms of stubborn heroism; of killed, wounded, and missing (yes, many still missing); and of artillery fire, measured in thousands of tons per attack and defense. We lingered at the statuary of the long tombs and walked around to the back of the building, to peer through the low windows and contemplate the giant mounds of dry, white, shattered skeletons. Only seeing is believing. Then back to our camper, where we studied our road map and set off for Nijmegen.

The route we took from Verdun to Nijmegen runs past Bastogne. I wanted to fill in some details for a chapter of *Air Assault*, and for the most part I did.

17

Belgium: Supreme Commanders Goodpaster and Haig

"A study in contrasts"

South of Brussels, in the flat beet fields of French-speaking Belgium, twenty-five miles from Waterloo, there is a sleepy airfield that once played a key role in Hermann Goering's strategy for stopping the British and American bombers that overflew the field in many of their attack routes into central Germany in 1944. During World War II, German construction engineers had gathered up a small army of local Belgians to build widely dispersed runways, taxiways, and revetted parking spaces for scores of Messerschmitt and Focke-Wulf fighter interceptors. This enlargement work did not stop until the airfield was overrun near the end of the war, and by that time it was a sprawling base, bigger than Napoleon's last great battlefield. After the war, the shattered runways and bombed-out buildings remained, to be overrun once again by the returning farmers and their beet fields. One small part of the airfield became operational again under NATO's Allied Command Europe. I landed at that field, Chièvres, in February 1974.

Headquarters had sent a car for me, and as we rode past the fat brick barns of the town of Ath, I rehearsed in my mind for the last time the things I might say to General Goodpaster, the supreme allied commander, Europe, who was looking for a new speechwriter. I had never met the general, but I knew that he was a Rhodes Scholar, that he had won the Distinguished Service Cross in World War II during heavy fighting in Italy, that he had a PhD from Princeton, and that he had been staff secretary to President Eisenhower. He also had worked for Ike earlier, I knew, helping with the creation of SHAPE and Allied Command Europe. Going over some of these facets of his life only made my mouth a little drier than it had been during the flight to Chièvres. I decided I would look for a chance to mention my work for General Ware and with the Pentagon Papers and for Stanley Resor and General Norton. First, I would find a glass of water.

At his headquarters at Casteau, I thought General Goodpaster would ask me all kinds of questions about NATO issues and programs and about policies of the Alliance, so I had created a cram course for myself and I studied it hard. Now, in his outer office, I waited to report to him—but he surprised me by coming out to look for me. He towered over me, but his affability seemed to make us equal in height.

Our session lasted only five or ten minutes, and his questions had to do with whether I thought I'd be comfortable in the position, how it affected my family, and my thoughts about the future. Then he called in his executive officer and said, "Jack will take the assignment." Period. And through the years, I saw that he was always that way. After we both retired, we served together on the board of the Institute for Defense Analyses, where he often deferred to me, although he knew much more than I did on the institute's areas of interest. It was just his way everywhere, and it encouraged communication. His quiet manner prevailed. He was a leader whom from then on I always tried to copy.

I told General Goodpaster that in my spare time I was writing *Three Men of Boston*, but that, with this assignment, I would stop. He said, "No, keep going. That is just what you should do. It will help you write for me." In preparing himself for a meeting, he would sometimes give me a half-dozen yellow legal pages of his precise handwriting and say, "Maybe we can work these in." I would informally get in touch with the people in the staff section where it belonged and learn as much as I could about the issue involved, then rewrite his draft, send it back to him, and wait to see if he liked it or not. Usually he had changes, and I would get yellow legal pages back again. Then I made sure I had sources for backup information on the subject. On some of the subjects I anticipated questions the general might get and prepared responses; in some cases I formed a team to keep the answers up to date, as most of the issues or "positions" involved were dynamic and under develop-ment. In others I expanded the information that needed to be available and what could be released. I was always trying to pick out subjects that I thought should get more of his attention, ones he was likely to need to address; I brought them up as "add-ons" to his ever-changing cache of possible public statements. I was continually asking myself: How can I round out his thinking here? Where could I go to find out more? My admiration for Goodpaster drove me to the highest levels of learning—and production—of my life. For his part, he would often say, "This is a thought that Jack Galvin tells me I should mention," knowing how much I would appreciate that acknowledgment and support.

Goodpaster arranged for my predecessor, Colonel Andy Remson, to stay on for a full month to allow me to go through his notes on hundreds of subjects. I learned from Remson: He was scholarly, diligent, articulate, and singularly aware of what was in Goodpaster's mind. He took me under his wing for the first few weeks, walking me through his files on all kinds of subjects. I took his papers, one issue at a time, and hunted down the staff officer who knew most about the history of that subject. All of this was sensitive work that had to be checked with the chief of staff and the executive officer (Major General Gerrity, Brigadier General Bratton), as well as with everybody else who had an interest in the action. Sometimes I stood in for Bratton to take notes, such as this memorandum for the record:

> 28 November 1974
>
> Resor arrived with Bruce Clarke Jr. and MG Crittenberger in town, after a T39 flight from Vienna. Although he and AJG [Goodpaster] have known each other for years, no small talk at all, simply quickly seated and into the business at hand, with SRR [Resor] talking rapid-fire fashion on the latest exchanges with the Soviets on force reduction.
>
> Resor said last time that he thought the only move we can make is to say we'll withdraw nuclear weapons in exchange for a reduction in the common ceiling. He repeated this. Soviets have made two moves themselves, first the 20,000 reductions, then the freeze at current levels. We can't keep saying "No buy" without advancing something ourselves, or they'll say it is we who are blocking progress.

General Goodpaster taught me much of what I know about politico-military relations, about the role of senior military leaders in contributing to strategic decision making at the higher political levels. In the years that followed we stayed in touch, and at the end of his distinguished life I went to see him at Walter Reed Hospital. But in his last days, I found him undergoing procedures that prohibited my presence and allowed only a telephone call from one room to another. I said, "It's Jack Galvin." He said, in a cracked voice, "Take care, Jack," and put the phone down, and that extraordinary human being, to whom I owe so much, reached the end of his life a few days later. One of his many fine characteristics I will never forget was his gentle, roundabout, but very encouraging way of telling you that you had made a mistake, or that whatever you had done could be done better.

In an abrupt changeover in December 1974, General Alexander Haig was named as a replacement for General Goodpaster. Haig had been a lieutenant colonel and operations officer of the 1st Infantry Division at the time of the Phu Loi fight in August 1966. I was a major, operations officer of 1st Brigade in the same unit. I thought that his arrival as supreme commander would mean my departure as speechwriter, and his first comments to me indicated that. It would be accurate to say that General Goodpaster and General Haig had not very much in common. In fact, the two were opposites, a study in contrasts. Goodpaster was a Rhodes Scholar, internationally minded, avuncular, philosophical, gentlemanly, thoughtful, warm, and measured in his ways. Haig was combative and suspicious, and conspiratorial in outlook. The title of his memoir, *Caveat*, fits him well.

In his first comments to me after his arrival, Haig said, "I had six speechwriters in the White House, and I didn't use them. I knew what I wanted to say. I don't need that kind of help here either."

I replied, "Sir, I think I can help in some ways, and I'll try to."

In a memo on 11 December 1974, I laid out for General Haig the schedule of the first five occasions at which he would be called on to talk. To this I added a series of paragraphs that could constitute the core material of his remarks. To this I added: "After your editing I will adapt these for your remarks next week."

Haig then issued a staccato series of instructions for crafting his forthcoming speeches, mixed with thoughts for the long run. For his address on the occasion of his accepting command, he said, "Give me four to five remarks and an emotional conclusion. Find out what Andy [Goodpaster]'s going to say." Then he fired off a series of examples:

"Full ingredients imperative to maintain every link in the deterrent chain."

"For the staff: Fill the empty spaces."

"Détente has to be the fruit of strength, not the substitute for strength."

"Humility, no. People have respect for determination."

"The Alliance will be sorely tested."

"Coming at a time of great challenge."

"Say your conviction."

"Rationalization: careful. Caution on standardization."

"Anomalies distort. Anti-tank over-emphasis now. The gap in low-level suppression is interpreted for massive demand for ECM [electronic countermeasures]."

As he was called in to another meeting, his parting words were: "Go heavy on Q&A."

I kept on writing and traveling with the general.

Haig felt that the Warsaw Pact exercises were intimidating to observers, and he wanted to increase the size of our own country's military exercises by linking several of them together. In spite of reluctance on the part of some of our allies, he created the Autumn Forge exercise, a spectacular biannual show of strength that proved sobering to the Soviets. His directive: form a working group composed of staff representatives from all subordinate units of Allied Command Europe, and link the NATO exercises together by holding them all at the same time of the year.

I remember the day in early 1975 when a large group of officers met at SHAPE to work on Haig's idea. At noon of that day, Brigadier General Bob Schweitzer, an old friend of mine, appeared in Haig's office. "I have to see the boss," he told Major General Gerrity. "The meeting is not going well. These officers are working toward a conclusion that will say there is no feasible way to bring all of our exercises together."

"Let's go," said Gerrity, accompanying Schweitzer into Haig's office.

There, Schweitzer began his story, but Haig didn't need to hear it through. He was out of his chair and on the way down the hall to the conference room, where he strode to the front of the group, ignoring the lecturer.

"I have just one thing to say. I told you to find a way to hold the major portion of exercises in the same time period. I want you to tell me how to do it. I didn't bring you together to tell me how *not* to do it. I would like the answer before this meeting is finished, however long that takes."

Haig also saw through the arabesques of reasoning regarding the numbers of nuclear weapons in Europe. "Why do we need seven thousand?" he asked, and he wasn't happy with the many answers he received from the staffs and commanders.

18

3rd Infantry Division

"Jack, you don't like it here, do you?"

On 4 February 1975 my name came out on the command list. I was surprised by my promotion to colonel and assignment as commander of Support Command of 3rd Infantry Division, and both surprised and elated to find I would be working with Major General "Shy" Meyer in the Marne Division, headquartered in Würzburg, Germany. General Meyer and I had been company commanders together in the 501st Battle Group of the 101st Airborne Division, and we were together in the 1st Cavalry Division in Vietnam in my two tours. "I chose you because you're an infantryman," Meyer told me, "and you need to know logistics. I know you can learn this, and you'll be worth a lot more to us, because none of the senior infantrymen know anything about logistics. Now go out there, and for Christ's sake learn it." With a smile he said, "Shut your mouth and open your ears. Remember that I could have picked someone who knows a lot more than you do about maintenance, supply, transport, and medical." As an aside, he added, "When it comes to logistics, most of us think you just order it done, demand whatever we want, and we don't care how it comes about." I found that he was right.

I wondered how I would do and what the battalion commanders would want from me. All I knew was the receiving end, not the delivery. I had the authority, but not the expertise. There were parallels with the Admin Tigers, which Meyer remembered.

My three battalions mirrored the division's mechanized infantry brigades along the Main River at Aschaffenburg, Kitzingen, and Schweinfurt. We worked and reworked our plan for defending the area allotted to us, which was the flat valley of the Main River between the hills of the Spessarts and those of the Steigerwald. These formed the left and right side of our "sandbox," as we called it, with the mountains of the Thuringerwald to our front and open, rolling country to our rear. Our mission was to defend our box, as far forward as possible. We inherited the planning of our many American predecessors, who for three decades had held this ground with the same mission: in the event that the Soviet and East German forces came through the Thuringerwald and down the Main Valley, we would stop them. The plan had been refined many times over, and we made only minor changes.

We knew, of course, that the plan would serve to get us ready only for the opening moments of a fight, and that we would then be in a dynamic situation. The early battles would be fought with conventional weapons, but if the enemy employed nuclear weapons or if we determined that we couldn't hold our ground, we would request nuclear fire. Our request would call not just for a single weapon but for a package, a mix of artillery shells and air-delivered bombs, laid out in advance.

As head of Support Command, I was focused intensely on the logistical side of the 3rd Infantry Division. If the division ever had to put its war plan into heavy action, it would need thousands of gallons of fuel per day, along with a thousand tons of ammunition. In practice the cost of spare parts averaged about $25,000 per day. All of this would have to be moved into the fight, and then there was nuclear ammunition that would have to be hauled to firing locations.

As we practiced this in our garrison war game simulations—and especially in our field exercises, where timing was easier to measure—I kept trying to find the confidence that this packaging of nuclear strikes was feasible. The strikes always came at the end of the exercise, the assumption being that the use of nuclear weapons would defeat the enemy and solve our problem. The exercise normally stopped when the request for nuclear weapons reached the senior Army commander in Europe, in order not to prejudge the decisions that would have to be made by political leadership in the countries of the Alliance. Sometimes we within the military provided a theoretical homegrown "approval" in order to complete the loop of communication, but it was always clear that such decisions were not ours to make. In fact, we used to discuss the importance of not showing any indication of what the political decision might be. Deterrence, we said, was enhanced by the unpredictability of our response.

It didn't take long for me to realize that I had excellent subordinate commanders: Lieutenant Colonels Jim Durham, Maintenance; John Erskine, Medical; and Duke Mooradian, Supply and Transportation. I told them, "I'll tell you how I am going to act. I want to command in such a way that you will feel glad you served under me." I added, "You get to command your battalion. I get to command you, not your battalion. Besides, running the Support Command, to include commanding you, is going to be hard enough for me."

It was the way Shy Meyer would talk, a recognition of interdependency. It was like my father, too: in the plastering team, the Syndicate, my father was a worker, just like the rest, except when he went off to compete for new work (i.e., for estimates).

Coming out of the back gate of Leighton Barracks in a military sedan one day at mid-morning, I saw a young woman standing on the corner in a well-beaten spot of frozen mud, in the area marked for the military shuttle bus. She was pregnant, bulging under her heavy coat. I pulled up and rolled down the window, and felt the icy air pouring into the car.

"Going to Kitzingen?"

"Yes . . ." She must have been waiting for some time. He face was ruddy and her nose running. She wiped it with a soggy piece of Kleenex.

"Hop in. I'm going that way."

"Thanks." She was not hesitant, probably recognizing me or the driver, and besides, it was very cold on the top of that hill. She got in awkwardly, apologetic. The cold cascaded from her clothing.

"Coming from the hospital?"

"Yes. My checkup day. I should be having my baby soon."

"It looks like very soon."

"Very soon, yes." She wiped her nose again. She was about eighteen. Her accent said maybe Georgia. She said she lived in Kitzingen, not in military housing. I told her it wasn't far out of our way and that we would drop her off.

"What does your husband do?" I asked.

"He's in the Engineers. He drives a dump truck." This meant he would be out on the road all day.

"How are you going to get to the hospital when the time comes?"

"There's a phone booth near the apartment. I'll go out and call him."

"But if he's out on the road, they may not be able to get him. Do you know people in his company?"

"No. I've never been to the company." Every soldier was supposed to have a sponsor, but she had never heard of this program. I thought, up to now she has met very few people in the neighborhood. When she feels her first contractions, she has a few coins to make a telephone call to her husband's unit, to talk to someone she doesn't know.

After I let her off at her door, I drove over to the Engineer Company. The first sergeant there was surprised to hear my story—he had no idea that this young woman existed. The system had broken down somewhere.

We fixed this problem, the first sergeant and I, but I was still worried. Was this just an isolated case, or did we have a lot of American families living in the local German towns with not enough contact with the units to which the father or mother belonged? I put the word out through the command: be sure we know who we have, and where everybody is.

Then Shy Meyer was gone, and a new division commander came in.

P. W. Crizer was a devoted soldier who worked very hard, and his people worked as hard as they could work. Everything was his number-one priority. I got to know him quickly, and I admired his tenacity. He was like a beaver, gnawing everything, big and small. When he was at his top chewing-out performance, you kind of knew he didn't mean it all that much—maybe. He was everywhere, starting with nuclear weapons storage and movements, maintenance, security, and the troops dedicated to the weapons.

Crizer was a good, dedicated commander, but an opinionated one. Following Shy Meyer, he reluctantly agreed to try out a new approach to the Reforger exercise and a change to the Support Command that was an idea conceived by the Supply and Transportation battalion commander, Duke Mooradian. "Here we have three battalions in the division Support Command," Mooradian explained. "But when we go out in the field, we don't go out as three battalions. We take a little of the Medical battalion, some of my Supply and Transportation battalion, and some of the Maintenance battalion, and we put that makeshift force in support of a brigade and we pick one of our officers to make up what we call the forward area support team commander," he continued. "He meets the people he's going to command as they get to the field. Anything else we do, we try to work the same way in training as we would in combat." Mooradian wanted to develop mixed battalions—maintenance, medical, supply, transportation—commanded by battalion commanders who trained and worked with them all the time. It was a radical move, but under Shy Meyer we reorganized the September Reforger around it.

Crizer was a traditionalist, not an innovator. Reforger '75 was coming up, the first big operation with him as the division commander, and with him a new idea was like a fish out of water—not dead, but in trouble. It wasn't working as well as we had hoped.

From the beginning General Crizer wanted to stop the test, regroup to the standard organization, and salvage what we could of the exercise. The test would be inconclusive. I argued that our mistakes and problems in trials were all correctable—that we were in a learning phase—but this was General Crizer's first field experience leading the entire division, and he wanted it to go well. A Reforger exercise was first a demonstration of capability, he said, and only secondly a learning opportunity. It was directly linked with the strategy of deterrence. For that reason, there were many visitors to the exercise. Also, on such exercises, there were other things at stake. Someone won and someone lost. Crizer was a new commander, and here he was, saddled with a change that was only a supplemental afterthought to Reforger, not the main theme—and it could go badly wrong.

Reforger '75 began—the biggest field operation of the year, in which a division from the United States joined us in Germany to demonstrate our plan for quick reinforcement in the event of war. It was more than a training exercise; it was a show of force, a keystone of NATO's deterrence plan. It was also a way of judging the leadership at all levels—including the division commanders.

At dusk, General Crizer helicoptered to the Division Forward Command Post at Uffenheim, in the yard of the lumber mill. He was tired and upset. We commanders had arrived and were waiting to meet with him over the map to work out the issues of the day.

General Crizer turned to me first. "Your new setup's not working."

I knew there was going to be trouble. It wasn't *our* setup; it was *mine*. He went on, crisp and quick.

"I've been to all three brigades today, and there are complaints everywhere. Nobody knows what they're doing. Vehicles are down; no parts, no mechanics. Fuel trucks don't show up when they're supposed to. We've got at least eleven tanks down, or stuck, and the maintenance people can't find 'em."

"I've had enough," he went on. "This is a disaster. I want you to go back to the old setup, right now. Get started now, and have us back to our standard structure by tomorrow morning. And clean up these problems while you're at it."

"Sir—"

"No, no, don't talk to me about it. You're wasting time already."

He walked away, and I walked with him.

"Sir, I saw the same dumb things, and all of them can be fixed." I proceeded to give him example after example, what the problem was and what we were doing to fix it. Crizer waved me off and kept walking, but more slowly. At some point he stopped, and I knew I had a chance. I assured him we could make it succeed if he would give us another twenty-four hours. He finally did, and we worked it through. We came out of it reasonably well and completed a major report on the exercise, and the Army changed—it went to a main support battalion and three forward support battalions, Mooradian's way.

My notebook entry for that day also has a different kind of comment:

Walked through NUC Ammo storage area. Thought of how complex their use would be. The moves by helicopter for remodeling the organization for this. Complex? Suppose a request for use was approved. A security, maintenance, transportation, and positioning challenge; in the event of armed conflict, the (changing) location of enemy positions and friendly units would have to be reckoned, along with the weather; damage would have to be coordinated, and the post-strike situation evaluated. The whole range of nuclear procedures.

Approval of the request for the use of a nuclear weapon, with whatever changes have been imposed through the levels of command, arrives at corps command post and is relayed, with additional detail, to subordinate divisions. All units are informed and directed to take protective action. Corps and division artillery select the firing unit, based on estimated location of the target at time of fire. Artillery moves to the firing location. Division provides transportation of the required rounds from the special ammunition dump to the artillery firing position. Signal to all units; military police accompany the artillery. Target is obtained and the artillery rounds are fired.

"As simple as that," I said to myself, and I set about to better prepare to carry out my part of these moves.

One day Major General Crizer announced, "We're going out to the field on Tuesday. We'll be back when our performance equals our standards."

I thought, "This can't work out too well. We know when we're going out, but we don't know when we're coming in." So I went to see him in the field. I told the chief of staff, Brigadier General Bob Elton, who happened to be a good friend of mine, what I wanted to talk to the general about, and Bob said, "You know, I'm beginning to think you have kamikaze tendencies."

When I got to the general, out in the woods, I said to him, "Sir, I need to set a time that we're going to come back."

And he said, "You already heard what I said on that subject."

I said, "Sir, we've got a lot of people out here who are married, who have children, and if they're not married they have friends they want to be with. They want to try to make dates to do things. They have to have some kind of predictability. It's not World War III."

And he said, "It's the mission that we're talking about here. We have to be ready to do the mission. And until we are, we're not coming back in."

And I said, "I find it hard to see that you would cause that much disruption, unless we're really in such a serious state that we would have to do this."

The argument went along like that. And it really was an argument. I was self-righteous. Finally he told me in no uncertain terms to go back to my job and get it done; but in a few hours he did set a time for coming back in.

Although there were several more events like these, when the time came to select a new Chief of Staff Crizer picked me, much to my surprise—and exchanges like this continued. The Headquarters Company ran two miles every morning, or every other morning—I can't remember which now. Some units were different. General Crizer hated physical training. He was not in bad shape, but he didn't like to run. He played tennis, but he didn't like to exercise. And this was a two-mile run. It was supposed to be a two-mile trot, but we had turned it into a two-mile race.

The general lived just outside the fence of the tiny former airfield where we used to make this run, but to reach the start of the run he would drive his car around the fence half a mile when he could have gone through the gate in the fence and walked there, less than a quarter of a mile.

One day when I was fairly new in the job, he said, "Jack, who measured this two-mile course?"

I said, "Sir, I don't know. I'll find out."

"Get it fixed. It's longer than two miles."

"Yes, sir."

The next time we went out to run he said, "What'd you do about the measurements?"

I said, "Sir, I got two jeeps and we drove them around the course side by side. The odometers read exactly the same. It's two miles."

"So that's what you consider a measurement? Jeeps? Don't you know how the engineers measure something?" He meant the bicycle wheel with an attached device for measuring. We got the wheel and took it around the track and it read two miles. The next time he was huffing, and at the end of the run he said, "Well, did you change the course?" I told him about the wheel, and concluded, "Sir, there aren't any changes to be made."

And he stopped and replied, "I cannot believe that you're so stubborn."

"Sir, I cannot believe that we're even talking about this. You're the division commander. You're setting the example. But you don't like to run with the troops."

And he walked away. After getting a shower and putting on my fatigues, I started my work. Crizer had a little buzzer that rang on my desk, although it was right outside his office. He buzzed the buzzer. I came in. He was looking out the window with his back turned to me.

I said, "Yes, sir."

He said, "Jack, you don't like it here, do you?"

I said, "Sir, I like it here."

He said, "Why don't you just figure you'll be doing something new." His comment did not sound like a question.

I said, "Yes, sir."

I went out and walked across the airfield to my house. When I came in the back door, Ginny said, "What are you doing home at this hour of the day?"

I said, "I've been fired by P. W."

She said, "You can't be fired. We're supposed to go to a dinner at their house tonight."

I heard her call Mrs. Crizer and say, "What are we to do about tonight? Jack got fired."

Frances said, "Oh, tell Jack to forget that. Be over here tonight. I'll talk to Pat."

When we went over there that night (they lived next door), the general was affable as always. I just didn't say anything—and the next day I went back to work.

The Supreme Allied Commander, Europe (SACEUR), at the time, General Bernard W. Rogers, had a good sense of humor and was a likable person, but in those days, when even only mildly perturbed about something, he could be tight-lipped and taut-jawed. In such times his characteristically soft-spoken and precise manner conveyed a message of imminent doom to the recipient of his attention. He was a well-versed scholar, a sensitive gentleman, and a man of absolute integrity, but people were intimidated in his presence.

In the fall of 1976 General Rogers visited a field exercise and was scheduled to spend some time with us. On that day, while we arranged extra folding chairs in our command post, we received a radio call from a neighboring unit informing us that the SACEUR had just left their location and was on his way to us. Our neighbors also wanted us to know of an event that had taken place during his stay with them. While General Rogers was speaking to the commanders and key staff, he had stopped in mid-sentence and said to a young officer, "What are you looking at?"

"My watch, sir."

"When you were speaking, did I look at my watch?"

"No, sir."

"Then why can't you let me speak without looking at your watch?"

"I'm sorry, sir."

The visit continued, and the word went out to all commanders: "We're in the doghouse. Be extra careful. He's not happy."

Our staffers asked me, "What do we do now?" They were all smiles when I said I would take over the briefing. When General Rogers arrived, General Crizer and I went out to meet him. Rogers did have that grim look. When it was my time, I shook his hand, saying, "Sir, welcome. Colonel John Rogers Galvin, chief of staff."

He nodded, slightly puzzled, as we walked up to the operations tent. Inside, all came to attention and stayed that way until the general sat down. There was a heavy silence.

I said, "Sir, we're happy to have this chance to brief you. Before we start, I'd just like to mention that although everyone here knows my middle name is Rogers, none have known until now that you're my uncle. I hasten to say, though, that we don't expect any special treatment because of that."

He laughed, and then the others laughed, and we went on with the visit.

General Rogers could *listen*—which is a skill in itself, and one of the hardest things to do, not least because we so often assume we *are* listening. I was giving a briefing once to some VIPs that was being televised. There must have been six or eight officials at the briefing. I was talking about something that had to do with a map, and I was pointing to things on the map. They were asking questions and contributing comments. Some time afterward, I had occasion to watch the videotape of that briefing—and I heard things then that I didn't even know had been said. I realized that while others were talking, I was thinking about what I was going to say next—so I never heard some of the things they said. Often I was so concerned with how I was going to phrase my answer that I didn't hear the entire question. I didn't hear comments people were making to each other. I didn't realize how little I was listening.

As I neared the end of my assignment with the 3rd Infantry Division, an Army selection board met to choose a new group of brigadier generals, and when they finished, my name was on the list. I felt one of the deep satisfactions of my life: this meant that I would join the inner team of leaders who would direct the Army in the coming years. This realization cast a powerful, euphoric spell over me, until one of my friends brought me down to earth. "I'm so glad you'll be a general officer," he said, "because no one needs an aide-de-camp more than you do."

My father, John J. Galvin, left tackle, Wakefield High School, 1922.

Photos from author's personal collection unless otherwise noted

My mother, Josephine Rogers.

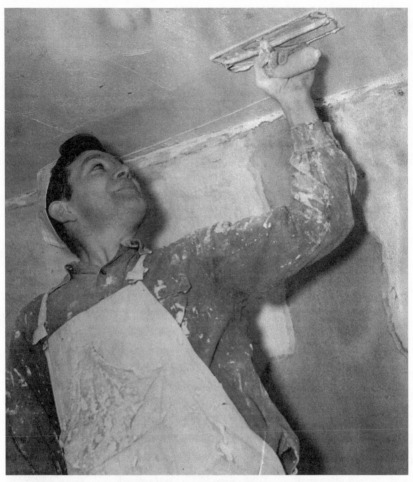

My father at the art of plastering, which he would not teach me.

With Barbara at
Newfound Lake,
New Hampshire.

Protecting the home
front. The Pleasant
Street Army: Gerald
and Donald Shanahan,
Elvin Brown, John
D'Alessandro, James
Galvin, Georgie Muise,
Jackie Galvin (top row,
center, commanding).

Bennet Noble, one of my early high school cartoon characters, featured in the *Journal of the Kennebunks* (produced with my friend Bruce Morang) and used in other publications.

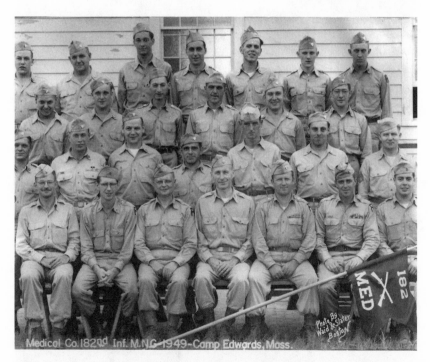

With the Medical Co. 182nd Infantry, Massachusetts National Guard, Camp Edwards, Massachusetts, 1949. PFC Galvin is top row, third from right; Sergeant Smith is second row from the front, fourth from right.

Cadet Lieutenant Galvin designing the class crest, West Point, 1954.

With my fellow Lanceros instructors, Tolemaida, Colombia, 1956. Ralph Puckett taught us: "The word impossible does not exist."

Sergeant Dies and I getting ready for my twenty-first jump, 29 April 1959.

Sergeant First Class Edwin Russell, Admin Center sergeant major, on field maneuvers, Spring 1959. "Strac" was our byword.

The "Iron Squad," B Company Headquarters, February 1959. Selected as best in the division. L–R: Maier, Lt. Chuck Campbell XO, Lt. Galvin, PFC Quiñonez, PFC Lincoln, 1st Sergeant Reavey, SP4 Timlin, SP4 Falkenstein, PFC McGovern.

Major General William Westmoreland, our division commander (at head of stairs), escorts General Lyman Lemnitzer, chief of staff of the Army (in rear), inspecting my company at Fort Campbell, Kentucky, March 1960.

Groom and bride, Fort Knox, Kentucky, 1961, both heading for Columbia University, Ginny to work on her German and I on a degree in English so I could instruct cadets at West Point.

Jungle volleyball, as styled by Brigadier General George Casey, Phuoc Vinh, Vietnam, Headquarters, 1st Cavalry Division, 1969.

With Secretary of the Army Stanley Resor (center) at the perimeter of Fire Base Mo. Second tour in Vietnam, October 1970 (Galvin at far left).

With my good friend George Stotser in Bong Son, Vietnam, 1st Cavalry Division, working out a detail in Operation Pershing II, first tour in Vietnam, early 1967.

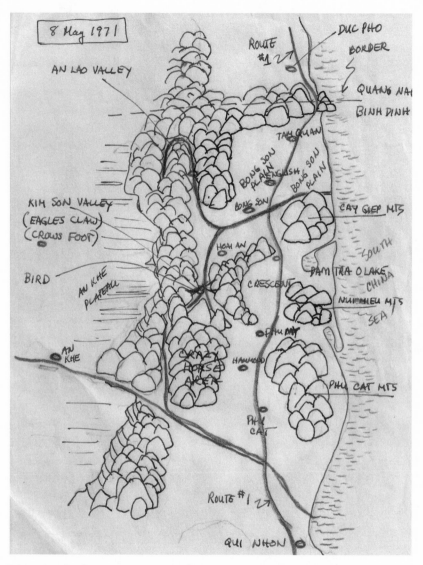

Map sketch of Vietnam to explain Operation Pershing II, pacification of the Binh Dinh Plain (drawn later, on 8 May 1971).

Presenting a visual aid to secretary of the Army Stanley Resor, Vietnam, 1st Battalion, 8th Cavalry Regiment, summer 1970.

Addressing soldiers at Tan Son Nhut, the airfield outside Saigon, as they ready for a three-day rest, October 1970.

Demonstrating the challenges of soldiers' packs for Secretary of the Army Stanley Resor, October 1970.

Being promoted to colonel by General Andrew Goodpaster at Supreme Headquarters Allied Command Europe, 1975.

CRISEX: Observing an airborne jump with Spanish King Juan Carlos and Crown Prince Felipe (center front), near Mojacas, Spain, 5 November 1979 (Galvin is second from left).

L–R: Brigadier General Bob Elton; Major General Gert Bastian; General George Blanchard; Major General Pat Crizer; and Colonel Galvin, chief of staff, 3rd Infantry Division (Würzburg), February 1977.

Receiving the flag of Support Command, 3rd Infantry Division (Würzburg) from Major General E. C. "Shy" Meyer, 1977.

The 24th ID team at the National Training Center, Fort Irwin, California, in the Mojave Desert. L–R: Colonel Pete Taylor, Colonel Taft Ring, Major General Jack Galvin, and Command Sergeant Major Clarence "Pohaku" Wilhelm, 1982.

Saying good-bye to aide-de-camp Captain David H. Petraeus, June 1982.

Reviewing troops at Victory Week 1982, Fort Stewart, Georgia, 27 October 1982. L–R: Major General Galvin, Brigadier General Douglas S. Smith, Lieutenant General Jack V. Mackmull.

Meeting with the commander of the Honduran forces during the U.S. airlift of his troops, 26 March 1986.

A low-key, but important, visit. Meeting in civilian clothes with the contras along the Honduran-Nicaraguan border, 16 September 1988.

An awkward exchange with General Augusto Pinochet, who had rebuffed the American ambassador to Chile, 6 August 1986. There was little meaningful discussion between us that day.

With President Reagan in the White House discussing my assignment to Southern Command in Panama, February 1985.

Maneuvers near the Fulda Gap on a practice exercise, 1988.

My father at a Wakefield, Massachusetts, Fourth of July parade.

After Malta: Briefing President Bush in an annex to the Royal Palace in Brussels, December 1989.

With Secretary of State James Baker and President Bush at the NATO Summit in Rome, 1991. (*Stars and Stripes*, Friday, 8 November, 1991, cover page, accompanying the article "Bush urges NATO allies to define U.S. security role." Associated Press photo.)

Welcoming General Mikhail S. Moiseyev, commander of the Soviet armed forces, to my headquarters, 26 October 1990.

Visiting with Red Reeder, hero of the Normandy landing, and Bob Sorley, master of military biography—two friends who have figured strongly in my life.

With John Eisenhower, my old West Point English professor, after attending the ceremony dedicating Ike's statue in Grosvenor Square, London, on a visit to the house used by his father in Paris when he was supreme allied commander of NATO, June 1990. In this photo John looks remarkably like his father.

Meeting with Senator Carl Levin in my office at Supreme Headquarters Allied Powers Europe, a place where politicians and soldiers often cross paths.

Prime Minister Margaret Thatcher visits Supreme Headquarters Allied Powers Europe, February 1988.

Talking with international troops during an Allied exercise.

SHAPE ceremony in honor of Lord Carrington, departing NATO secretary general, June 1988. (Also pictured, at left, is General Paul Cerjan.)

Change of command, June 1992. General Colin Powell flew across the Atlantic to speak at a farewell for me at my American headquarters in Stuttgart.

Waterloo Battlefield tour with NATO Secretary General Manfred Wörner, 24 June 1989.

With Pope John Paul II at the Vatican, 16 June 1989. His question: "Are you a man of peace?"

With Lieutenant General John Shalikashvili in one of the Kurdish refugee camps along the border of Iraq and Turkey, April 1991.

With statesman and author George Kennan during a visit to SHAPE, to talk to my commanders, May 1989.

Delivering an address as dean of the Fletcher School of Law and Diplomacy at Tufts University.

Back at Newfound Lake again, more than fifty years later, thinking of Barbara.

8th Infantry Division

"The new boss is a little nutty, but he'll be OK."

Word came that I would be reassigned somewhere in the United States, since I had by then spent five years in Germany and Belgium. I told the Pentagon staffers that, from my point of view, there was no need to send me back home; my family was happy in Europe, the two younger girls were in German kindergarten, and the older two were also content to stay. Many of us, officers and NCOs, had spent long tours in Germany and had come to love the country. We jokingly called ourselves "The B Cadre," the castoffs who were never invited back to the United States, but in fact we considered ourselves lucky, something special, out on the front line. Word came down quickly: I was to be sent to the 8th Infantry Division stationed in Mainz, with duties as assistant division commander and commander of the American Community.

The chain of command at this point was a reminder of Vietnam days. My division commander was Major General Paul Gorman, who reported to the V Corps commander, Lieutenant General Sidney Berry, who in addition controlled all American communities in his corps area, including Mainz.

General Gorman welcomed me with a summary of my new responsibilities.

"Out of nine communities in the Corps, yours is rock bottom. Five thousand troops, five thousand family members, all kinds of problems." Those he proceeded to enumerate with a flourish: "Fix all that."

"Furthermore," he went on, "your office in Mainz is in the same building as the brigade commander's. You're right upstairs over him. When you look out your window, you see the barracks and shops of 1st Brigade—his brigade. You need to get out of his way, let him command his troops, and find a new place to hang your hat. Now, getting down to business, our mission is to defend the Fulda Gap. From the Gap to the Rhine is only fifty miles."

Gorman went to his wall map. "1st Brigade is on the wrong side of the Rhine and the Main. We have to cross over both rivers and go through a built-up area and get up the Kinzig Valley and into position at Fulda. Your job is to make this happen fast."

He pointed out the essentials of his defense plan, which he called "the catcher's mitt." We were to form a strong point, a barrier, in front of Fulda to clog and stop the enemy there, and then pivot on our strongpoint and hit them from the flank. General Gorman also had another task for me. "I want you to take our Infantry and tank companies, one by one, to our training area at Baumholder and show them the proper way to build a strongpoint and get it done quickly." What he wanted was far different from digging shallow rifle pits with little entrenching tools. This involved expert consideration of the terrain and support from engineers. I was taken by this challenge and worked hard on it. Usually the exercise would start around Thursday evening and go until Sunday morning, with a dig-in and then a defensive operation. For me it was the best training of that kind since the lessons Lieutenant Colonel Bill McKean had taught me in the 101st Airborne Division, which became the fundamentals of these weekends at Baumholder. One day during a visit at Baumholder, General Berry asked me to step aside with him. By coincidence the date was 26 August, the anniversary of the Vietnam fight we shared. Smiling, he wanted to know if my banishment from the division was the correct decision at the time. Astonished, I mumbled something like, "I had a lot to learn."

I needed to get to work on the defense plan, the quality of life in our community, and the strongpoint training, so I drove my Volkswagen Bug up to Fulda on weekends to get to know the terrain. Route 40 goes up the floor of the valley, climbing over a saddle at Schlucturn. The shoulders on each side of the valley are forested and crisscrossed with lumberjack trails. Beyond Fulda to the east was the catcher's mitt, a curving, dominating piece of terrain carved out by the Kinzig River's Pliocene scouring. We would block and attack with minefields covered by fire immediately in front of Fulda, hold the enemy in a long column by putting pressure on both sides, then counterattack deep into the flank and rear of the echelon, and then pull back and reconfigure our forces to do it again.

I spent many days driving the farm roads around Fulda, studying the terrain and going over the defense plan in my mind. On weekends I took Ginny along, although on a beautiful day one weekend in Fulda she said to me, "This is not fun. I'm talking about the lovely country-side, and you're thinking about war." One day in February 1979 I drove up alone, through the logging trails past the three crosses to the catch-er's mitt, and then followed the swing of our planned counterattack and thought, if we did stop them, would they respond with tactical nuclear weapons? What about Fulda? We would hold on to Fulda at all costs, but there might not be much left of it.

My reconnaissance went late in the day, and I spotted a perfect place to spend the night: a rustic inn, nestled in a wooded corner of the Kinzig River valley near Schlüchtern. A sign announced an extra attrac-tion of some sort. At the bottom it said, "Mit Kugelbahn." I knew that Bahn means road, as in *autobahn*. I said to myself, maybe the reference is to walking trails. But Kugel? I wasn't sure what it meant. Maybe some kind of tree? In any case, walking through the woods would be a nice way to end this day of driving.

Wherever you may be, it is always advantageous to study the lan-guage. Doors will open for you—indeed, whole new worlds. I turned in and parked my VW Bug next to a lush little winter garden in bloom, then went inside to find everybody very pleasant, and yes indeed, *Zim-mer frei* (in terms of vacancies), there were some rooms available—and yes, *natürlich* (of course), there were excellent walking paths in the for-est that surrounded us.

My room was small and Spartan but comfortable. Pine walls, pine ceiling, quaint little window, tiny bath, no closets, a wooden hook for my coat. I did go for a walk along a stream, but not far, since the hills to the west had already cast their shadows.

I was back in my room, ready to shower before dinner, when I heard a rattling crash that made me think a waiter had just dropped a heavy tray. Such things happen. But then I heard a second waiter drop a second tray. I had a vision of the whole kitchen now spread out on the dining room floor. While I contemplated what this might mean for my evening, I realized that my comfortable room was just above the bowl-ing alley.

It was during this time that I searched out the Baumholder train-ing area and found a rugged, knobbed hill with steep-sided fingers extending in all directions, and got permission to dig there. I studied it carefully and wrote out a number of ways to attack or defend it from various directions. I then brought in a test company, to demonstrate that this was not the usual infantry kind of foxhole digging; I called it "sophisticated groundwork." We included engineer squads using front loaders and a rough-terrain forklift. We supplied barbed wire, stakes, sandbags, long-handled shovels, camouflage netting, and a large pile of logs.

The most important part of the work was the location of weaponry to the best advantage, covering the gullies and ridges. We reinforced the company with tanks, artillery, and mortars, which were also dug in. For weeks, every Saturday was readiness day for one of our companies. I climbed in and out of all the diggings, and after a string of discussions of the tactical decisions and the construction, we restored the hill and made ready for the next occupant. In the end we left the hill well ploughed and ready for a few years of rest.

In between trips to Fulda and Baumholder, I traveled through the installations that made up the Mainz American community. In addition to the brigade barracks, a former German Kasern in the middle of town, and family housing areas close by, we had a maintenance depot, an airfield (Finthen), a small local training ground, a church, the commissary, the officer/NCO club, a youth activities center, a child care center, and a firehouse.

Taking over an organization is harder on the people of the outfit than it is on the new boss. A leader has to think about what the moment means to all the people who will be affected: subordinates, peers, bosses. In this case, the social (and political) aspects were unusual. This was a military unit with a mission of defending Fulda. It was also a town within a town, with everyone anxious to know what was coming next. The tension became evident in various ways. How could I loosen things up? How could I communicate a message of change? I wanted to exert as little of my structural, statutory authority as possible—rather, to try to show who I was in a personal sense.

A few days after Ginny and I arrived, we attended a reception intended to welcome us. All the officers and senior noncommissioned officers and spouses were present in formal dress. Ginny and I, while still in our house in Würzburg, had been asked to approve the arrangements for this event; people in Mainz were concerned about the details of the evening. We told them that anything they wanted to do would be all right. On the evening of the reception I took along with me a plastic set of vampire teeth, the fangs that kids wear at Halloween, and wore them in the receiving line, shaking hands with the guests. More than a few ripples of laughter went along the line, and I think the conclusion was, "The new boss is a little nutty, but he'll be OK."

Colonel Sedgwick was my deputy. My first talk with him convinced me that the makings of a team—good people with plenty of experience—were there. He knew the staff well, and he himself was a fine soldier. For officers and NCOs, assignment to a community staff carried a blemish; the job was looked on as a lesser responsibility than a leadership or staff position in the line units. At the same time, the communities themselves were faced with an unwieldy load of problems: tight budgets; vacancies; the magnification of normal family problems by the overseas environment, especially for those who were living "on the economy," meaning in housing rented from local Germans; the clash of interests between the military units and the community. Our backlog of needed repairs to facilities was big enough to be close to unmanageable. The child care center was a remodeled firehouse. I visited Fort Meade, Maryland, during this time, and the contrast was dazzling. I looked at the broad acres of grass there and the lake with its swans and thought of the brigade of tankers and infantrymen squeezed into a single city block in Mainz-Gonsenheim.

The United States came to Germany at the end of World War II as conquerors and stayed, first as occupiers and then as cautious allies and later as partners and close friends. At the same time, we Americans were in many ways our own best enemies. We have lived in Germany, we used to say, not for forty-two years, but for a single year repeated forty-two times. We had a radio frequency of our own, a television channel, and a newspaper; we had American gas stations, American churches, American ice cream.

In many ways our insistence on constructing American microcosms made things harder for us. Germans asked, "Why do you Americans live in ghettos?" I answered that we needed help in finding good housing in Mainz, and that our soldiers needed more contact with Germans in their off time, not in bars but on athletic fields. I suggested allowing more Americans into the German sport clubs. "We have a language problem," I admitted, "but every sport has a language of its own." The Germans agreed, and we got a foot in the door in the exclusive sport leagues.

Our family was quickly absorbed into the neighborhood. We lived in Gonsenheim, just off the main street, Fintherlandstrasse. Our pet duck, named Quack, was instrumental. We had been given Quack, a

Peking duck, three years earlier in Würzburg. She had been the pet of a family returning to the States, and we offered to adopt her. She lived in a small enclosed space in our yard, and slept inside a wooden doghouse filled with fresh straw. One day one of the girls accidentally left the gate open, and Quack took off, running down the road. Ginny chased after her, worried that she would run out onto the main street, which was busy with traffic and trolley cars. Quack, always a few feet ahead of Ginny, ran flapping her wings and quacking loudly. People stopped, laughed at this funny sight, and pointed as the duck ran down the middle of the trolley tracks. The trolley came to a stop just as Ginny finally snatched the duck into her arms. There were smiles all around when Quack was safely carried back to our own yard.

I had a discussion with our community staff on the actions we would have to take under wartime conditions. When the military discussed evacuation of dependents, the briefer said,

"Pets will not be allowed to travel."

"What do we do, for example, with the family dog?"

"Sir, we have to dispose of pets. We can't just leave them here to run loose."

"So we dispose of them. How?"

A pause. "We will have to shoot them."

"So at the moment that the family is under a good deal of stress, we help out by shooting the dog. Who came up with that?"

"Sir, that's what the plan calls for."

"OK, thanks. Make it call for something else. There will be enough shooting going on if this thing ever happens. Let's leave the dog out of it."

We cut that part out of the plan. You don't have to include everything. Whatever happened, we weren't going to shoot pets around Mainz. I would have let the families take them as far as they could. Was this just shifting the problem to somebody else further along the line? Maybe. But it just might be feasible to let the dog hang on all the way. Who knows how the situation would be at the airport or seaport or wherever folks actually end up in a circumstance like that? At least the family would feel that they gave it their best try. (And yes, our family had a dog. In fact, two.)

While I worked on the Fulda plan and community matters, I looked for a place to put my office. One of the members of the staff, Colonel Sullivan, took me through Dragooner Barracks, a battered old two-story building that almost qualified to be a ruin—something that we had never managed to give back to the Germans. As it slowly fell apart, it had served as a dwelling for Turkish temporary workers. I went to corps headquarters with plans to resuscitate the building and found that the officers on the staff at Frankfurt were Colonels Chuck Fiala and Jim Sibley, my two mathematics coaches from cadet days, who had saved me from flunking out of West Point in the fall of 1950. I appealed to them once again for help and managed to get the money to restore the building and move into it.

Not far from our house on Fintherlandstrasse was a path that ran through a wildpark, a beautiful place for walkers and joggers, a trail where I spent many a happy hour. It was my custom to take some note cards with me, because my regular run almost always inspired thoughts that I wanted to preserve. I was fifty years old that year, so I marked those cards "R+50" and saved them all. As I read them now, I can feel the emotions that dominated those days.

I would jot down a word or two, and when I got back to my desk at home I would expand the note enough to preserve the thought for use later on. I have sometimes wondered if I could tie two or three hundred of the notes together, more or less in the order they were stored, to construct an informal "R+50" essay on Germany. A dip into those cards at random looks like this:

> Sports (a German-American sports club)
> Babies in Germany (Ginny's baby brother is buried in Frankfurt)
> Wilk (where we should next go camping, a shorthand reference to
>   our Volkswagen camper)
> German dead (how German youth spend summer vacation finding
>   and identifying and burying dead soldiers)
> *Über allen Gipfeln* (over all the hilltops – Goethe's poem "Wander-
>   er's Nightsong"; learning late in life)
> Gone forever? (what the Germans preserved, resuscitation of post-
>   war Germany)
> *Grundschule* (German grammar schools)

I now have more than a thousand cards in my R+50 file.

In my dozen or so visits to Berlin, I took advantage of a long-standing agreement that allowed senior officers from all four military sectors of the city—British, French, Soviet, and American—to pass through border control points, as long as they were in uniform and traveled in an official car. I usually went through at night, accompanied by an American liaison officer, and was never stopped for more than a few minutes to prove my identity. Inside East Berlin I was as close as I could get to the daily activities of Soviet military units. I was not allowed to enter Soviet military headquarters or other installations, but I was never challenged as I rode or walked nearby. I learned much from my firsthand looks at motor pools, barracks, and storage areas and got a feel for the normal details of life among the deployed Soviet forces. I expected that the East Berlin motor pools would be models of efficiency and would comprise the best troops of the Group of Soviet Forces in Germany (the Soviet Army in East Germany), since these troops were the main reserve for any battle—and any battles would likely occur there, in East Berlin. Instead, though, I looked out over the military motor pools in East Berlin and was surprised to see disarray.

In some units, for example, the workday activities stopped in the late afternoon and the soldiers disappeared like magic, leaving their vehicles and equipment wherever they were at the signal for day's end. Cargo trucks were left sitting at the fuel point, tanks were parked with main guns pointed in various directions; some turrets were under tarpaulins while others were not, buckets hanging on pintles of some, barrels in travel lock on some. Tanks were parked hub to hub, showing a lack of daily maintenance—everything was frozen in time.

This was true only in some installations; other places were spick-and-span, as any good sergeant would expect. Still, it left the impression that perhaps the Soviets were relying too much on their own self-image from the Great Patriotic War (World War II), convinced that soldiering didn't require much training and that the thing to avoid was softness, or decadence: soldiering was more a matter of physical hardiness and Spartan living. Suffering was predictable, and furthermore constituted good training in itself. Deprivation was to be expected and endured. Having been overrun so deeply in World War II appeared to have had a lasting effect on the Soviet military psyche.

This sense of stopping time came to me over and over on these visits to the other side of the wall. And this was just a drop in the bucket. What we needed, and never had, were some knowledgeable, thoughtful, articulate, reliable writers who could have, over time, produced a literature on the Soviet politico-military scene: not just organizations and capabilities, but outlooks and philosophies—some sense of their understanding and their thinking.

In early May 1979, my new division commander, Major General Bill Livsey, sent word that higher headquarters had a mission they wanted to assign to me. I flew down to Stuttgart, to European Command headquarters, where the chief of staff told me that I was to go on temporary duty in Madrid to help plan and carry out a field exercise—CRISEX-79—involving Army, Air Force, and Navy elements from the United States and those of Spain. Right away I left for Spain to meet the exercise commander, Spanish Army Major General Manuel Saavedra. I liked him immediately and knew this would be a memorable experience. Together we made a weeklong reconnaissance along the Costa del Sol, selecting areas we would need, from Cádiz eastward to Almeria and on to Mojácar. Then, over twenty days in Madrid, we laid out the rough structure of the maneuver, which would be an amphibious assault across the beach at Carboneras, followed by a 35-kilometer attack inland. Saavedra spoke little English, but he loved to talk at length about Spanish words and phrases, Spanish slang, any aspect of that great language. I learned plenty, as I had in Colombia twenty years earlier.

The next assignment for Saavedra and me was to gain acceptance of the plan in all its details, on both the American side and the Spanish. I was given quarters in CESEDEN, the Center for National Defense Studies, in Madrid. The building was quiet and dark—and hot—and thinly populated in those July days of 1979. My Spartan lodging was a high-ceilinged room with a tall window on the outside wall and a crucifix over my bed. I could walk across the street to the Army headquarters, Estado Mayor del Ejército.

Commanders and staffs were cautious about the selection of officers who would guide and coordinate the buildup to the exercise. Since there was no precedent, every decision, big or small, was something new that warranted discussion and mutual agreement on the part of the armies, navies, and air forces of the two countries. A growing list of undecided issues faced us every day, and often the resolution of one problem gave rise to a host of others. Nevertheless, the more we worked together, the more we saw opportunities to expand the team effort. General Saavedra was happy that the Spanish as well as the Americans wanted to get more out of the exercise. I of course urged both sides to make the experience as valuable as possible for all of us. This put pressure on headquarters at Stuttgart for more commitment: more staff, more participation from units, more logistical support, more unplanned lines in the budget. No message came down to me saying,

"Stop this thing from growing"—that's not the way bureaucracies work. Instead, support began to dry up on the American side. Everything got a bit harder to do.

I was not on the European Command staff's team. They felt that they had gained nothing from the operation and saw no reason to scurry around supporting it. On one of my flights back to Mainz, I made a stop at Stuttgart, carrying a letter I had written, but not sent, to the U.S. European Command chief of staff, describing in some detail the slowdown from my point of view. I let it be known to some of the staff that if things didn't improve, I would send the letter. It worked, but looking back now I see that there was a better way to have achieved the outcome that I wanted. On my flights back to Germany from Spain, I should have stopped at Stuttgart to meet face-to-face with the command staff and talk over the value of the exercise and the need to make the most out of this opportunity to get closer to the Spanish. I didn't communicate well. As it was, I got my way but paid a price for it.

In one of my trips home to Mainz, at the end of August, we held a ceremony at the 1st Brigade barracks to say good-bye to Major General Horst-Bodo Schuwirth, commander of the German territorial forces that had supported us in Mainz. We gave him a U.S. Army saber on that occasion, and he said to me afterward, "I'm very happy to have this saber. I lost my own when my unit was driven back near Moscow in 1941."

I couldn't help but ask, "What were you doing with a saber?"

He said, smiling, "We carried parade uniforms to be ready for the victory march in Red Square."

By September 1979, the number of Spanish and American participants in CRISEX-79 had reached 42,000. The amphibious landing on 4 September included Marines and SEALS from both sides and a brigade from the U.S. 7th Division. On the six days of combined operations we had a battalion-size parachute assault, along with air sorties from the U.S. carrier *Nimitz* and support from the entire Spanish Air Force, totaling more than 2,000 sorties. Midway through the maneuver, we held a day of demonstrations attended by King Juan Carlos and Crown Prince Felipe. As a special event, we conducted an operation in which a downed pilot was rescued from behind enemy lines by an aircraft that hooked him off the ground with a cable. In this case the "downed pilot" was U.S. Army Special Forces Lieutenant Colonel Ray Quijano, and the aircraft was a four-engine turboprop C-130 Hercules piloted by U.S. Air Force Captain Jack Whalen with copilot Lieutenant Randy McKeviee.

I stood with the king and others on a knoll, watching the field below. Colonel Quijano prepared for the pickup. He opened a kit bag he was carrying and took out a small steel bottle of hydrogen that he used to fill a balloon, which he attached to a long nylon cable he retrieved from the kit bag. He attached the other end of the cable to the harness he was wearing and let the balloon rise about a hundred feet. The king then asked, "Is he actually going to do this?" He later said, "I thought all along that it was going to be a dummy."

The airplane, the C-130, came in sight, flying low. It had a V-shaped apparatus on its nose. The pilot aimed for the cable as he roared along, caught it at a point about thirty feet below the balloon, and lifted Quijano off the ground and into the air, accelerating him from zero to 120 miles per hour in the matter of a heartbeat. The plane continued on in a straight line, with Quijano trailing behind, a tiny figure at the end of the long curving cable.

We all stood in silence. The king asked, "What happens to him now?" I said, "In the C-130 the crew will open the tail ramp and hook on to the cable, pull it in, and connect it to a winch. Then they'll draw him in."

In about ten minutes, the pilot radioed that Quijano was aboard and feeling fine. The king said, "I want to see him when he comes back. Is there any trouble in arranging that?"

I answered, "That we can do, Your Highness."

The king talked with his military adjutant, who hurried to a telephone. Juan Carlos wanted a motorcycle messenger sent immediately from Madrid with a medal for him to present to Quijano. "This man is a true hero," he said, "risking his life to show the feasibility of a rescue."

The plane landed at Almeria, and Quijano got back to Carboneras Beach in time to get his award. He recounted the story of his flight with his characteristic nonchalance. "They pulled me up near the ramp," he said, "but the turbulence kept me twisting and banging underneath for a little bit; then they got me in and strapped me in a bucket seat because they thought I was dizzy. When they closed the ramp, I went up to see the pilots. They were in a cold sweat, both of them."

I said, "How about you?"

He looked at me. "In a cold sweat? Not me."

This program for retrieving pilots and crew members with a cable and hook was later ended due to fatalities in field exercises.

Letter to my father, 2 January 1980:

Just before Christmas, on the 23d, the Gonsenheim church had an international Christmas carol "sing-in," and people from 10 or 12 different countries sang carols in their native language—Portuguese, Italian, French—even a Russian family sang a song that the head of the family said was forbidden in his own country—"Silent Night"—and got a rousing, emotional ovation. But the greatest thrill of all for me was when the Deutschland choral group from Gonsenheim grammar school sang "Was soll das bedeuten" (What does that mean?)—and there in the front row, singing their hearts out for Deutschland, were your two Black Irish granddaughters, with Macroom eyes and hair but with a lilting German laced with a Mainz accent. That was an unforgettable moment, and it brought down the house, which was packed to the stained-glass windows. At the program's end, choruses of "Silent Night" were repeated in all languages, with Kathleen and Erin singing "Stille Nacht," and myself with a great lump in my throat, standing in a side aisle and watching that scene.

The television station Südwestfunk called with a suggestion: How about an interview at home before the Galvin family departs from Germany? The interviewers would like to come to the house and show the family in home surroundings, casual and at ease. The idea had a lot of appeal, and that evening I asked Ginny about it.

"They'd better do it pretty quickly," she responded, "or all the furniture will be gone. The movers will be here next week." It was clear that she liked the idea, too. The following night when I got home from work, the parlor was full of light stands, cameras, and wires. Cameramen had rearranged the room. Kathleen and Erin were conversing in German with the crew. That always made me proud of them—in fact, I was forever urging them to speak German to me and Ginny at home, but to no avail. They were too young to fathom a father who had always spoken English and now wants to talk school language instead of home language. My attempts to break into their German conversation normally resulted in "Ach, Dad, das ist aber schrecklich!" (That's just awful) or some such comment. They were excited and interested in the lights and cameras. I thought to myself, "This is going to be fun for them," which turned out to be correct.

The camera crew was ready, and we seated ourselves in the stuffed chairs under the lights. It was already quite warm. The questions were good ones—about school, the town of Gonsenheim, vacations, all the things we usually talk about on most evenings. Then, near the end, there was a question for Kathleen.

"How do you feel about going home?" asked the interviewer.

"Home?" Kathleen was surprised.

"Yes, home—home to the United States."

"Hier ist meine Heimat"—I'm home now. "We will be leaving home to go to the States."

The smiles on the faces of the crew told me that Kathleen's response was sure to be a part of the program.

In early June I wrote to my father, "We are all set to go now; our furniture and VW Bus have been shipped to Norfolk. House is empty and full of echoes. Everything in Germany is looking so beautiful that we are trying to enjoy our last days to the fullest. Kathleen and Erin and Beth are full of worries about trying to become 'an American,' and no word of mine or Ginny's seems to alleviate this. Mary Jo graduated from Wiesbaden U.S. High School in a very impressive ceremony in downtown Wiesbaden—in the middle of an unusually hot evening with thunderstorms circling around."

In May 1980, when I was leaving European Command, U.S. Air Force General Jim Allen, the European Command (EUCOM) deputy commander, sent this message to General Meyer and me:

Shy: Last Wednesday, I participated in a ceremony in Madrid in which Brig. Gen. John R. Galvin, ADC, 8th INF DIV, received a high Spanish award for his work on the combined Spanish-U.S. exercise staff for CRISEX-79.

It was a splendid performance, both in a professional military and in a very sensitive political context, which has resulted in greatly enhanced military-to-military relationships between Spain and the United States. Spanish authorities are still glowing over the experience and success of CRISEX-79.

Warm regards, Jim

20

24th Infantry Division

"Heavy-light operations"

In the summer of 1980, it was hard for the family to pack up and leave Mainz for a new assignment. Our new station was Fort Monroe, Virginia, which was once a fortress guarding the mouth of the James River across from Norfolk—but in 1980 was the beautiful headquarters of the Army's school system. I was assigned to the training department, where my boss, Brigadier General Howard Crowell, generously awarded me half of his responsibilities, saying, "There's enough work here for both of us, so let's just split it." Five years earlier I had followed him into command of the support command of 3rd Infantry Division.

I thought I had left Vietnam far behind me, but not so. Something happened around this time that gave me a better understanding of Vietnam veterans and our syndromes. When we first arrived at Fort Monroe, Ginny and I went out for an early morning jog alongside the walls of the old fortress, and by coincidence we trotted close under a parapet just as a crew up on top fired the reveille cannon. I immediately pushed an unsuspecting Ginny to the ground and fell on top of her. She emerged from this event with knee and hand scratches and some scolding words for me.

It was also at Fort Monroe that Ginny and I discovered that our two youngest daughters, the twins, did not know how to spell. Their four years in kindergarten and first and second grade had given them a good grasp of German, and they could read and write in English—only their writing followed German spelling rules, which are stricter and closer to the phonetic, with initial-letter capitals for the nouns. Even their cursive handwriting style was different from conventional English cursive. We had thought the change to English would be easy, even routine, but now we began a nonstop spelling bee, with ten new words every evening, along with leftovers from previous misspellings. Over time we became dictionary bugs. We conversed about meanings, which led us in all directions of thought. There was, and still is, always something to talk about in that regard. We all still quiz each other and talk of words and their meanings and roots—and we know how to spell.

After ten months we moved once again, this time to Georgia's Fort Stewart, near Savannah, where I took command of the 24th Infantry Division, the unit that would eight years later make the long sweep to cut off the Iraqi Republican Guard. During that earlier summer the division was getting ready for its first series of brigade training deployments—to the Florida panhandle in October, to Egypt in November, and into our own very large reservation in December.

Before I left Fort Monroe, I had a call from my friend George Stotser, the other half of the Gold Dust Twins of Vietnam days with 1st Cav. He was then a brigadier general, the assistant division commander of the 24th. "There are lots of administrative details on your move down here with us," George said to me. "I'd like to get you a temporary aide-de-camp to help you settle in. There's a captain I have in mind. He has just recently come out of company command. His battalion is not going to be happy about letting him go, but I'll take care of that. I personally think this captain is the best we've got in the division. His name is David Petraeus. If you OK it, I'll put him to work. Later, if you aren't happy with him, we can always get you someone else." I thanked George for the help and told him, "Sure. Good idea. I'll take the captain and we'll see how it works out."

Not long after that, Ginny and I and the girls packed up and drove down the East Coast to Savannah and Fort Stewart—trailering our boat, which was full of bicycles and other Galvin paraphernalia. Stotser and Petraeus met us there, and we enjoyed an easy integration. One of our earliest family experiences at Fort Stewart was a large picnic for newcomers to the division, one of several summertime get-togethers arranged by established families to meet and assist new arrivals. Invited also were homegrown local Hinesville kids and their fathers and mothers. On that occasion, the weather was great, the food was plentiful, and everybody had a good time. Military assignments are based on a change every three years, but the length is variable and often shorter, so the traditional picnics were well populated with new folks. At this one we heard a boy from town say to his newfound friend from overseas, "It must be hard, not to have a home." The reply was memorable: "Oh, we have a home. We just don't have a place to put it right now."

I looked into Petraeus's background. He stood high in the West Point class of 1974. It was about six years since he'd been commissioned as a lieutenant of infantry. He'd been to jump school and Ranger School, then to the airborne battalion, the 509th, at Vicenza, Italy—the only American parachute battalion combat team in Europe. Then he was off to Savannah to company command, and then selection as a battalion operations officer. He was getting along pretty well, with the kind of solid start that opens the door to good follow-on assignments. I sensed that he was not excited about the prospect of being moved out of his newly acquired job as operations officer of his battalion to an aide position. We had a talk about that.

We got into the history of aides-de-camp, which is a glorious one. Their main job was battlefield communications, I said. Being a student of command in battle, Petraeus was aware that Wellington beat Napoleon at Waterloo with the help of several aides, who were mounted and ready to carry his orders out into the fray—a dangerous experience from which several did not come back. In that same fight, the Prussian general Blucher, personally leading a cavalry charge, went down and was saved under his galloping horse by his gallant aide, who stood over his boss and fended off the oncoming French lancers. We talked of Major William W. Blackford, aide to Jeb Stuart, and Moxley Sorrel, who stayed by General James Longstreet in the Battle of the Wilderness. We noted that Custer himself had been an aide early in the same war, where he carried messages and often volunteered to take part himself in leading the action called for.

I then told my new aide that I wanted to make clear his mission. I said, "My job is to run this division. Your job is to help me do that." I added that I don't see the aide-de-camp as someone who clicks heels and lights my cigarettes, which I don't smoke anyway. "When we go someplace," I said, "move off on your own. You've been a company commander. You can read the signs wherever we go, and be another set of eyes and ears, and we'll talk about it afterwards."

Petraeus turned out to be a good sounding board. His sharp and often original perspectives afforded me a point of view other than my own. I came to see that his consistently accurate judgment was the result of a constant inflow of information, brought about by a restless intelligence, a wanting to know, accompanied by a latent store of energy strong enough to let him roam over a broad spectrum of sources of information; he was forever following up and absorbing ideas.

It was not long before I saw the extraordinary intensity of this young man. He trained himself physically with a regimen that would punish any athlete—concentrating not on muscular strength alone but on stamina above all, and initiative. He wanted to be able to go non-stop, with no respect for the clock. He combined this advantage with a sharp, searching, voracious intellect and a curiosity that propelled him into every cranny of his environs. As quickly as I got to know him, he was faster in understanding me. He soon was answering my questions before I had a chance to ask them.

We ran mornings, joining the rear ranks of companies as they passed by. You can learn more running at the rear of a formation: there you find the soldiers that are having trouble keeping up the pace for one reason or another. Petraeus lived in Hinesville, so when he linked up with me on those mornings he had already run some miles at a good pace. We would then catch up with one of the units, where the first sergeant or one of the officers would drift back along the files to give us a running salute and a "Good morning," then stride up to the front rank again. On dark days the troops might not know of our presence, so we would hear interesting chatter. One winter morning we were on the run behind the rear rank of an artillery battery when a hefty soldier called out in cadence, "Let's go by the general's house—wake him up! Wake him up!" Then he sensed our presence, looked back, pulled his head in like a turtle and said, "Oh, my God," to the rippling laughter of his comrades. Petraeus and I later agreed that this kind of moment makes it all worthwhile.

In one of our early days, I told Petraeus that I had a list of things that I needed done.

"Shoot, sir," he said, and I handed him a little package of 3x5 cards. He looked at them, murmuring, "Done, done, done, done . . . ," and handed the cards back.

"Got it, sir. They're all done. HOOAH! If your horse goes down, don't sweat it. I'll be there."

Petraeus's habit of challenging soldiers and officers to test themselves against him in push-ups or running was a way of pulling them closer to him as well as underscoring the importance of battle readiness. I used to ask myself, "Would Napoleon get off his horse to hit the ground for push-ups? Would Rommel? Would Patton?"

Later on, when he gained his stars, Petraeus was closer to his soldiers than any military officer I have known.

I asked that Pete Taylor be sent down from the Pentagon to be my division chief of staff. He was highly respected for his dedication to his work and for the precision with which he carried out his missions, large or small. A few years later, Pete would be commanding the division, after Norm Schwarzkopf and then Barry McCaffrey, who led the 24th into Iraq in the first Gulf War. Pete could read my mind, and I his. We had been through Vietnam together, which was good—he was seeing things that I missed.

John Marsh, secretary of the Army, came to inspect the division and to see how we were coming along in absorbing the new equipment and adapting to the other changes. He was from Virginia, home of the Blue and Gray Division, and he held that unit in great affection.

I routinely asked brigade and company commanders what they had on their plates; I asked soldiers what they did yesterday. If they struggled to remember, there was a problem. I asked, "What can I do to help you do your job?" It was fun. It was great.

I had never met Lieutenant General Larry Welch, then the commander of the 9th Air Force. In early August I called and asked him if I could come up for a visit. "Well, sure. What's up?" I told him I'd like to talk about Air Force and Army training—just some thoughts. We set a date, and I flew up to Shaw Air Force Base at Sumter, South Carolina, his headquarters. Thus began a lasting friendship. We talked about teaming, and specifically about an ongoing arrangement called Quick Thrust, in which the Air Force flew about 1,300 sorties per year over the firing ranges at Fort Stewart. These were practice flights—either dive bombing and strafing using training ammunition, the kind that provides just enough explosive strength to indicate point of impact (wet runs), or simply going through the motions of identifying targets on the ground and "attacking" without ammunition (dry runs). Junked vehicles at Stewart served as targets on the live fire ranges, and the dry runs enabled air activities over regular maneuver training areas. From up and down the East Coast, fighter-bomber aircraft came, usually in pairs, for crew training over the 285,000 acres of Fort Stewart.

At this meeting, the gist of our discussion was to figure out ways in which Army training could be of more benefit to the Air Force and vice versa.

When I came back from my meeting with General Welch on 7 August 1981, I made a note to myself and to my key officers:

Subject: Visit with Lieutenant General Welch at Shaw AFB, 3 August 1981.

We at Fort Stewart are in an ideal position with reference to the Air Force. We have a division located here; we have a very large training area which, incidentally, has excellent air routes of entrance and egress. We are also very close to the Atlantic Ocean, which presents vast air space areas that are relatively free and easy to control by the Navy. We are within striking distance of a number of very important Air Force bases such as Eglin and Shaw, and also the Navy and Marine Base at Beaufort—and half a dozen others, including those used by air reserve components. In fact, Fort Stewart is so important to the Air Force that they are willing to fly A-10's all the way down from Massachusetts to take part in exercises here. For these reasons we ought to be at the forefront of Army and Air Force cooperation.

The A-10 "Warthog," a plane designed for close air support of ground troops, was able to take off from short airstrips. These aircraft were flying in from distant bases, where the weather might be quite different from our own, resulting in cancellations that didn't help training. I asked our engineers to look at a small, unused, overgrown airfield at Stewart that could become a forward operating base. It was less than five miles from our ranges. Someone said, "If we fix it, the Air Force will end up owning it." I said, "Let's hope so," and we fixed it. Later, an A-10 got too close with 40mm training ammunition. Two practice rounds hit one of our M-60 tanks but didn't penetrate the armored hull. I again flew to Shaw to tell Welch, "Don't let this stop the good relationships and good training. The last thing we want you to do is back off."

The 24th Infantry Division was about to become part of the Rapid Deployment Joint Task Force under Lieutenant General Bob Kingston (the captain who had trained my Ranger class twenty-five years earlier). This meant we would join XVIII Airborne Corps as part of the strategic reserve, along with the 101st and the 82nd, both airborne divisions. We were the heavy division in this high-readiness outfit, prepared to go anywhere, including Southwest Asia. The corps would have to be light enough to move across long distances quickly, but heavy enough to fight an intense armored battle on arrival. We studied possible deployment areas almost as vast as the United States, working hard on our capability to get there. The logistical problems were tougher than anything I had ever encountered in my time in seven different divisions.

We went immediately to bar coding, minicomputers, and every

innovation we could find to improve supply procedures and keep a heavy division moving. General Jack MacMull, a star fullback in his days at West Point, was a heavyset, square man, not the typical lean airborne trooper. He didn't think much of the 24th Mechanized Division with its tanks and other heavily armored and tracked vehicles that were arriving at Savannah daily, doubtful that their tactical ground mobility would do him much good. "How are they going to fight if they can't get there on time?"

We had been given high priority on a list of new equipment. There was no shortage of people; we were at full strength. Fifty-two construction companies were at work on the installation. The old wooden barracks erected by swarms of carpenters in 1941 were coming down, and brick dormitory buildings were sprouting up at such a pace that my main problem was keeping contractors out of each other's way. There were three-soldier rooms and other innovations that the Old Army wouldn't recognize: child care centers, learning centers, craft shops, family housing areas, shopping malls, and wide new roads to handle the tenfold increase in traffic. There were signs pointing out the activities center for families, the post nursery, the office of the Association of Federal Government Employees, the alcohol and drug abuse center. Beetle Bailey's Camp Swampy of the cartoon strips was becoming the most modern post in the Army.

The Army and the Congress were interested in the cost of this destruction and construction to the degree that we underwent forty-four audits in two years. I provided continuous office space for the teams that descended upon us. I also installed a "Dial the Boss" answering service that anyone could use to complain about anything. It was not necessary to give your name; an operator took notes and left them on my desk. One of the anonymous calls said, "Get the pool fixed, Dad!"

I asked my good friend Ben Schemmer, editor and publisher of *Armed Forces Journal*, to come down from Washington for a visit. Thirty years earlier we had entered West Point together; there we discovered that we had many of the same interests, including writing and languages. Ben was an excellent, prolific writer who left the Army early to buy the old and fading *Army and Navy Journal*, which he renamed and turned into a hustling, know-it-all, attractive monthly magazine that everybody with a military connection avidly followed. Ben was working on an article on innovation in the armed services, and in his habitually provocative way, he presented himself as already convinced that there was none whatsoever.

I had invited Ben to Savannah to see the changes going on in the 24th Division as it was coming to life again after its hibernation at the end of the Korean War. Brand-new tanks and other weaponry were everywhere.

Ben was intrigued with the chance to observe this circus and took me up on my offer. We roamed through the rebirth of Camp Stewart, now fast becoming Fort Stewart, and Ben was duly impressed. George Stotser, Pete Taylor, and I took turns showing Ben the new approaches we had under way: training in heavy-light operations; linking our mechanized heavy forces with the light airborne units of XVIII Corps; putting together air-land training with 9th Air Force; bringing the computer into play, especially in logistics; and instituting what we called "chain training," in which each level in the hierarchy trains the next level below.

Ben was attentive, polite, and supportive, but it was when we went over to the mess hall that he waxed enthusiastic. When we sat down to eat, I let him know that every officer and NCO sitting in that wing of the hall, more than thirty, had one thing in common: they had written at least one article for publication in the past year. How did that happen? he wanted to know, clearly surprised and excited. I told him that Pete, George, and I, whenever and wherever we found something inventive going on, tracked down the people involved and applauded them—and asked, "Why don't you tell the world about this?"

Ben in his way grew more and more exuberant—and so did all of us, as he went from table to table asking about the writings and congratulating everyone in sight. He then said, "You guys are wonderful! I want to know who among you got the highest number of rejections. Starting now, to that person the *Armed Forces Journal* will give an annual prize of $1,000!"

3 September 1981. I remember Captain Ralph Puckett's advice to me when I found myself in trouble with our Army mission headquarters in Colombia: "Invite your bosses down to see what you're doing; give them a chance to size you up." I got in touch with four-star general Robert M. Shoemaker, head of Army Forces Command, and sent a note asking him to visit. I liked Shoemaker. He had helped me with advice when I was writing *Air Assault*, and I had given him a copy of the published book in Vietnam. He accepted my invitation and arrived in early September. It's a good thing we were on easy terms because there were a couple of unexpected but marvelous moments during his visit. He let

me know ahead of time that he would like to see soldiers, soldiers, and more soldiers, and he would dislike sitting around listening to briefings, so I arranged an early morning run and exercises with a rifle company, followed by breakfast with an artillery battery. On the run, led by a sergeant, we called out the cadence for a while, the usual poetry of all troops, and then the cadence calls became more creative than usual:

> I don't know, but I hear rumors,
> I don't know, but I hear rumors,
> Gen'ral Shoemaker's wearin' bloomers.
> Gen'ral Shoemaker's wearin' bloomers.

I wondered if Puckett's advice from the Lancero days had led me to my doom, but when I looked across the ranks the general was laughing. When we finished and broke ranks to walk around and cool off, Shoemaker asked one of the soldiers, "Is this the battery that's all screwed up?" The soldier quickly answered, "No sir! That's Charlie Battery!" Again, laughter saved me.

There had to be a third unforgettable moment, and that came at breakfast. Shoemaker had asked to be seated with the most junior soldiers, and this I arranged. As he rose at the end of the meal, the general turned to a private first class and said, "Well, son, have you ever had breakfast with a general before?" The soldier replied, "No sir," then hesitated a moment and added, "Not that I recall, anyway." Shoemaker could not have been more pleased, and the day went well.

During this period we moved in three directions at once: Bold Eagle, to Florida; Bright Star, to Egypt; and out to the far reaches into our own training areas of Fort Stewart against some of the 82nd Airborne. We had to show our value as part of the Rapid Deployment Force. We started with Bold Eagle, where we would begin to practice loading out of Stewart. To do this we would, for the first time, move tanks and other tracked vehicles along the forty-five miles of road to ships docked at Savannah to take us around Florida to the panhandle port of Pensacola, then roll along the forty miles from there to Eglin Air Force Base, where we would fight a mock battle with the 101st Airborne and return.

The National Guard 48th Brigade of Georgia and 30th Brigade of Tennessee were part of these maneuvers. The regulars were fond of saying, "If the Guard can be ready enough after 38 days of training each year, what gives with our 280 or so days?" I needed to show the

48th Brigade, the 30th Brigade, and everyone else what I thought of the Guard, which was this: the Army trains to standards that are set forth clearly for the specific tasks we expect to be called on to accomplish. The tasks are wide-ranging, so the commanders have to set priorities and select the tasks to be emphasized. No single unit can be equally prepared for all the possible tasks at all times. The National Guard in peacetime has a total of thirty-eight days a year for training, which means the number of tasks for which the units can be expected to prepare must be limited. For some units—including engineers, medics, transport, supply—the required tasks closely resemble those of civilian life. This is not so for "maneuver" units and fire support, such as mechanized infantry, armor, and artillery. These units face a harder challenge, but not an impossible one.

We had never done a move like this. We had no experience to rely on as 3rd Brigade set off for the Florida panhandle. We needed to show Gorman that we could be quick and that we could absorb the 48th Georgia National Guard Brigade along with other Guard units. Also, we wanted to prove the value of a heavy and light combination—to show that we, a mechanized "heavy" force, could operate with "light" airborne troops from Fort Bragg.

On one side was our 2nd Brigade, with the 30th Brigade of the Tennessee National Guard and units from the 101st Air Assault Division and the 194th Armored Brigade. Opposing them was the 48th Brigade of the Georgia National Guard, commanding the 2nd Battalion, 34th Infantry, and other elements of the division—the first time regulars from the division were commanded by the Guard. The structure worked out well in the free-play exercises or maneuvers.

Then came Operation Bright Star, in Egypt. While we were preparing to load ships docked in Savannah, Egypt's president, Anwar Sadat, was assassinated. We were told to continue to march. Our task force left for Alexandria on 19 November. Bright Star was another display of our ability to move over large distances, and for us it was also proof of our ability to link up with our own military forces and those of our allies. Interoperability, it was called, although a simpler name would be teaming. After we arrived in the Sahara west of Cairo, a battalion of the 82nd Airborne Division, 850 troops, parachuted in along with 180 tons of supplies and joined us and Egyptian forces for maneuvers in the desert.

On 23 November 1981 I wrote to Gin, "Camels are wandering around here all by themselves—about 30–40. I wonder whose? Ugly as sin. I went to Alexandria today and it was just as squalid as in Durrell's

Quartet. The port is chaos, and I can only admire all that the troops have done in getting all the vehicles here through that mess."

In another letter to Gin, I told her of my surprise to see the petrified trees lying exposed in the sand. Tall trees, they had been. Most of them were now broken into many two- or three-foot lengths, some still aligned after thousands of years and resembling giant necklaces.

Letter to my father, 23 November 1981:

> I'm at our tent camp in the open desert about 40 miles northwest of Cairo. It is 10:00 p.m. and I just came in from farther out on the desert where we're attacking some sand hills tonight, Egyptians and Americans together. It's interesting and strange. They have mostly Soviet equipment, so all the U.S. and Russian tanks and armored carriers and artillery trucks are in formations side by side, intermingled with MIGs flying in support of us.
>
> Our troops have done really well, and I am as happy as can be. Two good exercises in a row—Florida and Egypt—both involving a sea move, both complex—and the officers and men have risen to the occasion both times. It is winter on the Sahara, with temperatures reaching 80 by day and 50 by night. The troops are enjoying it. I just came back from an hour's ride in my jeep across the night sands, with the stars all sparkling. Beautiful sight, like being at sea, with rolling dunes in all directions.

The deployment of a brigade to Egypt gave us all a chance to see a variety of Soviet military vehicles in action, and to drive and maneuver them ourselves. I drove a BMP, a Boevaya Mashina Pekhota troop carrier or infantry combat vehicle, built by the Soviets in the 1960s and first seen in public at a parade in Red Square in 1967. These vehicles smoked and roared and rattled, they punished their occupants—but they were durable and uncomplicated. Viktor Suvurov, a former Soviet military intelligence officer who defected to the U.K., called these export vehicles "the monkey version." Suvurov's books on the Soviet Army are pedestrian, but they were still better reading than most of our own intelligence analyses, and they filled a gap by giving us an extensive commentary from a worm's-eye view. He helped me understand some of the weaknesses of the training of combat soldiers who were drafted for a term of two years, with an intake of one million every six months—all at one time. This allowed for four training cycles, followed by two deployments in Central Europe each year.

In my notes, this comment: "Heading east toward Cairo, flying low in a helicopter over the undulating and seemingly endless waves of sand, we become accustomed to the sense of being alone, seeing nothing. Then the tops of the pyramids appear ahead, looking like small brown tents at first, but quickly looming up higher than we are flying, great masses of stone—and then just beyond them, farther to the east, a green horizon, the Nile."

In the summer of 1982, the Army announced that the 24th Division would receive the improved model of the M-60 tank, and I decided that the first seventy to arrive would be assigned to the 48th Brigade. This caused a certain amount of comment. Caspar "Cap" Weinberger, then secretary of defense, and Shy Meyer, chief of staff, came to visit the 48th at Fort Stewart during its summer training, and at that time Meyer said, "We can't go anywhere without the National Guard. If there is a national emergency, the Guard will be committed at the same time as the active force."

2 March 1982. I was still in my fatigues and boots, sitting at dinner with the family, talking over the day, when the bell rang, followed by banging at the front door. Kids' voices. Must be friends of the children. Ginny said to the girls, "Go see what they want. Tell them we're having supper."

Our girls came back. "They're crying. Something's the matter. They want to see you."

We got up from the table and went to the door. Two little girls from the neighborhood were talking at once, very agitated. Their sister was hurt, in the woods. A man took their sister. I said, "Calm down. Where's your sister?"

"Behind the house," they said, and Ginny and I started off with them. We rounded the corner of the garage, and they pointed to a copse of tall, skinny pines and low brush about forty yards away. I saw figures there, on the ground, and I started to jog. I said to Ginny, "Call the MPs." She turned back to the house. Our German shepherd was loose now, and excited about the commotion. He, too, ran for the woods. As I got closer, I was thinking, What's going on here? A girl and a man in the woods. Making love? This could be . . . anything. This could lead to some kind of fiasco. I thought, Well, here we go, Don Quixote. At this point I almost fell over my German shepherd, who was enjoying the run.

When I was twenty yards away, the man got up and ran. Still unsure of what all this meant, I followed him, running as fast as I could.

He cleared the far edge of the trees and headed across a field toward a parking lot and deeper woods beyond. In the trees I passed the girl, who was lying on the ground. I saw blood on her face and on her white blouse. She was trying to pull up her jeans. The man was now across the street, among the parked cars. I was losing the race.

The parking lot belonged to the officers' club, and there was a side door. I saw two young officers coming down the steps, and I yelled, "Stop him!" and pointed to the man. They immediately ran out into the lot and intercepted him. I can't resist commenting here that my teaming instinct worked even in this strange circumstance—a man in uniform chasing another through a parking lot. He didn't struggle much. I caught up, winded, and saw that he was a young soldier, a private. When I could manage some words over my heavy breathing I said, "Bring him back." We started back toward my house. We could hear sirens, and there were flashing lights in my driveway. Neighbors had arrived, as well as police, including two detectives who happened to be driving by and heard the radio calls. The girl was by then on her feet. She was about fourteen. Her mouth was bloody, her blouse spattered with blood, and there were flecks of blood also on her white sneakers. People were helping. We turned the soldier over to the Military Police.

That day was the soldier's twenty-first birthday. He had arrived at Fort Stewart only a few days earlier, sent back from his unit in Germany, where he had been disciplined for assault. He had seen the girl in the post's bowling alley with her sisters and, when she left, had followed her toward her home, near ours. At a point he thought opportune, he told the younger girls to go along home, and when they hesitated, he threatened them. Then he forced the oldest girl into the thin treeline that marked our backyard. The little girls showed good presence of mind. They ran for the nearest house.

After everybody left and things got back to normal, Ginny told me, "I called the Military Police and said, 'This is Mrs. Galvin. The general is chasing a rapist in the backyard.' The sergeant said, 'Thank you, ma'am,' and as he hung up I heard him say, 'Holy shit!'"

The soldier could not be taken to court at our post, because I was the ranking officer. He was tried elsewhere, and I was not asked to testify. He was sentenced to ten years in prison for attempted rape.

In April 1982, a few days before speaking at a military conference, I talked with General Shoemaker about the things I was planning to say. His comment was a laconic "I'll be listening."

My turn came when we reached the question of training. I said it was not realistic to get into details of how to improve training when the obstacle impeding any progress was inherent in the structure of the Army itself. Aviation training was split into fragments. Troop lift helicopters were assigned to the infantry branch; heavier lift ships and fixed wing to Transportation; attack and scout helicopters to Armor. The branches do not "necessarily" (I said) award a high priority to aviation training; yet aviation (and the third dimension of air power) is becoming more and more decisive in Army operations. It is changing faster than any branch—or than any facet of ground force tactics. (A year later, on 12 April 1983, the chief of staff of the Army made the decision that aviation should become a separate combat branch of the Army.)

It had never occurred to me that I might be associated with the division that General Bill Dean had led so well in the opening months of the Korean War. Finding myself actually commanding the division, I invited the general's son, my West Point roommate Bill Dean, and Bill's mother to visit Fort Stewart as guests of honor at the opening of Dean Field, a helicopter training area.

One Saturday evening in March 1983, Ginny and I were having dinner at Tassie's Pier down on the riverside below Savannah with General MacMull and his wife. I got a call from Pete Taylor, who gave me a number for Paul Gorman in Washington. I called Gorman. "Jack," he said, "I just wanted to let you know that you're going to be getting a call from Shy. We'd like to send somebody to El Salvador, and I think it's going to be you. This would be a temporary duty for three, maybe six months. You're a trainer and you speak Spanish. You might or might not turn over the division."

"OK. I'm all set. When does this happen?"

"We're talking about Monday. We want you to be up here to see us on Monday morning. You'll probably get the word tomorrow. I'll tell you the rest of this when I see you."

Walking back to the table, I could feel the impact of Paul's words in a heightened awareness of everything, a sharpness of light and shadow. The adrenaline was running. I sat down and tried to rejoin the conversation. The pelicans were stumbling around on the shrimp boats, settling in for the night. Lights swung along the docks.

"What was that?" Ginny asked.

"Just Pete with some stuff. Nothing really important." I didn't want to get into a discussion over something that complicated. Ginny looked at me quickly, as if to say, "Don't give me that," but she said no more, and we went on with our chat with Jack and his wife. At home that night, Ginny didn't mention the telephone call, and I figured that we'd both get a better night's sleep if I didn't say anything more.

On Sunday morning at 4:30 a.m., the phone rang next to our bed. Ginny picked it up. It was Shy Meyer. (The general never liked to have other people make his calls for him. "I'm not that busy," he'd say.) "Hi, Ginny! Is Jack around?" She handed me the phone. I struggled out of a deep sleep and sat on the edge of the bed, trying to sound awake as I croaked a hello into the receiver.

"Jack, this is Shy."

"Yes, sir. Good morning."

"How's the Victory Division?"

"Sir, it's fine."

"Good. How's your Spanish, Jack? Still OK?" He sounded preoccupied with something—as if another subject was more on his mind than his talk with me. The conversation stumbled along. "Look," he said, "we are thinking about having you go down to El Salvador. It would be for a short while, I think. If we did that, who would take over for you there?"

"Well, Dick Sharp has just arrived, but he can do it. He's got his feet on the ground already."

"OK, yeah—I'm sure he could do it. Then again, maybe we'll have you turn over the division. It's about time, anyway."

"I'd like, if possible, to make it temporary and short, at least at first. I could get down there quickly that way, but more than that, it would give Ginny a chance to stay here in the house. That way, the kids could finish out the school year."

"Well, maybe we could start it as a temporary and then turn it into permanent later."

"That'd be good, sir."

"All right. We'll see. We're working on it this morning here. We'll call you later in the day."

I hung up and turned to Ginny.

"What was that?" she said. "Wait—let me guess: Lebanon."

"Would you buy El Salvador?"

"Really?"

"Yup."

"When are they talking about?"

"Tomorrow."

"Oh, come on."

She took it the same way she always has: we started to figure out how to get ready. I kept thinking of the fragmented and preoccupied way in which Shy told me what was going to happen. He didn't sound quite convinced himself, as if he were still weighing other possibilities. There was no follow-up call from Washington that day; in fact, there was no follow-up call ever, not on that subject. My guess is that someone up the line said, "Forget it," and they forgot it. Four or five weeks later, Shy called to tell me I would take command of VII Corps in Germany.

That gave me two months to prepare the division for a smooth handoff to Norm Schwarzkopf, who would be my successor. I made a list of areas in which I felt the division needed to get better, things that I would be leaving undone. The top few included strengthening the overall computer support, especially the automation of logistics; improving the capability for strategic deployment; bringing the 48th "Roundout" Brigade deeper into the division; incorporating heavy-light tactics; and pushing the division's role in joint operations with XVIII Airborne Corps.

But for now, Germany beckoned, again.

21

VII Corps: Warrior Preparation

"Dusting off our procedures"

In early July 1983, I took command of VII Corps. It was my second assignment in Stuttgart, and it took me back to areas of Germany I knew well; I had friends there in and outside the military. My mission was: defend the West German border with East Germany and Czechoslovakia along the mountains of the Thuringerwald with both conventional and nuclear weapons. On the other side of the Gaps at Meiningen, Coburg, Hof, and Cheb were Soviet, East German, and Czech forces that I knew from my Fulda Gap days three years earlier.

I had thought all along about the possibility of World War III and the use of nuclear weapons, but it was at corps command that the specifics of that possibility all came together with intensity. I asked myself what chain of events, what decisions, what details of implementation, what responses might ensue—all in all, what the battle would be: the battle in which I would be the leader of 73,000 American troops and more.

A Defense Intelligence Agency study came out at about this time, which my close friend and West Point classmate Bill Odom, at that point Army Chief of Intelligence, sent me—one that impressed me more than any other I had seen. In twenty-two pages it outlined the Soviet plan of attack, which would force us to fight in two directions at once: it called for their getting rapidly into our rear areas with raiding forces while supporting their successful incursions with everything possible. Other aspects of their plan indicated that they doubted that tactical nuclear weapons would be used by us or by them, but if they were, the raiding forces would aim at ours early on.

The planning on the Soviet side made sense to me, especially since on our side we were relying so much on our General Defense Plan, which called for a strong frontline battle with practically no reserves and little mobility. On the map we were a north-south line of the forces of countries in a daisy chain, dependent on using tactical nuclear weapons if our line showed signs of giving way. I, however, had never believed in nuclear planning other than for political or psychological purposes.

After the change of command ceremonies and with all this in mind, I flew to Munich and joined the commanders and staff officers who were conducting a war game in a German schoolhouse that the corps had rented. (The students were on summer vacation.) In one of the classrooms was a large map of Germany and Czechoslovakia. There was much discussion—very interesting and well serving its aim, which was to refresh our ability to follow the procedures set forth in our extensive planning for carrying out our mission.

Carriage Trade, the war game, was under way. I listened. The battle marched along in a predictable way. The enemy, the red team, drove us back a bit, but not too far. We caused heavy attrition in their ranks, both in the air and on the ground. They committed reinforcements and pushed us back a little more, but we reinforced and held on to our new positions. It was what I called "tree rings." We concentrated all available intelligence on the question "Is the enemy likely to break through anywhere?" We gave the air forces plenty of credit for attacks that weakened the oncoming enemy echelons.

Our procedures were all working well. The exercise was a good opportunity not only to practice our procedures but also to socialize, to network, to get to know each other better: Americans, French, Germans, Canadians, and other allies who visited. Twice a day we stopped for an hour or so and talked about what we were doing, right and wrong, and what we were learning. We were fighting an enemy on paper, of course, with some of our own people acting the part of our opponents. The word most often heard was "procedures." We were dusting off our procedures, making sure we were all tracking together.

The commanders at all levels were trained to see the war in terms of a tactical fight along the front, followed by—if it were ever necessary—a nuclear exchange. In other words, we win or we nuke. The plans emphasized readiness, rapid deployment from garrison locations to assigned defense positions, and the kind of fighting that might occur in the first two or three days. There were small-unit counterattacks. Covering forces—usually cavalry, which is traditionally light and swift—had been given the main battle tanks and otherwise strengthened to the point that they were as heavy as any of the tank and mechanized infantry units in the main defensive forces. These strong forces functioned as a first line of defense, since we had given away the advantages of a light and wide-ranging covering force that might help us see where the main attack was coming. We were close-up on the border, so there was little room for that. Reserves were small—at corps level a brigade or two, at Army level a division—mostly in shallow positions close behind us.

Our exercises were constructed to take into account the concepts we felt were embedded in our strategy and were intended to bolster our procedural efficiency. We had a turnover in the units of more than one-third of the entire force every year. So we took to the field to practice the same plan over and over: alert measures, assembly areas, movement to defensive positions along the border, and then our tough up-front fight, with a commitment to hold fast in forward locations while conducting local counterattacks to restore any lost ground.

With the exception of a handful of innovations over the years, the defense of the West was like a Maginot Line without the concrete. In fact, there were many who thought we should build a thousand-kilometer-long barrier along the boundary between the two Germanys, and there were times when the Germans had to quietly explain that they did not want to have such an endorsement of the separation of the two parts of their country.

We routinely scheduled a monthly meeting of the senior commanders of the corps, down to the brigade level, for talks about our responsibilities: problems with logistics and administration, questions concerning our military communities, analyses of intelligence reports on the Warsaw Pact, directives and other information from higher headquarters. After watching the end of this exercise I proposed that we add an extra day each month to this meeting, so that on the second day we could pick up where we left off in the war game. "If we estimate it will be twenty-one days before we are adequately reinforced," I suggested, "why not try an exercise in which we fight for twenty-one days with what we have, plus what we think we might reasonably expect to arrive in the way of help?" We talked about this, and decided to add 1st Infantry Division to VII Corps in our game, assuming it would arrive early, since it was assigned to us and could be assisted by its 1st Brigade Forward, already stationed at Goeppingen, Germany. We also added to the simulation a National Guard division, the 38th.

As we took other steps to prepare for an extended game, I found that not every leader in the corps was happy with my plan for continuing the exercise. One general officer complained to me privately that we did not have time in our heavy schedule to take out a second day every month for game play. My response was, "If we can't take time one day a month to talk about our defense plan, do we have our priorities right?" He had a point, though. VII Corps was the largest combat unit in the U.S. Army. We had 262 military installations, thirty-three family communities, and a total strength of almost 200,000. We trained on 155 local training areas, spread all over the place. We ran forty-three schools for 29,000 students. We had hospitals, depots, airfields, pipelines, and maintenance facilities. West Germany was about the size of Oregon, and there was also V Corps, almost as big as we were, so there was plenty of administrative leadership involved.

Although our mission came first, there was a whole world of responsibility that came second. Some in the military tend to think leadership and management are two different responsibilities, requiring different personalities: the manager organizes, explains, implements, reviews, and controls while the leader inspires, envisions, decides, and creates. But the leader needs to be aware of the tasks and skills involved in the implementation of any decision, and the manager leads all day long.

We did go ahead with the extended war game. We began a series of meetings that made it possible for us to stay continually productive in our tactical and operational thinking on the most elemental questions of our mission responsibilities. To improve the monthly simulation day, we installed computers at corps headquarters, with support from General Glenn Otis and the Army staff at the Pentagon. With the extra day each month, we saw how immobile we were. We had not done much thinking beyond the first battle of a campaign, believing that either we would be reinforced or we would "go nuclear." Now we started to get a sense of the long campaign that might ensue if we fought the war without considering the use of nuclear weapons. Under most of the attack scenarios that we could imagine, our defense far forward made us too brittle, disallowing us the depth that large, well-placed mobile reserves could give us. We were forced to face the limits of a forward defense. No plan was ever made for offensive operations.

I called for a terrain ride. We spent three days studying the lay of the land thirty miles behind our front lines, considering how we would fight if we found ourselves driven back to that area. After the ride, more of the officers, including the Germans and Canadians, were convinced we could adhere to our defense plan while at the same time better prepare ourselves for mobile operations. I also asked the question "What if we were successful in defeating the attack against us right away, and our higher command wanted to employ us somewhere else along the front? Would we be ready to pull off line and move?" We considered this. VII Corps had 2,500 fighting vehicles and an additional 4,500 trucks and other administrative vehicles. If we put them all on one road, with proper combat spacing between them, they would stretch across the entire central front from the Austrian border to the Baltic Sea. We had much work to do in planning how the corps would move.

Then I got a call from George Stotser. When we left the 24th Division, Stotser had moved to Heidelberg as operations officer for General Otis. George was watching our goings-on, however, and also keeping his eye on the work on battle simulation that the Air Force called Project Warrior. For the fourth time, as in Vietnam and in the 24th Division, Stotser and I teamed. The Air Force was asking for players who could represent the ground units that aircrews normally would support, and my old friend called me about it. Would VII Corps like to take part? "They say they just want a few Army folks to make the ground portion of the game a little more realistic," George said.

His call had come at exactly the right moment. With each passing month, we were becoming more and more adept at enacting the corps simulation, and we were learning a great deal from the exercise. Participating in the wide-ranging Air Force game would carry us along even further. I thought it was a great idea.

"We don't want to be just a ground presence," I told George. "We want to work out better ways to operate together."

"I'll pass it on," he said, and he got back later that day to say, "It's a go. They're interested. They want to talk about it."

Lieutenant General Harry Goodall, commanding 17th Air Force (Allied Air Forces Southern Europe), an open-minded innovator with a lot of joint experience, brought all his wing commanders to see the game. At first they were uneasy and insisted they could stay only a half-day, but a few hours of play convinced them that this game could be highly productive. After a long and full day, we all agreed that indeed we had a treasure of a game, one that could teach us plenty about working together.

Our first exercise at the Warrior Preparation Center brought together leaders at the brigade and wing level for several hours of simulated air-land battle, followed by a half-day of discussion that stretched into a full day and turned into an unforgettable learning experience for us all. This became the first of a series of exercises that proved so successful that the Army joined in with the Air Force, took responsibility for half the funding, and shared the staffing. We linked our software models with those of the Warrior Preparation Center and integrated the VII Corps game into a much broader and more complex one. A little later, V Corps joined us, and German units came in also. I realized for the first time how much more mobile and flexible the air operations were. As one of the pilots said, he could fly along our corps front from one side to the other in a matter of a few minutes.

The game improved with each iteration as we integrated our fighting capabilities. It was very much ad hoc; we were making each other's acquaintance and sharpening our ability to combine our operating skills. Our main problem had been our tendency to plan and fight independently of each other, even though we knew the achievement of maximum combat power lay in our ability to work together. We talked about "stiff areas" of Air Force and Army doctrine, where what worked quite well for one side was an awkward fit for the other. We figured out ways we could change computer scenarios so as to focus the training on things we needed to know. We made mistakes, and there were some embarrassing moments; but we helped each other, critiqued each other, and learned from it. In those days I kept on my desk a small model of the Wright brothers' first aircraft. Ad hoc can become Kitty Hawk.

How credible was our fear of the Soviet Union? For my part, I believed that the Soviet Union did not want any given conflict to grow into war. Yet there have been numerous occasions that bore a potential—sometimes small, sometimes very serious—for escalation: Berlin in 1948 and 1953—and again in 1958 and 1961; Czechoslovakia in 1948, 1962, and in the Prague Spring of 1968; the Korean War, 1950–1953; the Hungarian uprising of 1956 and the subsequent Soviet invasion; the U-2 flights in 1960; the Cuban missile crisis in 1962; the Soviet invasion of Afghanistan in 1979; the response to the Solidarity movement in Poland, 1981–1983; the shooting down of Korean Airlines flight 007 in 1983. These were all times when a much more significant escalation could have happened, even if it resulted from confusion or misunderstanding.

If war had resulted, would the Warsaw Pact have fought together as an alliance? Throughout the 1970s and 1980s, I thought it dangerous to assume that the Central European countries would not have fought, even though later events made it clear that the Pact was held together more by coercion than by the solidarity of their respective Communist governments. In the 1980s, the Soviets were giving Central and

East European countries more and more real tasks and responsibilities within the integration of forces. It appeared that the military institutions of the various Pact countries were drawing closer together. Then there was the question "Since part of our defense plan was a deep air and missile attack to break up the follow-on forces—their reserves—including knocking out bridges and the rest of the infrastructure, would this turn Pact countries against us?" I had not forgotten the Prague Spring and the rapid movement of Soviet force at that time.

Much of what I learned about Soviet tactics came from the work of Lieutenant Colonel David M. Glantz and his team at Leavenworth. There, in an old building next to the cemetery, we discussed aspects of Soviet military history that were of specific interest to us both.

I was also happy to discover the writings of Chris Donnelly, a British intelligence expert. His work was a welcome change. Most intelligence people always wanted to talk about iron: weapons and armaments. Donnelly was not writing about iron. He knew the Soviet leadership; the hierarchies; who mentored whom; who served together and when; what their ideas were, as expressed in their writings and pronouncements; and how individuals changed and developed over time. I sought him out at Sandhurst, the Royal Military Academy for officer basic training outside London, where he was a senior lecturer in the Soviet Studies Research Centre. Much of the writing in the Soviet military journals seemed to me a rehashing of routine doctrinal material, tinged with an air of showing off. Donnelly, sans airs, put things together.

Would we ever use tactical nuclear weapons in Allied Command Europe? There were upwards of 5,000 of them in storage under my janitorial responsibility, which certainly indicated that the answer might be yes. If the time ever came on my tour of duty, what would I recommend?

Such a decision would have to be political—and in my opinion would be an impossible choice. If nuclear weapons were not to be used but only threatened, we would be faced with the question of how to survive a massive conventional attack that we believed the Warsaw Pact was capable of mounting, involving echelons of armored and mechanized forces that would come rolling across the border. Meeting such an attack would require the ability to outmaneuver the attacker at the corps level in order to seize the initiative through counterattack at the right places. Without timely political guidance that would allow us to conduct one form of defense or another, we would stand a good chance of being caught between the two: that is, assuming the early use of nuclear weapons (in other words, believing in our own threatened early use), defending too long in forward positions, giving away flexibility, and using up reserves to force the enemy to concentrate, then changing to a war of maneuver without the ability to fight it.

If we were to employ a single, artillery-size nuclear weapon, here's how it would go. I would calculate where the enemy would be three days hence, along with the locations of everyone and everything that might be affected and where our own forces would be; give orders to units involved in the moving of warheads and in the follow-up attack after the weapon was used; then I would pass all that on, via Allied Forces Central Command at Brunssum in the Netherlands, for approval and dispatch to Allied Command Europe and thence to the chairman of the Military Committee and on to the secretary general of NATO. In the meantime, I would be making adjustments within the corps in response to the changing situation.

That's what the book said. Reality said that all these steps would have to be close to simultaneous, as every top-level leader in every nation of the Alliance, plus the whole chain of command, plus everyone in the world (including Warsaw Pact leaders), would be clamoring to know what was going on. And the classified-message traffic necessary to keep information flowing to all those who had to know would have had to be moved by banks of teletype machines that in the 1980s were already ancient.

One factor in the equation would be the amount of damage inflicted on friendly territory. Here's a question. What hurts us less: the destruction resulting from our own use of nuclear weapons or the damage we would sustain from heavy conventional fighting in the depth of our own territory? Cohesion might be lost, and it would need to be restored by conventional action, such as retreating and reconsolidating. In the reality of such a momentous decision as one involving the use of nuclear weapons, our strategy's motto—"Direct defense, deliberate escalation, and general nuclear release"—of which we so often spoke (as a deterrent more than a strategy we were actually committed to, I think) would have been smothered in debate. As for the Soviets, I concluded that we would never know their thinking or intentions regarding the use of nuclear weapons.

There were few chances to meet, and gain any personal insight into, the Soviet military leadership. "No military contact" was a quick and easy option when the United States wanted to show disagreement or anger (usually referred to as "concern"). Connections, as a result, were tenuous and sporadic. For years we missed opportunities to understand on any personal basis what the senior Soviet military leadership was like. They remained distant and enigmatic until the end—as we were to them.

Major General Pyal'tsev was the first Soviet general I ever met, and when I did I had been an Army officer for more than thirty years. I had never tried to learn Russian, thinking, "Where would I use it?" As a joke, when I was a cadet, I memorized the phrase "I'm just a stupid guy" in Russian because, I thought, "If I'm ever captured and interrogated, I'll need a remark for openers." Pyal'tsev was Chief of the Soviet Military Liaison Mission in Frankfurt, and I eventually succeeded in getting a meeting with him.

From my notes, 18 February 1984:

On a Cessna flying up to Frankfurt I fumble through the folder of loose papers, among them a few one-page biographical sketches of the members of the Russian liaison group, illustrated with passport-style photos. I turn to the first, and it is the head man, Major General Pyal'tsev. One glance at his photo tells me that this might turn out to be a long day. The set to his jaw, the heavy jowls, the flat hair combed straight back, the narrow eyes with their piercing look, the faintly pugnacious air—a man with a permanent look of incipient exasperation. Every inch the American stereotype of the Russian general. Birth date: 1927. He is two years older than I am. Promoted to major general at age 42. Very early, yet the bio says his last command was a battalion. Could be a mistake, or maybe we just don't have the information.

I read the other pages in the same fashion, wary and cynical, not wanting to be taken in. In the thirty-six years since I joined the National Guard as a private in 1948, I had known no Soviet military people. Zero. Not good, but that has been the policy. Studies of the Soviet military leadership, yes, a little, but meeting them, no. The Soviets I know are the ones who drive past our convoys on German roads with a flash of yellow "Soviet Military Liaison Mission" license plates on their jeeps. Always looking for new intelligence, they dog along the fringes of our exercises, taking photos and scavenging in our old bivouacs.

Now I am on the way to meet their chief.

We, of course, have our counterpart, a group of liaison officers who drive the roads of East Germany picking up whatever information they can, and probably scavenging in the Soviet bivouacs.

Our flight route takes us over the hills south of Heidelberg and then across the Neckar Valley just east of the city. The forested hills are covered with a light dusting of snow. We set up in the Frankfurt landing pattern, and after landing we taxi over to the U.S. Air Force hangar area, a few minutes early. We should time our arrival to exactly the appointed hour. Bad form to be late or early. We drive the sedan down a few extra streets on the way, to use up time, and arrive on the button.

Even though I had studied an aerial photo of the compound, the place is a surprise to me. Three rectangular flat-roofed buildings, each three stories high, surrounded by a twelve-foot fence. We drive up and stop at the security gate, a massive steel framework that opens like a sliding door. The guard is a member of the West German civil labor force. I get a smile as we pass through.

The high fence makes the compound seem even smaller, hemming in the buildings. The leafless trees, which must lend a little natural beauty in the summer, add their skeletons to the starkness. Across the compound I can see a small group of people at the doorway of the center building. The officers, wives, and children are lined up there to meet us. I say half of the ten words I have been supplied in Russian, hoping that Pyal'tsev's English or German is good enough to help us carry on a conversation.

We pull up in front of the door. Pyal'tsev steps away from the group and salutes as I struggle out of the car to return the salute and try out my Russian phrase. It seems to work. He smiles and says through his translator, "I see you have picked up some Russian!"

"No," I respond, "I really don't know any. Wish I did." His smile shows a line of gold caps on all his front teeth, upper and lower. A little more gold than I have, but not much.

The officers are lined up on the left side of the walk, the wives and children on the right. I use my single phrase over and over again as Pyal'tsev introduces me first to all the officers and then to the wives and children. When I get to the children the first little girl shrinks away, and I remember the words of one of my young daughters that morning as I was leaving the house: "Why are you going to see the Russians? I hate them!"

Mrs. Pyal'tsev stands in the doorway with her eight-year-old daughter. She is matronly and quiet; all the women seem subdued, passive. Several are pretty.

The visit starts with a walk in the compound. Our path takes us past the playground, where the kids, apparently intrigued at the sight of their leader and a strange American walking and chatting, simply stand in small groups and watch us. The children are all below school age. I comment on this and am told that the parents have left their older children in schools in the Soviet Union.

Pyal'tsev asks me if I would like to see the interior of the building, where the officers and their families live. I'm very interested in that, I tell him. The first floor of the building is a wide room with heavy benches lining three walls, like the nineteenth-century railroad station in my hometown. Women and children are sitting there, quiet, filling the benches. I at first take it for a meeting, but Pyal'tsev tells me they are waiting for the dining hall to open. On the second floor I see that each family is given a sitting room and a bedroom, sparsely furnished, patriotic pictures on some walls. Everyone is smiling and polite.

For lunch we go to the headquarters building.

I have been told that Pyal'tsev loves anecdotes, and this becomes quite evident.

Pyal'tsev speaks little or no English. I try out my German and find that like us he knows a fair amount, but is not ready to try to keep up an extended conversation.

He is open and talkative, responsive to every question, not asking any himself. Service in West Germany is desirable, sought after. Wives are allowed to shop in the city. They go there in groups with an escort. The West Germans are receptive. The Americans are relatively easy to deal with. They know who we are and they stick to the rules. "Following along on your maneuvers, we sometimes have minor misunderstandings, but these are quickly resolved with good communication," he says. "We have nothing to complain about, and we hope the same is true for you."

We exchange amenities along the same lines, nothing of substance, but a good sizing up of the general, his troops, and the Soviet way of seeing things. It was a good start, and I would have liked more chances to talk, sensing that it could be productive. As we parted company I invited him to visit me in Stuttgart, and later he sent word that he had asked his side for permission and was turned down. With the Pentagon's permission I then invited him to the ceremony when I turned over command of the corps—and to my surprise he managed to come. At our customary parade, I said a few words of farewell, including a memorized comment in Russian welcoming him to our headquarters. In response, he stood up, smiled, and made a slight bow.

In November 1983, the U.S. Pershing II nuclear missiles arrived in my area and were located near the small village of Mutlangen. Immediately a siege by demonstrators began. The U.S. weapons and equipment sat in a muddy field on the top of a hill, surrounded by vocally unhappy Germans. The controversy was heated. One day the demonstrators showed their strength by linking arms and forming a continuous chain from Stuttgart to Ulm, where the other Pershing II unit was garrisoned—a distance of about forty-five miles. There was strong Soviet pressure on Germany as well, but the German government stood by its decision to accept the missiles, a show of solidarity that, as it happened, helped bring about a major move toward nuclear arms reduction.

During this period I enjoyed a diversion that connected me once again with West Point, through Red Reeder, the school's former athletic director and a prolific writer who helped me early on with my own writing. In the Normandy landing on 6 June 1944, VII U.S. Corps, commanded by General J. Lawton Collins, fought its way across Utah Beach. Within the corps, then-Colonel Red Reeder led 12th Regiment, 4th Infantry Division, over the beach and into the German defenses. On the fifth day of that assault, Red—who refused to be anywhere but up front—was hit by cannon fire and lost his right leg. He was invited to be present at the fortieth anniversary celebration of the landing on 6 June 1984, but he couldn't physically make it; his good leg was giving him trouble. As the current commander of the corps, I was invited, so I showed up for him, too. In the course of the commemoration, I attended the official addresses and a helicopter tour of the battlefield.

I took along my pocket Dictaphone and described for Red as much as I could of the historic events that would be of the most interest to him, especially the Utah Beach landing and the inland fight from there. In the process I was lucky enough to run into General Collins, who praised Red. I sent the tape I'd recorded to Red—along with a transcription, so that if he couldn't read my words (his eyesight was not good), he could at least hear them. Some excerpts:

> Tops of the clouds coming into Normandy are at 2,600 feet. We're coming down through those. Bottoms out at 1,900 feet at Deauville. The pilot says we're going to have to fly up off the coast, so I'm sitting near the left door. And now we're coming up on Omaha Beach at 1240 hours and into the long curve of Omaha Beach, sunlit today with the shadows of the clouds, but the sun coming down in different spots of brightness about a mile apart along Omaha, and now I can see the American cemetery at Omaha. . . . I have never been to that cemetery, but I see the American flag flying.
>
> The crosses so close together, as if it were a white field, just a white field with a few trees in it. Now coming up on the monument at Pointe du Hoc. Here the beach is impossible, only about 50 meters wide and covered with gray stone. We're circling in now to land at Pointe du Hoc.
>
> OK, Red, on the ground at Pointe du Hoc a few feet from the cliffs. They've got the cliffs marked off now with barbed wire fence, like a cow fence so you won't fall over. A few seagulls sailing up over the top of Pointe du Hoc. OK, Red, not too far from where you brought the regiment ashore. I just ran into Lieutenant Colonel Brower with his yellow braid; he turns out to be the President's aide.
>
> And, Red, I'm standing now with some of the Rangers who took Pointe du Hoc, and let me ask a couple of these folks to say hello to you.
>
> A hello to Colonel Red Reeder. "I was the battalion surgeon with the 5th Ranger Battalion, Reeder, and I enjoyed myself at Omaha Beach."
>
> "Red, this is General Collins. Red, I wish you could be here. Red was one of our fine soldiers on D-Day. Did a wonderful job, and like all good men he was up front, that's how he got wounded. Red was a great fighter and a great chap."

General Collins, he will like to hear those words from you, and I thank you very much for that.

". . . The only difficulty is Reeder isn't here himself." No, he made the twentieth reunion, but he couldn't make the fortieth.

And now the President is talking to General Collins. And the President has lifted off in his helicopter, heading for Utah Beach. The Dutch Cavalry Band playing, of all things, "Won't You Come Home, Bill Bailey?" "I know I'm to blame. Ain't that a shame . . ."

They line up with Reagan on the left end of the line. In fact, Mitterrand leads them in there himself.

All walking down towards the water. And Reagan stops and salutes our armed forces contingent, and now they move off. And the President walks down the line in front of the troops with the Queen and Mitterrand, and he's approaching the American Colors now.

Back aboard the helicopter again, and now we're heading up towards Cherbourg, so that we're going right along the lines of the way that the 12th attacked. So we're headed up towards Montebourg. So the line of attack of the 12th is right out my left door now.

Just crossed over the creek which leads inland from Quinéville and about at the location where the German 709th Division and 77th Division are on line on the map that I have. You probably remember those units pretty well. They had some long days during that period, I see. And now we've got clearance, and we're heading for the west coast. . . . And I see the hangars of Cherbourg field up ahead.

I felt good, making this recording. In some small degree, I had paid back my mentor.

Part 5

Southern Command

22

Southern Command, Panama

"Four countries in the area were facing insurgencies."

Coming out of VII Corps I was promoted to four stars and assigned to Southern Command, with headquarters in the Panama Canal Zone. I landed in Washington on 23 February 1985, with the family. The day was an usually warm and sunny one, with a hint of spring, so we decided to drive out to Mount Vernon. We had lived close by between 1969 and 1972, in Stratford Landing, in a little ranch house that I discovered was on land once owned by George Washington, the part called "the south farm."

The day after we arrived, I spoke to the chiefs of the services at their meeting in "the tank," their conference room. I started by admitting that I didn't know much at all about the Pentagon and the Washington scene, having served less than two years in the building some time ago. One of the chiefs, I forget which, commented that I was probably much the better for not having served there, and there were some chuckles. At that point they all seemed to settle back more comfortably, and their exchanges with me became, I thought, avuncular. The session went well. In the afternoon I went over to the hill to see Newt Gingrich, at his request. We talked about the history of the United States in its relationships with the rest of the hemisphere. Later I met with General Paul Gorman, whom I was replacing as commander of Southern Command. As in our meeting in Mainz when I went to work for him as assistant division commander, I enjoyed both what he expressed and how he said it: he had a great sense of the dramatic.

Paul Gorman is, without doubt, the most brilliant of all the officers I've known: not always right, not always free of diversionary predispositions, but the most brilliant. He is also the toughest, with a view of the world that can only be called pugnacious. His quick mind—ever conceptualizing, synthesizing, and innovating, and full of ideas—has no room for tolerance. But these qualities—his irascibility and utter lack of patience—must be put aside in favor of his sheer intellectual heft.

I remembered him at Ap Bo La, Vietnam, standing in the road next to a crater that still smelled of cordite and fresh earth. His face was sunburned raw, blistered and peeling, and he licked his split lips with a thick, dry tongue. The cracks spread out from the corners of his mouth like those around his squinting eyes. He seemed to me now little changed.

We went over to the Old Executive Office Building, with its high ceilings generating echoes as we walked down the ornate old hallways. There was an argument going on as we came up the staircase to the second floor, and it resonated all around us. I met an obviously busy Marine colonel, Oliver North, who said he would help me when there were issues involving the contras. He would indeed, running afoul of the law as he sought with near evangelical fervor to bring down the Sandinistas. He did much toward that end, but in so doing nearly brought down the administration.

I met next with Robert (Bud) McFarlane, the National Security Advisor, in the White House. We talked longer than expected, and then Bud looked at his watch and said, "Oops. I'm due to be in with the president. Why don't you come in with me?"

It was my first visit with President Reagan. Tall and wide-shouldered, he seemed to take pains not to be overwhelming; he had the gift of being both impressive and unassuming. His hearty handshake and down-home smile made you feel good, and his corny jokes conveyed an assurance that he liked you right away and was truly happy to be talking to you at that moment. His ease cured your *un*ease; his ordinariness allowed you room to be *your* ordinary self, too.

The president walked over and stood by a chair opposite his desk and waited while the other people drifted out. Vice President Bush took me by the arm and guided me to the chair next to the president. I felt lucky and full of anticipation to be heading for Panama, three decades after my time in Puerto Rico and Colombia in the same command. It allowed me to see those days from a quite different point of view—then from bottom up, now from top down.

We landed at Howard, the Air Force Base near the Panama Canal, and drove over the Bridge of the Americas, then through the town of Balboa and up Ancon Hill. Although I had spent a month in Panama as a lieutenant three decades earlier, I had no idea then that the Southern Command headquarters was in an old quarry on this majestic cone-shaped hill overlooking the Miraflores locks. I had never thought to ask; such questions were beyond my scope of interests in 1957, when I served as an umpire on a parachute exercise at Rio Hato, a dirt airstrip on the Pacific side, some seventy miles north of the Canal. I remembered the barracks of Fort Clayton, where May winds continually rattled the open screen-work and drove papers or anything loose hard against the screens on the other side of the room. I remembered the "Panamax" ships—built with a beam just under 110 feet wide, the width of the locks—shouldering their way through the tall grass of the fields to slip between the massive doors.

Panama is, from ocean to ocean, a geographical quirk, and the Canal is a place where the things you see every day are hard to believe. I remembered close-knit houses in Balboa with their meticulous stucco-and-tile construction. I remembered the sense of quiet contentment there—until a look down the hill to the slums of the city made for an uneasy contrast. But I did not remember the quarry, or even the hill itself. From the air the quarry is a gash in the side of the jungle-topped hill, carved out in 1915 to supply concrete for the Miraflores locks. From a distance it looks as if it had been chopped out by a giant axe, with one scythe-like horizontal swing followed by a downward vertical chop. It doesn't seem logical to think of a quarry enclosing a hamlet of beautiful old white wooden homes, green lawns, palms, great oaks, and tennis courts.

We drove along a street lined with tall, sentry-like palms all at attention, and turned into the circular driveway of what looked like a warehouse. My daughter Erin said, "Wrong place. This must be the officers' club or something." After some hesitation we accepted the driver's assertions that this was indeed our new home. Later I learned that the neighborhood had originally been built about twenty miles away during the excavation of the Canal, and was then later disassembled and moved by rail to the quarry. We walked up the broad stairs and onto the screened porch that surrounded two sides, then proceeded into the house, where my eye caught a plaque on the wall listing former tenants. Paul Gorman was number 37, so we were the thirty-eighth family to live in the house over the past seventy years, well under par for the Army. I wondered whether it was Colonel Gaillard's home in the Canal-building days—then later found a photo of the Gaillards, he in his high-collared white uniform, she in white muslin, with the staircase in the same place.

When one of the ceilings sagged after a heavy rain, the engineers came and took it down. This gave me a chance to climb up among the roof rafters and joists, to get an idea of how the house had been taken apart and moved from the Gaillard Cut to Ancon Hill. I saw that the numbers painted on the various sections didn't match, and in many areas the old notches in the timbers had not been used, but new ones had been cut. The house seems to have been reassembled from portions of several houses. The builders must have picked and chosen the trusses and walls from what was most easily available as they came in on railroad flat cars.

The screened-in porch was eighty feet long, and was cooled by sections of a canvas awning that was raised and lowered by large cranks. One former resident had painted one of the crank handles bright red so that he could theoretically explain his control over the north-south flow of the Canal. It was still red, and made for interesting conversations about the sense of humor of someone among my predecessors. There were, however, termites—and not just in the walls. Although they fear the daylight, termites are astute and brave wanderers, willing to take all kinds of risks. We had had cockroaches in our Manhattan apartment (they nested between the fold-out extension panels of our dining room table), but they were nothing compared with these Panamanian termites, who tunneled rapidly into the walls, filing cabinets, and rafters, and even burrowed into a misplaced and forgotten box of Kleenex.

My new assignment was an abrupt change in many ways from the standoff on both sides of the Iron Curtain and the related face-off between massive nuclear missile armories that characterized the Cold War. I had moved from a countersuperpower strategic environment into a coalition for democracy ambience, with a focus on internal national relationships and the political versus military struggle for control over infrastructure. I was leaving Germany and the command of a U.S. Army Corps of 83,000 troops to assume command of a joint force of Army, Air Force, Navy, and Marines amounting in strength to 9,154. This was, clearly, to be a different kind of posting. Four countries in the area were facing insurgencies of significant size: El Salvador, Nicaragua, Colombia, and Peru.

As soon as I started to talk with the U.S. ambassador to Panama, Ted Briggs, I knew we would work out as a team. I acknowledged that he was the president's representative in the country while I was the regional U.S. military commander, and that anything I did on the military side in Panama I would clear through him. He said, "I'll be glad to work things out together." I responded, "Yes, but you're in charge." And that's the way it went. I told my staff and commanders that, when it came to Panama, we were on the ambassador's turf, and he had to know about anything we were doing. No surprises for Ted Briggs, I said.

In Latin America I knew that in some cases I would be dealing with military leaders who saw themselves as the highest authority in their country. Panama's General Manuel Noriega was number one on that list. Panama was a crossroads, with all the troubles that came from being an attraction for elements that had little need or use for the locals. As far as the United States was concerned, the security and proper functioning of the ten-by-fifty-mile Canal Zone had been practically our only national interest, and all profit from the passage of about thirty-four ships per day went back into upkeep for the Zone—a manicured area that seemed frozen in the time when Norman Rockwell paintings captured the look of American towns. For Cuba and many other countries, the free ports of Panama and Colon welcomed marketing; for many others, drug trafficking had been a boon.

Another player on the American side was retired lieutenant general Phil McAuliffe. When, in 1979, Phil retired as commander-in-chief, Southern Command, he accepted an appointment as head of the Panama Canal Commission, a position he held for ten years. A veteran of World War II and Vietnam, he had commanded in Panama for three years and, at this point, with thirteen years in the Canal Zone under his belt, he had plenty of experience and was a great source of advice on Panama, on the region, and on relations with Washington.

Then there was Noriega, the cynic from the seamier side of things. He had seen many of us come and go. He had lived through years of corruption of all kinds, and he knew how to exploit it all. In my first talk with him I sensed that he saw me as another in a long line of transients in Panama, just passing through, one after the other. In the decades after the United States built the Canal, we created the Panamanian military, which, thanks to our indifference to all other national institutions, had become the only effective organization in the country.

I may have looked on Panama from my porch in Quarry Heights, but I had broader impressions of the situation in Southern Command in early 1986. Mexico was a next-door neighbor of special interest, albeit beyond my military area of responsibility. The same was true of Cuba, although both countries had a strong effect on the rest of the hemisphere. Guatemala was recovering from instabilities caused by its army's destructive interior policing. Belize was feeling pressure along its borders and getting some help from the British. Honduras was caught up in troubles and worries stemming from its role as a strategic pivot, and it also had its share of domestic challenges, including suppression of its own insurgency in the northeast area around San Pedro Sula and problems with the contras on the border with Nicaragua. To this might be added an unstable border with Guatemala in the north and some Nicaraguan gun-running through the Gulf of Fonseca in the southwest.

El Salvador, with the help of fifty-five or so U.S. military officers and NCOs, was dealing with troubles in several directions. Four insurgencies, loosely connected, challenged the government, which was seen as dominated by its own military forces and unable to provide for the needs of its citizens. Insurgents in Nicaragua had overcome a dictator and gained control of the country, only to then create a Marxist-influenced government that stumbled along and did more to cause anguish for its people than it did to help them. Colombia at this time was near exhaustion from thirty years of hard fighting to establish "Orden Público"—years that seemed to show gradual success, until the drug cartels came along. After a heroic effort, the Colombian armed forces seemed to be winning, until they were driven back by massive armed resistance on the part of vicious drug cartels. Ecuador, Bolivia, Venezuela, Paraguay, and Uruguay were to varying degrees likewise under pressure from the ever-growing drug traffic. Peru was wracked by the brutal, merciless campaign of the resurgent Sendero Luminoso (Shining Path)—a pseudo-Marxist movement that the government was trying to bring under control. Chile had General Augusto Pinochet, who was being gradually pushed out by democratic forces.

Costa Rica, with no military forces, was a calm ship in the middle of stormy seas, trying hard to keep out of the way of unpredictable actions in the rest of Central America. And the large and powerful country of Brazil was an inner-directed democracy that was successfully improving its national infrastructure.

And then there was Panama: a mess, dominated by the ruthless military leader Noriega, corrupt in its political structure and practically everything else, extending to heavy drug-hustling activity. The country was scheduled to take over control of the Canal from the United States on 31 December 1999; and it was badly in need of widening in order to serve ships of more beam; but basic planning for how to do this had not yet begun.

So much for a glance at my new surroundings. My mission could be characterized as "help our Latin American neighbors and thereby ourselves." My thoughts went back to my Wakefield High School days when Miss Caswell selected me as a graduation speaker, whereupon I picked out and memorized some words written by William Rose Benét, that began "America means good neighbors. It meant that long before we had a Good Neighbor Policy."

I saw my task as setting an example of the subordinate, but essential, role of the military in the government. This was not simple. In this region, the military sometimes saw itself as the protector of the constitution—only too ready to take charge if the governing structure did not seem to be following the rules.

Part of my mission required me to be prepared to respond if any of this unstable and complex, multifaceted mix of possibilities should expand into war. At the same time, another part of my mission was to keep the United States from being drawn into war—that is, unless we wanted to be involved, in which case we needed to have a plan for whatever the alignment of participants turned out to be. David Petraeus, then a major, was teaching in the Social Sciences Department at West Point. That department makes it a habit to send its professors off to the broader Army in the summer. Upon learning about this, Petraeus asked Colonel Kaufman, head of the department, to let him come down to Quarry Heights in 1986. In order to better understand the situation I was in charge of, I—with a great deal of help from Petraeus—wrote out my views on the challenges of security in Latin America.

I had to be ready to help the contras, but I was not allowed to communicate with them.

There were some experts I relied on. I talked for hours on end with Brigadier General Fred Woerner. Fred is a brilliant officer with deep experience in Latin America. He put together a team that I inherited. Everybody wanted to take part—Gabriel Marcella (International Affairs Advisor), Caesar Sereseres and Luigi Einaudi (from the Bureau of Inter-American Affairs at the State Department), General Bernie Loeffke, Admiral Richard Ustick, and Max Manwaring (an expert counterinsurgency advisor). I asked, do we understand our mission? After we've arrived at a consensus on that, what are the implications, what are the side issues?

General Wickham, chief of staff of the Army, had asked me to make a series of five speeches to British military audiences in honor of Kermit Roosevelt, President Roosevelt's son, who had served with British forces in World War II. I put together my usual stack of index cards, gave the five speeches, and with the help of my British friends I was able to visit with some of their best experts on counterinsurgency strategy.

One of these, Richard Clutterbuck, invited Ginny and me to stay overnight with him. I knew Clutterbuck from his visit to the Fletcher School in 1971, when he and I spent a day going over the strung-out Revolutionary War battlefields of Lexington and Concord. At Clutterbuck's invitation, we drove down to Exeter to spend two days with him in his stone house, with walls some four feet thick. At breakfast we had "free range eggs" from chickens who watched us with mild interest from the kitchen windowsill. We talked about the possible future of political violence and the mistake of thinking that a ten-to-one ratio of military to insurgents will overcome them, and the importance of communication with the populace. He asserted that if military action creates a public sense that the military is not accountable, the government will have lost the goodwill of the people and they will seek an alternative.

We also visited the home of Sir Robert Grainger Ker Thompson in the West Country, hunkered deep in a rolling part of the moors. He was another expert on counterinsurgency strategy. As we drove up to the front door, I remembered a well-meaning comment someone had just made in London about the Thompsons: "Don't be surprised—the wife is Irish." Being of Irish stock, Ginny and I took offense, and we both said as one, "We're Irish, too!" When we entered their home, we stepped by a saddle and trappings that were thrown over the banister rail leading upstairs. There were chickens again, this time walking around in the kitchen. Ginny and I felt very much at home, as if we were in Macroom or Georgetown, our Irish homesteads.

Thompson had two crowning points on the strength of government. First, you must have law, a penal code, and police standards. And the second? Commitment. Frank Kitson, a British Army officer who wrote extensively on low-intensity conflict, and his wife, Elizabeth, joined us the next day at the Clutterbucks', and again we had an excellent experience of give-and-take in the world of insurgencies.

A day or two later I went to Oxford to see Sir Michael Howard, a British military historian. Driving downhill into his courtyard, with its light-gray stone buildings, then looking for Michael, I got a few peeks into his Spartan and closet-like, yet comfortable, even enticing, book-lined rooms. In one of those I discovered Sir Michael. My notes on my visit begin with the words, "Right into substance." He wanted to set forth what he saw as indications of the changing nature of war, focusing especially on the ever greater importance and effectiveness of communication. He turned to the elements of power and I brought up the idea of "uncomfortable war." He moved to the development of third world governance. I talked about Central America and instability, with the contras as my example.

A few weeks after leaving my good friends in the United Kingdom, I gave a talk in Tel Aviv on technology in the current and future Army corps. The Israelis had published *Air Assault* in Hebrew, and I was happy to extend the connection. The working title of my address was "The Saber and the Computer."

From my time in the 24th Division, I had been pushing both heavy-light operational capabilities and air-ground combinations. David Petraeus and I often exchanged ideas about these issues, to the degree that we were able to read each other's minds and to converse in a kind of short-hand. As in our time in the 24th Division, Dave organized a stream of writing projects. Four of these papers he assigned to himself; he helped with the writing of most of the others—including mine, which together with our broader writing on the challenges of security in Latin America we made into "Uncomfortable Wars: Toward a New Paradigm," published in *Parameters* (December 1986). In the meantime, Petraeus wrote a comparison of El Salvador and Vietnam, focusing on the difficulty some military thinkers had, and still have, in giving more attention to low-level fighting.

Back in Panama, there were rumors aplenty concerning Noriega, who had vastly more money than he could ever have earned on his modest government salary. Nothing important in Panama could come to pass without at least his tacit approval. Some said that Noriega had worked for (and was paid by) the CIA and U.S. Army intelligence and may have been on salary with other U.S. organizations. His network certainly extended well beyond Latin America, and his life was laced with rumor and innuendo. Ted Briggs and I tried to see what records existed, but it was difficult to connect with Washington on this. We could not uncover any verifiable information.

In many ways Noriega was a menacing influence on the entire region. He knew how to manipulate greed and fear. He directly controlled the Panamanian port authority, the Army, the police, the prison system, the intelligence organizations, the international airport, the railroad, customs, and roads—and just about everything else that took place in the city and the rural countryside. Indirectly he controlled mayors and governors; he also was connected with the banks and major businesses. He influenced elections and political decisions and very likely controlled drug trafficking (which certainly couldn't have proceeded without his consent) as well.

Ted Briggs and I built a strong partnership for dealing with Noriega. We agreed to keep in close contact with him, but in ways that would not increase his importance. We would try to appeal to his pride, his sense of how he would be seen in history, his opportunity to usher in a new era. Step back, we said to him, start turning over control to a democratic government. Think of the life that has to follow your inevitable retirement. Concentrate on training and development of an army that can defend the Canal and deal with the drug issues. Set an example.

One of our early moves had to do with Noriega's officially scheduled retirement in January 1986. In April 1985, Ted and I had agreed to work together to make that happen, although we had intelligence advising us that Noriega would see to a "rearrangement" of his cabinet in order to provide enough support for his remaining in command of the armed forces for an additional five years. We talked about ways that we could possibly turn Noriega around, make him see that his service to his country lay in leaving a military organization well trained and prepared to take over the mission of protection of the Canal. If we wanted to influence Noriega to the degree that he would accept the proper place of the military within a Panamanian democracy, we would need to show him that we believed in what we were talking about. We would have to convince him of the importance of showing that he was subordinate to his own political leaders.

The main thrust of our argument went like this:

Omar Torrijos (the effective leader of Panama for over a decade, who negotiated the Panama Canal treaties with President Jimmy Carter) left you a legacy. You've made contributions: rural development, customs efficiency, railroads; but you have not allowed the government to develop. Canal 2000, the plan for its turnover, has many ramifications. If it is seen as enmeshed in corruption, the number of ships in the Canal will drop from the current thirty-four per day. A corrupt government can't deal with the Canal—it will deteriorate. Are you afraid of a democratic future? What will be said of you, compared with Torrijos?

On Monday, 4 March 1985, Azuero, a large peninsula southwest of the capital, celebrated the opening of a rural bridge. Panama's president, Ardito Barletta, was there—but Noriega took the spotlight and credit. Here I had my first opportunity to converse at some length with Noriega and to see something of his style. He had a scarred and lumpy face, with puffed eyes, a broad mouth, and a short chin. His nickname—and he had chosen to embrace it—was El Sapo, the frog, and his Panama City office was highlighted by his extensive collection of little frog statuettes—ceramic, carved wood, marble, plaster: colorful frogs, happy frogs, dull frogs, all sitting there on shelves and tables and on his desk.

Noriega delighted in his popularity with country folk. On this occasion, he cut and ate a chunk of roasted boa, stood close by as a cow was slaughtered, ambled along with an old man leading a pig on a rope, and posed for photos with a feather-decorated young girl.

I thought I might be able to make some progress with Noriega, and at any rate I wanted to keep up communications. What I tried to do with Noriega had much to do with how I saw my country's place in the world and the relationship between the United States and Panama. I stayed in close contact with Noriega, although there was much going on elsewhere in Latin America. Noriega's success as a populist was not to be discounted.

On 15 March I had breakfast with President Barletta, who at least was more open in speaking his mind, and with Bill Pryce, then acting ambassador. Barletta talked of favoritism, nepotism, cronyism, and cliques: "Business can't run on patronage," he said. Then, as if he wanted to forget it all, he looked out the window of the presidential mansion. "There are really three architectural styles in the city of Panama," he observed. "There is the old city, with its Spanish fort and cathedral and plaza; there is the new city, with its skyscrapers, hotels, and banks; and there is the old Canal Zone, with its homogeneous, manicured acres of concrete houses and tile roofs. One problem will be to maintain this beautiful combination."

That was Barletta. Nothing about the Panamanian people, the country, or, indeed, the slums *between* the old city and the new, slums that could not have differed more from the beautifully maintained swath of the country that was the Canal Zone.

The day before we met with Barletta, Pryce had told me that he wanted to look for an opportunity to discuss the president's lack of adequate communication with Panamanian industrialists, union leaders, and others. Bill said he felt that Barletta was not getting across to the people and was therefore causing the man in the street to believe that secret machinations were going on—or that Barletta was just too weak to do much of anything. I promised I would try to bring that up if the opportunity arose in talking with him.

Near the end of our breakfast discussion (which went on for two hours), Bill did bring up this point, telling Barletta that his lack of communication gave rise to a lot of suspicion. Barletta responded with a kind of mini-history of the months since he had taken over in late 1984. He described how as a new president he tried to move the country away from a paternalistic and conspiratorial view of business and finance and toward what he called more of an Anglo-Saxon approach. He knew, and tried to express to his people, that this would cause some initial sacrifice, but that it would be better in the long run. He admitted, however, that he had been defeated in this attempt, and that he had spent the early months of 1985 picking up the pieces of this effort. He now felt that industry and the unions were coming together in opposition to him because nobody wanted to make sacrifices of the kind that had to be made.

I responded that, as a military man, I was not sure I had the kind of understanding of the situation that he and Bill Pryce might have, but that it might be worthwhile to express the views of a newly arrived outsider regarding the political situation and the image of the presidency. Barletta expressed a lot of interest in hearing this, so I was encouraged to continue. I commented that I thought he had done some very important things and had had some successes, but that these were not well publicized because of a lack of communication and interface with the various groups that constituted Panamanian society. I shared with him the example of his visit to the United States, which had helped the country receive additional support from the IMF and the World Bank, and pointed out how little of the true importance and significance of this effort was picked up in Panamanian newspapers or other media. This was a great success early in his presidency, but he had not been able to take advantage of it in order to improve his standing. I added politely that I felt he needed to be communicating more than he was.

Though he nodded and seemed to agree, nothing changed after our meeting. Two months later, Barletta was ousted under pressure created by Noriega.

One day several weeks later, I received a call from National Security Advisor John Poindexter. He told me he would be flying down from Washington to deliver a message from the White House for Noriega, on the subject of the legitimate responsibilities of the military. Ted Briggs and I set up a meeting, not in our offices or Noriega's but in a small reception room in U.S. Air Force headquarters at Howard Air Field. The time was set for seven o'clock in the evening. Present at the meeting were the three of us and Noriega, with his aide-de-camp serving as translator: Noriega was articulate in Spanish but uncomfortable in English. Poindexter led off by setting forth the roles of the military as he saw them—seeing to the security of the nation, overseeing international participation in UN and regional structures, taking civic action in time of crisis—and then observed that there were limits, and that military leaders should be aware of those limits and observe them carefully.

Noriega responded, "The U.S. military built the Canal. They provided the leadership for running it. They built the railroad and ran it, and when they turned it over to us it was to the National Guard, not the government. They established the customs operation and the management of the airport and again turned it over to the National Guard. The Panamanian government has never created the infrastructure to provide governance and public works in the countryside; it has always depended on the Panamanian National Guard to do that. Should we stop? Who would take up this work? We are at it seven days a week. Who else is ready to work out there, seven days a week, for a soldier's pay? What are we talking about?"

Having delivered his message and used up the script to which he was tethered, Poindexter listened stolidly, calmly puffing his pipe while Noriega answered. He repeated several of the things he'd said earlier, and then stood up. The conversation was over. The word had been passed.

A month later, Admiral Bill Crowe, new chairman of the Joint Chiefs of Staff, visited Southern Command. He and I met with Noriega, but there was no repeat delivery of the Poindexter message.

Crowe had much on his mind beyond Panama and Noriega. His guidelines were "Keep things quiet—we've got enough going on in the Middle East, the Caribbean, and South Asia and across the Iron Curtain. Stay pointed toward the year 2000, when Panama takes over the Canal. Panama will need a security force, so let's not try to put it out of business now. Just put Noriega in his place."

On 13 January 1986 I had a long talk with Noriega. Ted Briggs had OK'd my attempt to deal with him one-on-one, soldier to soldier. I started with his conduct at the ceremony to open the bridge at Azuero. From my notes just after the briefing:

G: You took the credit. The President looked like a casual visitor.

N: I invited him to do more. He could have claimed all the credit he wanted. That's one of his problems. He doesn't like to be out front, and he doesn't enjoy being with people.

I then turned to the murder of Hugo Spadafora, a political activist who had been critical of Noriega.

G: The only way to respond to the pressure is for you to support an independent investigation of his death.

N: Spadafora was involved in so much dirty politics that there could never be a valid conclusion about him. Besides, he was killed in Costa Rica. There are many strange things that occur across that border. Some German killed three little kids up there not too long ago. Part of the trouble is the drug trade. Spadafora was deeply involved on the international side. It would be a never-ending investigation. Anyway, I'm not the one to speak to about that.

G: Admiral Poindexter was right when he said you are too involved in the government of Panama, and also on the business side. These are not the responsibility of soldiers. It can only lead to confusion or worse.

N: If we get into anything, we get back out as soon as possible. It was the President who requested us to take control of the railroad, for example.

G: It has been your action [the ouster of President Barletta] that caused the U.S. to reduce Panama's $10 million in assistance to $4 million.

N: I know what it really is: bureaucracy. The bureaucrats in Congress—here, and in the U.S.

G: How is [replacement president] del Valle going to have

influence when it's obvious that you were the force that made this change?

N: We'll make it. The new President is looking good already.

G: The economy of Panama is not looking good.

N: We thought Barletta could succeed, but he played to the politicians.

G: There should be a national plan and a set of periodic meetings to guide the implementation of it. Your President and cabinet and you and our ambassador could meet and exchange ideas. It has been done elsewhere.

N: Let's do it here in Panama. It would help your embassy to separate the wheat from the chaff. Some of what they get is good, but much is *boliche* (valueless).

G: Your military role and mine should be basically the same. We should set an example of good civil-military relations, protecting democracy.

N: Any president needs to be out front, needs to utilize his people, not just the military. He needs to understand history and also the present. The military in this country did not create the problems of the last sixteen years; we are in fact trying to address the problems, get them resolved. Several new small political parties have sprouted up. We are helping these parties. The next president will fly on his own.

G: Admiral Poindexter's visit shows you how far away the thinking in Washington is from the thinking in Panama.

N: We have tried to maintain the best possible relationship during this lapse. The [U.S.] ambassador is listening to one side only.

G: You must show movement along certain lines: suppressing corruption, allowing democratic development, response on the Spadafora case, moving the army out of government and business and out of using civic action as public relations for the Army instead of the government.

To my notes recapping our conversation, I added the following:

His overriding characteristic was a deep cynicism, a lack of trust in anyone, and a conviction that Panama politicians are entirely corrupt, making it useless and dangerous to believe that anything but sheer power could keep the country out of chaos. When he worked for Torrijos he "saw what was really going on," he once told me, and he became convinced that nothing could stop the succession of corrupt political leaders. This he saw as justification of his own actions.

Noriega remained confident that his system was working well enough to keep him in charge. As for the pressure from the United States, which had cut off some of its aid money and had grumbled a bit, the gringos were too involved with El Salvador, Nicaragua, and Colombia, too dependent on cooperation with the anti-drug effort, and too close to the year 2000 turnover of the Canal to do much of anything about Panama, especially because it would look like just another foray into the historically sensitive countries to the south. It couldn't happen, he told me.

Noriega wanted power, but he was content to stay behind the curtains and let the political side work for him. He had connections in the U.S. The same Americans who criticized him were willing to support him in many ways, and this helped cultivate in him a deep cynicism.

It was not, of course, just in Panama that problems existed in the United States Southern Command (SOUTHCOM) region. On 18 February 1986 I went to the Colomoncagua camp on the western border between Honduras and El Salvador, a hilly and forested place where Salvadoran refugees, mostly families of insurgents but also people who wanted to escape the conflict, were stopped by Honduran soldiers who were fighting guerrillas on their own side. The camp had dwellers who had been there for as long as six years, protected and assisted by teams from the United Nations, interrupted by sporadic outbursts of internecine violence. The camp was a microcosm of the troubles of Central America in the 1980s. Suspicion and fear cut communication. No one would talk about the future. It was difficult to get a response even to the greeting "Bien día," because it wasn't a good day for any of them. My aim for the visit was to stock up knowledge and vocabulary for use later.

On 28 January 1987 Ginny and I were staying with U.S. Ambassador Clyde Taylor and his wife, Ginny, in Asunción, Paraguay. It was late when we closed the door of the guest room, and as we prepared for bed, a dark-shouldered mantel clock over the fireplace informed us, in a rich and solemn tone, that it was, in fact, one o'clock. When we turned out the last light and climbed into bed—a bed so grand that it seemed like a barge—the only sound was the heavy tick of that clock, which grew ever louder as we lay there. After a while it was too much for me. I told Ginny that the clock had to go.

"But where?" she asked. "We can't put it out in the hall."

"No, but we can put it in the bathroom." I lifted the clock off the mantel, carried it to the bathroom, set it on a small shag rug, closed the door, and returned to our barge. But now the clock, its sounds reinforced by the echoes off the tile of the bathroom walls, was louder than before. This would not do. I rose again, fetched the clock, wrapped it in the shag rug, and tucked it under the giant bed. I could now barely hear the faint muffled ticking, and sleep came easily.

In the morning, we forgot completely about the clock, and it remained in its hiding place as we went to the airport with the Taylors. In an hour or so we were in El Chaco. It was only when we arrived home in Panama that we remembered, to our chagrin, the clock! I jumped up, reached for the phone, and put through a call to Clyde and Ginny. Clyde answered. "Clyde," I said, "I want to confess something." I explained what happened to his clock, and where it was now located. He laughed long at this.

"Aha!" he said. "You have resolved my problem. Thank you. Our housemaid came to see me after you left. She said, 'Your *good friends* took the guest room clock when they left. I can see why. It is a very nice clock. But they also took your bathroom rug. *That* I cannot understand.'"

23

Honduras

"Maybe a fresh face will help."

For Honduras in the mid-1980s, the most likely trouble spot was Nicaragua: a threat fueled in part by our military investment and strategy. The Soviet Union was supporting the Sandinistas in Nicaragua via Cuba as part of its strategy for gaining ideological ground in Latin America; the United States was calling for stable democracy but was backing the status quo throughout the hemisphere in the name of anti-communism—without much regard for conditions among indigenous peoples, which were the source in great part of the unrest. I asked to be present at the meetings of the U.S. interagency group tasked by State, Defense, and others to deal with this situation. Elliott Abrams, assistant secretary for Inter-American Affairs and the leader of the interagency team, immediately agreed, and even changed the meeting day to Monday so that I could fly in from Panama on Sundays. Another person sometimes present was Colonel Oliver North. Admiral Crowe's advice to me was, "Stay laid back." He meant: ease up, we want to be a part of any decision making.

The contras in Nicaragua were growing stronger as a threat to the Sandinistas, who were trying to build a political infrastructure. Daniel Ortega and the Sandinistas had built a political party around a cause, and they knew how to articulate the ills and needs of a populace and to promise attractive goals. They had fought and won in July 1979 a sustained battle against a powerful dictator (President Anastasio Somoza Debayle) with a nationwide network of henchmen in the form of landowners. Ortega took over the governance of a country at the edge of collapse and a Sandinista political structure run by fledglings. Their collectivist moves to improve an entire population's quality of life failed to show much initial progress, while their efforts to empower themselves by enlarging a new army smacked of the kind of regime they had overthrown. It was hard to move ahead when the methods and results looked like old times.

The rough Sandinista style had spawned several opposition groups in support of parties that were absorbed into the political wing of the contra movement, but that resistance would never be powerful enough militarily to defeat the Sandinistas. With substantial, if sporadic, help from the United States, however, the contras were able to harass and distract an ineffective Sandinista government for the better part of a decade.

In Honduras, the army, 17,000 strong, was faced with trouble on all sides. The western borderlands were crowded with Salvadoran refugees, while in the south the contras sought a haven, spending much of their time on the Honduran side of the border, which triggered attacks into Honduras by Nicaraguan forces seeking to get at them. In the Pacific off the port city of Union, speedboats out of Nicaragua supplied the insurgents in southern El Salvador; Guatemalan refugees built huts and farms along the northern side. Honduran president Suazo Córdova and General Walter López Reyes, commander-in-chief of the armed forces, were faced with their own Honduran insurgents. Palmerola is a small airfield in southern Honduras, very well located if anyone needed sustained fighter-bomber support in that vicinity. Working with our Honduran counterparts, we had improved the base so that it could handle a battalion-size task force of U.S. Army infantry, engineers, a field hospital, a helicopter unit, and other troops.

So: we, the United States, were supporting the contras, who were fighting the Sandinistas, who had wrested control of Nicaragua away from Somoza. The contras were using bases inside Honduran border areas as sanctuaries, whence they conducted raids against Nicaraguan government forces, and from which they also robbed Honduran farms to sustain themselves. We were also attempting to calm the frustrated Honduran government by supporting its weak military forces, in a sporadic way, in their attempt to secure the country's border. For this we exacted the use of Palmerola, an airfield where we stationed Task Force Bravo, a mixed battalion-size U.S. force. (Another of our task forces was engaged in building a mountain road as a kind of partial payment to Honduras for our presence there and in various other parts of the country.)

To carry out this arrangement, we depended on our own government to partially finance the Honduran forces and the contras—as well

314 Southern Command

as, of course, our own forces. This outlay was effected by Congress, which at this time had appropriated $100 million, with $40 million to be released during 1987.

The Nicaraguan contras also were in Honduras, and something was stirring. In mid-March 1986 I made a trip to Washington and saw sixteen senators and seven congressmen in sessions, as well as eighteen senators and twenty-seven congressmen in office calls, all requested by the respective members. It was not clear which way the Congress would act on these appropriations. On 20 March, the U.S. Congress voted no on the bill that would have given $20 million dollars in military assistance to Honduras. When Elliott Abrams and Admiral Art Moreau, assistant to Bill Crowe, came down to Honduras the following day for a much-needed consolation visit, they were met with a vitriolic expression of Honduran frustration. Honduran Army chief General Walter López called the situation a *porquería*, a disgusting mess, which prompted Bud McFarlane to walk out. My view of López was that for him the release of those funds was a matter of survival for the Honduran military—and though the United States was vacillating in its support for the Army, some level of Honduran military acquiescence was needed in order to get support to the contras. I therefore advocated openness and patience, but Art Moreau's response to me was adamant: "No! I was there! It was sustained invective and abuse for two hours, followed by dinner—we tried to stave it off, and were met with a new assault." I said, "Let me try. Maybe a fresh face will help." U.S. ambassador John Negroponte agreed, and I met with General López in Tegucigalpa on 13 May.

Our meeting started out in a goofy way. After my years in Germany, and now talking for the first time with López, I said, "Veo que el Presidente Reagan va a hablar con su embajador heute Nachmittag, und. . . ." (I see that President Reagan will be speaking with your ambassador this afternoon, and . . .). Without realizing it, I had shifted from Spanish to German. The general's wry laugh broke his pained silence, and I joined in.

"Some of you tell us you'll support us," he said. "That is your part of the bargain. Others on your side then cancel it." He nevertheless released a convoy of sixteen trucks with supplies for the contras that had been stopped on the road to Las Vegas.

The meetings with the Honduran military commanders continued to be little more than complaint sessions, however. For some weeks they had been calling for the contras to leave the border areas, citing the problems caused by their incessant robberies of local farmers, and of course the illegality of their presence.

On Saturday, 22 March 1986, Nicaraguan army forces chasing contras crossed the Honduran border and created a salient about fifteen miles deep. This incursion was not entirely unexpected. There was little resistance on the part of the Honduran border guards, who fell back and merely reported the news. The contras in the area also offered weak opposition.

My preparations for such an event were in place to the degree necessary, given that we in Southern Command were under orders that kept us away from the contras—in other words, we were just to help Honduras improve its ability to be secure militarily in a time of troubles in Central America, when "being secure militarily" meant being lucky enough to have a democratic government where political leaders and military leaders knew where they stood in relation to each other, and where the people ruled.

I got in touch with Admiral Crowe to get his thoughts and give him mine. "Let's watch it for a while," he said. "See what intel comes up with."

I was prepared to airlift Honduran forces to the border areas where contra camps were located. Tactical plans were sketchy at best, because we had no contact with the contras and had done very little in the way of planning with Honduran authorities. Elliott Abrams hurried down from Washington, and we met with General López at Honduran Air Force Headquarters to keep the situation calm, then flew to El Salvador to meet with Ambassador Ed Corr and then President José Napoleón Duarte to exchange news and ideas. We followed this with a flight to Costa Rica to see Ambassador Lou Tambs. Together we made the rounds, calling for a cease-fire and a restoring of the border.

On Tuesday, Honduran President Suazo gave the order to move a battalion-size force into the area, and on Monday, 25 March, at 0600, General Regalado Hernandez launched his ground troops in sixty sorties of U.S. helicopters out of Palmerola. By then the Nicaraguan force was showing indications of withdrawal. We conducted the airlift on schedule and in good form, taking pains to keep out of contact with the contras. The Nicaraguan Sandinista forces pulled back, the contra troops pulled back, and the U.S. and Honduran forces pulled back, and nothing happened. All grew silent on the front. This confrontation was the closest we came to war: if we had engaged, we might well have seen the beginning of a war that no one needed. There was a smaller encounter a few months later, but it was quenched. By 27 March the border was once again secured. It was, all in all, a tiny operation that had contained large possibilities.

Early in the morning on the 25th, I had received a telephone message from Colonel North through the embassy in Tegucigalpa:

> Item 1: President has signed a letter to Congress on intent to use authority under 506A Foreign Assistance Act to provide Emergency assistance to Honduras to the sum of 20 million. He (President) will sign Presidential Determination tomorrow at 0930 Washington time. 20 million includes: emergency use of U.S. Military Aircraft as required to provide troop lift for Honduras. LCMs, Stinger missiles (22), 7000 M-16 rifles, 300 M-60 MG, 30 AIMG P3, Helo armament for 412 helicopters, UH-1 spare parts, 2000 2.75 Rockets, 200 Rockeye bombs, 200 MK 82 Bombs, 10,000 30 MM OSP ammo. [A laundry list of arms and munitions that we were now on tap to supply.]
>
> Item 2: Buy will start tomorrow, if Commander in Chief Southern Command desires to change any of the above must inform North tomorrow.
>
> Item 3: Message to be released tomorrow will state: troop lift if necessary, will be "to areas of very low risk of hostility."
>
> Item 4: SOUTHCOM was a routine addressee on message from Chief of Staff Honduras, Commander in Chief should see message before leaving tomorrow for Honduras. North will have message retransmitted. He does not have communication means.

I had been pressing for a visit with Enrique Bermúdez, the field commander of the contras. After the close call along the border, I found it easier to get permission to visit the major contra camp along the Honduran border. The meeting with Bermúdez took place on 16 September 1986. I helicoptered to a tight valley still inside Honduras. Huts in fog, light rain. Bermúdez was worn, tired, inarticulate. The troops gathered as for a ceremony, ragged. Bermúdez was the only leader with any status as an "inside" hero; the entire political leadership was in Miami, and it was difficult to fight a war from there.

My notes:

> Bermúdez says he has to withstand a constant lethargic grumbling about the lack of support ("the 100 million") by the U.S.

or anyone else. "Our mistake," he says, "is being too optimistic, then having to back off. The result is one disappointment after another."

My sensing: Bermúdez doesn't spend much time with the troops. Doesn't know names or otherwise show regard. We climbed a hill to the command post, a vulnerable, open, makeshift bunker. Maps on the walls. Ragged. Seem to have selected their locations as far as possible from the decisive areas, the places they would need to operate [in] if not control in or near the urban west. No knowledge of the Sandinista forces. Bermúdez stumbles in explaining what their troops are doing at the moment. At this point Mike Lima breaks in. "We had been forced out of the more open areas in the north center, Nueva Segovia, Jinotega, and thereabouts," he says, "so we moved to the borders and found them more lucrative. We have no support in the south, nothing like a structure. Everyone thinks we're rich, that we have lots of money, 100 million dollars." Mike is short, wiry, wearing a prosthetic bandage on his badly damaged right forearm. He was a field commander and is now the top logistics officer. "The limits are choking us," he continues. "Five million has to go to the Misurasata, and 30 to humanitarian aid. No more than 20 million left for operations, and that's not coming to us until a year from now."

Bermúdez talks of four "operational" commands controlling nineteen "regional" commands, with a total of 101 "task forces." He says he has 248 qualified leaders he can depend on to accept missions and carry them out, although there was apparently no campaign plan beyond these uncoordinated missions. Mike Lima has little to say beyond some wishful thinking about what the force could do if any support became available. He points out where he would collect supplies, move and store them, and put them to use. Food is the top concern, followed by munitions. Other staff officers standing around have little to say. Everything depends on small fighting teams operating with no backup for their vague missions.

In reply to a question from me on planning, Bermúdez replies, "I don't have anything like a regional strategy. I have commandants, and they have enough soldiers to constitute a good-sized fighting group. I send them on a mission. They do what they can. When they return, we give them some rest, do some reorganizing, and send them out again." He points to one of the maps hanging on the wall and another lying on the table. They are unmarked. "The veterans train the newcomers."

On 5 October 1986, a C-123 two-engine cargo plane carrying military supplies for the contras was shot down inside Nicaragua. Only one member of the crew, Eugene Hasenfus, survived, and he was captured by the Sandinista armed forces. He proved to be the key that unlocked a wealth of detail about a fantastic operation intended to get around the congressional prohibition blocking support for the contras. High U.S. political leaders were involved in this adventure.

Many things were happening at the same time. While I was dealing with the Honduras problems, U.S. Ambassador Harry Barnes had Augusto Pinochet to deal with in Santiago, and he had his hands full. He asked me for some help.

6 August 1986. The acting ambassador, Alex Watson, couldn't get access to Pinochet, so we came up with a plan. Alex set up a protocol visit for me. Pinochet sent a last-minute message to our embassy, saying, "I'll see General Galvin, Commander-in-Chief of Southern Command, but I don't feel he needs to bring the Ambassador with him or that the Ambassador needs to have anything to do with this." I sent back a note saying that it would be entirely out of the question and awkward to consider seeing him without the ambassador. This caused a waste of time, but Pinochet finally agreed, and we went to see him.

As a conversation goes, it was almost entirely one-sided. Pinochet was past his prime by a long way. I had the feeling that it had been a decade or two since he last listened to anybody, and that he didn't have the slightest interest in me or whatever I might have to say. I was a convenient receptacle into which he dropped names. And once he began to talk, it was nonstop. "I've known a few Americans before you, General," he informed me. He started with Franklin Delano Roosevelt, and then we talked our way through Truman, Eisenhower, and every president since. He mentioned a litany of every prominent American politician, at least the top four or five people from every political generation. Pinochet's monologue was a string of pomposities, a recitation, fascinating and useless. He was an international strategist, as his several books indicated. (He provided copies, which I did not read.) Pinochet assured me that he served his country at great personal sacrifice, having been the savior of Chile. He keened over his loss of importance.

24

El Salvador

"Do what's right. You don't need a lawyer for that. Your heart will tell you."

2 March 1985. Before our first meeting with President José Napoleón Duarte, Paul Gorman and I had talked over the situation, and my notes say this: "El Salvador is building, and hopefully sustaining, a national military force of about 50,000." I compared this with what information I could collect about the Salvadoran military's opponents, and they looked like a loose organization of trouble. Foremost among them was the FMLN, 10,000 fighters under the name of a revolutionary hero of the past, Augustín Farabundo Martí, whose aim was national liberation. Members of the FMLN were everywhere, and they had plenty of help. In the eastern part of the country was the ERP, the People's Revolutionary Army, with 4,000 troops. In and around San Salvador was the FPL, the Popular Forces of Liberation, with 3,000. The FARN, Armed Forces of National Resistance, was in the south around La Union, with about 2,000 under arms. The FAL, Armed Forces of Liberation, had 1,500 members in the north central part of the country, around the Guazapa volcano. The PRTC, the Workers Revolutionary Party of Central America, was present in every region, with probably 500 to 800 members. In sum, the insurgent forces were close to half as large as the Army. El Salvador would be a day-by-day battle.

The country's leader, José Napoleón Duarte, I was impressed with from the start. He looked the part of the besieged, beleaguered head of a state that was at war with itself. He had the body of a retired welterweight boxer: wide shoulders, big hands, and a face that had absorbed a career of hard punches—powerful but saggy, with bright eyes framed by a strong brow, prominent cheekbones, and sad, drooping eyelids. It was not a happy face at all. My first thought was, "This man has been through a lot. He's all scar tissue."

Having heard much about Duarte from Fred Woerner, I wasn't starting from zero; but early into the first meeting, I recognized that El Salvador had a remarkable leader: he was a communicator, a man with a strong will and a profound understanding of his country and its possibilities. As soon as we were seated, and while someone brought a tray of coffees, Duarte went straight to his central themes, the message he carried on his weekend visits to the countryside: the principles of democracy, the importance of mobilizing the citizenry, and *concienciación*, or a commitment to follow your conscience, a word that he further defined as humanitarianism in the face of wartime conditions.

Duarte faced the need for instituting and implementing a revival plan for El Salvador. The Salvadoran leadership, civilian and military, recognized that the fight against the insurgents was a national responsibility that involved the entire infrastructure of the country, from the president out to the grass roots and back. Fighting and working alongside the military had to be others, too, from the ministries of education, health, transportation, finance, and public works. The military could provide security and protection; the rest was up to the civilian leadership. In El Salvador the armed forces recognized that they were not simply fighting *against* a guerrilla enemy but also *for* the Salvadoran people, carrying out the will of the citizenry.

Duarte also talked of political "space," something that I found he often mentioned in different contexts. On this occasion he meant pluralism, while at other times the meaning was more personal and meant: enough time for him to prevail. He insisted that the most important aspect for all of us was our contact with ordinary people, that politically we had to show the people that the guerrilla ideology was wrong.

Duarte clearly felt that status meetings on the progress of the revival plan and communications on that status should emphasize that military thinking is not characterized by simplicity. "*Obras*" (public works, like bridges and roads) don't make sense unless a message to the people comes with them.

"Psychological warfare!" he would say. "What a name! Call it 'politico-military conjugality.' And while we're at it, the engineer battalion is still a battalion in the people's eyes. Why can't it be called the technical support team?"

Elected in March 1984 after winning a run-off against the Nationalist Republican Alliance (ARENA) party's candidate Roberto D'Aubuisson,

Duarte took over from interim president Álvaro Magaña in June. How did this come about?

The answer involves the one person Duarte needed most, the one person who did what Duarte could not do: Carlos Vides Casanova, chief of staff of the Army. Vides was practical: he saw that there would be no chance of success without substantial support from the United States, and that U.S. support was never going to be enough unless El Salvador became an exemplary democratic state.

Vides was moving the Salvadoran military officer corps in a new direction—a complex task. And nobody knew the officer corps of the Army better than he did. Vides had been head of the military academy for an unprecedented eleven years, and he had kept book on the stream of officers passing through. He also headed his own *tanda*, meaning in this case his own graduating class and those just before and after him, and those who served with him in the other assignments of his career. In some ways, he was the classic mentor; at the same time, he was a shrewd bureaucrat who knew people by their strengths, but also by their weaknesses.

Duarte had learned long ago that, for all these reasons, Vides alone could deliver the Army. So everything that Duarte wanted depended on Vides, but it was Duarte's political skill, understanding, and sensitivity that made the relationship work. For his part, Vides was far beyond most of his military brotherhood. His pragmatic sense told him that Duarte could bring the focus of the world, and definitely of the United States, to bear on the realities of El Salvador.

Early in January 1986 I had a talk alone with Vides. I asked him, "Where do you think we are now: the people, the government, the Army, the FMLN?" Vides replied, "Let me start with where we were six years ago, and how I think we arrived at today. Six years ago, nobody thought the armed forces could understand that they had to respect human rights. We were not called the Army of the people; in fact, we had been fighting *against* the people for fifty years. We were called 'the Army of the fourteen families' [a reference to El Salvador's control at one time by dozens of families, at least in part for lack of infrastructure to reach its outlying areas]. We couldn't defeat the guerrillas, and our excuse was that they were being supported from outside. That was not the problem. We were seen as dominating *señoreados* [big shots], even more so than the landowners. We were fighting with everyone."

"Nevertheless," he continued, "it was not simple to arrive at the conclusion that we, the military, had to change. But we did change. We supported a national coalition, and then the elections that were won by Duarte. It was hard to convince people, some of whom said at that point that we not only supported the election process, but we conducted the campaign of Duarte. Not so. The elections were clean, and I think it changed world opinion of El Salvador. Duarte became an international figure. He confirmed for us in the military that respect for democracy and human rights was the way to win the people to our side and bring the conflict to a close. Democracies have the advantage of being able to change themselves, and that is what we have done. Newspapers don't say anymore that we don't support democracy or that there isn't any democracy to support."

Ed Corr replaced Tom Pickering as U.S. ambassador a few weeks after I came into Southern Command. Corr, a short Texan, was a fiery Marine and he wanted to show it, which made him a bit rough around the edges—proud to be a solid, predictable, hard-nosed manager of U.S. interests in a country at war. On the wall behind his office desk he hung a large sketch of a hard-faced Texas cowboy, rough as can be. The words beneath said, "If I'da know'd I was goin'ta live this long I'da taken better care of myself."

It was clear to me that Pickering and Gorman had given Duarte strong support with respect to the implementation of the country's revival plan, and I wanted to keep up the momentum. Much of the credit for organizing and managing this signal change toward a far more democratic approach to government should be given to Duarte's courageous leadership and vision, and to his ability to communicate that vision to the people of El Salvador. To the armed forces he insisted, "Counterrevolution has to be a revolution of its own," and added, "I can't see calling what we are doing 'counterinsurgency.' It is a fight for democracy. Willingness to accept the rules of conscience. Not to 'beat them at their own game'—that's too shallow. Do what's right. You don't need a lawyer for that. Your heart will tell you."

The vehicle for accomplishing this change was a group of leaders who met monthly to exchange information and evaluate the implementation of the national plan. The membership of the Combined Planning Commission included President Duarte, Generals Vides and Adolfo Blandon, Ambassador Corr, and me, along with the six brigade commanders. These monthly meetings allowed us to come to agreements that encompassed far more than just military tactics and operations. They were agreements on the meaning of our actions: the collective philosophy that guided our communications all the way to the soldier and the individual citizen—including the insurgents.

Duarte led most of the sessions. He insisted that the effect of a military force is not based on its physical power alone. There is a *moral* power that must be considered—and, in fact, put in the forefront. The battlefield conduct of the leader and his soldiers says much for the cause—and wins support that makes the struggle easier.

The Army leaders believed in the meetings, which were ongoing when I arrived. They saw that their survival lay in the strength of the plan and in understanding the needs of the population. In our continuing conferences, we pulled together the ways we would measure progress on meeting the objectives set forth in the plan. We wanted to get a better grasp of insurgent activities and then communicate this information to the six brigades. We had to have a handle on logistics, so that the forces could be assured of ammunition, food, medical care, mobility, equipment, and maintenance. We had to make the new training system work. And we needed good tactical leadership at all levels. Even having all this would not be enough, however, without the coordination of military operations and communication with the development of much better civic relationships.

To meet the requirements of the plan, my commanders and I set our overall schedule to include a visit to El Salvador every three weeks, and we kept to this routine. The places we visited were different, but the issues were pretty much the same: a brief rundown of current operations and plans, but leaving enough time for other aspects. Are we winning? How do we measure that? What are we doing right? What needs improvement? And what about the soldier now coming out of centralized basic training? We asked: How can we help? What do you need most—intelligence, communications equipment, mobility?

We walked around, stopping to talk and showing proper respect for the host. We also tried to visit the local towns and talk with people—taking notes, of course, as always—and the response we received was always good. *"Otro punto para mi tableta,"* as Governor Muñoz Marin of Puerto Rico used to say: "Another point for my notebook." The comments we heard always had to do with the people's quality of life: problems of poverty, crops untended, power lines down, bridges out, sickness rampant. Government leaders gone, markets closed, fathers and sons taken away. No reliable news from outside. Taxes demanded by both sides, hurtful events always happening. No stability. No law.

The fifty-five military trainers, commanded by Colonel Jim Steele, found themselves in a complex environment. Spread across the country-side in the headquarters of the Salvadoran brigades, they were forbid-den to take part in tactical operations, permitted to fire their weapons only in self-defense, under orders to help the six brigades of the coun-try's armed forces build up their fighting capabilities while engaged with a tough and spirited enemy. Fifty-five trainers over 14,000 soldiers is a small fraction, but the trainers were successful.

Steele's job was hard. He led the American trainers; he took orders from Ed Corr and also from me; and, like all of us, he sensed that there was some kind of U.S. covert operation going on. At Toncontín air-port, unmarked cargo planes were landing, refueling, and taking off for points unknown. Part of Steele's mission called for him to oversee U.S. military support for the Salvadoran air force, and Toncontín was the most active military airport. Steele was there often. People who were unmistakably American would ask him questions about airport proce-dures, would request newer maps of the area, or would simply engage him in conversation. What was he to do in these awkward situations? It was easy to guess that some of the U.S. support for the contras in Nica-ragua was passing through El Salvador.

When news of this activity became known, Jim's name was removed from the Army list of promotions to brigadier general. I went to the Pentagon to object to this treatment and was told, "There are things you don't know." I was later called to Washington for two four-hour ses-sions on the contra affair with agents of the FBI. My wife, Ginny, was also "interviewed" by the FBI. More on that later.

Not many U.S. armed forces senior officers knew as much about Latin America as did Fred Woerner. He had served in Colombia and Gua-temala in the 1960s, in Uruguay in the 1970s, and in El Salvador and Panama in the 1980s. His ability with the Spanish language was excel-lent. His academic and military studies had focused on Latin America. Jokingly, it was said of him that when he was a captain, the Army gave him a jeep and told him, "Head south of the border, and don't come back until we call for you." Woerner had worked out a plan for helping El Salvador turn its armed forces into an organization that could defeat the insurgents. His plan also called for military cooperation in rebuild-ing governmental structures that truly accommodated the people of the country.

The plan, envisioned by Duarte and devised by Woerner, Vides, and a team, grew to be much more than that; it became a message that would change the war and would lift the image of El Salvador. But first it had to be put into action. That took a historic effort that belied the parameters of this small country, which had managed to move from the verge of chaos and collapse to a strong democracy, with a fitting and effective military establishment. Along the way in that struggle, there has been every kind of violence, tragedy, and mistake in a long, painful, and finally successful journey.

When I arrived in El Salvador in March 1985, Woerner had returned to help with an expansion of the plan he had worked on four years earlier, called "United for Reconstruction," and operations to carry out the plan were getting under way. I began a series of what turned out to be about thirty visits to help keep the focus of Washington on support for implementation of the plan.

A few months after my arrival, on 20 June 1985, in a part of downtown San Salvador called the Zona Rosa, a car moved away from the curb next to a sidewalk café, allowing room for a truck to pull in and occupy the vacant space. This was a planned act. Eight men in military uniforms and armed with M-16 rifles piled out of the truck and opened fire on people at the tables outside the restaurant, killing four United States marines, along with two other U.S. citizens and seven Salvadorans. They then drove away. One Marine had been hit twelve times.

Two weeks later, on 2 July 1985, I received a message from the White House asking me to meet White House staffer Tony Motley in El Salvador and proceed with him to deliver a message from President Reagan to President Duarte. I took off at 1800 from Howard Air Force Base for San Salvador, where I met David Passage, the Deputy Chief of Mission (Ambassador Corr was on leave), and Tony Motley. We talked, then went to the palace.

President Duarte had retired for the evening, but he came down to meet with us, and Motley delivered the message verbally. It was a question. U.S. intelligence had been able to intercept radio messages from the guerrillas and to plot their locations. U.S. Special Forces possess the capability to strike against them from the air and ground with precision. Do you want us to attack them in their locations?

The following day I dictated a note over secure telephone to Colin Powell. It follows here, word for word, as close as I can retrieve it.

> Tony Motley delivered the message to Duarte; he delivered it in a very persuasive and articulate way. Nobody took notes, because it just wasn't the kind of situation in which you would

want to sit there taking notes. Duarte had been upstairs; it looked like he might have been napping, I don't know. Anyway, I wrote some notes when I stayed with Dave Passage last night. This morning I took some time in the helicopter and wrote some more notes. On the airplane on the way back I wrote down what I thought Duarte said. . . . I don't say that everything . . . is absolutely correct, but it's pretty close to it. I'll add a little more than what's in the message.

Duarte was sitting there, and later Motley said, "I could read it on his face that he wasn't agreeing with us," and that is correct. You could read it on his face from the moment Motley started talking that Duarte didn't like what he was hearing. He listened patiently all the way through, and then said, "OK, you want my point of view?" and Motley said, "Yes, sir, I do." And this was all in English, by the way. Duarte said, "Alright, I want to tell you first of all from a personal point of view. In order to do this thing, I think if we did it this would be the end of me. For years my party fought against violence, and in fact 600 of us were killed. During the time I joined the Party till I became the president, we never, my people never responded in kind to that kind of violence. For years I've condemned the idea of a violent response in avenging somebody else, some other act. I will never condone that kind of action. I have preached democracy and freedom, I've preached negotiation, and if I went back on that now I'd be finished, I would be absolutely finished. What could I say to my own people, what could I say to the people on the street? What I would be saying is, the guy who has the power is the guy who rules. But I don't want to say that, because I don't have very much power. In effect I'd be encouraging power solutions to problems, when we in El Salvador are incapable of those solutions. A move like that would demonstrate my weakness and my country's weakness and would make me a puppet. I would not survive that. I don't occupy a strong political position with a strong political party and a strong political base. What I do represent is an ideal. An ideal that says let's turn away from violence, let's respect humanity, let's respect human rights and the aspirations of the people.

"Now let me tell you how my country would respond to it. I think that we're doing quite well against the guerrillas right now, but I think if direct action by the U.S. came into it, it would tend to show that we're not doing very well and that we need U.S. help. Now let me tell you from the point of view of the Salvadoran people, the average guy on the street. They would respond negatively. They will not be on our side or your side. They will see this thing as a change in policy, a return of the idea of repaying violence with violence and substituting violence for powers of persuasion. Right now the people support the armed forces of El Salvador because the soldiers are fighting out there against the guerrillas and the people know it. But a direct involvement of the U.S. would change the equation in their eyes.

"Now let me give you a point of view of what the guerrillas would say. First they'd say, 'The U.S. Marines have arrived, and they're killing campesinos.' Then they would do their best to hide the bodies of the guerrillas and hide any trace of the fact that it was a headquarters that was struck, if indeed one was struck. Then they'd say when you fired on those people, even if they turned out to be guerrillas, you had no way of knowing for sure at the time, and therefore it really wasn't important to you whether they were guerrillas or campesinos.

"Now let me tell you from the point of view of the Salvadoran military. Some of them might want to do it. . . . But if you could look at it in the long run, you've helped us to carry the war to the enemy. Wouldn't it be better to continue that way? Give us maybe the aircraft, I don't really know—I'm not a pilot and I'm not a military man. But maybe train us in its use, if that's the kind of armament that the Salvadoran military needs. I'm not going to try to second-guess that, but give it to us and we'll do it, just like you've been doing. Why change that?

"Now from the point of view of Central America. You have to understand that this part of the world still sees the relationship with the U.S. from a historical vision of interventionism and the intrusion of U.S. power. The response in this region would be negative.

"Now from the point of view of the U.S. and the rest of the world. The other nations will tend to view this not as a response to terrorism per se, but as the beginning of a direct involvement of the U.S. in the war in Central America. I've worked hard, visiting Europe, visiting the U.S., visiting other areas to present a view of El Salvador as an independent small nation worthy of support, striving towards national unity. Such a U.S. direct action will tend to show us as too much under the influence of the United States.

"Now how about from the point of view of the USSR and our Marxist enemies. You know the picture they would paint of this, I don't have to tell you. Their worldwide program with this information is already strong, and they'll have new fuel for the program.

"Now how about from the point of view of the U.S.? I think I know the U.S., and I'll tell you that I believe that opinion will be divided. Americans will not like this idea. It is a violent idea. Congressmen will come here on fact-finding business. They'll want to talk to me about my opinion and they'll want to talk to everyone in El Salvador about it. They will take it back and bat it around the Congress.

"Now from the point of view of the media. Thousands of press will descend on us here in El Salvador, as they did before when we had problems like this. They will all want to go to the scene. Some will want to go to the guerrillas to get their opinion of the attack. Accusations of all kinds will come from that. Others will go talk to the campesinos or talk to anyone they can find to get their opinion. And all these different opinions will be expressed and comments will be made on these opinions, and comments will be made on those comments."

That's about what he said. Now Tony weighed in again, and he argued valiantly that really what we're talking about here is something isolated from all of this. It's just an isolated attack on terrorists; it has nothing to do with the war in El Salvador. And in effect, Duarte said, "I could never buy that. I just don't know where you think you're coming from on that." So then Motley said, "Mr. President, I appreciate your time. I would tell you again, and I've said this many times, the president of the United States didn't tell me to come down here to tell you what to do. He sent me down to get your opinion. I'm very glad to have that opinion; I'll take it directly back, and tomorrow I will talk to the president about it." And Duarte said, "OK, my friend, let me give you one piece of advice. Your president is under a lot of pressure. Do not advise your president, and do not let anyone advise him, to think about hatred and revenge. Your president is a symbol to the world, as America is a symbol of freedom and democracy. He should act to strengthen and preserve this symbol of an admirable America to whom others look for example." And then he said, "I apologize for my response to you tonight. I've just been rambling. . . . But you have to remember that you came here, and this was a complete surprise to me, I had no idea that you were going to talk about anything like this, and therefore I had to talk while thinking and think while talking, so please forgive me." And that was at 2215, 45 minutes after our arrival. We shook hands all around and left. Now that's what I'd like to put in a message to you. If you want it I can get it in the typewriter now and I'll send it. OK?

Powell wanted it, and I sent it via back channel. We did not send in Special Forces.

October 1986. Earthquake.

It was a big tremor, with its epicenter right in downtown San Salvador. I was sure that the U.S. response would be quick, and that with an American Army field hospital in Honduras, I would get orders to respond. I alerted Task Force Bravo at Palmerola to assemble a team and three C-130s to get ready to go. I asked Corr what was needed. There was no word from the State Department or the Pentagon, but I knew that we would respond, and anyone could tell what Duarte needed. On that day, on my own initiative, I sent Corr two UH-1 helicopters from Task Force Bravo in Honduras, followed the next morning by a CH-47 Chinook that was rigged for internal and external loads. By eight o'clock on that day we also had sent four C-130 Hercules aircraft from Panama with 72 of our troops—mainly medics and engineers. By that time, we had a message from the State Department that the numbers being reported by the Red Cross were 400 dead, 6,000 injured, and 20,000 homeless.

The State Department had created an on-call operations center, which gathered itself together and recommended what to do. My decision to send immediate help from Palmerola is what I would have done if an emergency occurred near any U.S. troop concentration. I felt that my gesture of quick assistance would in any case be a drop in the bucket compared with what was bound to follow from Washington. But I was wrong, at least from the perspective of the rules. I soon heard from Julia Taft, who was in charge of the State Department's Crisis Management/

Operations Center: "You can do whatever you want, but the Defense Department will foot the bill. You're not in charge. We are in charge."

She was right. I should have waited for orders, but my days as an Army medic told me to get going—medics don't wait. She invited me to stop by the State Department and see how she ran things. I did that, and though the meeting got us back on the right foot, this tension would surface again in our painfully slow response to other Latin American disasters.

25

Colombia

"Homecoming to tierra Colombiana."

I think big cities have their own collective smell. Manhattan has the smell of a steel mill. San Juan has the smell of the endless wind off the sea. Even in the rain, Berlin smells dusty, maybe because of Teufelsberg and other hills of war debris. (The "devil's hill," Teufelsberg is a gigantic artificial mound composed of the rubble created by the pounding of bombs and shells in World War II. To say that the city "fell" would be an understatement. Virtually all the city's structures came down in ruins that, as was the case in all of the many targeted cities, had to be carted away to make room for rebuilding—but carted away to where? Often the answer was a hill nearby.) Bogotá smells of burning eucalyptus wood and raw gasoline. Why? My theory is based on altitude: automobile carburetion is different at 6,000 feet. On my first time back, in April 1985, I didn't need to see the mountain barrier—Cristo Rey, Monserrate—or feel the upland chill or smell the eucalyptus or gasoline to know I was in Bogotá.

Awaiting me in the capital was a group of officers, all immediately recognizable as old friends across thirty years of soldiering after their experience as cadre instructors or students at the Lancero School. After lunch at the officers club and a wreath-laying ceremony at Quinta Bolivar, we went together to military headquarters. There we sat around a large, ornate table and talked as old companions will. We might as well have been seated around the formica-top table at Tolemaida, so familiar were the faces. "Pollo" Fernandez Guzman, my closest friend of them all, now a retired cattle farmer. Manuel (Manolo) Guerrero Paz I had known as a captain in Tolemaida; the rest were then lieutenants, like me. Now we were generals all. Guerrero Paz was chairman of the Joint Chiefs; Brigadier General Carlos Augusto Narváez Casallas was direc-

tor general of Army Schools; Major General Sergio Mantilla Sanmiguel
was head of the Escuela Superior de Guerra, the Superior School of
War; José Nelson Mejía Henao was comandante de las Fuerzas Milita-
res (head of the armed forces); Rafael Samudio Molina was minister of
defense. It was a homecoming to *tierra Colombiana*, more a reunion than
a briefing. Guerrero Paz, the senior of us all, later to become his country's defense minister, said, "Jack, your Spanish reminds me of the way
we talked, our style, thirty years ago." We were overflowing with reminiscences. It took us a while to get down to business. When we did,
Guerrero Paz led off.

As a lieutenant, I had written an article on the structure of the Colombian army entitled "Guerra Completa Con Seis Brigadas" (A Complete War with Six Brigades) for the Colombian army magazine *Ejercito*
(Army). In it I compared Colombia's forces with those of Israel, which
also had six brigades. Now, thirty years later, the size of the Colombian
army was up to ten brigades. The mission was the same, but the opposition was far different. Opposing the ten was a monster, with money,
and power, and arms that the drug trade had given it. The atmosphere
became grim as the leaders sitting around the table in Colombia's top
military headquarters turned to what they were doing in service of the
mission: *restablecer y mantener el orden*, reestablish and maintain order.

I had followed developments in Colombia to a degree since the late
1950s, but the changes were more all-encompassing than I had imagined. Colombia was a different place, and the difference was drugs. It
was the *violencia* plus money. The insurgency had become big business,
with chemical technology, armaments that could match the Army's,
and dominion over enormous tracts of terrain throughout the country. The drug lords had a presence in some of the biggest cities. As they
grew rich and more powerful, the guerrillas had become gangsters.
They were no longer as interested in running the country as they were
in carrying on the drug trade. To protect the narco-trafficking industry,
they improved tactical training and logistical support for their fighters.
They also began a systematic assault on local police, lawyers, judges,
mayors, politicians—anyone who could interfere with their business
operations. Under this kind of expansion, the armed forces were stag-
gering. The undermanned and underequipped Army and police were
so thinly spread that their only workable tactic was to conduct raids
against a growing matrix of insurgent groups in what we would call
spoiling attacks, trying to at least keep some of the guerrillas off balance—at least some of the time.

The generals had a tough but respected commander in President Virgilio Barco Vargas. They liked his activist approach, even though he scolded them often. General Mejía Henao said, "Any one of the president's ministers can expect to be called at any time of the day or night. He has called people at three o'clock, four o'clock in the morning. Four o'clock! He is normally at work by five o'clock, six o'clock, or earlier. By six o'clock he has read all of the Bogotá papers, has annotated articles, and has sent them to his ministers for action."

Someone added, "Barco calls, chastises the local brigade commander for not having enough information, and hangs up on him. Another time he says, 'You let a hundred of them take over a town?' That was Rio Frio."

Our conversation went long and the subjects were plentiful, but the single most often repeated word was: helicopters. In the end we centered on the most trying of issues, the mobility of the force. The insurgents were widespread. "When we move against them they attack in other locations, and our response is slow." All nodded. Helicopters. Must be able to move fast from place to place. Admiral Tito García Motta said the Navy's mission was to confront and stop the drug movement by sea and also support the intelligence screen with radar reports. He was working from the Archipelago San Andres to the little Gulf of Uraba on the Caribbean side and along the Choco area on the Pacific. He proposed expanding the connection with the carrier *Eisenhower*, which was supporting radar testing and monitoring. The police commander discussed current operations in the Llanos.

I did a lot of listening and came away with a bushel of ideas on how I could help. Before I left Bogotá I met with U.S. Ambassador Charles Gillespie and found that his views on the needs of the Colombian armed forces were close to mine. I said that I knew what the generals thought, but I needed to get out and see for myself. The best way, I felt, was to compare the activities around Melgar with what I knew from three decades earlier. I took this up with Ambassador Gillespie, who agreed that troop-carrying helicopters were the most obvious necessity.

On the second day of my visit, a Colombian Air Force helicopter pilot flying a Bell-212 took me from Bogotá to Tolemaida, home of the 10th Brigade, commanded by Brigadier General Roman Gil Bermudez. Flying low under the clouds, following the highway, we went over the town of Fusagasugá, where we used to stop for refreshment on the way up to Bogotá or down to Melgar. There were tollbooths near that spot, although most of the highway was still just two lanes. Not far below

Fusa, the hills begin to climb into the long mesa, with the Sumapaz River running alongside the bottom. I wondered why I didn't know the lay of the land very well, but then I remembered I had never flown the route—we always went by jeep or truck. We circled the mesa and I saw that all had changed. The little airstrip in the middle of the mesa had blossomed into a long runway. The brick buildings of the Lancero School, under construction when I was there, were hard to see, hidden by shade trees and mixed in with a parachute training tower, warehouses, and barracks. I asked the pilot to make a second, wider turn. On the west side of the mesa, the new buildings of a training school for junior leaders (sergeants) more than doubled the size of the small town of Nilo, which in my day had seemed far away from Tolemaida. Nilo, where we rode horseback through the gullies and walls of the mesa to pick out routes for Lancero student patrols.

Melgar, across the river on the east, had grown into a bustling market town surrounded by summer homes. I saw "La Roca," the cliff where we taught rappelling. The training center on the mesa was now also the main base of the tactical air support helicopters, of which there were only a few, but enough for me to have a look at the teaming of ground and air forces and also of commissioned and noncommissioned leaders. Roberto Fernandez Guzman, "El Pollo," was waiting for me at the old mansion, where we used to have English classes at the formica table and compared our bachelor lives and stared up at the sky, trying to see Sputnik. I spent a wonderful day with the 10th Brigade. I came away convinced that the one thing missing was air transport for these well-trained forces.

Later that year, on 12–13 November 1985, I flew with General Samudio to Washington, where we had a session with General Wickham. I wrote a memorandum of our exchange and sent it to John Wickham, Bill Crowe, Elliott Abrams, Nestor Sanchez, Tony Gillespie, and General Philip Gast. In it, among other things, I noted the following:

> Samudio feels that the Colombian government has made a fair and equitable distribution of available resources; nevertheless, the Army still lacks the wherewithal to operate against the guerrillas and traffickers in the numbers now appearing. Samudio especially cited his inability to provide air mobility and airmobile fire support when he is confronted by actions in different parts of the country at the same time.
>
> Samudio acknowledged that there had been problems with

financing the necessary helicopter repair parts and also diffi-
culties in coordination between the Colombian Air Force and
Army. At the same time, he stressed his conviction that the critical nature of the situation in Colombia at the moment—the
growth of insurgency and trafficking in drugs, and the con-
comitant expense of ammunition and other logistical support—goes beyond the capabilities of his country to support
at the levels required. His frustration at his inability to provide
adequate response to the threat was obvious.

I added, "The Colombian Armed Forces require a substantial assist in
improving their air mobility, which is key to the military operations
that must take place soon, or the situation will worsen."

For months I discussed the helicopter question with, I think, everyone who had anything to do with U.S. military assistance to foreign
countries. In short, I ran into the epitome of bureaucracy.

In the first week of November, the M-19 insurgent force attacked
boldly into the heart of Bogotá, firing their way into the Justice building. We supported the Colombian response, but in a minimal way—
supplying explosives and equipment. In the second week a volcano
erupted, melting a wall of snow that became a gigantic mudslide in the
town of Armero.

The horror of death in the mud—a gigantic, irresistible, merciless
flow, crushing and suffocating—was inescapable, except for a pitifully
few miraculous escapes. The U.S. response was disappointingly, colos-
sally slow. As in El Salvador, I felt we could not await bureaucratic
action. A military commander who has an emergency in his local area
should be able to respond more quickly and more generously in the
initial response. In the case of Armero, we waited until we got the go-
ahead from the State Department and arrived at last with twelve Blackhawk helicopters—but by then it was four days after the quake.

On Friday, 14 November 1986, I was in the Pentagon with John
Wickham. "Your problem is," he told me, "and the criticism, frankly, of
you is, that you don't know how to work this building. Paul Gorman
had everyone mad at him, but he knew how to get what he wanted. But
the pressure built up against him. . . ." My notes following that meeting read:

What does that mean? What do you have to know? Friends in
the right places? The collective psyche? Everyone has a pro-

gram. If the building liked me, I'd feel uneasy. "Tension," Gorman told me [to expect] back in Vietnam. Maybe Gorman's right. Seems that a lot of people don't know the building. I'm back in DC every two weeks—interagency group, Capitol Hill, White House, Joint Chiefs, Secretary of Defense. But John's point has merit. How to "work" a bureaucracy. How to deal with a turf issue. How to disagree.

It is easy to stay down in the ranks—to keep to "soldiering" activities: address the schools, visit units, receive briefings, inspect training—[and] stay away from the press. Set an example of the senior general. As what? As a soldier, of course, first and foremost and always, a soldier, skilled in the arts and sciences of war. Soldier . . . if not that, nothing; yet all advice, all influence would have to be based on what? Mere military experience has never been enough. To be influential I know I must be able to convince, to move ideas, and that means I need to be seen as objective, balanced, educated, aware of the questions of the day in their larger contexts—[and] of some intellect, some impartiality, and perhaps even some empathy. Back to my mission, which I should constantly re-study. Deterrence and defense. The "defense" part, actually, is easier. I have been trained for that all my life. Deterrence is another matter, involving politics and psychology and coordination with the kinds of people I have never really known.

I look at my notes from just a few weeks ago and they seem naïve, anachronistic.

In March 1987, Tony Gillespie and I made another of our assaults on Washington. Subject: Helicopters. After much time and effort, this latest round met with some limited success: we were given some UH-60s for troop transport and counterinsurgency efforts.

Two months after that visit, in May 1987, when I made my last visit to Colombia, Tony Gillespie arranged for us to have a chance to talk at Casa Nariño with President Barco, who told us he had a plan to defeat the insurgency: Do the good actions that attract the countryside population. Barco said he should "give the people an alternative by providing minimum social services"—roads, electricity, health care, primary education. This will displace the FARC (the Revolutionary Armed Forces of Colombia).

I say it sounds good, but a truce with FARC? Wouldn't that give them breathing space? FARC would then have time to strengthen their infrastructure.

The president's parting words to me were: "Thanks for the helicopters." The road had been rough at times, but Tony and I had come out on top. Still a question of the numbers, though: there was a continuing need for rapid movement of both the armed forces and the police, and helicopters would remain in short supply.

Ever since earliest days, the shape of Panama confused arriving voyagers, who would become lost in the jungle. This has not changed. The skinny isthmus has a twist, so that looking at its rolling hills from the front porch of the house on Ancon Hill we could see a little piece of the Pacific Ocean out to the east. The sun rises over the Pacific Ocean and sets over the Atlantic. At breakfast on our porch one morning during a visit from Senator Ted Kennedy, I nonchalantly said to him, "We like breakfast out here, where we can enjoy sunrise over the Pacific." He agreed, and our chat went on until he said, "Pacific?" We had a good laugh.

Part 6

Supreme Commander

26

Buttressing

"Reykjavik made the unthinkable thinkable."

After we knew that the Soviets could produce nuclear weapons, and especially after the successful launch of Sputnik, the question "How many nuclear weapons are enough?" was answered by the slogan, "No gaps." Our national strategy was to be rendered in terms of numbers.

This mathematical approach was nothing new. It had served us well in terms of conventional (non-nuclear) military forces, with respect to which we counted and compared soldiers, tanks, ships, and aircraft. This is where we were in 1977, when the Soviet Union deployed a new and more powerful missile, the SS-20. This was a weapon for which we had no counterpart. Now we had a gap that shook our "numbers" strategy.

The sporadic arms control meetings seemed to be going nowhere, so the United States decided, and the allies agreed, to fill the gap by fielding in Europe the new Pershing II missile and some cruise missiles. Amid public opposition by those in the West who believed that the nuclear buildup had to stop, Alliance solidarity became the issue of the day. Political leaders stood together, insisting that nuclear weapons had to be deployed for the sake of deterrence; but they eventually concluded that ordinary people would understand and support this policy only if it were seen as part of an overall effort to make progress in arms reduction. We therefore settled on an arrangement that became known as "dual track." We stated, in public, that if the Soviets withdrew their SS-20 missiles, we would do the same with Pershing II. This declaration succeeded in overcoming stiff resistance in Germany and elsewhere.

This hit General Rogers, still SACEUR, hard. He saw it as "folly," and he said so. He felt it would open a door; he called it a slippery slope. Like him, I worried about the idea of a mutual pullback of any kind—

and I wondered why the Soviets hadn't proposed it before. Once we move out of Europe, I said to myself, we will never return, but it would be easy for the USSR to move back in. We would have an ocean to cross, while the Soviet forces would have only a few hundred miles of land. I had been commanding VII Corps around Frankfurt when the Pershing II was fielded in my area, at Mutlangen, in the Swabian hills, and at Ulm, in Baden Wurttemberg. The arrival of these missiles in November 1983 had ignited new resistance on the part of some Germans. Crowds of dissidents, in a panoply of often soggy and windblown makeshift shelters, kept a vigil for weeks along the fences of the American Pershing missile unit.

As 1984 came around, while the Pershings and cruise missiles continued to arrive, a small group of Soviet politicians took a trip to London. On that visit, reported in the *Times* of London on 18 December 1984, one of the group said that the USSR was prepared to look at "radical solutions" in quest of a ban on all nuclear weapons. It was John Gaddis who pointed out that the speaker was Mikhail Gorbachev.

Three months later, following the death of Konstantin Chernenko, Gorbachev became the general secretary of the Communist Party of the Soviet Union. What followed was a series of surprising events, beginning with the Geneva Summit in November 1985, where President Ronald Reagan and Gorbachev talked about a 50 percent cut in strategic nuclear forces. Then, after the nuclear disaster at Chernobyl, came the meeting of the two leaders in Reykjavik, Iceland, in October 1986. After that summit, secretary of state George Shultz told the North Atlantic Council that nothing had happened—but some important things *almost* happened. The media, picking up on leaks, told the world that the two heads of state had talked about the complete abolition of nuclear weapons. Whatever happened at Reykjavik, it made the impossible seem possible, the unthinkable thinkable, and the world a different place. A euphoric shiver spread through Europe and out into the rest of the world.

At my headquarters in Panama, I was absorbed in trying to attend to my own responsibilities, but fresh out of Germany, I was also still following events in Europe, especially after Gorbachev announced that he would take the SS-20 missiles back to the Soviet Union and called for the withdrawal of the American Pershing II and ground-launched cruise missiles. Would the United States pull out its two best weapons? Who will have "won" in this case? My own conviction was that anything we withdrew from American forces in Europe would be gone for good—so we would be seen as having taken a step back in our commitment to our allies. Still, although Reykjavik represented a substantial risk, it was also a reaching out on the part of both sides, which would drive everything else in the agreements that followed.

General Rogers had been supreme allied commander, Europe, for almost eight years, longer than any of his predecessors, and his assignment as SACEUR was coming up for renewal. In February 1987 the White House put out the word that he would not continue in the position. Sometime after that, the Army chief of staff, General John Wickham, spoke to me about his own upcoming retirement. He said that I might be asked to come in and either replace him in the Pentagon or take Rogers's job. He asked, what was my preference? I told John I felt much better qualified to go to Europe than to Washington. "I know Europe, after spending seven years there out of the last eleven," I said to him. "I know the officers, the plans, and the terrain. Others know the Hill and the Pentagon much better than I do. I've spent only two years in the building, and that was eighteen years ago." John smiled. "Maybe that's an advantage." But he and I both knew that I could not resist leaping at the chance to command NATO forces in Europe.

I didn't know how seriously they were considering me for John's position. Later that month, Admiral Crowe called me. "The Army chief's job, however satisfying, is management," he told me. "The SACEUR's is strategic leadership."

"We have to replace Bernie," he continued. "He's been there eight years now, and we need someone like you to go over there. Anyway, you'll hear from us."

About a week later, Crowe called back and told me that Caspar Weinberger, then secretary of defense, wanted to see me. "He's going to tell you you've got the job. Get on his calendar and go talk to him. Better do this pretty soon. Make a special trip up here if you have to."

A few days later, I went to see the secretary. We had spent some time together, starting back when I was commander of the 24th Infantry Division in Savannah, and I liked him. When I came to his office he invited me to sit at the ornate little round table near one of the ceiling-to-floor windows and we talked, first of amenities, then about the situation in Panama, and then on broader issues. After a most enjoyable and relaxing chat, he told me how good it always was to see me, as he walked me to the door.

I returned to Bill Crowe's office, and the Admiral said, "Well?"

"I went to the secretary's office," I told him. "I saw Cap."

"Good. What'd he say?"

"The subject never came up."

"Well, why didn't you *bring* it up?"

"Come on now, that's not up to me."

"He forgot. Well, we've got to do it again. I'll remind him, and you get on his calendar for tomorrow."

Next day I went back. Weinberger laughed at himself. "I had such a good time with you yesterday that the Europe job completely slipped my mind. Anyway, I'm glad we get a chance to talk twice." He told me the president had liked the idea of my taking the job in Europe, and that I should be ready to go in June. At one point he said, "Bernie's done a great job for all these years, but the time has come. I think if we don't replace him now, the next SACEUR would end up being called "Son of Rogers."

"Well, my middle name is Rogers."

"See? We're almost there already."

As I left, Weinberger's military aide hurried up to me. "Did he do it?"

"He did it."

"Oh, good—very good."

I went downstairs to see Crowe, who said to me, "Jack, now that Cap has done his part, you need to mark on your schedule a briefing for the president sometime around the end of July. The 28th looks good." Crowe told me that, given the recommendations in the 1986 Goldwater-Nichols Act for shifting some of the power from the chiefs in the Pentagon to the four-star commanders out in the field, the president wanted to demonstrate this change by inviting the top commanders, one by one, to the White House to brief him in some detail on the duties and requirements of his assignment.

"He's asking all the four-star commanders to come in and talk to him about their wartime mission and the way they plan to carry it out. You'll be first."

"OK, but July 28 is less than two months away, and I haven't even taken over yet. What's the hurry? Why don't some of the others see him first?"

"Well, frankly, the president is going to need to know how you stand on the missile question, and this is a good way to get that to happen. You want to keep him waiting?"

"No."

"All right. I'll get you a new date." Crowe never asked my views on the Pershing II missile. He didn't have to.

I went back to Panama, and in the weeks that followed I squeezed in some homework—not much, actually—on the upcoming job. I sat on my porch into late evenings, reading such things as the *Terms of Reference* (what the job of SACEUR is all about) and the *General Political Guidelines*, which left no doubt that if we ever used nuclear weapons, all the allies in the Alliance would have a hand in the decision. Then the "alert measures": levels of response in case of attack and how, in the event of a surprise attack, I would take immediate control. Furthermore, I was free to visit all the allied troops designated for joint action (more than 1.5 million of them) and to form my own judgments as to their readiness—and to make my evaluations public.

When it came time to meet with the president, I had made a list of what I thought were the most vital things to do. According to my notes:

1. Above all, prepare for Reagan brief and give him an objective evaluation.
2. Keep the current NATO strategy. [If we changed it, I knew we would have to seek unanimous approval of a new strategy, a new force structure, and a new budget. Everything would be up in the air while we tried to negotiate the vast ramifications of arms control. I was aware that the last time we had revised our NATO strategy, in the 1960s, it had taken four years to get agreement on it.]
3. Do what I can to turn the negotiations toward a focus on conventional forces. [It was there that the comparison showed a large imbalance favoring the Warsaw Pact.]
4. Avoid controversy over the agreement to reduce Pershing II. What is done is done. If possible, keep from causing a Rogers-Galvin debate.

I laid out a rough plan to keep out of the argument. I would see the Alliance and U.S. subordinate commanders and hear them out on their views of our operational strategy for defense after the removal of the missiles; I would then talk with the NATO ambassadors individually, let them know where I stood, and provide them with information they could take back home. I would visit all the member countries of the treaty, talking to the military and political leadership in each. After that, I would make a public statement of my views, and then in August I would go to the White House. This sequence, to me, was essential. It was my short list as I arrived at Chièvres, Belgium, the airport of Headquarters, Allied Command Europe, on 25 June 1987.

As far as our personal plans, Ginny and I wanted to make a quiet, low-profile entrance on the scene. We decided to stay at the Hotel Amigo, hidden in a crook of forest a few miles from Headquarters. As hotels go, it was tiny and unassuming. Our rooms, on the third floor, were spare but comfortable. With the luggage inside, I settled into an armchair and reached for the television remote, which didn't seem to work. A blank screen continued its empty stare.

"Somebody show me what's wrong here," I said to the family, waving the remote.

"Let me see that," Gin said, snatching it away. Then she pointed at the little sign above the remote's button.

It said, "Duress."

Cars immediately pulled up on the patio under our windows, and a security man with a bullhorn ordered us to come downstairs. We tried to explain that all was OK, that I had simply pressed the button by mistake, but the security people insisted we leave our rooms and come outside. We followed orders.

The next day, the change of command ceremony went off very well.

In his words to the public, General Rogers did not surprise anyone. According to the Supreme Headquarters Allied Powers Europe (SHAPE) transcript of 26 June 1987, he said:

> Some of you were around when I mentioned it gave me "gas pains" in 1981 to think of the zero-level LRINF [Long-Range Intermediate Nuclear Force], and I continue to have that problem right up until this very moment—the political authorities within this alliance convinced our people that it was the way to go once we threw it on the table in 1981, and nobody thought that the Soviets would agree. After Reykjavik we realized how foolish we had been.

From *Stuttgarter Zeitung*, 27 June 1987:

> Disappointment and sarcasm, criticism of his President's course with regard to arms reduction, and concern for the secu-

rity of Europe could be heard loud and clear when Bernard W. Rogers, for the last time as NATO Supreme Allied Commander at his headquarters in Mons, Belgium, appeared before the European press, firing broadsides against the Reykjavik decisions, the double-zero solution, the threat of a denuclearization of Europe, and the lethargy and weakness of the Europeans, just as expected.

I was now SACEUR. In his time, Dwight Eisenhower had joked that maybe the title could be expanded to *Colossal* Supreme Allied Commander. Bill Crowe used to call me "the Proconsul," and his successor, Colin Powell, would phone and ask, "Is that you, Charlemagne?" My friend Bob Hunt, assistant to congressman Lindsay Thomas, used to address me as "the Emperor of Europe," and my West Point classmate Ben Schemmer christened me "SAC Universe" and in his letters to me addressed me as "Zeus." Best of all was a man whose name I didn't catch. He shook hands and said, "So you're the saucer!"

Over the next five years, the role of the supreme allied commander would continue to change and evolve to keep pace with a dynamic environment—so much so that I regularly reached out to the staff historians, Greg Pedlow and Morris Honick. I kept a phone on my desk with direct access to them, and they aided in my speechwriting and helped elucidate the historic context for our current-day decision making. Soon after I took command, I asked them to lay out the various changes in the past few years regarding the relationships among the North Atlantic Council (a political decision-making body within NATO), the Defense Planning Committee (its defense counterpart), and the Military Committee (a working group of officers from the various NATO countries). Their response took five pages of thick paragraphs. Right from the beginning I had elected to build a personal connection with the secretary general of NATO (Peter Carrington, later Manfred Wörner) and with the chairman of the Military Committee (Wolfgang Altenburg, later Vig Eide). This arrangement worked most of the time.

After the change of command ceremony on 26 June, which Secretary General Carrington had presided over, he asked me to come and see him "straight away." I went up to Brussels the following Tuesday, 30 June, for our meeting, which established an atmosphere of friendship and marked the start of a productive and enjoyable running conversation. Peter Carrington was my Irish idea of the quintessential Brit: genial, a quirky raconteur and master of repartee, open, easy to talk to, entirely likable—and at times also high-handed and sharp-edged. Carrington always acted the part of Carrington. He knew himself well and liked himself, and I liked him, straight away.

After a few friendly words, he put down his teacup with a loud clink and looked hard at me. "Do you think nuclear weapons are immoral?" While I considered that, he continued. "Why on earth would your president say in public that nuclear weapons are immoral? Of all things! And just when we're getting into what will probably be the most complicated negotiations we've ever had with the Russians."

We talked about the missiles. I told Carrington I would be meeting with President Reagan, and I outlined what I was going to be up to in the meantime, getting prepared for what my approach would be; that my predecessor, General Rogers, was correct, that the loss of the Pershing II was indeed a loss, but I believed there were ways to make up for it. We agreed that we should not comment on the reductions too early, that it should perhaps be as part of a speech. He suggested I see the Germans first—particularly Helmut Kohl, who had supported the stationing of missiles in Germany.

Carrington paused in thought for a long minute and said, "Good luck, then," and as I took my leave, he said in a low-voiced afterthought, "Don't tell them all you know. No use worrying them too much." Peter Carrington, I was to find, always had room for humor.

That same day I had lunch with Wolfgang Altenburg, chairman of the Military Committee. He had been Chief of Defense Staff for Germany during my time as commander of VII Corps. I was already convinced that Altenburg could lead any kind of team under any circumstance. He saw his position as not only chairman, but as a chief of staff and key advisor to the secretary general, and as a facilitator in helping me carry out my responsibilities.

We agreed that first on my docket had to be the Reagan-Gorbachev agreement on the missile reductions—how to handle this question without noise. I told Altenburg that when people asked me why I seemed to be taking a different position from my predecessor on the Pershing II question, I intended to say something like this: "He faced a different question. He was being asked whether or not he wanted to give up a very important weapons system, one that he strongly supported. I am being asked whether I am able to carry out the mission under the new circumstances."

As with Lord Carrington, I told Altenburg of my intent to see the commanders and their subordinates, to visit the member countries of the treaty. He nodded and said, "Remember, it's vacation time. You may not find anyone at work." I said I would look them up one way or another.

For the third time in my life, Dave Petraeus, now a major, showed up to help me in my new assignment, an act of generosity on the part of Army Chief Wickham. Dave had been on the ground in my Belgian headquarters for a week before I arrived, and the arrangement was for him to stay with me for a year before moving on to an infantry battalion in Europe. I put him to work on my most sensitive situation, the need to state my views on the arms control issues. Together with the chief of staff, U.S. Air Force General J. B. Davis, we created what we called the Round Table, made up of a team of staff experts, a gathering regardless of rank, which would change depending on the subject at hand and would discuss and formulate a tentative response to an issue, which could then be passed through the regular staff chain for normal perusal. Another team, often overlapping, was the Commo Club, an outgrowth of the public affairs office. The dynamics of that team were also effective. I would make a statement of some kind. The Commo Club would then examine it, compare it with previous statements, suggest adjustments, and put it on file, to be considered alongside future statements. The team would also recommend new "modules," or prepared statements, based on events of interest, ready for use.

The experts on the SHAPE staff—who were stronger in nuclear planning than in any other field—all agreed that we still had a viable defensive strategy. The Soviets would be giving up far more than we would. Our Alliance would lose the Pershing II and the ground-launched cruise missiles, a total of 420 weapons, but the Warsaw Pact would lose the SS-20 and three other types of missiles, for a total of 1,600. The Soviets would also likely lose some of their mystique as their Warsaw Pact allies saw them reducing their military power. They would still have nuclear bombs, short-range missiles, and artillery in Europe—but so would we.

I went out to meet with the senior commanders, as I'd planned. This took me to Oslo, Brunssum, High Wycombe, and Naples on the NATO side, and Heidelberg, Stuttgart, Ramstein, and London for the U.S. forces. There were fourteen generals and admirals in Allied Command Europe, heading the subordinate commands in the northern, central, and southern regions, plus the U.S. Army, Navy, and Air Force commanders and their deputies and my own chief of staff.

Many of my military colleagues were old comrades from earlier days in the Alliance and from maneuvers throughout Western Europe. Leo Chalupa, commanding the central region, had been a fellow corps commander in Bavaria and Baden-Württemberg. A Sudetenlander, he had been in command of II German Corps when I had VII U.S. Corps. Gerhard Brugmann, chief of staff of Central Army Group, had been my classmate at the Staff College at Leavenworth. I had served at SHAPE with Hans-Henning von Sandrart, who was head of the German Army and later the replacement for Chalupa as commander of Allied Forces Central Europe. I also knew Doğan Güreş, Chief of Defense in Turkey, from my earlier days at SHAPE working for Andrew Goodpaster. General Dieter Clauss (who would become my German deputy at SHAPE) and Admiral Dieter Wellershoff (later inspector general of the German Armed Forces) were friends I had met at the Führungsakademie der Bundeswehr (the General Staff College of the German armed forces). Because of the many ways in which NATO forces are integrated, we had shared experiences on command staffs, on maneuvers and terrain walks, in planning sessions, on firing ranges, in training centers and schools, and serving in various staff jobs.

These senior military leaders agreed that the arms control efforts carried some risks, but that the gains were obvious. Their concern was that we might move too fast with our conventional reductions, lose our negotiating leverage, and put at risk our chances of arriving at parity in equipment and conventional force troop numbers. We talked about Gorbachev and the Russian military. We felt fairly confident that, all the current activity aside, nothing much would change in the political and military confrontation of the past four decades. I suggested that, yes, Gorbachev was something new, though not entirely; yes, Khrushchev had repudiated Stalin's reign, which was a spectacular change; but, I said, the Soviet Union still existed, and if we imagined that Gorbachev's approach would result in a major change in the relationship, we were expecting too much.

We did anticipate that we would be reducing forces, and to me that meant that we would need more flexibility in our defense plans and capabilities. We talked of strategy: Should we be thinking about a change? Too early for that, we thought. Let's see if we can get the Soviets into negotiations on *conventional* forces, where the Warsaw Pact outnumbered us three to one. Until the aims of the Soviets became clearer, let's keep our feet on solid ground and stay with the forward defense and flexible response strategy. We had an infrastructure to continue to finance. The United States alone had 800 installations: not just barracks and training areas, but airfields, warehouses, port facilities, pipelines, and storage dumps (including several for nuclear warheads), along with a long-range communication network.

The military forces had seen fifteen years of negotiations under meetings labeled Mutual and Balanced Force Reductions, which had generated truckloads of communiqués and notes, during a period in which the Soviets mounted their most extensive modernization of nuclear missiles. We were therefore convinced that we were going nowhere with negotiations on these matters. We had said to ourselves for years that arms control was a cover for other activities—a placebo, and a dead-end. I felt it was going to be hard for us to change that impression.

My thinking at this time was still at the corps level, I'm afraid, and I had a strong temptation to tell the corps commanders how to do their business. I had been preoccupied with the sizable difference revealed in a comparison of U.S. and Soviet ground power, and I felt that our answer to this disadvantage would be found in a versatile mobile defense. This was a sensitive subject, because it assumed that, in defending against a strong Warsaw Pact attack, much of the initial conflict might well take place in West Germany. I was convinced that the possibility that either side would resort to nuclear weapons in the early days of war was small. More likely was a conventional conflict, involving a strong Soviet ground and air attack with or without the rest of the Warsaw Pact. Our defense plan would have to call for far more mobility than just a linear chain of forces up close along the border. We had the general defense plan, which gave us the initial orders, but a plan is only a plan, a starting point.

I challenged the senior commanders and my staffs to lay out for me how they envisioned the first two weeks of fighting if we were called on to carry out our conventional defensive mission. I wanted to see what they thought about the crises that might arise, the options we would find available to us, the decisions we would have to make, the means we might expect would be at hand for deciding among these options, and the results we would hope to attain. I wanted grist for the mill—a broad analysis that would tell us how to lay out, in priority, our requirements. If we didn't know how we wanted the battle to go, we wouldn't be able to deal with the critical questions of arms control, and our advice to the political leadership would lack a solid basis of agreement on what the early fighting would be like and what decisions might be needed. In this set of discussions, I was thinking in terms of the war games we had conducted at corps level.

Then, on 22 July 1987, President Gorbachev made another announcement: he was ready to negotiate a ban on intermediate-range nuclear weapons deployed in Europe without conditions. Gorbachev's announcement added a new dimension to our deliberations, as it took in not only the SS-20, but three other types of missiles. We studied the adjustments that the Soviets and the rest of the Warsaw Pact would have to make. They would lose 1,800 weapons, while we would give up 800.

Dave Petraeus looked for some place, some organization that could serve as a forum for me to state my views on nuclear arms reductions prior to my trip to Washington to meet with President Reagan. CEPS, the Centre for European Policy Studies, was just the right place. A think tank, it was located in Brussels, the capital of the nation hosting my headquarters, and it was the traditional place for an announcement of changes. CEPS recognized that I had a message that needed to get out. It offered me a speaking date on the shortest notice, within a few days of my request, even though most of its members were on their summer vacations. In the end, in fact, there were more journalists (some sixty or so) than Centre members in attendance; but that was fine, as the objective was to get my views on the public record, and the press was eager to hear my first detailed statement on the INF agreement (the Intermediate-Range Nuclear Forces Treaty between the U.S. and the Soviet Union).

Petraeus and I went over the draft speech at least a dozen times, working it back and forth, over and over again, in hard copy. (SHAPE headquarters was just coming into the digital age.) This would be one of the rare occasions on which I spoke from a text rather than from my beloved note cards, because I wanted what I said to be precise. I knew the press would parse my words, so I worked hard to close any seam between what I said and what the Alliance political leaders had stated. I sought to convey that I fully supported the agreement but at the same time recognized the need to strengthen our remaining forces in certain respects.

We searched hard for the right word to indicate that with one element of the deterrent mix removed, we would need to augment the remaining elements, that these elements determined both our capacity to deter and, if it came to that, our ability to fight. We considered a variety of words before settling on "buttress"—discarding others that might be taken to mean that the INF agreement was weakening our capability so much that we had to compensate substantially as a result. I thought that the resulting speech, after weeks of work, conveyed what I was seeking to convey.

On 30 July 1987, Petraeus and I drove together to Brussels. One of the requests he'd made when I asked him to work for me again was that he be allowed to ride with me to the venue at which I would deliver speeches he'd drafted (and redrafted, and redrafted). So we went together.

I began my speech with this comment: "I am, it is true, only one month into this new assignment, but I am 108 months into my experience as a field grade officer and general officer in Europe, where I have served under Generals Goodpaster, Haig, and Rogers."

I concluded by saying:

> If the negotiations at Geneva result in agreement on the "zero-zero" option—the global elimination of all U.S. and Soviet land-based longer-range (LRINF) and shorter-range (SRINF) intermediate nuclear missiles—NATO's strategy of flexible response will still be valid; however, the means to implement NATO strategy will require buttressing. Otherwise there will be a higher risk than we in the West should accept.
>
> On that basis, I support the conclusions of the NATO ministers at their June meeting in Iceland, and I support the current negotiations at Geneva to eliminate U.S. and Soviet LRINF and SRINF.
>
> There is no reluctance on my part in accepting the changes in the nuclear face-off of Europe, because I am confident that in buttressing the mix of remaining weapons, we will have kept our deterrent capability and also our capacity to fight using nuclear weapons in defense of the West if it ever came to that. In return for our elimination of some 350 Pershing II and ground-launched cruise missile warheads, the Soviets will give up over 1,400 SS-20 and SS-4 warheads, plus a substantial number of shorter-range Soviet missiles.

The word "buttressing," suggested by Petraeus, was a perfect fit. It implied the additional strengthening of a wall that is already in place and thus ready to receive even more security. To me it transmitted a vision of the famous flying buttresses of Notre Dame Cathedral.

I felt that we'd accomplished our objectives. I was on the record, but there was no battle with my predecessor. And the feedback from Alliance capitals and our commanders was positive.

27

The White House and Nuclear Arms Reduction

"The faster the better."

About noon on Sunday, 9 August 1987, I left for Washington via Kefla-vik. Flying with me were two of my staff officers, Colonels Tom Neary and Tom Lenny, who had helped me work up the charts I would show the president. As usual, I sent them to see their counterparts on the Joint Chiefs staff as soon as we got to Washington. Various staffs in the Pentagon took the gathering at CEPS (the Centre for European Policy Stud-ies) as an informational rather than decision-making meeting, and they were OK with that. In the afternoon I met with the chiefs in the tank, the windowless room deep in the belly of the Pentagon. The tank was a vault: a place where the top brass of the Pentagon—the Joint Chiefs of Staff and their assistants—met on major issues. Cap Weinberger and Will Taft, a legal advisor to the State Department, arrived to listen.

Tuesday, 11 August 1987. At a quarter of two we arrived at the White House. In the oval office, President Reagan glanced at my shoul-der patch. "That's the 1st Cavalry Division, isn't it?"

"Yes, sir."

"Well, I always feel confident when I see that patch."

Again, the president had found a way to put me at ease; in his face I saw friendly interest and anticipation. Besides secretary of defense Weinberger and Admiral Crowe, we were joined by Vice President George H. W. Bush, Secretary of State George Shultz, and National Security Advisor Frank Carlucci. In the opening part of my briefing, I talked about my peacetime missions, one of which was as custodian for nuclear warheads, the number of which silenced the group and led into my commenting on NATO oversight of "direct defense, deliberate escalations, and general nuclear response." I followed this with the dynamics of nuclear release, and then with a comparison between our warheads and those of the Soviet Union.

As I anticipated, what had been presented to me as a plan to "meet the President and brief him on your mission and structure" turned into an in-depth exchange on nuclear weapons, using charts that displayed the range arcs of missiles and aircraft from their likely launch bases. I spoke about my mission responsibilities first, then reviewed the structure and deployment of NATO and Warsaw Pact missile forces. These points were more or less routine reminders that provided the basis for a comparison of nuclear weaponry on both sides of the line in Europe— but the range arcs were not routine for the president. I then showed him a set of "before and after" maps of Europe on which I had superimposed the range arcs of missiles available to the Warsaw Pact and those available to the West prior to the planned reductions, and another set conveying the same information as it would be when the expected reductions by both sides had taken place. I said that the West would stand to lose its newest and best intermediate-range nuclear weapons, but the Soviets would give up four missiles for every one of ours. This would not only be advantageous to us in terms of numbers; it would set a precedent of reductions to parity or to zero by class, something that would benefit our side in just about every situation, nuclear and conventional, in the future, since the Warsaw Pact was a great deal bigger than NATO in both respects.

Secretary Weinberger commented that we needed to know whether our ability to deter war would be called into question as we reduced the numbers and types of these weapons. I responded that the planned reductions left no gaps in coverage, and the other side would be aware of that.

The president said he recognized the need to reduce conventional (non-nuclear) forces as well, but he said that his highest interest was to move quickly on nuclear warheads, "the faster the better." He asked about the time needed to cut back under the existing plan. I referred to envisioning the overall timing in years, and he was displeased with that. "Too slow," he said, "and the Soviets would be slow if we were slow." He added that if we brought any new nuclear weapons into Europe, the Soviets would do the same. Secretary Weinberger said he would have to agree, since that is what had been going on for two decades.

I saw how the president looked at my charts illustrating the range arcs: the area covered by the radii emanating from the Soviet side, covering all of Western Europe, and the opposing sweep of our own weapons capabilities. I don't think he had ever seen such a graphic layout. He pointed to my charts and asked, strongly, "When we look at these lines, are we making Europe uninhabitable in the future?" The message was clear to me—and clear, I think, to everyone in the room. There was a pause. I said (lamely)—not in answer, because there was no good answer—that we were taking out some of the shorter-range weapons, and now we should begin to look at strategic-level weapons. I thought of mentioning my discussions with Crowe about this, but decided not to. Secretary Weinberger noted that we had eliminated 1,400 warheads in the Montebello agreement. Frank Carlucci asked why we couldn't cut out the Lance missile and stop developing a modern replacement. Another pause. Then I said, "Nothing gets fired without your decision, Mr. President," and then I corrected myself by mentioning the weapons in the United Kingdom and France.

Vice President Bush brought the discussion back with his first question: "What would the Soviets respond with if we fired?" I answered that they would respond in kind. The president noted that there was the possibility they would go to the strategic level. Another pause.

Reagan seemed to still be thinking of his earlier question. In a soft, wry aside, he said, "I want to be at the ranch." His gallows humor was a signal to move along. We were all relieved.

The discussion next focused for a minute or two on a related issue. Crowe observed that "on exercises—war games—we have trouble getting people to fire nuclear weapons." He must have been thinking of my earlier comment on the command procedures. He went on to say that the biannual NATO-wide exercise called "WINTEX-CIMEX" (Winter Exercise, Civil-Military Exercise) was coming up soon, and as usual the political leaders of the Alliance were invited—but traditionally they sent substitutes. I agreed with Crowe that "WINTEX needs high-level involvement." No one responded to this issue, however.

I went back to my message that the European theater should be allowed to absorb the current planned nuclear force reductions until we saw how things went. Secretary Weinberger agreed, reminding us that we sent the warheads to Europe because we were outnumbered in conventional forces, and we still were.

The president didn't reply directly. He remarked that in his study of the Soviet experience, "All Soviet ideas depend on protecting their own homeland." Then, as he closed the briefing, he said of the reductions, "It is very important to be as swift as possible once arms control agreements are signed."

It had been a sobering exchange that went much deeper than just the content of the charts I had brought to the meeting. I came away assured that the president was appalled by the realities of the nuclear standoff and reinforced in his desire to do everything possible to get rid of the arms race while he had the chance. As for my briefing, he didn't like the answers he got; he didn't even like the questions.

Admiral Crowe, Vice President Bush, and I stayed after the briefing and discussed other nuclear matters, including WINTEX, the nuclear war game. Crowe and I scheduled a discussion on what we called "the SIOP question"—the bases for the numbers in the Single Integrated Operational Plan, which served as the justification for the number of nuclear weapons in Europe. I then went back to the Pentagon and joined the Army senior commanders conference, where I repeated for them my briefing to the president. They applauded me—it was the first time I had seen or heard of such a happening. I was stunned and happy. It was a heady moment for me, but a deeply serious one.

A day later, on 12 August, the president addressed the nation. As he neared the end of his talk, he said, "Let me tell you where I'm going to put my heart and my energies for the remainder of my term." He touched on five areas, including weapons reductions, about which he had this to say:

> I'm optimistic we'll soon witness a first in world history—the sight of two countries actually destroying nuclear weapons in their arsenals. Imagine where that might lead. . . .
>
> And I say to General Secretary Gorbachev, both our nations could begin a new relationship by signing comprehensive agreements to reduce nuclear and conventional weapons.

On 8 December, the U.S. signed the INF Treaty.

My first response was to study the numbers and storage locations of all the nuclear warheads in Allied Command Europe, the description of each target and the reason for its selection, and the readiness condition and capabilities of the land, sea, and air forces that would carry out the strikes. This took time and effort on the part of the staff.

When the work was done, I asked, "Who knows all of this?" The answer from the staff was what I expected: the higher staffs knew. There were copies of the plan in the major headquarters of the Alliance.

I went out to see the senior commanders one by one and said to each of them, "Here are the figures. Imagine a situation like this: A nuclear war is ongoing. We assemble in a deep bunker, and our staffs issue a report like this: 'In the last twelve hours, we have employed 75 nuclear weapons, and the enemy has answered with 100. The battlefield conditions are as follows . . . ' Do you find that to be realistic?"

"No, of course not."

"Then why don't we cut the numbers in half?"

"We need them."

"OK, then. What should the numbers be?"

"Hmm, well, there is a need for redundancy . . ." We should anticipate losses due to enemy action: destruction or capture of our ammunition storage areas; attrition of our nuclear-capable aircraft; weapons located outside the time-distance scheme of battle; malfunctions that might occur; missed communications and the possibility of other mistakes in the fog of war, including target inaccuracy, casualties, interceptions, wrong intelligence on targets, storage out of place for use, and misfires; as well as losses owing to other nuclear weapons exploding, losses to Soviet air defense, and destruction by detonation of other weapons. The reasoning was weak unless it was simply "We need to match the other side."

In October I had a good talk with Admiral Crowe in his Pentagon office, my first substantial discussion with him. He knew how power is generated, stored, and used. I showed him in detail examples of targets that were identified for several nuclear strikes, far more than would be required to ensure complete destruction. He was incredulous. He called in Air Force General Robert Herres, his deputy.

"Bob, is Jack right on these numbers?"

"I'll check."

"I can't believe this," Crowe said.

Crowe and I agreed that we had good reason to look into the number of nuclear weapons in Europe, but we didn't realize that we held differing views on the command and control procedures governing the employment of these weapons if such a situation ever came to be. This surfaced in a high-level war game that took place in Pensacola, Florida, just a few months after our discussions on nuclear stockpiles in Europe. The scenario of the game, attended by a number of civilian and military players, called for the employment of nuclear weapons in Europe. I described the chain of command on the U.S. side, in which I, as commander-in-chief of forces in Europe, reported to the secretary of defense, while on the NATO side, as supreme allied commander, Europe, I reported to the secretary general of the North Atlantic Council. This became a subject of hot dispute, with some players insisting that sole authority for approval of a nuclear strike resided in the U.S. president. I quoted NATO documents, long approved by the United States as well as by our NATO allies, that made it clear that all members would take part in decisions regarding use of these weapons. I added that in a real situation, there no doubt would be a very large amount of communication among the allied nations before a decision was reached. Others contended that such an argument was evasive, suggesting it must be clear that the U.S. president alone would make the decision.

This tension would resurface—the question of whether the Alliance strategy of threatening to use nuclear weapons was viable, when some members would not accept nuclear strikes on their homeland under any circumstances. In a sense we reached the same conclusion from very different starting points. For my part, I had become convinced that NATO could defend itself without the use of nuclear weapons at all. In this way, both camps looked ahead to prove our convictions in an upcoming WINTEX war game, two months away.

But there was much more to happen as we moved closer to the game.

28

Conventional Forces in Europe

"When they are all trying to get your attention, it's time to listen."

Talks on the reduction of conventional forces in Europe began in November 1987. As I looked into the questions that were bound to surface in those negotiations, I knew I had the support of the staff of Allied Command Europe and also the staff of U.S. European Command, as well as the help of the generals and admirals of the Northern, Central, and Southern Commands, along with their staffs. No one fully recognized the complexity inherent in coming to an agreement on the details of a massive reduction of opposing forces—and as it turned out, we worked for twenty months to arrive at that point. I had a mission—the defense of Western Europe—and everything else was secondary to that, but I did not want to get in the way of negotiations. My aim was to help stabilize the drawdown as it came along. Specifically, I held out for our taking a position of parity at the beginning of negotiations. As Gorbachev had said, the side with the highest number would have to come down.

In early December 1987, Reagan and Gorbachev signed an agreement to remove all short- and intermediate-range nuclear weapons from Europe—a cutback of enormous proportions, but one having no effect on the conventional forces in place along the line of confrontation. The nuclear forces of the West were intended to fill a gap in the size of our conventional forces vis-à-vis those of the Soviet Union and, presumably, the other Warsaw Pact nations. The Western military strategy, announced to the world, had been "deter, defend, and if necessary employ nuclear strikes to stop any attack into the soil of the Alliance members." A major reduction in the strength underlying that strategy would call for a revision of that conventional military strategy and the force structure backing it up, unless both sides achieved a parity of capabilities in some other way. In short, I needed to push for parity, and a new Alliance strategy and force structure compatible with it. But even General Eisenhower had been hard pressed with such a task. I sought out every way in which I could place the issues—national, civil, political, military, and diplomatic—squarely in front of every leader, making known my written rules of engagement, my general political guidelines, and my written permission to see heads of state, along with other such orders enabling me to get my thinking on these questions out there whenever it was possible and sometimes when it was (nearly) impossible. It worked better than I ever thought it could. In the case of relations with the media, for example, I was able, with the help of David Petraeus and many others, to publish articles in support of a new strategy and force structure.

The secretary general of the North Atlantic Council has his own military committee, with representatives from all member nations, to provide advice, along with a military staff to handle day-to-day analysis. My point in arguing for the change of strategy in the press was that with my two headquarters and all my commanders, I had the best collection of arms experts in Europe, and could be of great service. There would be hard negotiating to come and we had experience that could be of use, but we needed to be able to pick up on the new dynamics by being present during the negotiations.

We settled on an arrangement whereby officers from my staff, accredited by their own nations, sat with their national delegations, and we thus had an immediate sense of how the negotiations were proceeding.

The official source of the NATO position on details of the negotiations was the High Level Task Force, led by Assistant Secretary General Michael Legge and reporting to the North Atlantic Council. As it turned out, Legge was always starving for information. We increased the arms control section of my staff and turned its full effort toward keeping up a flow of information to his desk. My team, including the officers at Vienna, eventually grew to forty experts.

The job of searching out the numbers (we called it "counting iron") had its sensitivities. We had to have an accurate comparison of the military equipment in all the treaty categories: tanks, armored infantry vehicles, artillery, helicopters, and fixed-wing aircraft. I had several talks on this subject with Secretary General Lord Carrington and

Wolfgang Altenburg, recommending that we create a listing of equipment, country by country. They were not encouraging. Carrington said, "First, the Soviets won't give you their figures. Second, Bernie Rogers tried to get our own, and the Greeks and Turks didn't want to provide their totals, so we couldn't go on." I said, "How can I expect to command a force that I don't know in its full detail—against another force that I also don't know?" Altenburg agreed that I had every right to know—and encouraged me to search out and find the accurate figures.

"We do, in fact, have numbers," I said. "We have all kinds of them. With a quick search we've found 125 studies of the force comparisons, all different. If we don't get the correct numbers, we will be going into negotiating sessions without having done our homework. Just let me try it, and we'll see if anybody objects." There was some hesitation, however, and it was not just in the Aegean. We faced considerable challenges even in the United States in releasing numbers on the American equipment. My chief of staff, U.S. Air Force General J. B. Davis, picked German Colonel Peter Kuhn to head the team that would make what we called an "archival review," and my group sallied forth to make contacts with experts—political, military, and others—everywhere. Then began a series of point-counterpoint moves that often lacked the kind of politico-military coordination I was hoping for. We fell into the trap of the old pervasive tendency to make political decisions on military matters without any effective consultation. This was what had happened with the Greek reintegration of 1974. I remembered that episode well from when I was on the SHAPE staff myself. NATO authorities very much wanted Greece back in the Alliance, but there was no agreement in the eastern Mediterranean as to the details of the new command arrangements, especially in the Aegean. The situation became so difficult that at one point in 1974 when I was airborne in the C-54 with the SACEUR, General Goodpaster, on a flight to Turkey, our pilot informed us that his request for overflight of Greece had been turned down. He radioed to the Greek air controller, "What if I just go ahead and fly through your airspace?" and got the terse answer, "You risk being shot down." We took the long way around.

Regardless of the political uncertainties, my focus had to be not just on numbers, but on my mission. Above all, I had to be ready to fight for the defense of Western Europe, however unlikely such an eventuality might be. I stayed in touch with Chris Donnelly, the intelligence expert at the British Royal Academy's Soviet Studies Research Centre, and Colonel David Glantz at Fort Leavenworth's Soviet Military Studies Office, and asked everyone else I could the questions "What are the Soviet military folks really thinking? Are we seeing their willingness and determination to change, or is it our collective imagination?" It was hard to get precise data, hard for both sides. We kept changing our own figures as we discovered items that needed to be counted. Peter Kuhn's work would take a year, but long before he finished, the emerging numbers were of great use. The Soviet military saw what we were doing and launched into the same kind of study, which came out shortly after ours. This time, the numbers on both sides were more accurate than ever, and focused on the kinds of military equipment that would come into play in the negotiations. In rough terms, the comparisons showed that the Warsaw Pact armament was more than double the size of NATO's. Kuhn's "Blue Book" review showed the West (and the Warsaw Pact members) how important it was to demand parity.

The comparative study by Kuhn paid other dividends in ways I hadn't anticipated. Our support of Legge's task force was reflected in seventy-five papers on the details behind the numbers, and the list kept growing, convincing the Soviets that we were serious, prodding them into publishing their own listings. We had, at last, accurate lists from the United States, and from all of the NATO countries. Before this, all we knew was the force contribution each Western nation was ready to make to the Alliance, but not the entire national force structure of each country. We were also able to compare the figures we had gathered through intelligence means with the figures that were produced by nations on both sides, knowing they would be inspected in the verification program.

There was still the question of whether or not lists of military weapons systems are accurate indicators of combat power. The biggest error of intelligence estimates throughout the Cold War was the tendency to concentrate on the "iron on the battlefield" to the virtual exclusion of other considerations, such as the Soviets' strategy and their overall capability to carry it out—a factor that was affected by their relationship to their allies, their doctrine and operational art, their leadership, command and control, logistics, mobilization structure, and much else. It was too easy for us to simply rely on materiel, production of weapons and ammunition, and Red Square parades and other such indicators of power. Driven by a strong remembrance of past invasions to an overemphasis on armaments, the Soviets had concluded that "massive punitive response" was their only defense, and had consistently misjudged the rest of the world. They thought they were being helpful to their cause, but in fact they helped us maintain our solidarity within the Alliance. With our Blue Book study I could send a steady stream of data to Vienna by way of Legge at the task force. Our information was recognized as authoritative, especially when the Soviet study showed figures for NATO that were quite close to those in our report.

In the Pentagon in the fall of 1987, the sentiment had been "We're not going to get involved in this." Crowe told me, "Let the other side of the river come up with something, and we'll look at it." After the impulsive but vastly productive meeting at Reykjavik, where the Joint Chiefs of Staff had been left out, there remained little desire for the military to get involved. The Pentagon's interest in conventional arms control had not reached its peak. In early September I went over to the White House and met with the National Security Advisor, who at that time was Colin Powell.

In the White House you don't go very far from the Oval Office before you run into what I call the warrens, the small hallways with twists and turns, dotted by people at desks in corners. This was the first time I had gone in to talk to Powell in his White House job. I expected tension, but I should have realized that his office would be an island of tranquility, just as when we both were commanding U.S. corps side by side in Germany. I asked him who was working on the U.S. side of conventional arms control.

> Powell: We have a team in town.
> Galvin: Same people who are working START [the Strategic Arms Reduction Treaty]?
> Powell: Basically, yes.
> Galvin: Doing both? How can they work both negotiations at the same time? These are really two different issues. You need different expertise . . .

I started on the details of the Blue Book and the High Level Task Force, but I didn't need to. Powell didn't like lectures. He would jump into the flow of thought and take over.

> Powell: The focus has been on START, but we'll be turning to CFE [Conventional Armed Forces in Europe]. It's true that we

haven't done much yet. We do need to get going. And, OK, I don't think we can do it with the same guys. I'll talk to the interagency group this week.

Vice President Bush asked me to meet him in London on 2 October 1987 and fly with him to Brussels for a special session of NATO representatives to discuss the status of arms control negotiations. Al Keel, who was then U.S. permanent representative to NATO, and I flew to Heathrow and joined the vice president on Air Force Two to Brussels, which gave us about an hour with him. Air Force Two was like a European passenger railroad car: a corridor on one side, compartments on the other. My notes:

VP: "Talk to me about Scud vs. Lance." (I made a sketch for him, showing their respective ranges, and said Lance was old, cumbersome, costly, slow, and limited; it was obsolete technology.)

"What about France's Pluton? How does it compare?" (I said that Pluton was workable in the sense that anything with a nuclear capability is of enormous importance, because a single shot can change the thrust of a war situation.)

"What about the French-German brigade and the getting together of the two countries? How do you see that one?" (Anyone who knows history will not object, although it may involve a departure from the Alliance.)

"Will the Soviets now start after the British and French on their nuclear weapons?" (Yes.)

"Review for me the details of SNF [Short-Range Nuclear Forces]." (I provided details about Scud, Scarab, Frog.)

"Dual-capable aircraft. What's unique to them?" (They are configured to carry nuclear weapons; others are conventional only.)

"Where will they be stationed?" (UK.)

"Can't have circumvention?" [Isn't there some risk of violations?] (There will be a verification program.)

"Give me your view, the whys and wherefores of nuclear weapons in Europe." (Europeans want a strong conventional defense in Europe with U.S. strategic nukes as a backup. U.S. wants the same, plus short-range nukes in Europe as a deterrent. So far, we have a combination of these approaches.)

"Should we stay at current levels of nuclear weapons in Europe?" (We can afford to reduce.)

Later, General Altenburg and I sat in on the vice president's talk with the North Atlantic Council of ambassadors. The vice president praised the INF agreement—noting with approval that an entire class of nuclear missiles had been eliminated—and added that all that was left was an agreement on the details of verification.

Turning to his weeklong visit to Poland, Vice President Bush remarked that the president had sent him on this visit to emphasize that the American commitment to the Allies was as strong as ever, not declining—"not by a damn sight."

In early November 1987, I flew to Monterey, California, to attend a meeting of the planning group on nuclear weapons. On the way back to Europe, we refueled in Boston and I went home, where I found my father in a black mood. I had come across some photos of the old family house and barn, but he didn't want to see them. I took out our notes on a book we were hoping to write—a study of New England brickwork, something that had been part of our exchange of letters over many years. He said we could discuss that later, and turned to the subject of diarrhea and its various causes. The main problem, he said, was eating too much, and the solution was to cut back. At that point he weighed about a hundred pounds. I knew he was looking for a fight. Under white brows, his light-blue eyes were all that was left of color in his gaunt, unshaven face. He napped, we talked, and he napped again. Gradually his mood changed, and we revisited some of the old paths of our favorite memories. He asked about friends long ago dead, and I made up some news about them. We laughed over family stories I had heard many times before and was more than glad to hear again, and he showed me sketches of a fireplace chimney he was going to build when the weather got better. A few hours later, I leaned over the aluminum walker by his chair and kissed my father, the mountain. I said I would be back soon.

A month later I wrote my last letter to him. I wanted to be with him just one more time, even though he was gone:

You were laid out for all to have a last look. I didn't take much of a look for a while, but just waited till the place cleared out for the evening and then went up and knelt and looked you over.

And there we had our last communication, and it was a good one. I was glad to have it. Even though the undertaker is an old family friend, the ones who fixed you up didn't know you very well. Some stranger parted your hair in a completely different place and gave you a modish look, very up-to-date, a combing you'd have done only as a joke.

And I could swear that hovering on your lips there was just the slightest smile, as if to say, "How about that, Jackie?" I smiled with you, and I liked it. There wasn't anything you could do about it, so your secret smile was just right. No use trying to fix anything now. We're both part of the ritual; better to go along with it, and get on with our new relationship, the continuation under new rules. It's not as good as what there was before, but it's not nothing. . . .

It's hard to stop writing after 38 years, so I won't. I thought it was the end of the letters, as well as the end of talks to look forward to and anticipations of good quiet hours at the kitchen table talking about the neighborhood and the town, about history, about Isaac Davis at the Concord Bridge and Chamberlain at Little Round Top and Daniel Townsend at Lynnfield, repeating things we'd said before and feeling comfortable about it, talking about jobs you'd finished lately, fireplaces you'd built, the ordinary things, the stuff of life and love and fathership and sonship, talk to put the rest of my life in perspective.

I bought a copy of Gorbachev's book *Perestroika* in January 1988. I had read excerpts of summaries and commentaries and some of the speeches. Part of the idea of perestroika is to have an open mind, which I don't think I had, even though Gorbachev's words had been called expressions of hope for peace and a better world. In his efforts to explain himself, Gorbachev is both articulate and sometimes incoherent. He rightly calls the book a collection, and his rambling style, with its many repetitions, makes the book appear to be a cut-and-paste from speeches. I see now that in my marginal notes I focused on some of his occasional rabble-rousing. The European nations, he writes, have been abducted and are being carried off across the ocean; there is an onslaught of mass culture from across the Atlantic. "Indeed," he writes, "one can only wonder that a deep, profoundly intelligent and inherently humane European culture is retreating to the background before the primitive revelry of violence and pornography and the flood of cheap feelings and low thoughts." There is not much of this in the book, and what there is may be a result of hasty scissoring of the "collection." More important to me was his insistence in 1988 that NATO be dissolved, that the United States get out of the "European home," and that there should be no reunited Germany. At that time, I gave little credit to his many calls for new thinking and comprehensive security, but I did underline these words: "It is high time the great powers realized that they can no longer reshape the world according to their own patterns."

The following month, on 23 February 1988, we held a briefing for the NATO military committee on the work U.S. colonel Huba Wass de Czege was doing with the Warrior Preparation Center. By this time we had supplied answers to questions such as "What is the definition of a tank?" and provided schemes for getting accurate verifications of compliance with the treaty. We often suggested a question that would help the negotiators, then went ahead and drafted the response.

Some months later, on 2 June 1988, I attended the Bilderberg Conference at Telfs-Buchen, Austria, on the defense of Western Europe. These sessions bring together influential leaders from many areas—government and politics, defense, finance, and other industries. At the end of the day, Henry Kissinger said to me, "Let's go for a walk." I was happy to hear that. The paths there are beautifully organized and left rustic, as if they had been there for centuries, and the late afternoon was cool—sweater weather. As usual, I wrote down our exchange right afterward. Clouds were coming up through the valley, bursting through the pines and spilling onto both sides of the hotel. There was some light rain sometimes, some fog, glimpses of gray mountains with vertical strips of snow. A kind of New England day. I think that Kissinger's first question was aimed at showing me he did not want to talk about the conference. As soon as we started to walk he said, "What do military officers read?"

The question made me cautious. It sounded more like a complaint than a question. So I parried with, "That's simple. We all read [Kissinger's own] *Nuclear Weapons and Foreign Policy*. Beyond that, I don't know." He liked that. I went on, "There is a lot of professional reading. The service schools are always publishing new reading lists and sending out book reviews and asking folks for a list of their favorites."

Kissinger: On military subjects. Primers.
Galvin: Some of them, I guess. But most are pretty broad-

ranging—biography, history, strategy, leadership, some novels. Not too much poetry, I imagine.

Kissinger: So some officers read fairly widely outside of their direct professional interests?

Galvin: It's hard to know what other people read. I would hazard a guess that about half of us read a lot. And there is the question, how do we read? Do we dip here and there? Do we write notes to ourselves in the margins? Do we read the same books over again? I remember that Doctor Johnson said he had not finished a book, but put it aside instead. When someone expressed surprise, Johnson said, "Do you really read all of a book?"

Kissinger: What's your list?

Galvin: I don't have one.

Kissinger: No favorites?

Galvin: Not that I want to wish on somebody else. I do think you can't be too smart to be an infantry soldier. When I was a captain, I escorted Cornelius Ryan on a visit to West Point. He had been a war correspondent in Italy in World War II. He said he was standing with some other writers on a night somewhere near Anzio, when a truck pulled up and half a dozen second lieutenants climbed out. He listened as a sergeant pointed out soldiers who would guide these young officers up different paths into the hills to take over platoons in combat. It got quiet, he said, and then one of the correspondents said, "I wonder if they are well read," and we knew what he meant: The youngsters couldn't have had much training or experience for what they were facing next, but maybe the knowledge they had picked up through their reading along the way would help.

Kissinger: So you resolved to be well read.

Galvin: Have you kept an account of the books you've read?

Kissinger: No. Have you?

Galvin: I started once or twice, but it became a confusion of different kinds of books at different times. *The Golden Bough*, *The Singer of Tales*, "The Hedgehog and the Fox," *The Red Roan Pony*, *The Light That Failed*, Grant, Sorrel, Blackford. . . .

We both went on naming books and authors. I have been unable to find the lists, to my regret.

Kissinger: It strikes me as not useful.

Two weeks after the Bilderberg Conference, on 15 June 1988, John Shaud arrived and took over as chief of staff of the headquarters at Casteau. John and I had overlapped as cadets at West Point. He was the last Air Force general on active duty to have graduated from the Military Academy. In his time, West Point turned out lieutenants for both the Army and the Air Force, but by 1958 the Air Force had built its own school. I was lucky to get Shaud—an astute, fine officer, one of the best I have ever known, whose personal advice and help as well as his keen management of the staff made complex issues simple.

John taught me many lessons, one of the many he himself learned while flying an F-4 low level up the Ho Chi Minh trail. The ceiling was treetop, and he was caught in a crossfire from the ground. He pulled straight up into the clouds and felt lost as he watched his instruments. He didn't believe the needles and lights, but he obeyed the messages they sent, and he came out on the cloud tops OK. He told me, "When they are all trying to get your attention, it's time to listen."

29

WINTEX, the War Game

"Everything was changing."

The main purpose of the biannual series of "WINTEX-CIMEX" (Winter Exercise, Civil-Military Exercise) war games was to make sure that all senior political and military leaders of the Alliance were familiar with what would happen in the event, far-fetched or not, that nuclear weapons might be employed. There would be hundreds of decisions made up and down the chain of command that would affect the final decision at the highest levels to use or not use these weapons. But as long as we possessed these weapons, we had to be able to control them.

A secondary purpose of the war games was to deter war by showing the Soviets that we were serious about defending the West with nuclear weapons and that we knew how to handle them. I was aware that plenty of people in high places, in both NATO and the Warsaw Pact, did not comprehend the stark possibilities inherent in this confrontation of thousands of nuclear weapons, all available on short notice, and did not want to confront them. Some political leaders offered one or another reason for keeping away from the game. All of those reasons amounted to this: "I don't want to be in the position of making decisions in extremely hypothetical circumstances. My actions could be interpreted as a commitment on my part to what I might actually do in a real war. I prefer to keep such questions unanswered."

Preparations for the exercise always began about two years in advance of each game, and the long and complicated planning for the war game was a training exercise in itself. People on the political and military staffs came and went; there were always new faces and new relationships, as well as new ideas, and much to be learned in all the national capitals, and of course within the deployed military national reserve units themselves. In the case of WINTEX 1989, the Alliance commanders and staffs drew up a proposal and sent the draft to Alliance headquarters in October 1986. In the months that followed, players throughout the Alliance organized, reviewed, and refined a war game that did not reflect the unbelievable swirl of change in the real world. In particular, and naïvely, many did not take into account the political side of the game. But some of us, including Bill Crowe, wanted the game to demonstrate that Alliance members would not consent to the use of nuclear weapons under any circumstances. This should be, we felt, the last of this kind of war game.

On Thursday, 12 January 1989, at the Air Force One Complex at Andrews Air Force Base, the Reagans bade their farewell. Afterward, I had another talk on nuclear weapons with Bill Crowe. "In sum," he said, "we have to see whether we have the support of our allies; and the use of short-range nukes, which is what the strategy calls for, will either confirm it, or at least show us where we are with them on this." We had both told then–Vice President Bush that it would be good to take part in the game, and I had reviewed with Crowe in detail the overloads and redundancies in our nuclear planning and the concentration on numbers rather than targeting. I repeated that we had far more nuclear weapons than we needed, but as long as we had them we had to be ready to use them, and we would train ourselves to high standards of capability. We both knew that everything was changing. The Soviet threat seemed to be evaporating, but at that moment remained unpredictable. Until the mission changed, we would have to stand ready.

Time went on. Soviet forces pulled out of Afghanistan. Spain indicated that it wanted into NATO, but it wanted the U.S. Air Force fighter wing out of the Torrejón air base near Madrid. (Crotone in Italy turned out to be the proper location for the operating base of the wing.) In November 1988 we had begun working on the details of the agreements by which Spain would establish the coordination of its military forces with those of the rest of NATO. These coordination agreements stirred up questions surrounding Gibraltar and the security of the Canary Islands, along with that of the seas around the Iberian Peninsula. Great Britain and Portugal had long-standing interests in the geography of that complex region, and I wanted a quick resolution on the military aspects of the agreements. I of course remembered well the six months I had spent with the senior military of Spain almost a decade earlier, working out the doctrine by which Spain and the United States would coordinate the efforts of their armies, navies, and air forces in combined operations and exercises. At the ceremonies in November, I met with

King Juan Carlos, who remembered the amphibious training exercise in Almería. That effort between two countries was much simpler than what we intended to do now between Spain and fifteen other allies, but I was full of optimism and determined to do everything I could to make this full coordination of Spain's forces come about as soon as possible.

Many of the officers I had worked with at junior levels were now high up in the Spanish military structure, and that helped: we knew each other well, and we found it easy to team together. My old friends were very happy that I had kept up my Spanish over the years, although they smiled now and then at my Latin American idioms and talked about "the return of Panama Jack." I enjoyed the ribbing, and since I had fallen in love with Spain years earlier, I enjoyed the work as well as the renewed friendships.

Meanwhile, the Solidarity Party was legalized in Poland. Conventional and nuclear arms reductions talks were showing progress. Communists were being voted out of office in the USSR. There were political disturbances throughout Eastern Europe.

In September 1989, Colin Powell was on the cusp of replacing Bill Crowe as chairman of the Joint Chiefs of Staff, and he thereby became a target of my work of reminding everyone of the need to carry out the tasks of the commission called Conventional Forces Europe. I met with Powell in his office in the White House. Once again I told him that we needed support for the negotiations on conventional forces in Vienna. I talked about the days with General Goodpaster in 1974, when I helped him with speeches that were almost unchanging—where if I put in a new idea he might take it out, leaving a note, "OK as is." Now the things I said were often quickly overcome by new considerations, and logical constructs that once seemed clear and appropriate quickly grew antique and stale. The scope of ongoing change was both broad and seemingly instantaneous. How far can Gorbachev go? Whither Germany?

Monday, 23 January 1989. I was in Grosvenor Square in London for the dedication of the statue of Dwight Eisenhower that now stands in front of the U.S. embassy. Margaret Thatcher was there, along with David Craig, U.S. Ambassador Charles Price, John and David and Julie Eisenhower, Bob Dean (the sculptor), the Archbishop of Canterbury, and Vernon (Dick) Walters. Bob Dean and I knew each other well—in earlier years we were in the same cadet company at West Point. I said to him, "Bob, I never would have thought of you as an artist." "Well, Jack," he replied, "I never dreamed you would actually graduate from the Academy."

The statue of Eisenhower is well done. It represents him in June 1944, looking toward the Channel and thinking of the Allied troops assaulting the beaches of Normandy. His jaw is set, his brow is grim, his eyes piercing. At the unveiling I stood next to John Eisenhower, who as an Army major had been my English professor at West Point. As the covering cloth fell away from the statue, John said quietly, "I know that look, all right."

That evening at Chequers, I was trying to convince Margaret Thatcher that we could be more flexible about military-to-military contacts between NATO and the Warsaw Pact. I thought we could open up some communication and reduce the level of confrontation. I went through some of the moves we might make with the Soviet military. She was not excited about the idea, so I stopped.

"Do you think we perhaps are moving too quickly in these matters right now?" she asked.

"There's a lot to be done, Prime Minister," I responded, "and we need to get on with it. I don't think we want our military to look like old curmudgeons." That's as far as I got.

"General," she looked at me with that eagle stare of hers, "World War II was *won* by old curmudgeons."

We were getting closer to the opening of the WINTEX-CIMEX war game. Command posts in North America and Western Europe were setting up and rehearsing the communications network. I could not stop the game. Making that move could be taken to mean we did not want the political leaders to be involved, and would confuse everybody. But I could tone it down and still get the practice.

I talked again with Crowe, who said he wanted to use the war game to show what the relationship would be among the players when it came to the use of nuclear weapons. He held that any decision would be a U.S. decision alone. I argued that the game was a game, and by its nature would always be oversimplified. If in the event of an actual conflict we were reaching a decision point on nuclear weapons, there would be a great deal of communication going on—"tons of it," I said. It would begin at the slightest indication of war—and even before hostilities broke out, we'd have done an enormous amount of talk on what we might do. So why should we make the game something that was contrary to NATO procedures that had been created with the consent of the United States and of all the other countries in the Alliance? Among the other nations there would be consternation and damage to the Alliance as a result of our not keeping faith. What if other countries did this? Were we unwilling to stay with the principle of collective decision making? The UK and France had their own weapons. If they launched strikes independently, they could open a full exchange between NATO and the Warsaw Pact regardless of what the United States did.

My line of argument didn't work with Crowe.

The game started on 24 February 1989 and ran for thirteen days. War games are usually the work of military officers who need to practice their skills, review procedures, allow for teamwork, stay familiar with plans, and perhaps try out changes in those plans. All of this is usually a routine matter, carried out by players who are practiced, and who often change positions in order to broaden their experience. In putting together this game, we had succeeded in convincing senior civilians to take part. The players in the game took their places in their actual wartime headquarters, so that we could test our communications and try out the logistics. In the simulation, the main attack came in, as always, on the central front, aimed at the North German Plain, with a secondary strike toward Frankfurt and with pressure all along the line, from the Baltic Sea to Czechoslovakia.

Since the purpose of WINTEX was to keep ourselves up to date on our procedures for employing nuclear weapons, we had to make our situation continue to deteriorate. By 3 March, after a week of formulated fighting, I sent a message to NATO Headquarters, and also to all national capitals, warning that the scale of the Warsaw Pact attack was forcing us back from defenses along the border, that air attacks were heavy, that chemical weapons had been used against us, and that we had lost some terrain critical to our ability to sustain a forward defense. In another false report, I estimated that, unless we were able to stop the oncoming echelons, we could lose cohesiveness of our defense by 11 March.

The bank of antique teletype machines rattled away, keeping member nations in touch. On 5 March I sent another message, reporting that my earlier estimate was correct, that we lacked the power to hold on, that all available air and ground forces had been committed, that supply lines were interdicted, and that reinforcements had slowed significantly. Without the support of nuclear strikes, I said, our defenses would collapse. I asked permission from the North Atlantic Council to use the weapons and sent a list of specific targets.

At that point, as intended by the players, the war game began to come apart. The scenario had grown painfully relevant. For some of the participants, military as well as civilian, this was the first exposure to nuclear planning. The simulation was too close to possibilities that they had not considered. This was all fine for refresher training on civil-military procedures, ensuring that people could do their jobs, but it was earthshaking for political leaders, who now had to confront our idea of what lay in store if such a situation ever became a reality.

A training exercise had become for many a demonstration of what might really come to pass—but in terms of breakdowns on our own side. During the game, when I tried on the map board to move the forces of one country across a border and into the territory of another—because there was a situation requiring reinforcement—the sending nation disagreed with the move and demanded it be stopped, insisting that it created an awkward precedent. There was a failure to understand the absolute requirement for coordination and common purpose among the civilian, political, diplomatic, governmental, and military aspects of every endeavor. For some of the players of the war game, the possibilities became a prediction of a horrible reality.

These mistakes were bad enough taken one by one. Lumped together, they caused an even worse condition: a gap had opened up between our political and military sides. We were losing confidence in each other.

And if WINTEX 1989 evidently did damage to relationships between political and military leaders on our side, the message it communicated to the Soviet Union was evidently more one of belligerence than of serious resolve and deterrence.

From Moscow's *Krasnaya Zvezda*, 25 March 1989:

NATO General Galvin's "Credo" Criticized

The attempt to introduce new political thinking in the heads of people like J. Galvin will hardly succeed. His military-political credo has long been well known. You remember how when he was in charge of the U.S. armed forces in Central and South America, he threatened to occupy Nicaragua and personally led the bombing of that country's population centers from U.S. Air Force aircraft. And he viewed all Central America as nothing but a field in the battle against world Communism.

And *Pravda*, on 28 March 1989, noted: "Galvin and those who think like him are clearly devoid of the ability to respond flexibly to the challenge of the times, the changing circumstances, and the positive trends of international development."

30

Change: The Right Mix

"Don't make it harder for them."

WINTEX had its effect on much else that followed. It opened our eyes, broadened our understanding, took away much of our posturing, changed our mechanical approaches, and broke through the group-think that bound us. We recognized that we were all out of touch with each other. In the spring of 1989, everything turned to the management of change. The alliance ambassadors called me to a special session to demand, "How did we get to wherever we are now?" In a meeting of ambassadors on 10 March, I showed how bureaucratic we all had been in ignoring our many opportunities to see change coming and respond to it, and I accepted responsibility for misjudging the atmosphere surrounding our entry into the WINTEX game.

The topic was what we called "The Right Mix"—a way to reduce the size and number of field exercises while maintaining an adequate level of combat readiness. The right mix of what? From readiness activities as simple as marksmanship to complex decision making, and across the spread of forces from Norway to Turkey, we were breaking away from old ways, with less deployment but increased training. Cutting back on the numbers of people, weapons, equipment, and buildings as well as administrative activities, while maintaining fighting capability and readiness. There was much interest in all of this—not only military, but also political and diplomatic.

Right Mix made possible joint use of the Warrior Preparation Center and Computer Assisted Exercises and made us reconsider the basic rationale for our training. For example: Does using one hundred percent of the force in field training exercises guarantee the best training? With deep cuts coming and a heavier reliance on simulation, how should we plan for a more austere approach to training?

The work we had done at the Warrior Preparation Center now helped us alter many of our field exercises or replace them with highly effective simulations. I invited the North Atlantic Council members to visit the Center and see how it was in use as a testing ground, serving the conference tables in Vienna. We were able to compare force structures and levels by running them through simulated East-West confrontations, although we were still subject to the weaknesses of hypothetical situations.

With its new capabilities, the Warrior Preparation Center allowed us to enable participation by all regions of Allied Command Europe at once, partly with forces on the ground, but mostly simulated. This meant that we could, for the first time, get away from the scripted exercise, even at SHAPE. Up until this time we had worked our exercises at the higher levels by planning a war game in great detail and laying out the whole scenario in advance. Once the game started, everything would relentlessly follow a preordained scenario so that we knew that, no matter what decision we made, the "war" would roll on. Now that would all change. We would be forced to deal with a realistic and unpredictable situation and make the strategic decisions that would be required in wartime. From now on, we would confront the high hurdles as well as the low.

By the end of that session, the question had become "Where do we want to go and how can we get there?" Over the next eight months, under the guidance of Secretary General Manfred Wörner, we took on more aspects of change than I had ever imagined.

In the days that followed, I was concerned that the NATO ambassadors knew little about me and all the senior officers. We rarely talked to them about military operational or strategic matters. Our mutual interests and our contacts seemed always to revolve around the budget, the infrastructure, and our needs for this or that—bases and airfields and pipelines—making us seem like mendicants. In the comments I now and then heard, they saw us as parochial, cushioned by sycophants, full of pomp and circumstance. We in turn looked on them as stereotypical diplomats—the word itself rooted in the idea of "double," with overtones of duplicity.

I wanted to make better connections and to show them who we, the military side, are, because there was a strong need for teaming, not just for holding our hats out. The relationship between the political side and the military should not be antagonistic, though many then saw it as that. Better communication was needed. We would need to talk among ourselves.

On 10 April 1989 I invited all the NATO ambassadors to my house for a morning meeting. We gathered around the big fireplace, where we talked about our doings, our aims, and the way ahead. In the afternoon we visited the Waterloo battlefield, a place I know well, and talked of tactics and soldiering, of Napoleon's confidence, Wellington's responses, and Blucher's loyalty.

The excursion was coordinated with the owners of the property; we chartered a military bus to carry the guests from place to place. As would become the pattern, the first stop was always Hougoumont Farm, situated at the base of the slope where the contending armies first came together. Upstairs in the barn we had a light lunch and discussed the strategic reasons for the importance of this place. I talked about the twelve ways of looking at the battle and the political-military connection: as emperor, Napoleon was both a political and a military leader.

The second stop was the Lion mound, where we considered Wellington's tactical plan and battlefield position, Blucher's role, and Napoleon's strange, exclusive focus on the center of the battlefield.

Bill Crowe, who had once humorously referred to me as "the Proconsul," now became a little more serious about the nickname. Early in April I stopped in to see Brent Scowcroft, then National Security Advisor. We had our usual exchange, and as I was turning to leave he said, "I understand that you don't work for the president." I turned back around. He added, "Bill tells me you think you're the Proconsul."

I said, "I don't think I'm the Proconsul."

"Let me tell you something," Scowcroft said. "If you don't work for the president, you don't work for nobody." He smiled at me.

I thought, this is something that could become a very big issue for a lot of people, not just a "by the way" theoretical argument. I can't let that happen. I had a meeting scheduled for the next day, 7 April 1989, with Secretary of Defense Dick Cheney, and I thought this subject might come up then too, but it turned out to be a routine exchange.

A month later, on 10 May 1989, I was about to hold our annual meeting of the senior officers at my command headquarters. I had asked George Kennan to come and be our guest speaker. I had read a speech he had given at the headquarters in 1963; twenty-six years later, the thrust of his talk was the same. Be open and understanding with Russia. Don't look on Russia as a threat; make sure that attitude ends. Help them to change and to avoid instability. I noted my reaction to Kennan: "On one hand, the sense of innocence, fragility; on the other, a tough and uncompromising and insistent guy. He has a left lean and a right lean."

Kennan stayed with us for two nights. He was at ease with family talk and reminiscence. He told stories that he knew my daughters would like. He delighted all the family when he proudly told us that a Princeton fire engine was named after him.

He described his railroad trip from Berlin to Frankfurt after he was interned, along with his embassy staff, by the Nazis. The Gestapo controlled the train, he said, and the trip dragged on for seven days. He had to "squeeze the dog out the window" and hold him there so he could go to the bathroom.

He talked about his time as ambassador to Moscow and how he didn't like being trailed by five men every time he left the embassy. He felt imprisoned in his own embassy. Even Russian children who wanted to play with his son were turned away at the gate. In Berlin he was interviewed by a reporter, who asked him—off the record—how he felt about things in Moscow, and he replied, "Somehow you must not be aware that the mission staff is shut up in the embassy and can do practically nothing." This came out in the press ("The reporter knew it was off the record," Kennan said, "but said it was too good to leave that way"), and Kennan was declared persona non grata. "Not allowed to go back to Moscow," he said—"not even to move the household out, which I had to leave to [my wife] Annelise."

At one point, he and I took a walk behind our house and alongside a pasture where young heifers grazed. We talked about his book *Sketches from a Life*. He said his secretary and his friends urged him to publish more of his writings and helped him pick out the best of his remaining papers, some of which he had not seen since he wrote them. He felt that he should not add much, he said, so most of the editing consisted of correcting typos, or "just enough to provide coherence." He talked about the School of Historical Studies that was part of the Institute for Advanced Study at Princeton, noting that he "was picked up by Oppenheimer" for the Institute, and that he had hesitated when asked to commit himself fully, but friends convinced him, and he was now happy with that decision—because, among other things, it helped him keep his "liberty" and avoid stuffed shirts, having to shake hands at black tie dinners, "losing the ability to be a person and to read, think, and empathize." Don't let that happen, he warned me: get away from the bureaucrats, the sanctity of protocol and procedures. I liked his advice.

In his remarks to our commanders, Kennan said that much of future relations with the Soviet Union would depend on the way the West responded to what he anticipated would be the predictably lower profile of the Soviet Union, until the only thing left of the country would be its military machine.

He told the commanders, "Don't make it harder for them."

Kennan was brilliant, and it showed in many ways. Reading an article he wrote for *Foreign Affairs*, I noted that he could distill the essence of a century on a single page. He gallops through the last years of Stalin's horrific rule and then observes that the Russian survivors of the years and decades of Stalin's rule had been brutalized—and that you can see it in their faces as they walk the streets. George Kennan was never afraid to speak his mind.

In Berlin, along the lakeside of beautiful Wannsee, on a morning in August 1989, I wrote to myself: "We are on the outer fringes of the Cold War, at the edge, in a period of transition to something else. It is a period of promise, a period of danger. The ice is thin. It's like on Lake Quannapowitt, when you're skating fast over the white ice and then you find yourself over the dark and you hear it groan. There is no doubt that our old adversaries are entering deep into a period of change, a time of vast experimentation that has a scent of instability about it."

I talked with the secretary general in his office on 6 September 1989, and laid out the plan for the Right Mix. Wörner asked, "Do we have the flexibility, the creativity, to respond to the current situation and the future at the same time?" I told him that my aim was to cut back on the large-scale exercises that put hundreds of tanks and other heavy military vehicles on the fields and roads of West Germany. We could effect this reduction now that we had devised a combination of local training and computer-supported simulations that, to a degree, would maintain the readiness of our forces. I drew on what I had learned in theory at the Training and Doctrine Command and on my experiences gained from participating in seven of the yearly Reforger exercises, and told him that we had begun a review of our program of training exercises throughout the command.

The next day, 7 September, I was notified by an FBI agent that the agency wished to question me in a downtown Washington office concerning issues relating to the contras–Oliver North affair. My involvement, I was told, was as a witness. I replied that I would like to bring my lawyer, Lieutenant Colonel Barry Steinberg, along with me—to which the agency response was, "In that case, your category will change from witness to something else." This caused me to ponder: I could be one of the usual suspects. The situation seemed to be something that could drag out and even become an investigation rather than a questioning, and I had too much else to do. I decided to accept the invitation. The questioning lasted four hours. It concentrated on the various times during my tour as commander-in-chief of Southern Command when I had contact with Oliver North, and what the nature of said contacts was. My answers led the agency to request an additional four-hour session, which in turn led to a request to interview my wife, who had received a check from Colonel North in repayment for some Christmas shopping she did for him in Panama when he was too busy to do it himself. I am happy to be able to say that the questioning of the Galvins resulted in clean slates, so far as I know.

19 September 1989. Danish Rear Admiral Hans Jørgen Garde and I climbed into a Lynx helicopter and took off from Karup in western Denmark for a flight out over the North Sea. We had a date with the German destroyer *Kohl*, on a NATO exercise. Four or five miles off the coast, I saw a stream of oil come out of the overhead padding, whereupon we banked into a quick 180-degree turn back toward shore. While we looked out at the tilted ocean horizon, the pilot explained to us that the Lynx has two independent hydraulic systems, but when one system fails as copiously as ours, getting to the ground becomes a preoccupation. We agreed with that. The pilot radioed Karup to explain that we would need another helicopter, and as we neared the beach he decided he didn't like the slope. That part of the water is shallow. Still descending, we crossed the shore at a few hundred feet, turned back into the wind, and landed steeply but smoothly in a fenced-in backyard behind a cottage. A man and woman stood in their doorway looking as if our arrival had been expected, the woman protecting her apron against the helicopter's wash. The Lynx had been designed with a brake to slow down its rotor blades, which does seem more polite when your helicopter is sitting in someone's garden.

We were at the home of Mr. and Mrs. Magnus Nielsen, who asked us in for coffee and sent their son Paul Erik off to get some rolls. Nielsen served as a one-man patriot. Next day, the *Jyllands-Posten* commented:

> When the coffee and rolls were on the table, the four-star American General and the retired fisherman had a chat, partly about the life of a soldier and the circumstances of a fisherman.

The General and the Danish Admiral were picked up a couple of hours later by an S-61 helicopter from Aalborg, which took them to the headquarters at Karup.

Here General Galvin stated: "Let me be honest. I was sorry to leave the Nielsens. We had such a good time together."

I marked it down as a good civil-military operation.

On the evening of 3 December 1989, I traveled via sedan to Chateau Stuyvenberg in Brussels, the Belgian Blair House, at the request of President Bush, who was arriving that evening from his Malta Summit with Soviet leader Gorbachev. Earlier in the day I had watched on television as the president rode the wave troughs in a ship's boat—a U.S. Navy motor launch that carried him on the Mediterranean to a Soviet cruiser off the island, where he was to meet with Gorbachev. It was quite a naval maneuver, given the heavy seas of that day.

The president had indicated he wanted to discuss a special meeting of the heads of state of the Alliance. I waited for him in a book-lined corner off to the side of a large room. It was nearing eight o'clock and I knew he would be tired.

I squeezed my notes to a minimum, a single subject: the reduction of conventional forces in Europe (CFE). The May summit report had resulted in promises of action and things had moved along for a short while, but attention to CFE had slipped away—and it needed to remain uppermost. We needed to regain momentum. That would reveal what the Soviet military leaders had in mind. The key to it all would be the word "parity." If both sides reduced their tanks and other combat vehicles to the same number, that would cost the Warsaw Pact far more than the Atlantic Alliance. If I had my way, I would move right away on this.

As I waited for the president and thought about my susceptibility to seasickness, he wandered into the reception room and said, "Hello, Jack." Recovering from my surprise, I stood up and we shook hands. I said, "Sir, that was a great display of seamanship today, riding the waves off Malta. Sometimes you disappeared from the TV screen, the sea was so rough."

He said, "I did? It didn't seem so rough to me"—the right answer for a sailor. In his typically informal way, Bush had left his retinue behind. I don't think he had had much uninterrupted sleep on the trip, though he was trying not to show it. He motioned me to a chair, settled into another, and turned right away to the events coming up in the morning, when he would be addressing a special meeting of the North Atlantic Council.

"Well, how are you?" asked the president. "How are things in Allied Command Europe? What's the atmosphere in NATO?"

"It's fine, and I'm fine," I replied. "I'm glad to have this chance to see you. In the command there is much anticipation of the summit, especially concerning conventional forces. This is the first time that you have met with this group since the summit conference last May. The proposal at the May summit made things move—for a while. Now the effort has slowed significantly. We need to regain momentum. We need to get an agreement on conventional forces as soon as possible, and we have to insist on parity of numbers as we go down."

"The U.S. won't move unilaterally," Bush replied. "We've got to get the agreement on conventional forces, then move to the nuclear. How do the Soviets see this?" While we continued, the president took out his speech cards and shuffled through them. His cards were bigger than mine, 5x8 inches. He penciled a note and shuffled the cards again.

"I think we can add helicopters and aircraft into the negotiations without any real disadvantage to ourselves," I answered. "In both areas the Soviets and the rest of the Warsaw Pact outnumber us by a long shot, and the drop to parity would be big."

"What about the personnel cut?" the president asked. "How do you see that?"

That was the most important issue, as far as I was concerned. "If we can get the other side to come down from 600,000 to 275,000, we certainly ought to be ready to do that ourselves," I replied. "That means a drop of 30,000 for us and more than ten times as much for them."

"I don't know anybody in the military who will not fall into line behind this proposal," I continued. "It gives us the initiative and puts us strongly into the negotiations—together—at Vienna." He smiled at my quick response, and our talk continued.

Bob Blackwill joined us at about this time and we talked briefly; then the president left, and Blackwill and I continued to talk. My note cards for the evening list single-word or single-phrase subjects: transition, unity, armaments, harmonization, verification, strategy, burden sharing, and Right Mix. At the meeting the next morning, President Bush was strong on the need to keep up the momentum of change. When the question of numbers came up, they were accepted by all.

Listening, I was happy to have been of help the night before.

31

The Wall

"The Wall has a morality of its own that does not say good things about the East."

To understand the events leading up to the breaching of the Berlin Wall, we need to go back to the end of World War II, when Germany was divided into four sectors: British, French, American, and Soviet. Berlin, the capital, lay in the Soviet zone of occupation, and to resolve the awkward situation the city was divided into four zones. The Allies were afforded free access across the Soviet zone to and from the city. This worked all right until 1962, when the Soviets decided to block the Allies' access to Berlin. Why? Because living in East Berlin was dreary and unpleasant, with East Berliners under constant political and financial pressure and unable to travel outside the wall.

As a soldier in uniform I was permitted to enter the Soviet sector; and, in order to gain as much knowledge as possible about my Soviet counterparts by making use of the rules of liaison, I visited as often as possible, by railroad, highway, or air. Passing from West to East Berlin through a gate in the wall was, I often thought, like changing from color to black-and-white television, from beauty to gloom. East Berlin was a despondent, languishing piece of a city, forlorn and stripped of happiness. It was hard for me to see Germans without flowers. Around the barracks for the Soviet troops and officers, as in some of the nearby motor pools, things were spiritless and uncared for, with shabby buildings, cracked and broken windowpanes, front doors left ajar, and fences leaning—many indications along these gray streets of emptiness in houses that were full of people.

After the Soviet blockade of Berlin in the late 1940s and the confrontations it spawned, the United States, Great Britain, and France knew that they would need to be prepared for Soviet moves to isolate the city. The three countries, all of whom had troops stationed in Berlin, agreed to create a separate military headquarters under the code name Live Oak, which would be prepared to command troops in response to any further attempt to cut off Berlin, and which commanded a designated division-size ground force that would be ready to move through Berlin under any circumstances. The commander of this force would be the supreme allied commander, Europe.

Vernon "Dick" Walters was the American ambassador to Germany early in my tenure as SACEUR. I saw a lot of him, liked and admired him, and even borrowed an apartment of his in Paris. His German was far better than mine, his French seemed to me perfect, his Russian was good—and after all my years of studying and using Spanish, I found that his was better in style and vocabulary than mine. He knew how to use Italian and Portuguese and could get around in more than a dozen other languages. Walters drove his ancient Oldsmobile from Bonn to Moscow and then on to Leningrad with a bag of tools, a trunk full of spare parts, and his nephew along as a mechanic. He would talk to ordinary people along the way. "Every time I stopped for gas," he noted, "I got into discussions on world politics." Walters was the only person I know who insisted that the Wall would come down very soon. Secretary of State James Baker didn't like hearing that, Walters recalled. "When he came to see Kohl, I met him at the airport and we drove to see Kohl—only he didn't ask me to sit in on the conversation."

General Pyotr Lushev replaced Marshal Viktor Kulikov as commander-in-chief of the Warsaw Pact Armed Forces in February 1989. Three months later, on 2 May 1989, Hungary dismantled the fence along the East German border; the Kremlin didn't react. The British Royal United Services Institute for Defence Studies asked me to take part in a mid-May conference on NATO and the Warsaw Pact, to which they were also inviting my counterpart, General Lushev. I readily accepted, hoping that it would be a chance to see how he fitted into the top team of Soviet military leaders, what he was like, and how he was taking in the events in both Eastern and Western Europe. Well aware of the pages of NATO's Terms of Reference, which permitted and even encouraged me to communicate with senior leadership; remembering my long meeting with General Pyal'tsev in 1984; and aware that I was a NATO commander as well as an American commander, I decided to speak at the same place as General Lushev. When I arrived that afternoon, someone said on the way in, "Lushev's upset because he got there first. He expected you to be there, and now he's waiting around with an exasperated look on his face talking only to his own people."

The rooms were tiny, all angles and little corridors and corners. The British have big old, roomy buildings, which they assiduously over time convert into a maze of warrens. It took a couple of minutes to find Lushev. The British were serving tea, and Lushev and I had a good talk. I expected little and that turned out to be correct, but I followed my usual plan for such occasions, turning my talk into a set of questions to which I wanted to have answers. After all, he was my counterpart.

At my next lunch with Secretary General Wörner, Wörner began the conversation with, "Why did you meet with him?"

"Lushev? I had hoped to have a chance to talk to him in passing, but someone served tea." This was such a lame excuse that we both couldn't help laughing.

"Well, that tea has caused me grief with my colleagues," I continued, but Wörner was still smothering a laugh, and we got past that issue. I have to say again that I liked this man wholeheartedly—especially at times like that, of which there were a few.

In an interview in early June 1989 with Ohio's *Columbus Dispatch*, I said:

> I think the wall could come down. That might not be a real disaster for the East Germans and the Soviets. I think the Soviet Union is embarrassed by the wall. I think maybe in the near future there will be enough confidence on the part of the East Germans to think about taking it down. We ought to push that idea anyway and see if we can get it to happen. It is a terrible, terrible embarrassment [for] them. It's a sin against human nature. The wall has a morality of its own that does not say good things about the East.

On 10 September, Hungary allowed ten thousand East Germans to pass through to Austria and on to West Germany. The thing we all needed to know was, what would the Soviet forces in and around Berlin do? Would they support the East German forces and encourage them to protect the wall? Would they get involved themselves?

Was Gorbachev still in charge? Did he have a plan? Who was with him and who against him? He's taking things apart—but what then? And how do we get through this without big trouble? Judging from his comments at home in Russia and on his extraordinary travels during October, Gorbachev was sounding open to change, as was his foreign minister, Eduard Shevardnadze. On 6 October 1989, Gorbachev was in East Germany talking about reforms. By this time the question of the wall was the subject of rumbles of distant thunder. I asked Dick Walters, "Where do they go from here?"

"It's coming down," was his reply.

In Rome on Saturday, 7 October 1989, Soviet General Vladimir N. Lobov, chief of staff of the Joint Armed Forces of the Warsaw Treaty Organization and First Deputy Chief of the Soviet General Staff, and I were both scheduled to speak at the North Atlantic Assembly. The subject: the new force structure. I knew I would not have much time, or any at all, to talk privately with him, so I addressed my words as much to him as to the audience. In essence I turned our joint appearance into a debate rather than a sequence of two speakers, as the secretary general later pointed out to me.

Stars and Stripes for Sunday, 8 October 1989, described the meeting:

> In an address to lawmakers, Lobov described measures being taken to trim Soviet military might to a more economical and less threatening force. As examples, Lobov described the Soviets' unilateral cutback of 500,000 troops and 8,500 tactical aircraft and the removal of three tank divisions from Eastern Europe. The West is making no reciprocal reproductions, Lobov said.
>
> "What's this all about, comrade parliamentarians?" Lobov asked. "Are you trying to terrorize us, to start a new arms race? Maybe you're just being careful, but we're not just talking about things, we're doing them."
>
> In responding to the Soviet general, Galvin agreed that much had happened in the Soviet Union during the past year to encourage NATO, but questioned the significance of the Soviet military reductions. . . . "Across the board, combat power continues to roll off the Soviet production lines," Galvin said. "Where is all of that equipment going?" . . .
>
> He also said the Soviets should dismantle logistic systems and supply depots that are located so far forward that they could be used for only offensive purposes. . . . "Above all, allow each side to observe for itself that these changes are really taking place," Galvin said. "Let us both accept greater openness, both agree to an extension of greater confidence and stabil-

ity-building measures. . . . When things are unpredictable and uncertain, we in the West need to be as predictable and as balanced and as stable and as unified as possible," he said. "And that means the North Atlantic alliance. It is the way to face an uncertain future."

We concluded the event shaking hands, and an 11 October 1989 news summary of the press comments on 8 October included the following:

> *Il Messaggero* noted that the presence of a Soviet general next to the SACEUR at a NATO forum was unprecedented since the creation of the alliance.
> *Il Tempo* wrote, "The handshake between [General Galvin and General Lobov] may be the sign of a new relation between the military alliance shaping up for the 1990s."

A month later, at midnight on 11 November 1989, the East German guards opened the gates in the wall to the citizens of East Berlin, allowing them to cross through to the West side. An enormous celebration ensued, the most dramatic event in the postwar history of Germany.

That night we needed to know the answer to a critical question: What are the Soviet units in Berlin going to do? We were in touch with all our sources of intelligence, but we didn't have the answer. Then our U.S. Air Force command came up with a suggestion: "Templehof." He was referring to the Berlin Air Safety Centre, where a small Live Oak–prescribed crisis management and contingency planning staff was composed of representatives of East and West, including a Soviet colonel. "Let's ask him." It was easy to get in touch with him, and he said, "We have orders to stay in barracks."

On 16 November 1989 I wrote to my daughter Erin:

> The Berlin Wall, I'm sure, has been a big event for you. We've sat glued to our TV, just amazed at it all, and quite moved, as we watch people breaking up the wall, dancing on it, and hugging each other. It has been a great event, and the reverberations will go on and on. If the two Germanys are united, I don't see how Russian troops could be stationed in East Germany and U.S. and Allied troops in West Germany—so the future may bring some very big changes.

32

A Strategy for Change

"Deployed where? And to do what?"

"Strategy" has become a word of many meanings. It was for a long time linked with military thinking, but in the past fifty years its uses have grown far wider, so that these days everyone needs a strategy for everything. The old word now needs the help of more precise definition; we have to apply an adjective: "military," or "national," or "global." Nevertheless, the word still retains its old meaning some of the time. Political leaders argue about strategy, with opponents often accusing each other of having none.

So what is a strategy? I can call it a plan to use available resources to achieve stated goals. In the spring of 1989, after the hard lessons of WINTEX, the countries in the NATO alliance were talking about our national and Alliance goals and whether our collective strategy could achieve them given our resources—or, if not, whether we could provide the additional resources necessary to achieve them. You cannot have a military strategy without a national one. Can we go even higher than that—to a collective, Alliance-based strategy? These were meaningful questions. And what happens when you seek to change a strategy?

Secretary General Wörner tended to pontificate when he was worried or felt himself under pressure; but he also listened, especially at those same times. He had developed a speaking style that would descend to a whisper and rise to almost a bellow. He knew how and when to stop deliberation and drive a group to a decision, and when to simply assume a position—in which case I never saw him challenged. Wörner wanted to show the Soviet and Eastern European military and political leaders that the NATO politicians definitely held the reins on their militaries and made the major decisions. He said to me, "This new strategy has to be accepted as the product of the political side, not the military. We need all you can do to help, but the work has to be seen as, and the decisions must remain as, essentially political." He was right. I promised him I would follow his directions to the letter, and I mostly did. As with the arms negotiations, I wanted to be part of the team that created the new Alliance strategy—since, to begin with, I would be the one to carry it out. I think that his confidence in me allowed me to argue points with him, sometimes quite strongly; but when he said, "Enough, Jack," that was it. The development of the new strategy was a team effort, beginning with a working group at NATO under Michael Legge that included a key member of my staff to provide the military expertise. This gave me the opportunity to funnel the resources of the whole command to support the effort. It also kept me aware of the thinking within the group as I went ahead with the development of an interim operational concept and a force structure to put it into effect.

On 16 June 1989, I had an audience with Pope John Paul II at the Vatican. I took Ginny and her mother and our children and found it an incomparable experience. Not a churchgoing Catholic, I nevertheless had respect for the pope's intellect, political understanding, courage, and of course his leadership. We were guided into a reception room and from there he asked me to accompany him into a small office, where we were alone. After a short conversation, he asked, "General, are you a man of peace?" It was a question I had not expected. I found myself saying, "Yes, Your Holiness, I am a man of peace." There might have been a split second of hesitation on my part, because he then said, in quiet affirmation, "You are a man of peace." I answered, quickly this time, "Yes." He told me that his impression was that ordinary people want peace, but their leaders, some of them, tend to qualify their dedication to peace with other interests, and the result has been great suffering. His comment has come back to me many times since.

That month, Poland held its first elections in fifty years, and in elections in the Soviet Union voters replaced many of the hard-line Communist regulars with liberals. On 19 June 1989, I wrote to myself:

> Plan ahead for a new strategy—what will change? How? Close contact with Chiefs of Defense Staffs, ministers of defense, Chairman of the Military Committee. The ideal way to proceed would be to work out a new strategy, and from it derive an operational concept for the employment of the force. This concept would tell us what kind of force structure we need, which

then would dictate the infrastructure requirements. We could then come up with the readiness levels and from those the training needs, which would allow us to build a proper [exercises] program—and then we would have the supporting rationale for a funding level, the cost of maintaining the force in all its details, enabling us to explain coherently the military budget needs of the Alliance.

For the next several months, however, I stuck to the position that our current strategy was flexible enough to meet all possibilities. As long as we had a chain of command and high readiness, we could respond to any kind of threat. The most pressing problem was the budget. Without a plan, we had no rationale for continuing our support by Alliance countries, some of which were already moving to cancel large chunks of their budget contributions (such as for improvements in our long-range communications). So I held to my insistence that arms control reduction had to show progress—especially in conventional forces—before we could move away from a command chain that we all understood, and that right now it was versatile enough to meet any new situation. The senior commanders wanted to keep close to the existing strategy. They felt that the confusion of a major change would cause a loss of focus with respect to arms talks. They didn't want to be caught between two strategies, with one no longer considered valid and the other not yet agreed on.

At the same time, we worked on revisions of our military side of the international strategy—and so did everybody else. We were not at a loss for suggestions. One line of thinking took us back to the doctrine of the 1950s: *massive retaliation*. Any war with the Soviets, it said, surely would lead to the use of nuclear weapons, so it was useless to spend money to improve conventional forces when we would only be delaying the inevitable. Others were convinced that Gorbachev's call for *nuclear-free zones* would be a step toward greater security. The Soviets claimed that they had already changed their strategy to *"defensive sufficiency,"* which would make changes that rendered their force structure incapable of attacking anyone. How they would do this, they said, would be evident as things went along. This was attractive, even compelling, to some representatives in the North Atlantic Council, as well as to political leaders in Alliance countries.

Some called for a *"defensive defense,"* a posture that would provide for our security but would not threaten anybody. Under this argument, both sides would mark out defense areas in a kind of chessboard fashion and put static military forces in each of the squares. Since tanks seemed threatening, there would be no tanks. There would be no massing of ground forces. Neither side would be capable of military operations above the local, tactical level. True enough, this level of force would threaten no one, but it would also be subject to defeat in detail, square by square. Others wanted to *eliminate offensive weapons*, not concerned, or unaware, that counterattack is part of almost any kind of defense. We studied the different possibilities, including a few of our own invention, but could find no credible formula. Later, in talks with some of the senior military leaders in the Soviet Union, I asked them what meaning they took from Gorbachev's concept of "defensive sufficiency." They said they had no idea what he was talking about.

I was worried about the growing sense of euphoria in all countries, West and East, grounded in the conviction that our fondest wishes had already come true. I remembered 1945, when the Allied armies of World War II were so quickly dismantled, and U.S. forces, which were so powerful and capable at the end of the fighting, found themselves only five years later hanging on for dear life to a little piece of ground on the southern tip of Korea. I also kept in mind the earlier change in NATO strategy from the threat of massive retaliation to a strategy of flexible response. That earlier effort had taken six years of discussion before something had been developed that could be accepted by all the nations involved. I didn't want to see us repeat either approach— either too-hasty reductions or a prolonged effort to devise a workable strategy.

We were trying to act our parts on the stage while the stagehands changed the scenery around us. I told the commanders to concentrate on the basics of training and readiness. Yes, they said, but training and readiness for what? My interim orders merely told them to be ready to move to assembly areas from which they would be deployed. But deployed where? And to do what? To defend Alliance territory? To take on peacekeeping missions? To provide humanitarian assistance? To maintain stability? This plethora of possibilities was not an easy thing for the commanders to digest. Not only did we have much creative, innovative work to do; we had to undo a great deal of old Cold War thinking. And this was not just so for military leaders. This was true of everyone.

We did not have much time to devise and gain support for a strategy. The next summit meeting of all the Alliance's national leaders was scheduled for July 1990 in London. We could not come away from a summit at this phase of world developments without making a clear statement of where the Alliance was going. The teams working on the strategy stayed in touch daily. And we worked hard.

Using "Round Table" discussion teams, we covered a wide range of issues, including nuclear and conventional weapons and strategy. To the Commo Club (for information and public relations), we added the CFE Team (focused on arms control) and the Blue Book Team (to secure correct figures for both NATO and Warsaw Pact forces and equipment), and we assigned special assistants to serve as liaisons. To protect the organizational structure, all the teams had to see themselves as part of one overall team. It sounds complicated, but it worked.

It *had* to work, because we were moving along through a whirlwind of events. On 11 February 1990, Gorbachev agreed to German unification. On 14 February 1990, the Two Plus Four Agreement talks began on reuniting Germany (bringing together East and West Germany and the four former occupying powers). On 20 February 1990, the U.S. Congress approved radical infrastructure cuts in the Defense Base Closure and Realignment Act of 1990 (BRAC). On 27 February 1990, Gorbachev and Václav Havel signed an agreement stipulating the Soviet troops' complete withdrawal from Czechoslovakia by July 1991. On 7 March 1990, I spoke before the Senate Foreign Relations Committee on the matrix of negotiations—and the effect of these negotiations on the new NATO strategy. In March 1990, the Soviets started to pull out of Hungary, and Lithuania declared independence. Also in March 1990, Gorbachev was elected president. And in April 1990, elections were held in Slovenia and Croatia.

At a meeting of the German-American organization Atlantik-Brücke (Atlantic Bridge) in Stuttgart on 22 April 1990, I laid out some pieces of the new strategy, speaking from these notes: "1. Smaller forces. 2. Nuclear weapons, but small numbers. 3. Collective security. 4. Multinational governance. 5. Arms control. 6. Force generation (marshaling the necessary resources). 7. Crisis management. 8. Communication and consideration of the security needs of the other side. 9. Solidarity—cohesion—sharing principles, values. This would be enough—in peace, crisis, or war."

May 1990. The Latvian Parliament declares independence. Hungary says it will leave the Warsaw Pact.

"If we are going to deal with all of these changes," Secretary General Wörner said to me, reaching into his well-worn dictionary, "NATO has to be vivacious." It was the right word. He said that with no Warsaw Pact, no way to predict what the Eastern European states would do on any question, we needed to assure all of Europe, and all the world, of what we might do. We needed to send them a message of stability.

In June, Gorbachev said he would remove all tactical nuclear weapons from Europe.

I stayed in touch with James Woolsey, who was then serving as the U.S. ambassador to the Negotiations on Conventional Armed Forces in Europe (CFE), and in another meeting with Wörner I told him I was worried that the CFE negotiations were coming to a standstill, and I was convinced that General Mikhail Moiseyev, commander of the Soviet armed forces, and his military chiefs were pleased to see it lose momentum. "We have to make things move at the negotiations in Vienna," I said. "We are arguing whether to reduce to a level of 19,500 artillery pieces each, or whether the figure should be 20,000. When we are that close in numbers that we can trust, it's close enough."

We also had to make sure that the new strategy was general and versatile enough to meet the changes that the future would bring, or else we would find ourselves constantly rewriting it. As it turned out, the winds of change were on us right away. Starting in 1991 the United States began heavy withdrawals from Europe; the following year the Germans and French created a joint new army corps; and all nations of the Alliance began reducing their standing forces. To keep Alliance nations involved in devising the new strategy, we put out a progress report, noting these changes:

New: emphasis on *arms control*

New: concept of *crisis management* rather than focusing on an "enemy"—packaging of response.

New: *Force generation.* Concentration on surveillance and fast response.

New: *Nuclear guidance.* Political message of deterrence rather than war-fighting.

A forward presence, but much less.

New: *Mobility.* Ability to shift forces.

New—and disputed: *Out of area.* Forces designed to facilitate the move of units from their normal locations and missions to unexpected areas and new missions.

New: *Small but quality force.* Mix of active and reserve. Prob-

> ably a mix of heavy and light. Quality means equipment,
> but it also means training (right mix) at the right levels
> and in the right things (such as mobilization and deploy-
> ment and flexibility of operational employment). Also
> quality of manning and . . . organization and . . . logistical
> sustainment.
>
> New: *Strategic logistics.* A complete revision, possibly along the
> lines of the U.S. Air Force "wheel spokes" rather than the
> U.S. Army "pyramid" structure.

The London communiqué of July 1990 (the "London Declaration on a
Transformed North Atlantic Alliance" issued by the heads of state and
government participating in the meeting of the North Atlantic Council)
was good enough to set us on a track toward new operational guidance
and thus to the essentials of our future force structure after CFE. The
words were there, and we had moved quickly to establish the main elements of the new strategy. At the time, I wrote to myself, "We will look
back and see the London summit of July 1990 as the true watershed
for NATO, and for that reason I want to describe the politico-military
teamwork leading up to that meeting as I saw it. The summit proved
that NATO is healthy and strong, and that the leaders of the Alliance
can put aside their differences and set us on a good road for the future."

On 19 June, I joined Dick Cheney and Colin Powell in Brent Scowcroft's office to go through the text of the London Agreement. With one
small addition—a paragraph in which NATO made a commitment on
nonaggression and invited the Warsaw Pact to reciprocate—and a few
minor fixes, we approved the draft declaration.

My notes from the comments of President Bush on 5 July 1990
(which I did not capture word for word):

> We have transformed the alliance for its intense relevance in
> the 21st century. We have reached out to our adversaries and
> changed the character of the alliance. We have relegated our
> nuclear weapons to weapons of last resort. We have made a
> declaration of peace. We have altered profoundly the way we
> think about defense.
>
> We have seen the dissolution of the Warsaw Pact. We note
> the prospect of the withdrawal of Soviet forces from Eastern
> Europe and the effects of the CFE treaty. We want no dispro-
> portionate military power on the continent. We will handle

military strength in a stabilizing way. We will move away from forward defense.

From page 1 of the *Wall Street Journal*, 16 July 1990:

[Galvin] is rethinking the role of nuclear weapons, while planning to reduce and relocate his troops. Rather than dig in his heels and resist change, this general has become a radical reformer, pleased to help preside over the end of a dangerous and costly Cold War. . . . "We will, as you can see, have to restructure everything—not practically everything, but everything," he says, almost delightedly.

Moscow seems to agree. "One might say the ice has started to break," Soviet Foreign Minister Eduard Shevardnadze said. . . .

More than anyone, John Galvin must turn NATO's policy phrases into physical reality. . . . But after spending his first three years in office trying to build up the West's main military forces, his task now is to pare them back—while retaining enough power to deal with future problems that may arise.

Gen. Galvin now favors withdrawing all nuclear artillery shells and short-range missiles from Europe, and supports wholeheartedly the NATO decision to make nuclear warheads "truly weapons of last resort." . . . "The military has done an astonishing job of responding to political change," says one senior diplomat, "and Galvin is the key player."

In fact, he has assigned 40 staff officers to planning arms reductions, not war—a switch he said took "dynamite."

Yet just a year ago, Gen. Galvin seemed more a defender of the past than a campaigner for change. . . . But in today's environment he has joined the first line of a new debate.

He pushes peaceful initiatives while reminding politicians that the Soviet Union remains an overarmed and somewhat unstable nation that could yet, perhaps by accident, bring Europe to a crisis.

"I think we should applaud them for their efforts," he says, "but keep on counting their military."

I went across the Channel to see Margaret Thatcher. Chief of Staff John Fieldhouse had set up an appointment, and I went to John's office first to talk about the visit. I told John that among other things I wanted to say something about the decrease in the British military budget. We had talked about the evils of a flat budget, but now the line on the chart wasn't even flat; it had taken a distinct downward turn, and this boded no good for the force modernization program that was dear to his heart and mine. "Go right ahead," he said, "and you will be helping me." He said he had been trying to bring this issue up with Thatcher in the past few days, and she had cut him off each time. That put things in a less than optimistic light, but I said that I needed to get it off my chest, and besides, my comment might hit her at the right moment. "Who knows, we could be lucky," I said. "Right," he said, but he didn't look happy.

As we crossed the street, John said, "Here you can see the solution we found long ago to the problem of the civilians in the defense ministry versus the military staff: we walled them off. Things got a good deal better after that."

At 10 Downing Street, we found ourselves in Mrs. Thatcher's office without a wait and, as usual, got right into the business at hand. Mrs. Thatcher greeted us in her hearty way, and in the process told me, as she always did, that the primary responsibility of political leaders is the security of the nation. Following the plan that John Fieldhouse and I had concocted, I waited until things had gotten around to a point when a comment on the budget seemed logical. The prime minister and I talked of various things as I tried to work my way around to the budget, but it is hard to work your way anywhere when you're talking to Margaret Thatcher. Her style was to go directly to the issue and hold forth with a short, sharp declamation (in a style of elocution that certain British politicians and military leaders tend to use). She had her own way of speaking. She underscored her diction with a regular cadence, falling heavily on every third or fourth word—or more often on two or three successive words—in a way that gave an exaggerated sense of importance to her comments. It was mesmerizing.

"It seems to us, Prime Minister," I said, "that unless something is done, the British defense budget is going to suffer more than it should; I don't see how it is going to be more than flat, and I'm afraid it will be even less than flat."

Her response was sharp. "I *must* say that I *agree* with something that you said earlier, which is the *danger* that the Germans are not going to *hold steady* on their force structure. I am *most* appreciative of your making me aware of this *very worrisome matter,* and we all certainly need to *communicate* to the Germans and to our other allies our *deep concerns* with the *damage* which this could cause to us *all, especially* since the *Soviets* have not shown *any sign* of being serious about reducing their continuing *superiority* of *forces.*"

We did not manage, John and I, to get the prime minister back on the subject of the United Kingdom's defense budget. Soon after, when she came to visit my headquarters with John Fieldhouse, we decided I should try again. But a try was as far as I got. This time she did not talk about the Germans or anyone else. Her answer was, as usual, quick and strong. I felt as if I were being sandblasted. The problem, she said, was not the budget.

"Let me tell you something about the management of the British defense budget," she said, looking hard at John Fieldhouse. "It has been *terribly* wasteful. The British taxpayer has had his *hard-earned* money put into projects that were *poorly* thought out, *poorly* planned, *poorly* executed, to the extent that literally *millions* of pounds have been completely lost with *nothing* to show for it." She named some of the military production programs that were in trouble in the UK. "That," she concluded, "was poor fiscal performance. The losses have been such that if we were to take all the funds that have been *needlessly* spent on *abortive* projects and *ineffective* programs, and if we add this to the current defense budget, we have a line that is not flat at all but *soaring* upward!"

John glanced at me, and I had no trouble reading his mind.

On Monday, 26 November 1990, I met with Vladimir Lobov during my visit to the North Atlantic Assembly's meeting in London. General Lobov was present as an elected Deputy of the Congress of People's Deputies. This was his third appearance at an NAA meeting; I had met with him on the two previous occasions, in Rome in October 1989 and Brussels in February 1990. I was able to greet General Lobov and then have a private conversation with him, lasting seventy-five minutes. Also present was Kent Brown, my Special Assistant for International Affairs, and an interpreter for General Lobov.

We spoke of Gorbachev's position. Gorbachev's most serious point had been that he intended to use the military, if necessary, to stop unconstitutional activity from taking place. I said that my assessment of Gorbachev was that he was a man of courage and vision, faced with a rocky road ahead.

Lobov responded that Gorbachev's situation was difficult because all change is challenging, and it is in particular very hard to remove age-old, stereotyped Russian mind-sets. Most people prefer to stick to their habitual frame of mind; many are confused and afraid of the new way ahead.

Democracy is like oxygen, Lobov continued—and, they say, you can suffocate on pure oxygen, too. We need to adapt to this new atmosphere. People now have to think for themselves, make their own decisions, and react in a practical manner. Most people still expect the president to tell them what to do—while some others resent it when he does so. We think this is a transitional phase. In the military we are used to clear lines of command and restrictive boundaries. But Gorbachev is forcing us to see wider and deeper, and to act on what we see. The military, who are trained to respond with discipline and to defer to authority, can now suddenly have direct access to the president (as in the Kremlin meeting that morning) and can challenge his actions. Most want him to be more resolute. All of this would have been unthinkable five years ago and constitutes a real achievement in itself. The people had, and many still have, unrealistic expectations of more material possessions immediately as a result of perestroika. Many simply cannot grasp that this can come about only through their own efforts.

Personally, Lobov asserted, perestroika has allowed him and his colleagues to visit and experience the West—something that he had never dreamed would be possible in his lifetime. The economy remains the greatest threat to President Gorbachev, because the people still expect to see goods on the shelves.

Lobov and I spoke also of arms control and the German question. He said that he supported the arms control process, but that the level of armaments was not his primary concern. What caused him concern was the lack of control over the means of production of arms and the technology of arms production. He used as his example a united Germany, with a troop ceiling of 375,000 and no nuclear, biological, and chemical weapons, but with its military industry and military technology lying outside any oversight. With no controls of any sort over the militarization of its economy and population, Germany could, he asserted, mobilize 12 million men and could gear up to produce the necessary military equipment for an armed offensive in a couple of years. "A nationalist, revenge-seeking spirit" could produce a vast number of German armed forces all too quickly.

NATO had sixteen months to move from principles to a strategy complete in all its ramifications. My notes when we met the halfway mark, at the time of the November 1991 summit meeting in Rome: "Multi-purpose joint combined forces, trained in competency and sustainment. We are already into a new future—and who can say what the USSR will be next year?"

33

The First Gulf War

"It takes friends."

With the results of the London summit in hand, I had all the support I needed to work up recommendations for a new operational concept for Allied Command Europe, one that would guide our work on the changing structure of our forces—along with the supporting budget. Without the agreements from the London meeting, the command would have been cast adrift. Even though I knew we had a hard road ahead, I was ready to celebrate.

I was scheduled to see Colin Powell, chairman of the Joint Chiefs of Staff, in Washington in mid-summer 1990 to tie up loose ends on many issues that had been put aside during the final several weeks of concentration on the summit meeting. We were reviewing a draft of our new force structure plan, including the drawdown of both conventional and nuclear forces. We were also involved in what came to be called "harmonization," the sharing of the best fighting equipment among NATO allies (meaning that reductions would be concentrated as much as possible in aging equipment and munitions).

Any action by the United States in the Persian Gulf was the responsibility of General H. Norman Schwarzkopf at Central Command; NATO would provide his closest support. Orders would be coming in from Washington, but it was also up to us to recommend what we should do.

In the Gulf War of 1990–1991 I had the opportunity, given my American responsibilities, to be a "supporting commander-in-chief" on a large scale. At the same time, I had a role unlike that of any earlier supreme commander. Everything would be new and untried, and sixteen nations would have an extraordinary historical opportunity to improvise on the theme of crisis management.

I knew it could hinder the operation if I gave any sign that I was worried about losing my own capability to support NATO, or that I had "turf problems" about giving up some of the U.S. forces and assets assigned to me. The risk of a massive surprise attack against Western Europe was negligible; in fact, the possibility of moving forces from NATO's center to the southern region was what we had contemplated in drawing up the new strategy of crisis management and rapid response, and we were already getting ready for it. As SACEUR I was supposed to review and comment on any question of the withdrawal of forces, stocks, or bases that nations had committed to the Alliance—but not to fight along with the Americans in the Gulf.

I told Norm Schwarzkopf near the end of August, "We're looking at the best way to provide support to you. Just let us know what you need." My staff and I had figured out a menu—a list of things we thought we could do. "We can give you quick turnaround on just about all your equipment that needs fixing, including aircraft engines, tank engines, radios, things like that. The Air Force is bringing in extra maintenance crews so that we can run work shifts around the clock. If you need people with critical skills, I'll send them to you. We'll open up our parts warehouses. I'm ready to send rations and other consumables." I had told a packed meeting at my European Command headquarters that "we will be Norm Schwarzkopf's main support. Whenever he asks for something, our answer will be yes. The details can come later, but the answer is always yes." That "yes" was coming from me as commander-in-chief, U.S. European Command.

I contacted Powell about hauling Schwarzkopf's equipment from the Gulf into Europe for repair. This would save time and money, and would allow Schwarzkopf to keep down the size of the logistics base he had to deploy to the Gulf. At first, Powell was worried about interrupting the stream of cargo aircraft from the United States, but I told him we could use the C-130 Hercules turboprop planes on these shorter runs, and we wouldn't be in the way of the flow from the United States. I passed this word on to Norm also, and he said, "Sure would help if you can do that—let's get started and see how it works out." I knew there were many other areas where we could help him. I sent my U.S. staff planners down to Saudi Arabia the next day to meet with his and lay out the work to be done. "Don't wait for them to tell us what they need," I said to my planners. "Show them what we have to offer here in Europe." The flight time from Germany to the Gulf airbases by C-130 was only seven hours.

Over the years, and in the course of many meetings, discussions, and decisions, the Alliance had devised a pattern of working. Always faced with the possibility of a surprise attack from the Warsaw Pact, the Defense Planning Committee had perfected a plan for quick and comprehensive response—an automatic defense that could take effect immediately across the whole eastern front of NATO in a matter of hours. Alert measures, the detailed instructions to military units, had been distributed, practiced, and improved over the years, so that from the top to the bottom of the fighting organizations and their supporting troops, everyone knew exactly what he was supposed to do if we were on the receiving end of a massive attack by Warsaw Pact nations, led by the Soviet Union.

The first hours of war, in other words, would be push-button. All decisions on how to defend, what actions to take, what reports to send, had been made in advance. Once NATO declared a state of alert, the measures to be taken were automatic. Most of the political decisions had already been made and were codified in our defense planning books. This was the correct way to enable a military response fast enough to provide for an effective defense; but it was very much an inflexible response, one that assumed that all political alternatives had been exhausted. And at every level, from Alliance headquarters down through the military commands to the combat troops and planes and ships, procedures and preplanned actions had been laid out in great detail over many years of multinational planning and coordination. We were locked in, attempting to navigate a fixed direction in an environment that proved to be much more dynamic.

This was evident from the first move I made in response to Iraq's attack into Kuwait. With a warring country on Turkey's border, I needed to keep track of events, which in NATO's terms meant approval of "Military Vigilance Measure 001." We found ourselves cutting and pasting to make sense of the directions we expected the Alliance to give us, which then opened up all the military measures to a debate rather than yielding a sequence of specific instructions to Allied Command Europe. NATO Council members contacted their governments and made recommendations. Chiefs of Defense Staff offered their views. The secretary general called for additional meetings. Everyone requested more detailed information.

As for the reconnaissance aircraft, there were some initial complications. The aircraft were based in Greece, but would be flying their missions in Turkish airspace. As with many other things, the urgency of the situation made it easier than usual to come to a working agreement by which we flew the first mission into Turkey, landed and picked up an observer from the Turkish Air Force, then continued on to the reconnaissance area. After this, the flights became routine, and there was no requirement from Turkey for an observer. The Turks had made their point, and that was enough.

I knew that the Alliance permanent representatives, under pressure to keep their nations informed and to make recommendations, would be hungry for intelligence reports on Iraq, for details of coalition operations, for the views of other countries, for information on weapons systems—for anything that could help them understand or at least put in context the welter of reports and rumors and stray bits of information. My dual role afforded me moment-to-moment communication with the U.S. intelligence network, which guided my dissemination of daily reports to everyone.

On 14 August 1990 I requested activation of frigates from several of the Allied navies in the Mediterranean—those of the United Kingdom, the Netherlands, Norway, Greece, Italy, Spain, and the United States. Germany sent five mine warfare ships to the Mediterranean fleet; Portugal gave us unrestricted use of Lajes Air Base; the Netherlands sent two frigates; France agreed to work under U.S. rules of engagement; Italy moved F-16s to Sigonella. The Gulf War marked the true beginning of the change from a military to a flexible political NATO—something that had to happen, given the change in the world situation. Accordingly, we had to change our procedures, to invent a new way of working together that would meet the new requirements. The North Atlantic Council became a different place: it changed its way of doing business so dramatically that it became a kind of marketplace where, on a daily basis, nations could coordinate their responses on several levels to the needs presented by the Gulf War. As a full Alliance, the sixteen countries made decisions that sent the ACE Mobile Force Air— three combat aircraft squadrons—to Turkey; ordered multinational sea and air patrolling of the Mediterranean; and built an ad hoc communications and radar network to collect and disseminate intelligence from its southern region. As individual nations, but acting with the help of the North Atlantic Council, the Alliance sent additional support, such as air defense missile units and chemical detection devices.

On 17 August, I called Spanish Defense Minister Eduardo Serra Rexach at his vacation cottage in Mallorca. In my role as commander-in-chief (CINC) of U.S. European Command, and speaking for Secretary of Defense Dick Cheney, I asked Serra to permit a refueling stop at Moron Airfield for two groups of twenty-four A-10 aircraft on their way to the Gulf. After some discussion, he said, "All right. You can do it this time. But we will have to watch this closely and consider each request like this on a case-by-case basis. When will this happen?"

I told him the first of the aircraft were about four hours out.

"You mean they will be arriving in four hours?"

"Si, Señor Ministro."

"You Americans. It's always the same." He scolded me at some length and then agreed to clearances for Moron, Torrejon, and Zaragosa.

By 21 August, the French agreed to be part of the Gulf coalition and to operate under U.S. rules of engagement, and they also gave us clearance for the use of several airfields.

By early October it was becoming clearer that Saddam Hussein was not going to respond to any pressure to move out of Kuwait. We had been looking at other things that the European Command could do to help if the situation came to war. Intelligence showed that the Iraqi air force was locating aircraft in its far northern bases, a long distance from the Saudi border—no doubt to make them harder to hit from the south. This put them close to Turkey, where there were good airfields from which U.S. fighters from the European Command often operated. At Ramstein Air Force Base, headquarters of the U.S. Air Force in Europe, General Bob Oaks had been studying the situation. He and Jim McCarthy, my Deputy EUCOM commander, asked me, "Why not a second front?"

I brought up the subject in a call to Schwarzkopf. He was skeptical at first. "It would be great," he said, "but I'm not at all sure we could get the Turks to go along with it. Even if they did, they might change their minds at the last minute. We could never be sure it would happen." He agreed that it would be worth a try, though. On the same day I talked about it to Powell, and he said he'd take it up with Secretary Cheney. This idea would have to be worked at the highest levels in both the U.S. and Turkey.

The Turks had taken a tough stance vis-à-vis their neighbor, Iraq. They had shut down the two major pipelines that moved large amounts of oil from northern Iraq through Turkey to the eastern Mediterranean. Now, well aware that they were arousing Saddam's ire; knowing that an Iraqi corps of seven divisions was in position on the border with Turkey; and worried about their own ability to move forces and logistical support up to reinforce the border areas, they nevertheless said yes, they would allow U.S. aircraft to operate against Iraq from Turkey. I immediately sent key commanders and staff officers from U.S. forces in Europe to Ankara to work with the Turkish General Staff on plans for the operation, which took the code name "Proven Force."

We had a squadron of F-16s from the U.S. 401st Tactical Fighter Wing in Spain flown forward to Incirlik, Turkey. This unit became the core element of a composite wing that eventually grew to over a hundred combat aircraft, including F-111 bombers, F-15 deep penetrator fighter-bombers, and "Wild Weasels": specially configured aircraft for attacking opposing air defenses. Schwarzkopf assigned the missions, and we flew them. This powerful wing flew more than 6,000 sorties against targets in northern Iraq and was responsible in great measure for driving Saddam's planes to seek sanctuary in Iran—from whence they did not return.

On 8 November 1990, Powell advised me, "We've got a lot of forces over there now, but so does Saddam. We'll soon reach the point of buildup where our forces will be too big to allow for a sustained presence in the Gulf. We will have about half of our ground and air forces in place over there. If we pass that point, we won't be able to relieve the units by rotation. The other nations in the coalition are probably at that point or beyond it now. I'm telling the president that if the U.S. goes much further we will be in for the duration, and the duration will have to be short. The choice will then be to continue to build or to stop at that point. If we put more combat power in there and Saddam stays in Kuwait, we will have to use the force or it will look like a victory for him and his perseverance. The president will have to make the decision in a few days, and if he wants to continue to build up, we will need a corps from you. You ready for that?" I said, once again, yes.

I turned to General "Butch" Saint, the commander of U.S. Army forces in Europe. We agreed that our units were about as highly trained and ready as they could be: Every officer and NCO already knew what to do, and the nations in the Alliance knew how to help us. This turned out to be true indeed. When the time came to move the VII Corps, we resorted to the same procedures on the railroads and availed ourselves of the same contracts for use of port facilities, and we relied on the same assistance from the German territorial forces and police—in short, the same everything that we utilized in our exercises. We had top priority on rail lines for the 300 trains we needed, escorts everywhere on the highways, and plenty of help with the 300 barges that moved us and our supplies down the rivers to the ports.

General Saint was ready for this. He got his leaders together, and in a matter of hours created a composite force structure, using parts of each of the two corps in Europe and giving the mission to Lieutenant General John Shalikashvili. Planning was complicated by the drawdown of forces that was well under way. We had already announced a schedule of closeouts of units and installations; and, in military communities, families were leaving their homes in the German countryside or in the garrisons, loading up furniture, taking children out of school, and shipping cars home. To change this entire pattern of events would be absolutely chaotic; it had to proceed at the same time as we sent half our units off to the Gulf. Even then, some people would go to the Gulf knowing that their unit was due to be disbanded later. This meant there would be cases in which Sergeant Smith would leave his family in Germany, go off to war, and return to Europe just in time to uproot his wife and children, ship his furniture, fly home to a military post in the United States, and be told that because of reductions in the force he no longer was needed in the service.

Given the schedule of unit and installation closures, General Saint and his commanders picked the strongest armored forces that were still in good shape. We had trained all along with the understanding that our forces would have to be "tailored"—fitted to their mission by arranging a proper mix of units—and we therefore were accustomed to working in different teams, depending on the task. This made it easier to put together a fighting organization from different parts of the two corps.

Then there was the matter of the families left behind. We didn't want to take all U.S. military units out of any given area of Germany, since that would leave no support for the American community. Saddam Hussein had made a number of threats to use terrorism, openly warning that he would "take the war to the capitals of the enemy." We had to consider that he might well strike at our communities in Europe, so we would need to keep some of our forces for security. There was ammunition—four hundred thousand tons of it—to be moved to ports, last-minute gunnery refresher training to be carried out at the firing ranges, helicopters to be dismantled and loaded on flatcars and into airplanes, equipment to be put into storage while other gear was withdrawn from warehouses, vehicles to be prepared for desert fighting, and barges and trains to be loaded. Using several seaports, we would have to load 115 merchant ships, while at the same time keep the ports secure. And there were families and communities to be guarded. In the end, 19,000 troops were charged with the security of schools, housing areas, and garrisons.

The families of troops departing for the Gulf were faced with a difficult choice. Should they stay in Europe while the troops went off to war, or was it better to go back to the United States? No one knew when the fighting units would return. At home, an ocean away, they would be among fellow countrymen and relatives, but in Europe they would be together, helping one another through the experience of waiting, worrying, and anguishing. As it turned out, of all the military families of troops from Europe that waited for a loved one while the war went on in the Gulf, ninety-nine percent elected to stay where they were. And of the one percent who went back to the States, half returned to Europe during the war.

I got permission to slow down the reduction of forces in Europe in order to support the Gulf War, but the goal of 150,000 home by 1995 remained in effect, and I would have to accelerate the drawdown later in order to meet it. We sent Schwarzkopf 90,000 troops from Germany in sixty days, and he put together the main attack force from units I had commanded a few short years before, VII Corps out of Europe and the 24th Mechanized Infantry Division from Savannah, my old command. I thanked our lucky stars for the computer support that we had so recently built into our European forces and their communities, because we were living with unbelievable levels of change.

On 20 November 1990 I wrote my daughter Erin:

> I went up to Bremerhaven today to watch some of our armored cavalry troops load vehicles onto a ship in preparation for their move to the Gulf. It was raining almost all the time, and fairly cold. The soldiers and NCOs were working hard but in good spirits. They're tired but proud of their mission and [of] the fact that they have been selected, but concerned about the chance that a major war may break out. I asked a lot of questions about how their families felt—wives, husbands, kids—and I got some pretty straightforward answers: NCOs are worried about their families, but most feel that the community support structure will be strong and efficient enough to take good care of them. I promised that I would keep an eye on things myself.

Thanksgiving week I was very glad to get out and see the units. The strain on the leadership, troops, and families was going to be heavy. It was not just a matter of that particular week, of course, but all along, as the buildup in the Gulf continued. One sergeant first class said to me, "My eleven-year-old son is excited and envious about my sailing for the Gulf, but my five-year-old daughter just says over and over, 'I'll miss you, Dad.'" Another said, "My wife understands and is holding up OK, but I can see that the pressure is building up for her." An unmarried specialist four said, "I'd rather be going than staying behind."

The U.S. and other national forces headed for the Gulf were moving by air, land, and sea through my area of responsibility, utilizing ports and airfields in Western Europe and the Mediterranean. This transiting force needed help. The United States, for instance, would make 91,000 one-way landings of cargo and combat aircraft heading for the war, and all would need refueling and maintenance assistance, as well as clearances through the airspace of many countries.

There were seven Iraqi merchant ships in Mediterranean waters at that time, including a ship that had dropped mines in the Red Sea in an earlier crisis. On any given day, there would be about 3,000 merchantmen from countries around the world plying the Mediterranean; if one or more of these ships encountered a mine, traffic would freeze and a serious economic standstill would result. After discussion with the secretary general and the North Atlantic Council on 14–15 July, I requested the activation of NATO's on-call forces for the security of the Mediterranean.

On 17 January 1991, the Gulf air war began.

On 18 January, Tel Aviv and Haifa were hit by Scuds.

The possibility that Israel would get into the war now became very real; their entrance was, in my mind and I think in Powell's, imminent. In a matter of hours they would be going in with their fighter-bombers against the Scuds, and that would be just the beginning. After the Scuds would come any target that Israeli aircraft could reach. Israel felt it had to respond.

Powell wanted to know how long it would take me to move air defense Patriot missiles and launchers into Tel Aviv if I got the word. I said a couple of days. We had talked about this earlier, and I had alerted Butch Saint to put a Patriot battalion on standby without giving them any mission.

Powell said OK and hung up. He was back on the secure line in an hour. "Go," he said. I called Saint, and he passed the order on down the chain to the unit in Giessen, Germany. Giessen is up north, in the Hessian Corridor, about thirty-five miles north of Rhein-Main Airport in Frankfurt, the closest airfield big enough to take a C5A Galaxy. It was snowing in Giessen. The Galaxies, every one of them, were flying missions all over the theater. We didn't have the luxury of holding them for special flights, but it turned out that we had one at Rhein-Main, where it was being loaded with cargo for the Gulf. We unloaded it. It was snowing there, too.

The first Patriot missile trucks were out the gate at Giessen and on the road to Frankfurt within the hour. C5A transports were on the way to get into the stream of aircraft to Tel Aviv and Haifa. On arrival at these two cities, the Patriots fanned out to preselected firing positions. We were operational and ready with the first missiles to defend Tel Aviv 28 hours and 35 minutes after Powell said to go, but our missiles were meant for point defense of particular locations, not entire cities. Nevertheless, they provided an answer to the attacks.

It takes a lot to win a war. It takes friends. We were unopposed in transporting our forces 5,000 miles to the war zone. Had it been necessary to fight our way across the Atlantic and the Mediterranean and the Red Sea and up the Gulf, we would have needed our friends even more.

Some thought we learned from the Gulf War that we had more power than we really required for that conflict and that, with our impressive technological capabilities, we didn't need more than a small percentage of the land, sea, and air forces that we actually mustered to beat Saddam Hussein. But high-intensity warfare (if we define that to mean that each side owns more than 700 tanks, more than 1,000 artillery pieces, more than 400 combat aircraft, and more than 100,000 active duty soldiers) requires the readiness that comes of superb training from top to bottom of the armed forces, and the strategic mobility of a fleet of fast-deployment ships. And, as we would come to see in the second Gulf War, our battles were not limited to high-intensity conflict: we found ourselves fighting guerrilla-style forces and waging low-intensity combat. All of these elements pointed to the essential need for a high level of integrated training.

And for friends, sometimes a lot of them.

34

Red Square

"Let each go crazy in his own way."

11 November 1990. Norwegian general Vigleik Eide, chairman of the NATO Military Committee, and I were flying from Belgium to Moscow, invited by USSR President Gorbachev and Defense Minister Dmitry Yazov. We were at a critical point in the midst of an enormous sweep of change, at a time when all was dependent on the continuing stability of Russia—which in turn meant the strength of the tie between the Russian political class and the Russian military (or, perhaps better put, between the Russian people and their soldiers). We wondered how far we could go to show our own willingness to lay aside the sword—and how much we could depend on our counterparts for the same response. We knew that everywhere we went in the USSR, people would be wondering what we were really like, and for that reason we requested that Vig's wife, Aase, and my wife, Ginny, accompany us. After the meetings in the Kremlin we were to separate, Aase and Vig going to St. Petersburg and Ginny and I to Kiev and then to Sevastopol.

There were times when the policy change seemed to be moving along surprisingly well; then there were other times. This was one of the other times. Four days earlier, in Red Square, a would-be assassin had fired two shots that barely missed Gorbachev. Over the previous several weeks, a fiery debate had been stalling the critically important Soviet economic reform plan. On top of this, the military deputies of the Supreme Soviet (more than a thousand active duty armed forces officers) were calling for a separate meeting with Gorbachev to express their concerns, and it was scheduled for the same day on which we were to meet with him. And as for our side, the United States and other countries were preparing for war in the Persian Gulf.

Eide and I brought along with us teams of officers who were

experts in the fields we knew would come up for discussion. Mine were Kent Brown, political advisor from the U.S. State Department; Italian Lieutenant General Antonio Milani, my deputy for logistics; British Air Vice-Marshal Anthony Woodford, Chief for Policy and Planning; and German Brigadier General Manfred Eisele, Chief of Operational Requirements. They, along with Eide's team, had their own connections with their Russian staff opposites. I told myself to listen more than I talked, and as it turned out, on this occasion that promise was easy to keep. Everywhere we went, in meetings, at dinners, in airplanes, aboard ships, and in the streets, people—including our military counterparts—were more than ready to talk openly with us.

One question stood out in all our individual, one-on-one talks: it had to do with the possibility of a coup, although we didn't use that word. We would say something like, "Let's talk about the future," and the answer, in practically every case, was, "The military will not be involved in running the country." Their question to us was, "What kind of help can we expect from you?" Russian civil and military leaders had guidelines they were trying to follow: *perestroika* called for restructuring and renewal; *glasnost* encouraged speaking out; and *novomychlenie* demanded new thinking, abandoning old styles of doing things, becoming more effective. As goals, they said, these orders were confusing, especially when considered alongside the primacy of the Communist Party and the unity of the nation.

On 11 November 1990, we landed at Sheremetyevo Airport, outside Moscow, where General Mikhail Moiseyev, Armed Forces commander, met us at planeside. Eide and I shook hands with him and a dozen senior military officers, including Generals Maksimov (Strategic Rocket Forces), Varennikov (Ground Forces), Tretyak (Air Defense), Shaposhnikov (Air Forces), Chernavin (Naval Forces), and Colonel General Boris Shein, who was to be my escort. Moiseyev had made his first visit to NATO only three weeks earlier, and had spent a day with me at my headquarters in Casteau, where I found him soldierly, open-minded, and an easy conversationalist, articulate and aware of the world around him. From the start I felt very comfortable with his friendly self-assurance and willingness to discuss a wide range of topics, though we differed, amiably and constructively, on many points. Fortunately, on that day in Belgium we quickly agreed that we would discuss all matters in "soldier talk": simple, straightforward assertions, and responses having more regard for truth and clarity than for elegant obscurity. With that in mind, we had conversed for hours. A few excerpts from my notes, drastically condensed, follow here.

> Moiseyev: The Cold War is over, and Europe should not be divided. We need more East-West exchanges in the military field, with the aim of creating an environment of trust and cooperation. There is a good possibility for security through political means as the military balance goes down. We should be free from military blocs like NATO and the Warsaw Pact. A united Germany demands a united Europe. What is the future for NATO? Still aimed at the USSR? Why not a pan-European security system? (I reply that the North Atlantic tie will endure.)
>
> Moiseyev: "Pan-European security is a sacred endeavor." (I refer to the Atlantic Bridge, the transatlantic ties among NATO allies. I say arms reduction should get more emphasis in our collective strategy.)
>
> Moiseyev: Our military strength should be as easy to see as the lines on the palm of your hand, and we should do a joint study of conventional forces and security. New strategies should conform to the interests of all. (I agree, and this leads to a lengthy discussion.)
>
> Moiseyev: 500,000 of my troops and 170,000 of my officers returning from Eastern Europe do not have housing. We don't have experience as managers. A lot of our economy is a kind of barter: we are accustomed to sending lumber to Poland in exchange for other things. Now we don't know how much to charge Poland. The Congress of Deputies can't deal with this. Nobody knows anything about budgets.

Moiseyev, Eide, and I, along with Colonel Popov, a superb translator, climbed into the four back seats of a limousine. As we cleared the airport, Moiseyev rolled down the glass partition that separated us from the driver and said, "We are like that window—closed before, open now. It's good to see our soldiers mix with the people—not just here at home, but wherever they are, including especially our troops in Germany." Earlier in his career, Moiseyev had commanded a motorized rifle division in Group of Soviet Forces, Germany (GSFG), and he was hurt by the coldness that East German citizens had exhibited toward his soldiers—who were, after all, moving out. He also chided me for a lack of coordination concerning the crisis in the Persian Gulf. "If we had pooled our intelligence," he said, "we might have recognized what Saddam Hussein was up to. We could have stopped him with a relatively small cooperative effort. Now it's out of hand."

The highway leading from Sheremetyevo Airport into the city was quiet. I saw a few dump trucks carrying vegetables; there were no semi-trailers or large vans. A few days before this, I had been driving on an autobahn outside Stuttgart that was crowded with heavy trucks, almost bumper to bumper, heading into and out of the city, each bearing the name of a different firm. I had thought to myself, "There is no one in overall charge of these vehicles. They are registered by a department of transportation and weighed at various locations along the road network and monitored by police who regulate traffic, but no single organization manages their contents or destinations. They are on their own. That's why it works." Whereas, in traveling over Russian roads during the five days of this trip, I had seen only fourteen heavy trucks in the traffic. I wondered how the Soviets were going to change from centralized control of dump trucks to a private enterprise system that could put thousands of trucks on the roads and keep track of them. I understood a little better the things Moiseyev had talked about three weeks earlier, and the effort it would take to change from one system to another. In the center of Moscow, the sidewalks were lined with makeshift stalls, while many of the stores behind them were closed, their display windows empty.

I had asked the British to invite me to lodge with their ambassador, Sir Rodric Braithwaite, because I didn't want the Soviets or anyone else to assume I represented only the U.S. military; that was Colin Powell's job. I was the commander of NATO forces, and of the U.S. military in Europe. After unpacking at the residence, which looks out on the Moscow River and the Kremlin wall, we drove through the gates of the Kremlin and up the steep roadway into the yard at the top, where a light snow was falling and melting as it landed, adding a glisten to the roads and buildings. Nowhere had I seen such an amazing cluster of cathedrals, bathed in light: golden-topped towers against a black sky, like a caravan of giant kings gathering on this crag for the night. We walked through the vaulted Cathedral of the Archangel Michael and through part of the palace itself, whose art and architecture were enough to make me lose track of place and time. I thought of my bricklayer father and wished he could have been with us to see for himself the pillars and arches.

It was dark by the time we moved down to Saint Basil's Church, where again the grouped domes were illuminated by floodlights. With the wall on our left we went up into the center of Red Square, sharing that immense space with a few strollers, mostly in small groups led by guides. I walked in a trance. In my lifetime, I had always thought there would be only two ways that I would have an opportunity to visit Red Square: either as part of a victorious armed force, in which case the square and its Kremlin wall and its onion-domed cathedrals would be in ashes, along with a lot of the rest of the world, or as a prisoner of war, forced to march there. The square was as recognizable to me as Boston Common, yet at the same time as remote as a crater on the back of the moon. Now, at seven o'clock on a cold, dark evening in November 1990, I was here, wearing my American Army uniform, walking toward Lenin's tomb with the bust of Stalin lurking behind it. I tried to absorb it all as a single image: the looming wall, lit by searchlights, with its memorial plaques; the tomb; the clock tower; the GUM department store; the great cobblestone apron that envelops the structures; the cathedral all closed in and concentrated by the surrounding night, the colors black and gold.

I was surprised to see that the square is not level. The surface rises to a mild hump in the middle, with a slope downward in the direction of Saint Basil's. Watching Red Square parades on movie newsreels and then later on television, I had never noticed this. The slant must increase the difficulty of marching in massed troops and vehicles there.

On that evening there were few people walking in the square. The people we passed looked at us with smiling interest and curiosity, and some went out of their way to greet us with a quiet "Good evening." With the help of Colonel Popov, we told them how wonderful it was to be here in Moscow, and how impressed we were. They welcomed us, and some of them said, "What has kept you from coming for so long?" All we could do was smile and say something like, "Well, here we are, anyway." That night we dined with Moiseyev and others at Ambassador Braithwaite's residence. I sat next to Tamara Shein, Colonel General Shein's wife, and we had a long and enjoyable conversation. At one point, I saw that tears were running down Mrs. Shein's cheeks. I asked her if she was all right and she said, "Yes. It is simply that for all these years I have thought of you as horrible people, and I did not want to come here tonight. Now I see that you are just like us. There is really no difference."

Early the following morning, Eide and I paid a routine visit to the Guards Motorized Rifle Division "Tamanskaya" (named for a battle in which the division distinguished itself in World War II) at barracks on the outskirts of Moscow, walking with its commander, Major General Marchenkov, among the tanks and displays of weapons, and chatting with soldiers. This was the palace guard—the unit that would be seen on worldwide television nine months later, with Boris Yeltsin standing on one of the tanks. The commander, who had been praised in the Army newspaper *Red Star* for his efforts to raise garrison morale, told us that three hundred families of members of the division still did not have housing. Junior officers, we were told, were leaving for jobs such as driving buses, where they earned more money.

The news on that Monday morning noted that President Gorbachev was meeting with Yeltsin to discuss economic reform and the latest draft of the union treaty on the relationship among the republics (aimed at preserving the union of Soviet republics and countering moves to secession). Also, Iran announced it planned to conduct major naval maneuvers in the Persian Gulf from 12 to 22 December.

Returning to the city, we met with General Moiseyev and his staff, then with Marshal Yazov. In both instances we compared the size of our forces and theirs and came to the conclusion that the precision of our numbers was affected by the way we count such things. That in itself was helpful to both sides, I think, as we moved along on conventional arms control negotiations. Their main problem, they said, was their inability to see what the future holds—for them, but also in terms of their view of us. Nothing is predictable, they said; nothing is easy to fathom. For the military there was the challenge of national security and stability, and on top of this the military structure itself was under transformation. Furthermore, and more worrisome, their tanks and other military vehicles were piling up in depots east of the Urals, rusting away. They verified what we saw at the Taman Division: the quality of life—of the troops and of the career officer corps—was being hit hard. The saviors of the nation in the Great Patriotic War (World War II) were now penniless. Any Western-style relationship between the military and political leadership, especially on the budgetary side, was nonexistent, they said. The cost of nuclear weaponry, indeed the cost of all military technology, had overwhelmed them. On my note cards I scribbled, "Combination of so many things—idealism, romanticism, necessity, urgency."

Marshal Yazov talked about nuclear weapons. He started with a comment on Chernobyl. "Only one element exploded," he noted, "and for five years we have tried to overcome the disaster. We've spent thirteen billion rubles on it already, and the radiation has reached Tula and continues to grow, with worldwide consequences. And look at the levels of nuclear weapons. There is no way but peace."

"We are both reducing," I remarked, "so we're on the right road."

"If *we* possess nuclear weapons," Yazov replied, "how can we make others *not* possess them?"

Someone said, "But nuclear weapons do deter . . ."

Yazov's response was, "A few nations have them now, but tomorrow . . . and we both know what nationalism can mean."

Later, before we left, I asked Yazov in an aside, "What is the key to success for President Gorbachev?" "The economy," he replied. "Other problems are lesser."

After these two meetings, we were on our way to see Foreign Minister Shevardnadze when we saw him walking toward us down the hall. We met in front of a copy of the Greek sculpture of Laocoön and his sons trying vainly to escape the serpents. I pointed over his shoulder and said, "I have days like that, and I suppose you do, too." He looked back and said, "I do, indeed." No one knew then that he was three weeks away from announcing his resignation.

We followed him into his office where, in his unassuming and understated way, he began by welcoming us as examples of international military cooperation. He said it was good that Reagan, Shultz, and many other political leaders had pressed for military contacts. "We are not adversaries, and we have ruled out a return to the past," he said. "The new policy develops a new image for Europe. This is a top-priority task, one of our long-term objectives."

He then turned to nuclear weapons. "The Soviet delegation was stunned at Malta, as we had been also at Camp David," he said. "We assumed there would be little progress on strategic nuclear forces." I suggested that the reduction of conventional forces at this point, followed in my opinion by strategic nuclear forces, was the right way to address arms control. Shevardnadze ignored that opinion and continued, "The important thing is that we have agreement to go ahead. The inspections will be costly," he noted, "two and a half to three billion rubles in the next five years. And the destruction costs. And redeployment of forces. The cost of change is high. We should examine cost sharing." Then, in a stage whisper, he returned to my comment and said, "We have reached understanding. Troop strength, then follow-up with strategic nuclear forces."

After a few minutes on other subjects, he again turned to nuclear weapons discussions. "Let us get under way in successive stages. Whether or not we formerly have been hostile to the concept of deterrence, we are currently not overdramatizing this, and we recognize other views. We will see what's possible."

Before we left, the Foreign Minister brought up a new subject. "Domestic stability problems—including in the Soviet Union—may grow into instability in Europe, for example Yugoslavia," he observed. "We should not close our eyes to this, but rather settle it before it becomes an insoluble problem."

The next morning was cold and wet, like the previous one. Eide and I, in raincoats, laid a wreath at the Tomb of the Unknown Warrior and, along with all present, saluted the symbols of the soldier, the flag, and the notes of the Russian national anthem, as water streamed down the Kremlin's walls. The ceremony left all of us silent and moved as we shook hands all around and walked back through the monument's gates. It struck me that, when I was entering high school, these officers were fighting World War II. It was a moment of understanding and empathy that signaled the start of a most extraordinary day.

After a session with the ambassadors to Moscow from the NATO countries and an interview with *Red Star*, Eide and I went back to the Kremlin to meet with President Gorbachev. He was waiting at the end of a long, narrow office that was lined with cameras. After shaking hands and exchanging pleasantries, the president waved the scramble of media people out and led us to a table. Eide and I sat facing Gorbachev, with Yazov and Moiseyev flanking him. We knew he was coming from a session with the military members of the Congress of Deputies, who had asked to meet with him. He looked tired, worn, frustrated. From the moment he sat down, his right hand drummed the table, his fingers, reflected in the polished tabletop, galloping softly but continuously. He was obviously affected by the experience he had just undergone, and during our conversation, his response to the provocations of the earlier meeting now and then broke through. As we took our seats, Vig Eide said, "Mr. President, as a Norwegian I must congratulate you on being awarded the Nobel Prize. . . ."

Gorbachev answered quickly, "Yes. Perestroika. When I brought about the changes of 1985–86, everyone applauded, but now the time has come—inevitably—for the sacrifices that these changes make necessary, and no one likes that part. Just now in the Chamber of Deputies meeting, a colonel berated me about the Nobel Prize. A colonel! In the past, he wouldn't be a colonel by now." Yazov stirred, but looked straight ahead. Gorbachev turned to us and said, "And you, the USA and the West, with your talk about your great victory over us." Eide and I both demurred, saying we have consistently held that we're all on the same road, to peace.

"Yes, things have changed," Gorbachev replied "We are no longer adversaries. Even Cheney, your defense secretary, says that. Well, we need to move away from those days. We must unite in the effort to prevent conflict—for instance, right now in the Gulf. We need no war with Saddam. The military chiefs should have contact with the Security Council." I took out my note cards, as always, and he seemed to like that: a general taking notes. He went on, "We need to study the security structure so it can deal with future crises like this."

Colonel Popov's skill at translation was as smooth as I'd ever seen. He followed along quietly, just a couple of words behind Gorbachev, as the president ruminated about his worries over the Soviet troops in East Germany. "They are not respected by the local populace. I've known [German Chancellor Helmut] Kohl and [Foreign Minister Hans-Dietrich] Genscher since 1975. There should be more consideration for our soldiers." Then, quietly, "We've spent billions on Chernobyl, and it's getting worse. We've invited scientists from all over the world, asking them for help. This is what nuclear weapons could do—and a lot worse." Yazov nodded yes, and Gorbachev continued. "We will continue our support for reduction of nuclear weapons as well as conventional forces in Europe. General Yazov will be going to Vienna. We all need military reform, and"—turning again to Yazov—"we ourselves are well along on this. We will share this information with you. We need better military-to-military contact. We have a large overlap of interests."

Eide asked, "Sir, what do you think will be the main problems affecting the new military balance?"

Gorbachev was quick to reply. "There are three. First, there has to be a structure for security for the continent of Europe. Second, it requires military structural changes. Third, NATO must become a political organization. There is also a fourth, and that is, we need more contact, more communication. You are lagging in this effort. And there is a fifth: We must proceed with courage." With both hands on the edge of the table, he was again lightly tapping his fingers, almost as if he were playing a soft tune on a piano. He looked exhausted. He looked grim. I felt awkward taking up his time on this day, when what he needed was rest. "For the first time in this country's history," he said, "we have a chance to make this scale of changes without bloodshed. Can we do that? We don't need white against red. No civil war."

Then he erupted with exasperation. With lips pressed hard together, he took in a deep breath through his nose. He sat up straight and looked beyond us. "They call *me* indecisive? I know my society. I ask my critics: Are we not on a track of reform since 1985? *Yes!* Then leave it to us! You can't tell us what to do. We *know* what to do!" He relaxed a little, and said more evenly, "For stability, we need the Union treaty, a transition to a market economy, and a state governed by law. And the military *will* help. There are people . . . there are dangers of separatist elements, pro-fascist elements . . ." His eyes shifted away from us, beyond us. He seemed to be inspecting with some curiosity his own office, but he spoke with deliberation. "The military is a political instrument. We *must* operate resolutely against the threat to constitutional order. And we will be most resolute." He sighed. "Let each go crazy in his own way, that's the way we put it. But we must have orderly government, and the stance of the military will be of great significance. We must safeguard our national security interests, with forces of a size commensurate with the task."

There was an uncomfortable pause. The president told Eide and me that we needed to get out into the countryside and talk to people, communicate, let them hear from us, and listen to what they had to say. We both said we would do that. I mentioned that General Eide and I planned to split up: he would go to St. Petersburg, I to Kiev and Sevastopol. There were more amenities; then we took our leave. On the following day, Vig and I parted company at the airport and went our separate ways.

On our arrival at Kiev, General Gromov, commander of the Kiev Military District, greeted us with, "Welcome to the Ukrainian army." Gromov, forty-seven years old, had commanded the Soviet Army forces at the end of their campaign in Afghanistan, and he was proud to be the last soldier to have crossed the border back into the Soviet Union. At a long luncheon, I found he had a good sense of humor and wanted to be seen as a man of action. We talked of NATO's future, the Gulf, Afghanistan, Army reform, Germany, the quality of life of the Russian soldier, the media, our visit to Moscow. I asked him, "How do you see this winter? Is it going to be rough?" And Moiseyev immediately replied, "I know what you mean. We're not going to be trying to take over the government. First of all, we are going to be loyal just like you would be loyal. But to what? To the USSR? To Russia? Or the Ukraine, or what?"

He worried that his district forces had been tasked since 1985 with cleanup and reconstruction in Chernobyl and, in addition, with helping recovery after the Armenian earthquake in 1988. These diversions from military training troubled him, although he knew they were necessary. But "above all else," he insisted, "we must remember that we are the military, and we must concentrate on being excellent at that."

We next visited the high bluff—the height of Mamayev Kurgan over-looking the city of Volgograd—where the Victory statue ("The Moth-erland," commemorating the Battle of Stalingrad) stands with a raised sword. At one time it was the tallest sculpture in the world.

Then, in the late afternoon, we boarded once again our assigned Tupolev 154 and headed for the Crimea.

We flew from Kiev to the Crimea, landing at Sevastopol, where we were met by the commander of the Black Sea Fleet, Admiral Mikhail Khronopulo. We drove into the port past traffic control points operated by sailors, where signs read "Sevastopol Limited Zone." We toured the center of the city, enjoying the warm weather and talking to the people strolling there. I felt obliged to tell everyone I met that I was having a wonderful time in Russia. One woman asked Colonel Popov, "Is he running for office?"

Together with Colonel General Shein and his wife, Tamara, we lodged in a dacha with a fine view of the Black Sea. We had dinner, just the four of us, and talked long about the experiences of my visit. It was a conversation—and two people—I will never forget. At about one o'clock, Ginny and I went to bed, happy with the events of the day but grateful to get some rest. I drifted off into a deep sleep, but two hours later woke up with a start. One can harbor a lot of thoughts in two sec-onds; before I was fully awake, I had asked myself, "What am I doing here in this strange house? How do I escape from here?" Then I came to my senses and went happily back to sleep, but not before I promised myself that I would take an early walk. At sunrise I got up, dressed, and slipped out of the house. I walked through the garden and down to the edge of the sea, where some crooked stone steps led into the water. This was another place that I never expected to see, but I was determined to seize the moment and make it mine. I said to myself, "I can't have come all this way only to turn back now. I must put my toes in the Black Sea." I took off my shoes and socks and stepped down into the water—

where, it turned out, the rocks were mossy. My reveries were quickly over as I flailed around, seeking balance, and slid slowly into the Black Sea. I took it as a kind of christening, and gingerly worked my way out over the slippery stones. Fortunately, I had a backup uniform. Later that morning I was piped aboard the heavy cruiser *Slava* and graciously given the chance to tour the ship from stem to stern, chatting with the sailors as I went along and enjoying a welcome contrast with my unforgettable earlier Black Sea experience.

We had planned to visit Yalta, but I lingered too long aboard the *Slava*, so Admiral Khronopulo rode with me to the airfield, which I think was at Balaklava. As we drove along, I asked about the small huts sprinkled throughout the fields. They were the homes of squatters, he grumbled: Tatars who, arriving from exile in the north, were trying to reclaim parts of the farms they said belonged to them. Thus I ended the most interesting visit abroad I ever had.

On 29 November I was scheduled to meet with the foreign press corps in London. But a fog bank moved in, making my flight across the Channel impossible, so I dictated a fax from my note cards to the group, a summary of the main impressions from my trip to the Soviet Union:

> I will pick up now on the main issues as I saw them rather than give you a tour guide approach to the four and a half days that I spent in the USSR. Most of what I have to say concerns the single subject of the Soviet military mind and how they see the situation.
>
> First, the Soviet military thinks it's going to be a tough winter. They see a breakdown of the economy, and they do not know where that can lead. They are loyal to their political leadership but concerned about the political structure of the future—not in the sense that they want to control it in any way, but that they need to understand their own role in that structure.
>
> Second, military reform. Discussions of this made me realize how big and how widespread the Soviet military really is. It's going to take a long time for the ideas of reform to fully sink in and become meaningful in terms of changes in doctrine, training, organization, equipment, leadership, planning, and all the daily activities of Soviet military life. On top of this, the Soviets have to reorganize at the same time and reduce their

forces, which entails finding homes and jobs for former military people.

The military is discussing perestroika, glasnost, sufficiency, and defensive defense in more or less theoretical terms. At the top they insist that they are wedded to these ideas. But, as might be expected, in an organization as large as the Soviet military, these concepts suffer some attenuation as you go down through the ranks toward the bottom of the pyramid.

35

The Rescue of the Kurds

"Exodus from the mountains"

In late March 1991, as the first Gulf War came to an end, it was followed by two short internal uprisings in Iraq. A defeated and weakened Saddam Hussein found himself beset not only by the Shiite Muslim factions in the south of the country but—even more infuriatingly to him—by the Kurds in the north, who, encouraged by the United States, seized the opportunity to throw themselves into a battle for autonomy, convinced that their moment had (finally) come.

This ancient coalition of tribes, the Carduchi, had battled for centuries to gain autonomy for Kurdistan, a territory encompassing about 75,000 square miles of the border areas of Syria, Turkey, Iran, and Iraq. Finally promised independence by the Treaty of Sèvres after World War I, the Kurds were embittered when the pledge was not honored, and within years of the signing of the treaty resumed sporadic guerrilla warfare and a long succession of revolts in this area. In 1988, Saddam Hussein's answer was to attack the Kurds with spectacular brutality, shelling them with poison gas and leveling whole villages with bulldozers, with the result that the inhabitants took flight across the borders into Turkey and Iran. This event was followed by an uneasy truce, often broken by both the Iraqis and the Kurds, whereupon some, but not all, of the refugees crept back to their homes and farms, even as thousands of Kurds stayed behind in Turkey.

But the Kurds' moment had *not* arrived. In April 1991, after losing control of Kuwait in the Gulf War, Saddam once again selected Kurdish villages that he thought might be supporting the guerrillas and moved artillery batteries up to shell those areas into ruins. This time, when Iraqi troops began their systematic destruction, the Kurds, knowing only too well what havoc Saddam was willing to bring down on them, panicked and fled en masse. The population of hundreds of villages was almost instantaneously on the move, hauling what possessions they could carry in their autos and farm tractors and wagons or on their backs, hoping to find sanctuary in the mountains along the borders with Turkey and Iran.

Large numbers of Kurds made it into Iran, but when others—450,000 of them—reached Turkey, they were stopped by border troops who would allow them to go no farther. The Turks had accepted a wave of 80,000 Kurdish refugees three years earlier, but there was not to be that kind of help this time. The Turks knew that the refugees pouring into the border provinces would quickly overwhelm the weak government apparatus and consume more resources than their infrastructure could muster. Instead, the refugees huddled in forty makeshift camps on the steep and forbidding slopes, a choice for which they were eminently unprepared. In their hurry to escape they had carried very little with them, and this barren land offered scant supplies of food, water, shelter, or medicine. In addition, the battles of previous weeks had fragmented and dispersed the Kurdish leadership and their young fighters, leaving few able administrators for the makeshift camps.

Once in a while (though not often), you experience the luxury of an unencumbered decision. For several months the United States had been withdrawing thousands of troops from our European bases and sending them and their families home. We were anticipating instability in Eastern Europe and the Balkans. The migration of the Kurds would add to the border troubles of Turkey. Trouble draws reporters like a powerful magnet—and with stringers scattered everywhere, always scanning for new developments, the conveyors of the news are quickly on the scene when anything happens. Already, television teams from major networks around the world were in the refugee camps. The most helpful support for the Kurds at that point was the arrestingly stark and graphic reports that were going out over the media. The world saw the flies and sewage everywhere in the camps; the suffering and dying children; the haggard, despairing Kurdish doctors, who spoke of scores of deaths every day in every camp and begged for medical supplies. At one point I told Colin Powell about my worry that if no help came and the Kurds started to die in even larger numbers, there would come a moment—a point of no return—when the camps would collapse, probably all at once. He asked me to send him a "back channel" message—a rough plan of the actions I would need to take—and he enumerated those tasks in a message that he in turn sent me, ordering me to be ready to respond to the Kurds on short notice. "I don't know when we'll get a decision, but I think it's coming very soon," he said on the secure phone. "And when it does, we'll have to jump through our asses, so be ready to do the same."

President Turgut Özal of Turkey asked President George H. W. Bush for assistance, and on Friday, 5 April, Powell's deputy, Admiral Dave Jeremiah, called me to say that within a couple of hours President Bush would make a statement. "It will call for a major effort on assistance for the Kurds," Jeremiah advised. "A sizable package. This means you'll get the final order without any real changes from what we've planned; airdrops of food, tentage, clothing to the Kurds in their main concentrations. [National Security Advisor Brent] Scowcroft is going to get the word to the Iraqis in Baghdad that we want no interference. This will be your show, with Norm Schwarzkopf supporting you. Be ready to start on Sunday."

I checked in with Schwarzkopf and asked him for the military food rations he was shipping back from the Gulf and as many tents as he could possibly give me. "OK on the rations," he said. "We can send you plenty. But I'm scrounging for tents myself. I've even borrowed pilgrimage tents from the Saudis." Schwarzkopf diverted ships already sailing for eastern U.S. ports and also sent me radar early-warning aircraft to help us manage the airspace and coordinate the first supply flights. A few days later he sent twenty cargo aircraft, some aerial tankers, and four reconnaissance fighters and notified us that he had seven hospitals available. From our Stuttgart headquarters, Jim McCarthy wove together a rescue team from the ground, sea, and air forces in our European Command.

President Bush, along with Secretary of State James Baker and Secretary of Defense Dick Cheney, talked with political leaders around the world, and Powell and I followed up with the military leaders. I called Ankara at 11:00 a.m. on 6 April and talked to the Turkish Chief of Defense Staff, General Doğan Güreş, who gave me details of the situation on the border. We worked out tentative arrangements for the use of Incirlik and other airfields in eastern Turkey. I called General Bob Oaks, head of American air forces in Europe, and told him I needed a seasoned commander—and he knew that I meant Major General Jim Jamerson. During the Gulf War, Jim had led the American air operation out of Turkey that flew 6,000 sorties against northern Iraq. Bob's quick response was, "Jim's our man."

Only two weeks earlier, Jamerson had closed down the temporary camp just off the runway at Incirlik, from which 5,000 U.S. troops had supported the Gulf War. "Don't worry about rebuilding the organization right now," I told him. "Let's do enough to get started. Put what aircraft you have on hand into position to deliver pallets to the Kurds right away. Be ready to get the stuff into the camps however you can, and we'll smooth it out later."

Jim's reply was a laconic "I got it. We can handle it. No problem."

"When can you get started?" I asked him.

"Soon's you let me off the phone."

Later that day, I reached Admiral Jeremiah in his sedan in Washington traffic and let him know that we were set to go with the first airdrops by noon the following day. The mountains along the Turkey-Iraq border were shrouded in heavy clouds and rain, but we were confident we could get our supply flights into the camps. "I'm glad you got through to me," he replied. "I'm on my way to the White House right now to talk to the president about this." I went over the plans quickly with him as he drove up Constitution Avenue. We would fly the first supply runs to the concentrations of Kurds where we had an accurate fix on their location; in the meantime, we would send our air reconnaissance out to pinpoint the other camps. We had enough parachutes, pallets, and rations of food and water to cover the first few days. We broke off the conversation as he arrived at the White House gate.

That night, President Bush appeared on television to talk about the plight of the Kurds. "No one," he said, "can see the pictures or hear the accounts of human suffering—men, women, and, most painfully of all, innocent children—and not be deeply moved." He announced that we would drop food to the Kurds starting the next day, Sunday. We watched the president and heard his words, and we were already leaning forward in our saddles. By noon the weather in the mountains was good enough for six C-130 Hercules to take off from Incirlik with the first pallets of food and fresh water for the Kurds in the camps along the border. Secretary Baker flew in to look at the situation and sent back to President Bush a confirmation that the plight of the Kurds could only be described as horrible. He was concerned about the lack of water, the cold weather, and the scarcity of tents, medicine, blankets, and clothing, stressing that "much, much more needs to be done very quickly."

The airdrops were a godsend to the Kurds and arrived in the nick of time, but without ground guidance they were also awkward and dangerous. I told Powell that Jamerson and his air crews were trying hard to drop our parachute loads close to the clumps of people we could see on the ground, but we were never sure we were getting the right supplies to the right places. I then made my first request for a change: I asked to put some of our own troops under Brigadier General Dick Potter into the camps to work with the Kurdish leaders, checking the situation in each location, telling us what was required, and setting up electronic directional beacons and ground communications for accurate drops. The next day, 9 April, Powell called and said, "You've got the go-ahead to put some troops on the ground inside the camps." He told me to keep our presence as small as possible. Our drops immediately became much more accurate, but we knew that the most efficient way to support the Kurds was to bring our supplies by truck from the airports and seaports. By 11 April, American, British, and French forces had dropped 346 tons of supplies, and we were by then running trucks up from the Turkish ports of İskenderun, Mersin, and İzmir all the way to the border at Silopi, a drive of about thirty-six hours.

Meanwhile, the membership list for the coalition of forces in eastern Turkey was growing. The Turks were there to greet us and join us at the command posts. The British and French had come in, followed by contingents from the Netherlands, Italy, Canada, and Spain. More and more volunteer groups and relief agencies arrived: the Red Cross and Red Crescent, Médecins Sans Frontières (Doctors Without Borders), CARE, Christian Outreach, Global Partners, Operation Mercy, Save the Children, UNICEF, the World Food Program, Oxfam, the Centers for Disease Control—all in all, fifty humanitarian organizations. (We did not have the support of the UN.) These groups, operating with as much help as we could give them, went up into the camps and worked with great dedication, living among the refugees and putting heart and soul into the effort. Among them there was a desire to work alone, as self-contained agencies—to make a contribution without being involved in the general administration of the assistance effort, which they tended to view as overly bureaucratic and limiting their freedom of action. "Military operations and relief agencies are two different things," they said. "We'll just set up on the other end of the airfield and in the camps. Let's just keep out of each other's way."

We had some teaming to do. We tried inviting the leaders of the volunteer groups to attend our daily international military staff meetings to exchange information and resolve problems. They accepted, and began to see that there were many ways we could be of help to them without usurping any of their authority or restricting their flexibility. It was a new experience for some of us, a little shaky in the beginning but improving as we went along, and it was facilitated by a mutual recognition that this would be a big operation—one of the largest humanitarian efforts to date—calling for sophisticated handling of administration and logistics, relations with the Turkish host government, the need for security, and dealings with the Iraqi side. These volunteer organizations needed us, and we needed them.

We were only beginning to understand the problems that the Kurds were facing. When we inserted American and British Special Forces and French reconnaissance units into the camps, our operation improved by one great quantum leap. They set up drop zones, resupply sites, and storage areas; they established medical clinics; they gave the Kurds confidence that the camps were safe; and in many cases they helped Kurdish leaders establish the first real organization and discipline among these enormous populations. Most important, working together with large numbers of refugees convinced us all that getting food and medicine into the camps was not going to be enough. Sanitation was nonexistent. The refugees lacked pure water, and their living areas were unbelievably filthy and contaminated. We were at all times concerned about the possibility of an outbreak of cholera. The children had diarrhea, and many were dying of simple dehydration. At that point we had only rough estimates, but we could see that the Kurds were still dying in large numbers every day. They needed to be down on level ground, near freshwater. We had dropped pallets of water by parachute, lifted water by helicopter, and pumped water from small mountain streams, but we still could not adequately meet the demand, which we estimated at a million liters per day. I asked for yet another change of mission. We would need to enter Iraq.

We first had to agree among ourselves within the task force before we could recommend to the nations involved the actions we felt were necessary. Every move would have to be acceptable to the Turks, the supporting countries, the UN, the volunteer agencies, and—we would hope—the Iraqis. The key, of course, was getting the Iraqis to move their military units out of the way. We would have to bring in more ground troops to hedge against the possibility that at some point the Iraqi response could get us into a "High Noon" situation. Jim McCarthy flew down to Turkey to get a firsthand look. He visited Jamerson at Incirlik and then piloted a C-130 Hercules on a resupply mission himself to be sure he had a good understanding of the way things were going. Flying with him were Brigadier General Paul LePage, commander of the French forces in the coalition, and Staffan de Mistura, the UN representative. Jim called me on 16 April to say, "There's no doubt about it—we're going to have to move the Kurds." Jim then went on to Ankara to visit U.S. ambassador Mort Abramowitz and talk to him about this change. Abramowitz, who from the beginning had worked day and night to achieve the close coordination we needed with the Turkish political leadership, agreed that the best idea was to get the Kurds to more hospitable terrain—and also out of Turkey. He and Jim spread a map of the border area on the floor of the ambassador's living room and roughed out an area in Iraq south of the mountains that could be used for establishing camps. After listening to Jim, I called Powell. He got out his map, and I described the boundary of the area we had in mind; Powell transferred the information to his map and said he would discuss it with Cheney, Scowcroft, and Baker, and with Tom Pickering, our U.S. ambassador to the UN. It would have to go to the president for approval, Powell noted, because the other nations of the coalition would want to hear from the president on this if we were going to get consensus. All the supporting nations with troops on the border, without exception, told us they were ready to send more of their military forces to meet the new requirements—including entering Iraq.

On 16 April, Dave Jeremiah called. There would be a warning order coming to me that night, telling me to prepare to move the Kurds down to the designated area. We had asked for a complex and difficult decision that required international agreement among eight countries, and we had received an answer in the space of thirty-six hours. Tom Pickering took the plan to the UN. Now we had to see what the Iraqis would do. We were going inside Iraq, a nation we had recently defeated in war, and we had been ordered to defend the Kurds against any further attacks by the Iraqis. Meantime, the Kurdish guerrillas had kept up their attacks against Iraqi military forces in the area, and the Iraqis were searching out and attempting to eliminate the guerrillas. The UN High Commissioner for Refugees had not yet taken control of the operation and said he could not do so until the fighting stopped, the area was made secure from attack, and the Kurds were in decent, survivable camps.

At this point, we needed to get Saddam's military forces to back out of the region where we wanted to build the camps, approximately 1,800 square miles of Iraqi territory. We laid out a plan for the valley camps, estimating a need to provide for 500,000 refugees who would require 600 tons per day of food and supplies. We decided to build communities of separate villages, organized to encourage group integrity. The Kurds themselves, we hoped, would build the camps. We put the plan together in a matter of several hours and sent it out to the nations involved, arranging for them to do the detailed work in putting together the support that would be needed for this new phase. Admiral Jacques Lanxade in France said he could send 100–200 ground troops within two days, and this number could increase if necessary as time went along. Admiral Dieter Wellershoff in Germany said he could send forty helicopters, some tents, and some C-160 aircraft, but he could not send ground forces. He noted that Germany was working also in Iran with the Kurds who had fled across that country's border. Domenico Corcione, the minister of defense in Italy, said he could send C-130s plus parachutes and rigging, and he would also try to send some ground forces. Admiral Gonzalo Martín Granizo, Chief of the Defense Staff in Spain, said he would start with a company of infantry and probably build to a battalion. We (the Americans) at this time had 1,500 Army, 1,800 Air Force, and 2,100 Marines, along with a Navy contingent at sea as well as 35 Navy present in the land part of the action. On 17 April, we deployed the U.S. Navy carrier *Roosevelt* to the eastern Mediterranean for good measure.

General Butch Saint called me from Heidelberg and offered Lieutenant General John Shalikashvili, his deputy, to be overall commander of this growing force. I had watched John working under General Saint, and I knew he was a strong leader. In 1990, Butch had given him full responsibility for the complex logistical operations of the U.S. Army in Europe in support of the Gulf War, and I was much impressed with the way he moved in and took charge of one difficult task after another. He was an experienced soldier, sensitive to political issues, and cool under pressure—just the right person for this novel mission. Shalikashvili dropped what he was doing and left for Turkey on 17 April. General Jay Garner also arrived on that day, along with General Anthony Zinni. Jim Jamerson stayed on as deputy during this phase and would later take over again as forces were drawn down.

How to move the Kurds? Many of them had used their autos and farm tractors to get into the mountains, abandoning them when they ran out of fuel. With Lieutenant Colonel Bill Braddy, commander of 4th Squadron, 11th Armored Cavalry Regiment, in his command center, Jay Garner made a reconnaissance of the hundreds of cars and trucks along the clogged mountain roads and found that most of them were still usable. After we flew out teams of mechanics to fuel them and get them started, their owners came back to claim their vehicles. We also lined up all the buses and trucks we could get our hands on and set up helicopter flights to carry out older people and the sick. Along each of the roads out of the camp, we provided way stations and security patrols. The French volunteered to move their cavalry in to screen the roads from the mountain camps down to the new area. On 19 April, Shalikashvili went to the Habur Bridge, where a main road crosses the Turkey-Iraq border, to meet Iraqi Brigadier General Nushwan Danoun and deliver a demarche laying out our plan.

The 2nd Battalion, 8th Marines, Lieutenant Colonel Tony Corwin commanding, entered Iraq with two rifle companies, an 81mm mortar platoon, an engineer platoon, and the battalion staff. Another Marine rifle company was placed on standby on the Turkish side to assist if necessary. When the Marines crossed the border, they reported, the Iraqi troops were waving and smiling. British, French, and Dutch forces also went in—the British to patrol the city of Zakhu, the Dutch to keep open the road from Turkey, and the French to operate farther to the east, screening the new camps. We picked up the leaders of the Kurds and flew them on a reconnaissance of the proposed campsites and the security zone. For the next three weeks came long and colorful caravans of cars and trucks, augmented by our military vehicles, rented buses, and skinny mules, snaking down the mountain passes. "We're riding high with the media," Jim McCarthy observed.

While working in the camps we had acquired a general knowledge about the home areas of the Kurds that were in each camp, and we had located the new camps along return routes that would put each camp's residents in the direction of their own home area. American Army Colonel Dick Naab took up residence in a house close to the quarters of the Iraqi brigadier general responsible for the area, and we set up regular meetings. Naab's Iraqi counterpart had direct radio access to Saddam Hussein's headquarters, and we found we could get a message to Baghdad and receive a response very quickly, usually within twenty-four hours. This gave us a conduit that often worked better than any other connection. Dick's negotiating skills—and his courage—were the reason we were able to engage in such an unprecedented way.

By late May we were working hard to stay ahead of the exodus from the mountains. With more and more camp populations returning to the lowlands, we needed to expand security to the east, deeper into Iraq, encompassing the towns of Al Abadiyah and Sirsenk. We showed our new sketch to the Iraqi brigadier, who communicated with Baghdad and came to see us a few hours later. "This will be very hard to do," he said. "What you are asking for is a large piece of territory that is very important to us for many reasons. Foremost, our leader, Saddam Hussein, has a palace in this area. We could not abandon it and risk its damage."

"As far the palace is concerned," we replied, "we knew it was there, and we flew over it throughout the war and never touched it. It wasn't a target then, and it isn't now. You don't have to worry about the palace. We'll leave it alone. Tell him that." He came back later and told us that the Iraqis would "have to keep control of the palace with at least a company of guards. Otherwise, we would feel required to destroy it so that it would not be defiled." I got in touch with Powell. My view was that the palace had no importance to us, and we ought not to make a fuss about it. He agreed and said he would let me know if anyone in Washington had a problem. No one did.

The task force now had units from the United States, the United Kingdom, France, the Netherlands, Canada, Italy, Spain, Belgium, Australia, and Luxembourg. The roll call of other countries that were supportive in various ways had grown to include Austria, Bulgaria, Czechoslovakia, Greece, Hungary, Iceland, Ireland, Japan, Norway, Portugal, Romania, Saudi Arabia, and Sweden. We kept up our daily coordination meetings of the task force, at which leaders of the military contingents and the civilian relief organizations could take part in exchanges of information and ideas. The Turkish General Staff officers in our headquarters grew in numbers and helped us with solutions to the problems inherent in this extraordinary presence in their country. There was never an easy day, and we knew we owed a lot to the patience and understanding of these officers. On Sunday, 21 April, Jim McCarthy met in Paris with UN Secretary General Perez de Cuellar and High Commissioner Sadruddin Aga Khan. McCarthy went over the details and urged these UN leaders to take over as soon as possible. Jim then ordered U.S. Army Europe to take ten trucks, paint them white, fill them with relief supplies, and get an Air Force lift to Silopi, Turkey, where the UN provided its banners and began operations.

With the Iraqis, by contrast, we were hard-nosed about protection of the Kurds. The 44th Iraqi Division was then only a few kilometers outside the security zone, and we demanded that it back off farther to the south. We drew two lines on the map—one that demarcated what we considered to be a twenty-four-hour march toward our outposts guarding the Kurds, and the other a twelve-hour march. We said that if we saw troops moving toward us, at the first line we would warn them, and at the second we would have to attack them with air strikes before they got to our positions. We told the Iraqis to inform us of any kind of movement they intended to make and for what reason.

On 21 April, the last of the Iraqi military moved south from the Zakhu area and left the security zone, with the exception of the city of Zakhu itself. We were disarming the Kurds as they came into the new camps, and the Kurds didn't like it: they felt naked and vulnerable without weapons. We held fast to our policy, however: no firearms in the camps. We knew that we were thereby taking on more responsibility for protecting the Kurds, but we couldn't allow camps that were soon to be run by the UN to become bases for guerrilla activity. At the same time, we had not tried to disarm the Kurds or the Iraqis inside the city of Zakhu and, increasingly, fully armed Kurds were walking the streets with rifles slung over their shoulders, sharing the town with armed Iraqis and with coalition soldiers from the United States, the United Kingdom, the Netherlands, and Spain. There were some tense moments.

On 24 April, I went to London to talk to Prime Minister John Major and British military leaders. After the meeting I flew to Turkey to see Shalikashvili. On the way I called Powell and told him of my meeting in London, then passed on to him what Shali had told me about conditions in Zakhu; I noted that we would be watching this development. His advice was, "Keep the task force presence in Zakhu from becoming a big confrontation. We don't want a Dodge City there." I flew on into Incirlik in the early evening, and at the airfield I talked with Shalikashvili, who brought up a new matter of great interest. It was beginning to appear that, as we had hoped, some of the Kurds were making their way not to the main camps in the security zone but beyond them, passing through Iraqi lines and returning to their homes farther to the south. He wasn't sure how much of this was going on, but our troops reported that Kurds were approaching the Iraqi outposts, talking to the soldiers, and being permitted to pass. This was a good sign. I asked him to have Colonel Naab find out through his Iraqi point of contact whether a homeward migration of the Kurds was acceptable and would be tolerated. A little later, Naab came back with the word that Saddam Hussein wanted the Kurds to resettle on their lands and would not oppose it. His motive, I felt sure, was to get the coalition forces out of Iraq, and he knew this would not happen unless the Kurds were returned home.

Shalikashvili, Jamerson, Garner, Zinni, and I talked well into the night. On the morning of 25 April, Shalikashvili and I flew to Diyarba-kir and shifted to a helicopter for the flight to Silopi, where Garner had brought his coalition commanders together to discuss the situation at Zakhu. The population of the town was now 10,000, but it could grow to 100,000 or more as the Kurds continued to pour down from the hills. The British had been given the mission of security in the town, and they wanted to go in immediately and get started. I approved a plan to put pressure on the Iraqi police, to intimidate them and force them out of the town. The plan called for the Dutch Marines to take up positions surrounding the town and control entry and departure. U.S. Marines in light armored vehicles would control the interior of the town. The risks were mounting. In some ways it was hard to believe we had gotten this far with the Iraqis, but the thought of what could happen to the refu-gees made the risks worthwhile. The fear of cholera was always there.

After the meeting, Shali, Garner, and I flew a reconnaissance over the camps under construction near Zakhu and then on to Sirsenk and Al Amadiyah, about fifty kilometers deeper eastward into Iraq, where we looked for areas for new camps. We overflew Iraqi small units in their gun positions, and they waved at us as we passed. Then Saddam's pal-ace came into view: a spectral white cluster of towers and walls on the crest of a conical hill, very different in style from the surrounding agri-cultural area. We turned at the eastern edge of the security zone and flew back toward Turkey along the hills that marked the southern bor-der of the area that Powell and I had sketched out earlier, where our string of observation posts kept watch on the Iraqi forces farther south.

The next morning I boarded a Blackhawk with Shalikashvili and lifted off for the mountains on the border to see for myself the condi-tions in the camps. The ridges in this area climbed to fourteen thou-sand feet. It was a blustery day, and as we bounced along in the whorls of air currents in the valleys, climbing higher and higher, I saw in the distance, far up near the crest of a ridge, a sea of makeshift tents in the closest of the camps, Isikveren, which held 80,000 refugees. The word "camp" did not describe these places; "conglomeration" was more accu-rate. The multicolored mass slowly became more defined, and I could make out hundreds of hovels scattered along craggy ridges and nar-row, rocky ravines in a desolate array, a jumble of images of wrack and ruin. As we made our landing approach, a throng of people crowded into the helicopter landing zone, trying to be close to any delivery of goods. We circled and the people moved back barely enough to let us land, then surged in for the supplies we carried, while U.S. Special Forces soldiers and local leaders tried to organize the unloading and distribution of our cargo.

At the landing zone, I met the leader of this swarm of people, a short and muscular middle-aged man. We walked through the crowd to a hillock from where we could see most of the area. In spite of the bright sun, the weather at this altitude was cool. Here we met a doctor from the town of Zakhu who said, with a tired, wan smile, "Things are better, much better. We lost three today, though—children. It's the best day we've had since we got here. We were losing thirty every day until your people arrived. Thanks for what you're doing to get help to us."

The camp leader and the doctor took me for a walk along the rocky hillocks and gullies. There were very few young men in the camp; the doctor, who spoke good English, said many had been killed and others had gone with the guerrillas. I looked at some of the many ragged little children, most of whom were bare from the waist down. "Diarrhea," the doctor said. I thought of them as I looked at a slope on the outskirts of the camp, where I could see shallow graves that had been scooped in the stony earth. The ground—it was in essence an extensive dumping ground—was spattered with feces and littered with rags, paper, shredded sheets of plastic, bones, animal hide, trash and more trash, and fragments of everything imaginable. The smell of death and corpses hung over the place, along with other smells: smoldering garbage, excrement, urine, cooking odors, greasy fats, dried body sweat. I could see the absence of hope in the faces of listless, totally expended human beings sitting half inside tents that the word "makeshift" would flatter. Many sat in a stupor, staring straight ahead with the expressionless faces and haunted eyes of people who are deeply troubled, exhibiting no signs of contact with those around them. Exhaustion, hunger, sickness—we may have kept these people from dying, I found myself thinking, but we have a long way to go before they are on their feet again.

I talked to the American Special Forces sergeants who were helping out in the camp. Given the amount of work to be done, they had concentrated on essential things. Get clean water and food storage. Build toilets. Get medical help. Get plastic sheets to cover leaky tents. Now they were organizing the area to get better sanitation. But mainly, they said, they were waiting for the word to move. "The folks in this camp came from the cities," said one tired sergeant. "They have no idea how to survive out here on a mountaintop." I could look in any direction and see that he was right. "We'll move fast on this," I replied, convinced that nothing but an exodus could solve the problems I was seeing. I could not put aside a feeling of satisfaction that our decisions had been right, the risks we took justified.

We flew on to another concentration of tents lower down the mountain slopes, closer to the Turkish border. This was Yakmal camp, which at that point held 71,000 people. After we landed and started up a hill, we ran into a column of men leading small mules that were loaded down and laboring. The men stopped and squatted silently on the narrow path, close to their pack animals, warily watching us pass. Their dark, angular faces below their black-and-white headdresses were masses of deep wrinkles. The barrels of their AK-47 rifles were old and worn shiny. In this camp there were more leaders than I had seen in Isikveren. Discipline was better. Abdul, the camp elder, an engineer, carried one of our hand-held radios to stay in touch with his subordinates in other parts of the sea of makeshift tents. In this cold weather and muddy terrain, he was wearing a pair of light fabric sandals. In fact, no one seemed dressed for the climate; they still wore what they had been wearing three weeks earlier, when they streamed out of their villages and headed for the mountains and what they had hoped would be safety beyond the border. At the medical treatment tent, a long line of women with ailing children waited to see a U.S. Special Forces medic who was holding sick call. He told me quietly, "One of the women here just told me that her husband had forbidden her to bring the baby to see me. He thinks the baby is too sick, causing too much trouble for the woman, and he says it's best to let the baby die. There can be more children later, he says." The sense of desperation was pervasive.

I talked to dozens of people at all levels of the volunteer relief organizations working with the Kurds and running the supply line to the camps. The one constant question was "When do we move?" After a slow start, there had been a constant improvement in our relationships with the private and national relief organizations. Now, with the move of the Kurds down to flat ground, which all agreed was the solution for survival, we became a stronger team.

Back at Incirlik, I visited the hangars where crews were working around the clock in twelve-hour shifts, packing and bracing the sled-like pallets that would be flown into Iraq and parachuted in to the mountain camps. Parachute supply lifts were still necessary for a number of the far-flung camps. A U.S. Air Force sergeant proudly showed me how he had found a way to pack the small glass jars of baby food donated by a major U.S. food corporation, to keep them from breaking during hard landings. He took a slab of Styrofoam and hit it time after time with a small sledgehammer, with each strike driving a hole of just the right size and depth for one of the little jars; then he fitted another piece of Styrofoam on top as a lid, and the package was ready for delivery. "Can't disappoint the kids," he remarked.

The next day, back in Belgium, I called John Shalikashvili and found that UN representative Staffan de Mistura had visited Zakhu and was planning to raise the UN flag there on Tuesday, 30 April. The deployment of our task force troops into the widened area was already turning out to be helpful: Kurds from the Zakhu district on the Iraqi-Turkish border followed and settled into their old homes or with friends. We were successful in moving the Kurds along the border from makeshift aid on the mountains to more organized camps below and finally back into their regional areas and homes.

On 7 June we transferred our remaining responsibilities to the UN, and on the following day we started our military withdrawal. By 23 July there were no coalition forces in Iraq except for a handful of people who remained to maintain coordination with the Iraqi military, and in Turkey we kept a reaction force of only four companies, along with helicopter support. Not everybody was happy, of course. In rescuing and resettling the Kurds we returned them to approximately the status quo ante, which was the unstable standoff that the Iraqis and the Kurds had experienced for so many years. Kurdish leaders Masoud Barzani and Jalal Talibani said that dealing with Saddam Hussein was still the same treacherous road it had always been. And now, after yet another war, the issue of Kurdish independence remained unanswered. Nevertheless, at that moment in time the teams could say, "All quiet on the eastern front."

36

The New Force Structure

"The road ahead"

The work of creating the new force structure brought me close to NATO Secretary General Manfred Wörner. He came to meetings with two small but well-thumbed paperback German dictionaries, French and English, propped up in front of him and often in use. I liked this habit of his. No one else does that, I thought, but we all should. He was methodical—even with his tea bag, taking it from the cup and carefully wrapping the string tight around it, squeezing it into a figure eight, then placing it on the saucer the same way each time, as if he were calming a superstition. Later, I deeply admired his courage in the way he bore the pain of his illness (cancer), carrying on with aplomb all his leadership responsibilities. Wörner and I were not always in agreement, however.

He was not comfortable, for example, with my leaning toward opportunities to get face to face with the Soviet military leaders. Still, he regularly left his office and met with me at my own, and our meetings were fruitful.

In 1987 NATO had four thousand nuclear weapons in Europe. Three years later we were working our way down to four hundred. In June 1990, also on the president's orders, we began moving all chemical weapons out of Germany. We packed these into steel boxes and moved them by rail, protected by U.S. troops and the local German police, to ships that took them to U.S. destruction facilities. Between 12 and 19 September 1990 we moved two trains every night, each with forty shipping containers, each steel container holding either three pallets of 155mm projectiles or two pallets of 8-inch projectiles. Ten containers were packed into each MILVAN (20-foot shipping container). More than eighty U.S. Army, West German

Army, and West German Police vehicles moved the MILVANs to the railheads.

At the time of the Malta meeting of Bush and Gorbachev in December 1989 I had invited Secretary of Defense Dick Cheney to visit the Waterloo battlefield with me, and he had accepted. On this trip we had a memorable tour. At Le Caillou, the farm where Napoleon slept before the battle, in the back room of the home, leaning on the glass case that contains the bones of a grenadier, I laid out for Cheney the road ahead as I saw it. First, as our next step, push hard for an agreement at the Vienna negotiations that would bring the two sides to parity. This would mean, for the Soviets, the elimination of an enormous amount of military equipment, but they seem ready to accept this and carry it out, I said. If they did so, the destruction of 40,000 tanks and thousands of ground-fighting vehicles and aircraft would be a confidence-building step without precedent in history. I also brought up the issue of harmonization (focusing the reductions first and foremost on our aging equipment, even if that requires some shifting of armaments among the Allies).

February 1990. Meeting once more with General Vladimir Lobov at the North Atlantic Assembly in Brussels, I found that if you ask a serious question, you get a good answer. The Soviets are not evasive, and they expect us to be straightforward in return. At the assembly, Lobov and I found ourselves speakers together for the second time, and we managed to get together during a break. He brought up the issue of the American Navy being unwilling to be a part of negotiations. I fell back on the Navy's comment: "Numbers don't count when we have 3,000 miles to go to carry out our mission, with 18 nuclear submarines waiting at any given time." "What are you afraid of?" I asked, noting that "we're not sure of your stability." His answer, with a smile, was, "Ah, we've always had problems." He grumbled over what he called "arithmetic," but I noted that he didn't challenge anything I said.

A month after my seeing Lobov, on 31 March, Colin Powell told me that the president had sent a letter urging the Russians to keep moving with regard to conventional forces.

19 November 1990—from the Associated Press:

NATO's chief military commander in Europe hailed Monday's signing of the treaty to cut conventional arms on the continent as a "fundamental cornerstone" in a new European order and predicted that "there will be more to come."

Supreme Allied Commander, Europe, General John Galvin said the new conventional forces in Europe agreement, which will slash tens of thousands of non-nuclear weapons, "will enhance stability from the Atlantic to the Urals."

Seen as symbolizing the end of the Cold War, the treaty was negotiated in only 20 months during the collapse of most Communist regimes in eastern Europe.

"The fact that previous, less ambitious arms control efforts often languished for years demonstrates the mutual good will that guarantees the success of the CFE Agreement. There will be more to come," said Galvin in a statement from his headquarters in southern Belgium.

Now that we had the agreement settling the strategy and the force levels, we needed to create the military organization necessary to carry out the missions the Alliance might call for in the future. We turned to the issue of just what, specifically and in detail, would be the kind of battlefield units and their commands and logistics—and budgets, of course. In the history of the Alliance this last set of decisions, relating to the sharing of costs, had proved to be more trying than any other aspect. Even General Eisenhower found himself bogged down as he laid the financial costs before the member nations, and after a year he left this matter to his successor, General Matthew Ridgway, who after another year did the same. Anticipating the atmosphere surrounding this task, I did my best to bring it to the surface in good time.

We had six months before the next meeting of the North Atlantic Council, a very short time for sixteen nations to restructure military forces for a quite different strategic and operational approach. By August 1990 we had removed 77 of our 82 Pershing II missiles and 82 of the 209 ground-launched cruise missiles. That part was going well. Since we had no mission guidelines, I sent new orders to commanders to plan to move to assembly areas to await "Be prepared" missions— interim measures. The response was some confusion among commanders who were accustomed to the old General Defense Plan.

In July 1990, civil war broke out in Liberia. My U.S. command in Europe extended to most of Africa, and in this case we called on Marines to protect our embassy in Monrovia and American citizens in the country. As a result, 2,300 Marines evacuated close to 2,700 people, half of them Americans. At the same time, VII Corps, my old command, was sailing in 130 shiploads of equipment to the Gulf out of North European ports.

On 4 March 1991 I met with Colin Powell at his house on Fort Myer. Over a pizza we played catch-up on every subject we could think of, ending with the drawdowns in Southwest Asia and in Europe. The budget for U.S. Army Europe had been cut by 48 percent. With some exasperation, I asked him, "Are we staying?" We agreed, though, that despite these reductions we needed to maintain stability and security despite these enormous changes. How? For a start, by good communication.

The readjustment of forces under the new strategic concept was not difficult to conceive. It was the old defensive lineup along NATO's eastern border with a three-level design: a small immediate-reaction element, a main-force backup, and a reinforcing group of units at lower readiness that would anticipate a more drawn-out situation requiring augmentation. The mission: prepare for peace, crisis, and war. Simple enough. That is, until you decide in detail who will do what. A couple of days later I summed up our thinking with the chiefs of the Army and Air Force in a letter to Powell in my role as U.S. CINCEUR: "As we discussed, I got together with Carl Vuono and Tony McPeak on the bottom-line numbers (in thousands) for Europe. They agree on the Army-Air Force breakout of the 130 figure at about 92 Army, 38 Air Force. When the ashore Navy is added (17), this gives an overall of 147. Obviously this will take a White House decision, but this number represents the max reduction possible to keep a competent Corps (2 Div), three to four Air wings, and the fleet (CVBG and MARG), plus air defense, logistics, commo, intel, and NATO support."

After our early beginnings in the comparative study of the Warsaw Pact and NATO, the team at SHAPE published our document, "Conventional Forces in Europe: The Facts," in 1988. This booklet would undergo many corrections, but it served the purpose intended very well. It forced both sides to put their cards on the table in terms of military equipment in the categories of tanks, infantry fighting vehicles, artillery, combat helicopters, and combat aircraft. On 29 January 1989 the members of the Warsaw Pact published their list.

A month earlier, on the morning of 8 December 1988, I had listened to a replay of Gorbachev's speech to the United Nations from the night before, in which he told the world that he would cut back on Soviet forces in Eastern Europe by 500,000 soldiers, 5,000 tanks, 8,000 artillery pieces, and 800 aircraft and added that six armored divisions would be withdrawn over two years. I said to myself, "If he sticks to that, and if his military accepts it, this will change everything."

I resolved to hang my approach on "parity." The Soviets were roughly twice as big; they would have to reduce by extraordinary numbers to get down to our size. What Gorbachev had already done was astounding, and his willingness to cut back forces unilaterally gave me more confidence that we would see change. Yet it was hard to believe that the Soviet leader could announce a unilateral withdrawal of his own forces and have it proceed calmly and peacefully. Of all the possibilities, this seemed the most desirable, but the least likely. How to deal with Gorbachev's offer? What should be my recommendation to the political leaders in the U.S. and NATO? The *Frankfurter Allgemeine Zeitung* for Saturday, 3 December 1988 offered a good description of my job. A translation:

[The notion that] the office of the Supreme Allied Commander, Europe, is a difficult one not only from a military, but also from a political point of view has gone uncontested for many years. The time is long past when Dwight D. Eisenhower was elected President of the United States from that position. As the gap between the military mission and the assets provided to accomplish it is widening, SACEUR increasingly runs the risk of becoming the irksome admonisher, the scapegoat of both the politicians and the public. Bernard Rogers had to undergo that bitter experience toward the end of his term of office, and General John R. Galvin, Rogers's successor since the middle of last year, is well aware of the danger. In Europe he has to deal with a population that is about to lose the feeling of facing a threat and thus the need to be protected. At the same time, their rejection of the NATO strategy of deterrence and the weapons necessary to maintain it—nuclear weapons, in particular—is increasing.

Against this background, Galvin enjoys the non-negligible advantage that the only military aspect he presents is his uniform. If he wore civilian clothes, the fifty-eight-year-old general with the full white hair and rimless glasses would be taken for a scientist, an industrialist, or a writer. It is a distinct advantage for an officer who has moved so high up in the military hierarchy that, whenever it really matters, he cannot command, but must convince—at least in peacetime. In this difficult business, the General's experience and his temperament stand him in good stead: Galvin is no zealot. He speaks in a friendly manner and remains relaxed even if the conversation becomes controversial. He relies on the weight of the facts and arguments he produces to persuade.

Galvin is not only the Supreme Allied Commander for Europe but also, in a U.S. national capacity, Commander-in-Chief, U.S. Forces Europe, with a command area stretching as far as Israel and comprising the Mediterranean and the U.S. 6th Fleet—a dual function that is not only among the highest available in the U.S. forces, but is among the most critical, both militarily and politically speaking.

That in his previous assignment as Commander-in-Chief, Southern Command, Panama, he has had to prove himself for more than two years in a politically rather than militarily critical position now stands him in good stead, just as did previous assignments as military assistant to SACEUR and, above all, Commanding General, VII (U.S.) Corps, with headquarters in Stuttgart. At that time he had toured Swabia on bicycle and was planning to establish a secondary residence in the "Landle" once he retired, the rumor went.

But that will have to wait. Galvin will first have to enforce what the security of the Alliance demands, so long as disarmament between the Atlantic and the Urals remains verbiage while armament goes on in the forces—irrespective of whether that is popular or not.

Insisting on parity, over and over, I went back to my notes, taken in November 1974 when, as a colonel, I sat in on a meeting between General Andrew Goodpaster and Stanley Resor, secretary of the U.S. Army. I had written down the then supreme commander's words: "Common ceiling is still the frame to work for; freeze at the common ceiling." What was right then was now still the right road, I said to myself. If we could get parity, we'd be on the right path.

To reach parity at 20,000 tanks, the Warsaw Pact forces would have to get rid of 39,000 tanks, while NATO would cut back by 2,250. If that happened, the level of confidence that the Soviets would enjoy in the minds of Western countries would be very different from what it is in early 1989.

European leaders were pleasantly surprised by the United States's willingness to put forward new initiatives for CFE. In the transition period from Reagan to Bush, there had been a feeling in Europe that the new American administration was turning inward and that NATO and conventional arms control negotiations would get less attention. The Bush proposal brought the initiative back to the West and provided a much-needed unity and sense of direction to the Alliance. But there were worries.

In notes to myself at the time I wrote: "If the Soviets remove six armored divisions from the forward areas, that is good. But if they leave the whole infrastructure of the command and control and communications systems, logistical pipelines, bases, and airfields in place, along with the higher echelons of command and control, that's not so good—because that means they have just unplugged something that can be easily plugged back in. How do we take these things into account?"

Both East and West possessed a variety of tanks, some old and some relatively new. In destroying our 15 percent, we decided to keep the best we had, handing off the newer American tanks to other NATO countries, who would then destroy theirs. The redistribution would be complex, involving not only tanks but all of the equipment specified in the draft treaty.

I explained this to the UK House of Commons Defence Committee on 3 April 1990:

> Harmonization—the cascading or transfer of equipment—looks to some people like circumvention of the treaty. It is not circumvention. It simply doesn't make sense if some countries have old equipment and some have new equipment, and each one destroys the same amount.
>
> I have a fear that if we destroy new equipment—probably, for the most part, in the larger countries of the Alliance—how will those countries then be able to go to their legislatures and say, "We need to keep up with modernization"? They would get the answer, "You mean you want me to do some research and development and build an airplane, while you are destroying the one that was just built?"
>
> We should be looking at this from the point of view not of the budget, but primarily of the strategy, and be saying to ourselves, "How do we make this reduction happen in such a way that we maintain as much capability as we can and yet comply

with the treaty obligations?" Certainly that is what the Soviets would do. That is simply good husbandry.

This concept of sharing made eminent good sense, if we could get the agreement of the U.S. Congress, which had paid for the tanks, and of the countries of NATO, who followed the advice of their military experts. All soldiers know that exchanging equipment has to be accomplished with care and honesty. I made another circuit of the countries with forces in the Command, and Lieutenant General Robert Chelberg took his team to all of them except Iceland, which did not have armed forces, and France, which declined to participate. Our reception was excellent, but the arrangements depended on bilateral agreements.

27 September 1989. TASS, Moscow's news agency, responds in the negative:

Galvin's "Arms Redistribution" Plan Analysed.

American General John Galvin, Supreme Commander of NATO's Armed Forces in Europe, has proposed "redistributing armaments" among NATO allies, which would allow them to preserve up-to-date weapons systems when the conventional arms treaty, now being worked out in Vienna, begins to be implemented.

This would considerably reduce the significance of the treaty.

So, according to the General, each NATO ally would fulfill its quota of cuts under the future treaty by eliminating outdated weapons.

But this was the same plan the Soviet Union ultimately adopted.

While we worked on our new force structure, we also needed to assist the former Warsaw Pact countries as they put into place their departure from the military configuration they had experienced as Pact members. Czechoslovakia was the scene of our first effort, although Poland and the others came soon after.

Czechoslovakia, like all the Eastern European nations, was undergoing a multifaceted change in the way the country was governed. The West reached out to help with advice and support. The military part of this assistance marked the beginning of a close tie between Czechoslovakia and the West, as pressure from the East disintegrated. We had been watching the organizational struggles in the rebirth of these countries and were happy at last to be able to help.

Our NATO staff moved quickly. Working in Prague, we formed a team of twenty officers to match the structure of the Czech Ministry of Defense and the Committee of Defense and Security of the House of the People, along with the finance minister and other interested political leaders from the National Assembly and the Advisory Board of the President. The twenty on our side included four senior general and flag officers. At times we would be working with fifteen to thirty members of the Federal Assembly. As with our visits to the other countries in the East, there was much concern with budget interests, and there was invariably astonishment upon learning, for example, that the U.S. Pentagon had about 400 military officers assigned at any time on Capitol Hill for liaison purposes—to keep in touch with Congress, mostly on budget issues but also on quotidian matters, and to answer questions.

Ginny accompanied me and the team to Prague. On the way she remembered her only other visit, in 1974, when she rode a tour bus hired by the Würzburg Women's German-American Club and the Czech border guards took everyone's passports and held the bus for five hours, when the trip was purposely made dismal in many ways. This trip of ours proceeded under very different circumstances.

We flew into Praha Ruzyně Airport on 11 June 1991 and were greeted by the minister of defense, Luboš Dobrovský, and Major General Karel Pezl, Chief of the General Staff. General Pezl was the host for our visit, and he could not have been a better one. He was thoughtful, self-contained, considerate, accommodating, and quietly articulate. We discussed the restructuring of the Czech armed forces (which were cut approximately in half). As we moved among the discussion groups, I learned much about the lives and military careers of the Czech officer corps. Pezl had been an Army major in 1968. I was also a major then, and I could imagine what it would be like to have been put aside for twenty-three years and then be called back as the Chief of General Staff.

At one point, I wrote this note:

> Pezl on himself. In 1970 I was put out as a colonel, and now [as of two weeks ago], I am back as the Chief of Defense Staff. In the meantime I had all sorts of jobs. I and my wife weeded gardens, along with our children, to get enough money to put them into college. And then they were not allowed to stay. I worked as a stoker, and as a window washer. I know those who

came back after twenty years, and I know those who stayed—
and we are different people. I don't know the younger officers,
and they don't know me.

Now he was in charge of the future security of his nation, and he
was the right man for the responsibility. I learned a great deal from
our discussions. Although our two countries varied in their military
structures, there were several areas that revealed more or less the same
debilities. Pezl told me that the Czechs did not have the expertise or the
infrastructure for managing the country's civil and military airspace.
"How can we 'NATO-ize'?" he asked. "What do we need to do to come
up to NATO standards? I know where we want to go, but I don't know
how to get there." We discussed strategic planning, politico-military
relations, common systems of air defense, and much else.

At dinner that evening, the conversation turned to the imminent
break-up of Czechoslovakia into two countries: the reasons for such a
move and the need for it to happen. Most said that the Slovakian perspective reflected a yearning for separation and freedom on the part
of an agrarian region that would otherwise continue to drag down the
country's industrial side. They were determined to be Slovaks, and Slovaks only. For the Czechs, proud of their industrial reputation and of
an economy with great future possibilities, the Slovaks were stubborn,
"so let it be."

The next day, at a light lunch I attended with Ambassador Shirley Temple Black and Czech foreign affairs minister Jiří Dienstbier, he
asked when and how the Russians would cease to be a threat. We proceeded to speculate on the future development of the Soviet Union.
Dienstbier also wanted to know what I thought might come out of the
meeting in Prague at the end of the month to discuss the dissolution of
the Warsaw Pact. With a Czech Golden Tiger beer, we toasted "stability
in the unpredictable future." In the center of the city, a Soviet tank high
up on a pedestal had been painted pink.

On 13 June 1991 I attended a meeting at Prague Castle with Ambassador Black and Václav Havel, who had moved so remarkably a short
time before from prisoner to president. He was interested in our plans
for a rapid reaction force and what missions it might be given. I called
NATO the backbone of the new European security architecture. He was
interested in "compatibility with Western democracies in all ways." He
asked, "How do you deal with all of the competing interests of NATO
countries?" My answer and his reply filled the lunch hour.

That evening we had dinner with Ambassador Black at her residence. As is probably true of everybody who met her, I found her unpretentious, self-assured, vivacious, bright, and articulate, with some of the same mannerisms as in her acting days—a mature and impressive version of the girl who spent her childhood "on location" and took on the world with aplomb ever after. Like a good officer, she stood at attention, as she did in her movies as a child, and even her frown remained attractive. Because of her—and I told her so—my mother insisted that my sister and I take tap dancing lessons.

Later that year, on 25 November 1991, the U.S. Senate ratified the CFE Treaty.

37

The Coup

"Stand fast."

The Russian armed forces were in a deepening quandary, and there was little that anyone in the Western alliance wanted to do about it—except for the Germans, who quietly financed the construction of quarters for the troops departing East Germany for Russia and also supplied the rolling stock to return the troops and equipment. There was talk at Brussels about the possibility of sending a fact-finding committee to examine the living conditions in the army of our former antagonist, but this sputtered out. I discussed the option with the secretary general, who was among those who thought something could be done, and with several NATO representatives. There was interest and informal discussion, but the possibility of some form of help while member countries were demanding a reduction in their own defense expenditures was, in the end, nonexistent. If a NATO fact-finding committee went to Russia, the representatives said, it would come back with a report that doubtless would call for something to be done, thereby putting us on the spot. My staff observed that once a week a German cargo plane left the airport at Bonn for Moscow, carrying medical supplies and equipment. I discussed the possibility that this suggested that more could be done, but to no avail.

Soviet Foreign Minister Eduard Shevardnadze's resignation in December 1990 was another complication. As he left office, he warned that President Mikhail Gorbachev was drifting back toward dictatorship, along with the Army, the KGB, and the Communist Party. Gorbachev continued to lose support.

From the *Wall Street Journal*, 13 May 1991:

Galvin Sees Reduced Threat, Possible Cooperation

Gen. Galvin . . . told the permanent representatives of the 16 North Atlantic Treaty Organization member nations that the West should support the Soviets in coming to grips with their internal problems. Moreover [he said], they should avoid any action that could be misinterpreted as a threat, according to reports of those who attended the meeting.

To some surprise, he suggested that NATO and the Soviets may in the future see themselves as friends facing common enemies, rather than as rivals.

He suggested [that] the alliance needed to "communicate with the Soviet military on all levels," [attenders] said. In the interest of a more stable relationship, he questioned the wisdom of continuing the past practice of severing links to Moscow if it acted in ways disagreeable to the West.

Then came the head-turning specifics. One idea was to open one of NATO's most sensitive training schools at Oberammergau in Germany to Soviet and other East European officers. The symbolism wouldn't be missed by Moscow: in rooms where NATO officers were once taught how to handle nuclear weapons, former Soviet enemies would be schooled on matters of mutual interest.

"NATO has to look at the whole of European security, and a good workable relationship between NATO and the Soviet Union is of primary importance," [Galvin] said.

In the spring of 1991, Gromov became the military assistant to Interior Minister Boris Karlovich Pugo. Boris Yeltsin was elected president of Russia.

The *Atlanta Journal-Constitution* on 13 August noted, "[G]eneral [Galvin] said he does not anticipate a military coup. If Gorbachev falls, General Galvin was quoted [as] saying, 'It will not be military dissension; it will be political competition.'"

Six days later: Coup. The first word we got was from television early on Monday morning, when the intelligence staff said there had been some strange announcements out of the Soviet Union that Gorbachev had been ousted.

"Any activity that has to do with nuclear weapons?" was our first and lasting question. Then: Any troop moves in the western military districts along the border with Poland and Hungary? And: Could we expect refugees?

I did not want to do anything that would add new uncertainties to the crisis. We needed first to know what was going on. Our intelligence analysis and communications structure in Allied Command Europe, I knew, would give every senior commander all the information available. I put the word out to the subordinate commands: Keep your eye on the situation (an unnecessary instruction). Don't do anything other than absolutely routine operations and training unless you consult me first. "Absolutely no comment" is the answer to all media questions on the coup.

In Moscow, across the street from the new U.S. Embassy, thirty tanks were moved to Yeltsin's building. It was obvious that while they are dealing with this crisis, the Kremlin would be nervous about what the Alliance might do. They are certainly going to feel vulnerable. "Don't make any moves" was my response. Stand fast.

Leningrad and Riga appeared to be under firm military grip. No one had heard from Gorbachev. Airborne units were on the move to key cities, although not at the force levels that I would have expected.

My most consistent source, as always, was Colin Powell. The U.S. military, at the order of the president, was staying very low-key, low-profile. I told Powell I had put out the same word in my commands.

The first good news was that the Soviet military wasn't shooting. In Moscow, the troops in the tanks of the Taman Division were talking with the crowds that milled around them. Then more good things happened. The crowds increased, even in the cold rain. Yeltsin was still defying the hardliners, and nobody had arrested him. Intel was showing that the Soviet military didn't seem in charge of the coup activities. The left hand didn't know what the right hand was doing. Good news, indeed. We weren't seeing anything that would prompt the Soviet command to take action. A good part of the SHAPE staff was on summer leave, and we left things that way; no one was called back. I talked to Manfred Wörner regarding the upcoming NATO ministerial meeting. He felt it would be better not to have me or the other commanders present, so that the meeting would not send any message of military threat, which might only complicate the situation in the Soviet Union.

I shared with Manfred my views on what might be significant in the intelligence we were getting. I said that the Soviet Air Force didn't seem to be cooperating with the hardliners, who were having a problem getting aircraft to move Army troops to various cities. I also told him that there was less than the normal amount of activity along the western border of the USSR, and nothing unusual in any of the places we were tracking.

My notes on my discussions with Powell:

President Bush back from Kennebunkport.
19–20 August. Unrest wasn't spreading to other key cities.
No military alerts in western districts.
Paratroops active but not moving.
Air Force not responding to request for lift.
Army moving slowly, reluctantly. A kind of wait-and-see.
"State Committee" seems in confusion.
Public lethargic, even resistant.
Defection of army units to Yeltsin.
Yazov and Gromov silent.
Yanayev says Gorbachev is "resting."
Yeltsin says Gorbachev is "detained" in the Crimea.
Ukraine refuses to support coup.
Protesters against the coup surround Parliament building.
Yeltsin takes charge, dominates TV, orders Army to stand down.
21 August: Tanks withdraw from Moscow. Gorbachev returns.
Yeltsin demands Gorbachev be allowed to speak to Supreme Soviet.
Yeltsin says, "We have won!" Disbands Communist Party cells in Army.
Gorbachev supports Communist Party.
23 August: Yeltsin forces Gorbachev to read to Parliament a report that the Soviet government—and the silent armed forces—supported the coup.
24 August: Gorbachev resigns from the Communist Party.

As Lobov had said, all change is challenging. Intransigence and stalwart resistance among the Party faithful could not halt the momentum of perestroika; but in the absence of economic progress, the old ways rushed in to usurp the new.

Part 7

Global Perspective

38

Back to West Point—
by Way of Bosnia

"It was hard to put aside other interests."

In the summer of 1991, nuclear weapons were being drawn down on schedule. Soviet forces had backed out of Eastern Europe and were destroying tanks and other fighting vehicles, also on schedule, and we were cutting back on our ground and air units. Both sides had sent all chemical weapons to be destroyed. Our new Alliance strategy was in place, ready for acceptance. It was tempting to say, "We're on track, heading out of the Cold War." Secretary of Defense Dick Cheney said to me, "Jack, we're going to extend you in your position for another two years. Is that OK with you?"

I said, "Can we make it one more year instead of two?"

He was surprised. I didn't say that although Ginny and I had managed to put our four children through college while staying free of debt, we had no house and no investments of any kind. I didn't say that a big chunk of my retirement pay would have to go to Ginny's future support. I simply said, "I'll be sixty-three, which is old for a soldier, and I have some other things I'd like to do before I retire completely. My list of options, though, is getting smaller." We talked about implementing in detail all of the changes that had come about in the past few years.

Bill Perry, later to be secretary of defense, asked, "What's your plan for the future?" I told him that I hoped to be associated with some university so that I could teach and write, and that I'd also like to come home and join the family again, given that in the past two decades, Ginny and I had spent eighteen years outside the United States.

"What will you write about?"

"I think I have something to say about leadership," I said.

"Where will you settle down? In the Washington area?"

"I'm a New Englander. I'd like to go back there, maybe to my home-town, near Boston."

"Well, Boston certainly has enough schools to think about."

The secretary agreed to the one-year extension, and said he would talk to Secretary General Wörner about it. That would allow me a year to continue to work on implementing the changes—beginning with the new force structure and the reductions of nuclear and conventional weapons. Not long after this meeting, Colin Powell and I had a discussion about possible replacements for me, among them Lieutenant General John Shalikashvili. I told Powell what he already knew about my admiration for John as a leader, and then I said, "Why don't you go and see him in action—take a trip to Turkey?" Powell did just that, and in the end Shalikashvili was the choice.

I devoted my final year as SACEUR to following up on the mani-fold changes in the Alliance. Each decision we had made in these event-ful four years from 1987 to 1991 had to be implemented, which called for close coordination with our old adversaries and among ourselves. All the new issues and many of the old contentious ones were now merged in a mix—sometimes in grim quietness, other times in clamor. There was much still to do, both in carrying out actions agreed to and in addressing new changes that arose out of earlier ones. NATO needed to pull together political, economic, and military structures, addressing the future role of the United States in Europe, and factoring in Russia, which was part of both Europe and Asia. The United States also had to attend to verification inspections, to the NATO School at Oberammer-gau, to the turnback of U.S. bases in Europe, and to the rapid reaction force; harmonize the transfer of 2,800 fighting vehicles and their spare parts while supporting the development of the eastern European coun-tries' militaries and continuing support operations in the Gulf; and manage force reductions from 326,000 to 150,000, which entailed clos-ing half of the existing 1,400 installations, with their troops and fami-lies. In early November 1991, the NATO nations held a summit meeting in Rome to discuss these issues and many more. From my notes at that session:

President Bush is to arrive in 50 minutes by helicopter and I'll ride with him to the U.S. Ambassador's residence—Pete Sec-cia's place—Villa Taverna, about 10 minutes away.

It's 8:55 p.m. I'm sitting in a corner, writing last-minute notes on a desk blotter that I'm using for a lap board. Whatever it is, my message needs to be short. My 3x5's are full of notes, but I've boiled them down into an "intro" and about 5 things. (1) Need to stress how NATO's changed with a changing world. (2) Need to emphasize opening the door to the former Warsaw Pact countries. (3) European security identity, burdensharing, France, European Community, Western European Union—all of this is connected. (4) U.S. role. Commitment. (5) Nuclear matters. Then a few extras if there's time. . . .

[Bush] was as friendly and informal as ever. I rode with him and Barbara to the ambassador's residence and managed to get across to him all the things I thought were important (my 5 points). We were in his limousine with me facing backwards on a jump seat, facing the President and Barbara in the rear seats. He stuck one leg out to the center of the car in order to leave enough room for me. He was in a good mood, asking questions and chatting, with a good mix of attention to the subject but also good humor. When we met at the helicopter, for example, he held our handshake and then said, "I wanted to make sure we got a smile out of you for the cameras."

We went to Seccia's villa, and I had a chance to walk and chat with the President some more. Baker and Scowcroft and [White House Chief of Staff John] Sununu were there, and Pete and Joan Seccia and Barbara Bush, but at one point I had the President to myself. He was tired, though, and he told me he was fighting a cold. He and Barbara went upstairs at about 10:30 and the others followed soon after, leaving me and Pete and Joan to talk a while.

It's now Friday morning, and I have a forty minute meeting on the side with Secretary Baker to discuss the connection among the Western European Union, NATO, and the European Community. Then we have our final series of discussions, and later . . . a press conference.

During the meeting yesterday, Bush sent someone across the room to tell me he'd like to see me. When I went over, I found he just wanted to get me into the press photos that were bring taken. He said, "Get in here, Jack—photo op."

In the months that followed, the new strategy was laid out in more detail, but in content it followed the lines of the 1990 London version.

President Bush committed 150,000 troops to remain in Europe in a new force structure and announced further reductions in nuclear weapons.

My notes on what the president said on 7 November 1991:

> U.S. will not abandon its responsible interest in Europe.
>
> U.S. wants not followers but partners.
>
> To ascribe to the United States ambitions of power in Europe is to ignore the role we have played.
>
> A united Europe will not diminish the need for NATO.
>
> NATO has been more successful than any of us dared to dream. We defended our freedom. We triumphed over totalitarianism.
>
> We are seeing the struggle toward democracy of an immensely centralized state. We must help them, but we cannot ignore the dangers.
>
> We can't know what the Soviets themselves don't know; the Alliance is indispensable.
>
> How will we answer the call of the countries of Eastern Europe?

The president concluded his comments with the words, "If you want to do it alone, the time to tell us is today."

The summit meeting confirmed the new strategy in detail.

At this point, Yugoslavia fell ill, as had been predicted by all the doctors since Tito's death in 1980, and nobody knew the remedy. At first, NATO could not respond, because the major nations of the Alliance held differing views of what should be done. The European Community sponsored political action to resolve the crisis, which was unsuccessful, followed by UN sanctions and peacekeeping, also unsuccessful, then by action (somewhat tentative) on the part of NATO. We learned things we should have known all along about the nature of political crises. I came to understand that they are not resolved quickly. In addition, since the situation during such crises tends to change rapidly, we have to be prepared for flexible political/military action and for multiple missions.

It was "Yugoslavia: Descent into Chaos." Inspired by what was going on in the former Soviet Union and the Warsaw Pact nations, the various republics—Slovenia, Bosnia, Croatia, Vojvodina, Kosovo, Macedonia—one by one declared themselves independent. The Serbs in Serbia supported the Serbs elsewhere in the country and especially in the republic of Bosnia, where fierce, bitter, disorganized, and cruel conflict sputtered throughout the Balkans. The European nations tried—without success—to restore peace. For the next two years, the Serbs under Slobodan Milosevic in Serbia helped those under Radovan Karadzic in Bosnia create a bitter conflict in order to maintain as much control as possible over the former Yugoslavia.

In the fall of 1991, units from a Serb heavy weapons battalion, part of the old Yugoslav army, attacked the Croatian port of Dubrovnik with artillery and mortar fire. Many in the watching world called for intervention while at the same time remaining reluctant to take part in any military actions. It was obvious that the NATO on-call Mediterranean fleet could be sent to positions off Dubrovnik, backed up if necessary by the U.S. 6th Fleet, also available in the Mediterranean, to answer the Serb guns. This would have required a strong Washington initiative, however, and I was well aware that with the first Persian Gulf War barely over, with the August coup exposing possible instability in Russia, and with a drawdown of U.S. forces in Europe, support for a move in the Adriatic did not exist in Washington. Although there was much anguish over the violence in the dissolving Yugoslavia, and many a call to arms in order to stop it, there continued to be no effective support in the United States or anywhere in Europe for a strong military intervention. Besides, at that time the Croatian Danube city of Vukovar, far inland, had been under siege for weeks and fell to the Serbs a few days later. Any local success at Dubrovnik would have been tempered by our unwillingness to commit ourselves to the consequences of a campaign rather than a single action.

I told Colin Powell, "We're available." He knew that, of course. He and I had talked often about the situation in Bosnia and the Adriatic. He was well aware of my reservations, and I knew his. My duty was to describe how any intervention could be done, what resources it would take, and what results could be expected.

When the sporadic fighting intensified around Sarajevo, NATO took another hard look, this time much more in earnest, at what kind of military effort would be needed if we were serious about driving the Serbs off the mountains around Sarajevo and keeping artillery fire away from the city. We were hearing the same kind of thinking as there was with regard to Dubrovnik, except on a larger scale: do something to stop the Serbs from firing on a city, but don't get too involved. Sarajevo was too far inland for a naval gunfire action, but air forces, with bombs and missiles, could attack Serb guns whenever they fired. This approach would require a day-and-night presence of surveillance and attack planes and also a willingness to risk collateral casualties. I had been asked many times, "Why can't you just send in artillery and take on the Serbs, gun to gun, whenever they fire?" My answer was sometimes seen as shrugging off a good idea. It was difficult to explain that, in order to keep the city and its outskirts reasonably safe, we would need not just guns but target acquisition radars, ammunition, and other logistical support, in addition to security. In other words, we would need full military units. A force to protect the city would need a ground supply route about 100 miles long from the Croatian port of Ploče to Sarajevo—winding across forty-two bridges and through nine tunnels in the mountains. If we had put forces on the hills around Sarajevo, we could have pushed Serb artillery back far enough to put the city out of range, but the Serbs would have been free to move their guns elsewhere to shell other Bosnian cities, while we would have had to continue to protect Sarajevo.

The effort to address the security of Sarajevo was part of the platter of responsibilities that General John Shalikashvili inherited when he took over from me at two change-of-command ceremonies at U.S. European Command Headquarters at Stuttgart, Germany, and at Supreme Headquarters, Allied Command, Europe, at Casteau, Belgium, in early June 1992. Colin Powell, who presided over the Stuttgart ceremony, approached me after my impassioned good-bye speech to my command and to my American and German friends and was moved to say, "Jack, you are every inch an Irishman, a true Mick, I have to say!" Leaving these commands in the good hands of John Shalikashvili, I retired in yet another ceremony at Fort Myer, Virginia (with Defense Secretary Cheney presiding), and moved to West Point.

The European Community had sent Lord Carrington to the Balkans as a mediator; he was not successful. Later, the team of UN Special Envoy Cyrus Vance and European Community representative Lord David Owen produced a territorial plan; this was not accepted. Finally, the major nations—the United States, the United Kingdom, the Federal Republic of Germany, and Russia—formed what was called the Contact Group, with the mission of gaining acceptance of a plan for the end of hostilities and the future of the region, using among other resources an electronic map which could quickly adjust itself to changes during negotiations. The Contact Group succeeded, on the political side, in stopping the three-way war in Bosnia by uniting the Muslims and Bosniacs against the Bosnian Serbs, thus simplifying the conflict. Standing in the way, however, was the possible lack of support by the military leadership of the Muslims and Bosniacs, and there was a further problem to be resolved: Under this proposed arrangement, would the united Muslim and Bosniac military forces be sufficient to drive back the Bosnian Serbs, who probably continued to be supported by the old Yugoslav army?

In retiring from NATO, I stepped away from the situation in the former Yugoslavia—though, as things turned out, it was not for long. In the meantime my original plan to go to Ohio State University after retiring changed when Lieutenant General Howard Graves, the West Point Superintendent, asked me to spend a year at the Academy. I happily accepted a chair in social sciences for one year, which was subsequently extended to two years, back at the place that made me. I arrived with my family on a sunny July day at our military home, a large brick house facing out over the Hudson, with a beautiful pastoral view of Garrison, New York. Sitting on the porch, I counted up the forty-two years since I stepped off the train at the foot of the hill and climbed up into that mysterious gray fortress, wondering what in the world would become of me. Memories struck me, one after the other—stark details of those first days almost hour by hour, at first with the conviction that I would not last long, but slowly seeing a glimpse of the possibility that I might survive after all.

Now, with the years behind me, I began taking walks up into the hills overlooking the river and the gray buildings that I knew so well, allowing visions of earlier days to come back. Up in these hills I revisited hours of remembrances, my four years as a cadet and the three as an instructor. The trail that passes above Fort Putnam was our path for cross-country running and practicing, and higher above, another ridge links small outposts that provide magnificent views of the fortress and of the two sides of the valley below.

Like everyone, I guess, I had looked ahead to retirement as a quiet, restful time, with all the stored-up dreams of easygoing freedom of action, when clocks and calendars have less importance. I wanted to bring to life my 1948 Willys jeep, ready for hours of work before it could become our family's second car, and of course I had my thousands of 3x5 index cards, the source of any writing I intended to do. But I discovered that it was hard to put aside other interests.

Senator Mac Mathias asked me to take his place as chair of the American Council on Germany. I accepted. Shy Meyer asked me to take his place on the board of the Center for Creative Leadership. I accepted. General Larry Welch asked me to join the board of the Institute for Defense Analyses. I accepted. There were articles and speeches, and the Council on Foreign Relations. There were diplomatic trips with Henry Kissinger and company to Moscow, Kiev, and Beijing, and to Berlin for the American Council. Plus the Cox foundation and the business boards of U.S. Life, Seligman, and Raytheon—and of course there were my students.

I tried to bring to my classes visitors who would teach by their presence as well as their knowledge. These included George Kennan, John Eisenhower, Secretary of Defense Les Aspin, Senator Sam Nunn, Congressmen Ike Skelton and Newt Gingrich, Chief of German Defense Staff General Klaus Naumann, Ambassador Dick Walters, UN Secretary Boutros Boutros-Ghali, and Assistant Secretary of Defense Ted Warner. Beyond their classroom talks, the cadets were able to benefit from the intimacy of dinners with these guests at my house, providing not only education but moments that I hope they will not have forgotten.

With help from Mark Smith, an armor captain on the teaching staff, I created courses on strategy and on the future military aspects of alliances in Europe, concentrating on the question of the future security of the Atlantic nations. Sessions were loose and nonchalant, but topped off with cadet essays.

In early January 1993, Ginny joined a group of women who were traveling to Siberia with humanitarian supplies, aimed at providing support to Russian military families who were celebrating the Christmas holiday season for the first time in many years. On her return I picked her up at the airport. She looked haggard, but was glad to be home. She said she was hungry for some kind of snack, so we stopped at a local restaurant, and while we were eating she started to tell me about the things that had happened on the trip. Halfway along in her story, she burst into tears. Eyes turned to watch her and wonder what was wrong. Sobbing, she said, "Oh, it is so *hopeless* for them!" She was glad, very glad that she had had the chance to go.

Beginning in 1991, Harvard set up a program that invited a succession of groups of twenty or more senior Soviet military officers to a two-week course on United States government. I was asked to come over to Cambridge to speak to a group, which I did, and while there I saw an opportunity to enhance these visits, which were to take place once every year for an indefinite period of time. Wakefield, Massachusetts, is the hometown I never really left. In all my years in Europe, Asia, and the Americas, I was always the wanderer thinking of home—of my strong ties to my father, of my friends, of my plans for coming back. I talked with several of my longtime friends in Wakefield to see if there was interest in hosting a daylong Saturday visit that would show Soviet officers what a typical American town is like.

The word spread around. People became enthusiastic about the idea; there was news of it in the local paper, and the small group grew into a committee that created a rough agenda. We discussed the arrangements with Harvard, and we decided to try it out. In the months that followed, the committee worked out an agenda with the help of dozens of enthusiastic townsfolk. The first group of twenty Russians arrived on 18 September 1993 and dismounted their tour bus in front of the middle school, in Wakefield Square, wondering what would happen next. Our newspaper had prepared the town with headlines announcing, "The Russians Are Coming!"

A busload of officers would typically arrive at the middle school in time for an early breakfast in the school's dining room and a welcoming speech by committee members and their children, along with handshakes, plenty of photographs and introductory chatter, and waffles and other hearty breakfast foods. Then began the walk up Main Street, first to a hardware store, then a pharmacy, followed by a visit to the firehouse and then to the local newspaper, then to a lawyer's office and a doctor's office, both in between ordinary homes, and then back into the bus to travel to an automobile sales showroom and lunch at the golf clubhouse. Throughout, the visitors were accompanied by Wakefield's citizens in groups, and enough Russian translators to provide one for every three of our visitors.

Along the way, and never far from the center of town, the Russian officers on these visits often expressed surprise to see the houses that spread out from Wakefield's Main Street, the lawns and tree-lined roads, and the driveways with their flocks of automobiles. Often the question was "How many families live in that house?" and when the answer was "One," the next comment was "But there are two (or even three) cars in the driveway."

We walked by the common, with its monuments honoring the town's fighters in American wars, and beside beautiful lake Quannapowitt we visited the Congregational Church, where we heard a history of the several churches in the town; from there we proceeded to the Town Hall, to hear how an elected committee handles the decisions of governance. As the day began to darken, all the Wakefield sponsors and their guests went to dinner at a downtown restaurant (with speeches by both sides) and then, in small groups, visited the houses of the sponsors for dessert and drinks. The day ended with hugs and good-byes at the bus in Wakefield Square and with the officers' return to their lodgings at Harvard. A week later, the Russians reciprocated with a dinner at the Kennedy School, with the translators and many of the hosts of the Wakefield visit present.

These outings took place every year for four years, starting not long after the dissolution of the Soviet Union in 1991 into fifteen post-Soviet states—a period in world history when international relations were changing in unprecedented ways, hard decisions were everyday matters, and leaders could not see the future with any clarity. A total of 132 senior Russian military officers visited this small town and made Wakefield, for senior Russian military leadership, the best-known place in all of the United States.

On 4 March 1994, I was in the office of Paul Volcker in Manhattan, where we were discussing the American Council on Germany. Volcker was a strong supporter of the Council, and was much involved in its activities over the years. We were interrupted by a call from Secretary of Defense Bill Perry. I took the call, and Secretary Perry said he needed me to work on the military side of the State Department's involvement with the Contact Group, the representatives from several nations who were trying to resolve the conflict in Bosnia-Herzegovina. He asked me if I could meet with him the next morning. I said yes.

Paul told me it had begun to snow outside and predictions were calling for a heavy storm, so I lost no time departing to catch a train to Garrison, the town on the Hudson River across from West Point. In the station parking lot I cleaned off my old jeep's windshield and canvas top and drove across the Bear Mountain Bridge to home. Later in the afternoon I caught a flight from Newburgh to Reagan National, but as we approached, the airport closed—snowed in. Dulles shut down also. The pilot managed to get us into the Baltimore-Washington airport, which closed just after we landed, but there were no taxis or buses available for me to make the drive to Washington.

After some searching I found a U.S. Air Force officer who was leaving for Washington, driving an official sedan. He was kind enough to take me with him. We followed the plows down the interstate, and he dropped me off at my hotel at one o'clock in the morning. At eight I took a taxi to the Pentagon and met with Secretary Perry, who told me that the State Department wanted me to go to Bosnia. The idea was simple. The Croats and Muslims in Bosnia were beginning to get along better on the political side, but their military leaders remained aloof from each other. I was to see what I could do about this, how I could help pull them together. Later in the day we moved to an alcove in a Pentagon corridor, where I was sworn in as an envoy with the rank of ambassador, tenure of 180 days. Mission: to get the Croat and Muslim militaries on board with their political bosses.

The Muslim and Croat political leaders had agreed to put into action the Framework Agreement (establishing a Federation in the areas of the Republic of Bosnia and Herzegovina with a majority Bosniac and Croat population and providing for a Confederation between the Republic of Croatia and the Federation). A high-level Transitional Committee was meeting in Vienna beginning that day and hoped to reach agreement on unifying; but there were indications that the military sides were uneasy about the political decision making. Everyone wanted to be assured that senior military on both sides would not back away from the agreement at the last minute.

Charles ("Chuck") Redman was a member of this team, as the American Special Envoy, and I was his helper. The first step for me was to build a team of my own and get to work. The State Department gave me Colonel Jim Allgood, an Air Force officer who was on loan to State. This odd arrangement worked out very well. West Point allowed me to add Major Mark Smith as the team secretary. Mark had worked closely with me over the past year and quickly became our most indispensable member. I talked with Chuck on 4 March 1994. The press release from the State Department read:

> General Galvin will head the U.S. team to the talks on the transitional military arrangements called for in the Framework Agreement concluded in Washington on March 1 between representatives of the Bosnian government, the Croat government, and the Bosnian Croat community. General Galvin, who will have the personal rank of Ambassador, will join the U.S. Special Envoy for the Former Yugoslavia, Ambassador Redman, next week in Zagreb and Sarajevo for initial contacts with the involved political and military authorities.

IF ASKED:

General Galvin is currently engaged in consultations with the State Department and the Pentagon. After further consultations here and in Europe, he will undertake to arrange contacts between the military leaders of the parties. No times or places for meetings have yet been established. No specific arrangements have yet been made. We are relying on General Galvin, working with Ambassador Redman, to define the requirements and to establish a process for the implementation of the military arrangements as soon as possible.

We headed for Brussels first, to get the views of NATO. That part of the trip was like a homecoming. For ten days the team became a traveling Round Table. On the morning of 8 March we flew to the Southern Command at Naples. After comparing notes there with Admiral Leighton "Snuffy" Smith, we flew to Zagreb, where we met Peter Galbraith, the first U.S. ambassador to Croatia. Chuck Redman, U.S. Army Lieutenant Colonel Kevin Campbell, and I joined Croatian President Franjo Tudjman for dinner at his residence. Campbell, on loan from the Pentagon's joint staff, was very knowledgeable on the issues that we could expect in our meetings in Bosnia. After dinner I took him with me to the headquarters of French General Jean Cot, the overall commander of the United Nations forces.

Cot went over the possibilities, good and not so good, of my mission, adding that he believed the overall effort didn't have enough support from the United States. Redman was present, along with Lieutenant Colonel Rick Herrick, the U.S. Defense Attaché, and Lieutenant Colonel Campbell. I asked Galbraith if I could borrow Campbell and take him with me to Bosnia. Galbraith agreed, and Herrick also went along when our team met with the special representative of the UN secretary general, Yasushi Akashi, at the United Nations Peace Forces headquarters, and then accompanied me to see General Janko Bobetko, head of the Croatian Army, who was hesitant about supporting the Federation of Bosnia and Herzegovina, probably because of his distrust of the Bosnian Army.

In the early afternoon of 9 March, I left Zagreb for Sarajevo in a propeller-driven Tupelov with a Russian crew. This service was nicknamed "Air Maybe." The plane was carrying a cargo container with a boxy refrigerator powered by a small combustion engine on top, which dripped fuel on the plane's floor until we landed. I then drove to the headquarters of Lieutenant General Sir Michael Rose, who poured us both a drop or two of Canadian whiskey as we discussed the situation.

I flew down to Split in the mid-afternoon of 10 March and went to the Villa Dalmatia, Tito's favorite vacation house, a beautiful place on the Adriatic, where I joined our team. There we worked and reworked the draft of what we wanted to say in our first discussion. The next morning we listened to the positions of the Bosnian and Croat military leaders and responded with our own. I began by saying, "Our presence should show the clear U.S. commitment to this effort; we are mediators, here at your request, to chart a course for success in support of the Framework Agreement. We hope you will see the logic of our approach."

On Friday, 11 March 1994, we concentrated on confidence building with the military representatives from both sides.

In the evening my team and I continued working together on a final draft summarizing the agreements we reached in the mediated discussions, emphasizing civilian control of military forces. After thirty-six hours together we had a conclusion—or better, a group of conclusions agreeable to all parties—that would be daunting under any circumstances: for the Bosnian and Croat military leaders to accept the Framework Agreement; to approve the creation of a Federation of Bosnia and Herzegovina; to agree with steps leading to a confederation with a neighboring country; and to create a combined force out of two opposing forces—all while fighting a war against a force at least as powerful as their own. And on top of that: to establish a unified Bosnian-Croat military command; pattern it after in-place command structures and draw on any existing unified arrangements (e.g., where Bosnians and Croats are already fighting together against the Serbs); and show keen support for the concepts of political oversight, combined centralized control, and decentralized execution of operations. Furthermore, the Bosnian and Croat senior leaders agreed to establish joint command staffs, determine a disengagement sequence that included a cease-fire, and designate withdrawal areas for troops and heavy weapons.

Mark Smith worked around the clock in the basement of the villa throughout the discussions, keeping in touch with the outside world via his laptop while drafting and redrafting through change after change as we moved toward a series of straightforward concluding statements:

> The main military arrangements in the Framework Agreement are supported and accepted as the foundation for future military agreements. . . .

Forces of the sides will disengage from one another immediately, with the aim of withdrawing a safe distance to be specified in the military agreement.

We confirm agreement on a separation of forces and weapons from designated confrontation lines.

In the transformation to a Federal Army, a Joint Command
from the existing armies of Bosnia Herzegovina and the Croatian Defense Council will be created and [will] be responsible
for control of all operational military regions.

On Saturday morning of 12 March we made minor last-minute
changes, signed the plan, and held a press conference to further nail
down the signatures. I was able to tell Chuck Redman in Vienna that
the Muslim and Croat military leaders were supportive of the Federation Agreement and were committed to the joint command. General Ante Roso of the Croatian Defense Council told the media that
same day, "Solutions for all the problems have been found. The military arrangements in the Framework Agreement are supported." During the following week, the Framework Agreement was confirmed in
Geneva with the full support of the Federal Forces.

The *New York Times* for 13 March 1994 carried this comment: "In a
statement issued in Split, General Rasim Delić, commander of the Mus-
lim-led Government army, and General Ante Roso, the commander of
the Croatian Defense Council, said they had agreed on guidelines for
combining their forces into a 'joint federal army' with a joint headquarters that would eventually work toward creation of a combined command structure, intelligence gathering, and planning of operations."

I headed home, via Paris. Now the question was, if the two sides do
follow through with the union of their forces, would the combination
prove strong enough to stand up against the Bosnian Serbs, who held
more than half the country? Our team asked ourselves, can this shot-
gun marriage hold?

In April the agreement was signed at a ceremony at the White
House, and during the first week in June, I went to Geneva, where the
Contact Group met with all three sides. I tagged along in order to talk
again with the military leaders—Delić, Roso, and Ratko Mladić (the
Bosnian Serb military leader), if he decided to come. He did. I met with
him for about an hour as he listed his complaints: the Clinton administration did not sufficiently support the Bosnian Serbs; the cease-fire
was too lengthy; and the UN force was not acceptable as a peacemaker.

Three months later, in early July 1994, our team got together again and headed back to Bosnia, this time to size up the viability of the new Muslim-Croat military linkage as it faced the Bosnian Serb forces.

At the Joint Army Headquarters in Sarajevo, the senior commanders gave us a detailed report on the status, plans, and problems of the Federal Army joint staff, now several months into its existence. As we expected, the staffs were working reasonably well, but connections to the forces in the field were weak. With the help of General Roso, we then went out to see the forces and talk with their commanders.

We found that the two forces, even after the linkage that freed them from the need to keep troops poised against each other, were extended in defense of the territory they held to the degree that there was little possibility of seizing more. Unlike their Serb opponents, they had very few tanks, and were therefore unable to maneuver in open ground, such as the flat valley of the Sava River in the north—though they were well supplied with light antitank missiles and had far less trouble holding the wooded hills. At that time they had few troops available to organize and hold more terrain, so that any gains would be minimal or would weaken the defense structure in other places. The Serbs, occupying 70 percent of the country, were spread thin. They knew that if they took more ground, they would have to organize and defend it, making of every new success another liability. At the same time, both sides were trying to gain and hold the initiative.

Among my impressions from those visits, some of the most vivid and surprising were the many destroyed houses within the Muslim and Croat zones. In some areas, as in Mostar, it was easy to see that gunfire in the many battles that had raged over the area had brought down the houses; but in the great majority of cases, as in the Kiseljak pocket or near Brčko or around Travnik on the western side of the Bosnian government area, the houses had been systematically dismantled by hand, neighbor against neighbor. A distinct pattern emerged: the houses of the dominant group, mostly on the best land, remained untouched, while others, on the less fertile slopes, were roofless, windowless skeletons, destroyed not by gunfire but by people. It was the same in the Serb areas, which did not surprise me—but what the Muslims and Croats had done to the Serbs had not always been well reported. On all sides, the extent of this devastation was gripping.

Near Brčko we climbed a knoll to greet a platoon and came upon one solitary rifleman in an outpost. "My son," he said, "was killed in this area. I have taken his place." On another hill, a soldier who was even more wrinkled, more patched, and skinnier scrambled out of a tumbledown log bunker, snapped to attention with a stiff-armed salute, and shouted a toothy "Heil Hitler!"

In order to learn more about the new Muslim-Croat Federation's ability to defend itself, I needed to get some idea of the Bosnian Serb military organization. General Roso and I visited General Mladić in his headquarters at Pale, on the eastern outskirts of Sarajevo. He was wearing a black rose on the lapel of his uniform. I learned later that he was in mourning for the death—by suicide, I was told—of his daughter. On that day he was alone except for a translator. He said that the fighting had been costly for all sides, and he hoped that a way to peace could be found. I said I had seen the new organizations of the Bosnian Muslims and the Croats, which seemed to be doing pretty well, and that the Federation was taking its first steps and looking good. I asked him to give me his view of the Contact Group proposal, and whether he thought this could be a basis for further negotiations. Instead, Mladić felt the need to pontificate, to recite a well-worn list of grievances, and to threaten—but when I said, after a few minutes of listening to diatribe, "General, this conversation is beginning to deteriorate," he stopped, and we resumed our discussion on the productive terms we had established at our earlier meeting.

Mladić had some messages that he wanted to get across. He insisted that there would be no peace in the Balkans that did not include communication with the Serbs. Also, he stated emphatically, "We don't want to talk with the Russians. They can't help us much; they have too many problems of their own. We want to talk to the Americans." My reply to him was the same as what he was hearing from the Contact Group: there has to be some movement by the Bosnian Serbs on two issues—a cease-fire and territorial negotiations. I added, "The U.S. is ready to do more, including troops and reconstruction, but only after we see some response, some goodwill on your side on these two matters. We know the solutions will be complex, but these issues have to be taken up first." He said the United States was backing the wrong side and was rattling a saber. I asked him if he thought we were moving toward peace. He responded by saying that there had been "too much war," but that it was hard for the Serbian side to respond to something when they had not been adequately consulted. He added that the area must not become an Islamic or German-dominated state, and that the United States and United Kingdom, he was sure, wanted a Christian state in the Balkans. He asked me for my impressions, both political and military, of the situation. I took note of past tension between the Croats and Muslims, but told him that I felt the Federation was helping to alleviate these tensions.

On 27 July 1994, on our way home, we wrote a memo to Secretary of State Warren Christopher summarizing our team's impressions:

> The Federation Army as an organization is fragile; it has made good progress, but needs concrete support to maintain the momentum of integration.
>
> Both sides are extended; neither can make large territorial gains against the other, and they know this. [Muslim-Croat] Army attacks are countered by Serb artillery attacks on villages. Both sides are receiving outside help, and both have indigenous production capabilities.
>
> Our general approach to Bosnia should encompass the following actions: contain the fighting; suppress it; attenuate it; continue humanitarian support; and force the combatants to the negotiating table without causing UNPROFOR (the United Nations Protection Force) to withdraw.

Perhaps we can say with some accuracy that when a place becomes for any reason ungovernable, the people grow afraid; they group together in traditional ways and look out for their own. At such times it doesn't take much to start a fire, and the tinder was already in place in Bosnia, as it is in so many other places in the world.

Yet the joining of forces did come about, and it has held together through many contentious years of political and military patchwork.

39

Ohio State University and Global Strategy Seminars

"Bringing together the cogitators and the agitators"

In 1994, I left West Point after an eventful two years to join the Mershon Center, a think tank at the Ohio State University, keeping a promise I had made before retiring. There I created, along with John Lewis Gaddis, Paul Kennedy, and Francis Fukuyama, a traveling team called the Global Strategy Seminar, dedicated to building a closer connection between university professors and senior political decision makers. We set up the Seminar with the help of the Smith Richardson Foundation, founders of the Center for Creative Leadership, where I was for some nine years a member of the board of governors. With no fanfare, we invited small groups of senators, congressmen, and other Washington leaders to join our team for dinner meetings and seminars on the Hill and at other locations, where we could get to know each other and establish ties that could help understanding in both directions.

The purpose of these seminars was to provide a chance for the foremost academic strategists to become better acquainted with Washington leaders (we called this "bringing together the cogitators and the agitators"). We hoped that these sessions would in some cases, at least, result in long-term associations between the global thinkers of academia and the influential (but busy and harried) senior movers and shakers on the Hill and at other places in Washington.

We emphasized that these were not tutorials or briefings, that there were no records kept—that we were looking for free discussions in an informal and relatively unstructured atmosphere. "As I see it," I wrote to the other Global Strategy Seminar participants, "one of us will lead off and talk briefly about the work he is doing (all of us are writing and teaching). That should open up a conversation in which I'm sure you and the others will want to bring in your own views, as will we. It usually turns out that John Gaddis focuses on what he calls the tectonic forces which cause both integration and disintegration in the world, while Paul Kennedy's more recent comments have been on what he calls pivotal states on the international scene. Kennedy will also want to talk about the United Nations and American national interests. I will also be waiting to get a word in edgewise, and I'm sure we will have a most interesting exchange."

We did one of these seminars with Newt Gingrich and congressmen Christopher Cox and Doug Bereuter in July. In a letter to me later, Gingrich commented, "If we in the Congress are to make informed decisions which ultimately benefit the American people, then we need to continually educate our members on the current thinking in the foreign policy arena. Your program is one of the best ways to make that happen. I hope you will be able to expand this program, as there are many here on the Hill who would benefit from participation in these seminars." We also held a seminar that included Senators Sam Nunn, John Warner, Chuck Robb, Carl Levin, and Joe Lieberman, and another with Secretary of Defense William Cohen and Chairman of the Joint Chiefs of Staff John Shalikashvili.

When I found that Brigadier General Paul Tibbets, who had piloted the *Enola Gay*, lived near Ohio State, I was tempted to call on him, to round out my own experience with nuclear weapons. A proposed visit proved acceptable to him, much to my gratification. To visit with Tibbets, I drove with two Ohio State colleagues a mile or so to a 1960s-style low ranch house in a modest and quiet neighborhood of parallel streets lined with high, arching trees. His wife held the aluminum screen door open and let us in. In the hallway there were photos of Medal of Honor flyer Joe Foss and other great World War II pilots, as well as of the *Enola Gay*. The interior of the house was neat and spare.

Tibbets was waiting in the den. He was small in stature, maybe 5'7", with iron gray hair—not much of it lost, if any. It was the third of March 1993, a warm day. There were two cats and a dog in the house, and each had a bed. Mrs. Tibbets brought us tea, and when she saw our interest in the pictures on the wall, she mentioned having lived in Karachi, New Delhi, and Beirut. The sparse décor also included Asian prints and ceramics. General Tibbets had dry lips, cracked and peeling; a handsome, very regular face; hearing aids in both ears; and a slight potbelly. The greetings were formal but not unfriendly—businesslike. He knew none of us and was not curious, not interested in knowing anything about visiting think tankers. We were simply interviewers, and his job was to tell the story he had told many times.

Tibbets talked of his twenty-six combat missions in B-17s in World War II, flying out of makeshift airstrips in England and North Africa. He knew that aircraft well: the Pratt and Whitney piston-driven propeller engines, how to nurse them, get all four of them running well together, coax them to maximum output—make them sing, as he said. At that time, Boeing assembly lines were turning out the B-29, the follow-up to the B-17, and the Air Corps needed experienced pilots to test them. He was a logical choice, I thought, for the war-closing mission that was his.

He warmed to the story of the first B-29s. There were problems, he said. Boeing was trying to pack more and more power into the new engines, and it was causing some trouble; they were prone to overheating. They needed cylinder changes every twelve hours. Actually, he said, the engines of the first ones off the line were each like two B-17 engines strapped together. They needed a lot of fixing—new wiring harnesses, other parts. He liked the job, and enjoyed helping figure out the changes that could make the B-29 a better aircraft. And then he was obviously proud to have been selected for a special task.

The challenge had fascinated him. He was told only what he needed to know in order to prepare himself, his crew, and his aircraft to carry that newly developed bomb against Japan. The size and shape of the bomb, and its weight, he was told, would be extraordinary.

Tibbets was assigned a hand-picked air crew and given the latest B-29 to come off the line, along with permission to make alterations on the plane as he saw fit. He said that to get used to the plane they had given him, he sometimes trained by flying against American pilots who flew captured Japanese "Zero" fighters. He found that by stripping the B-29 of all armament, he could significantly increase both airspeed and altitude. He was delighted to hear his opponents, in their Zeros, radioing to the exercise controllers, "Slow him down, or we can't catch up to engage him." When he returned to base from these runs, he continued to strip off more and more excess equipment from the plane. He said little to us of his thoughts on the mission itself. He had a job to do, and he was completely absorbed in the mechanical details.

Sent to Tinian in the Marianas, he practiced takeoffs with heavy loads. "I knew," he said in his laconic voice, "that if I lost one of my engines on takeoff with that load, I wouldn't stand much of a chance of getting up off the runway. It wouldn't lift off on three alone." Beyond getting the plane into the air, Tibbets was preoccupied with navigating to the assigned target, outrunning any Japanese fighters that might appear (none did), putting the bomb on target, and getting his crew home safely. As to what the bomb might do, he said he had been told that it could have the equivalent of twenty thousand tons of TNT. He flew the mission with some escort fighters and a plane to take photos. He said that years later at MacDill Air Force Base, he was introduced to a Japanese pilot who said he had led the attack on Pearl Harbor. "Jakaza was his name. I said, 'You sure surprised us,' and he said, 'What the hell did you think you did to us?'"

In the conversation, which was more of a monologue, Tibbets let us know that he had not been treated well in visits he made to Ohio State. The students had taken him to task, calling him a war criminal. He was also upset about the display of the *Enola Gay* at the Smithsonian, which he felt overemphasized the cost of civilian casualties, insisting that the plane should be presented in the context of the times. "They can say it killed a lot of people, because it did. Of course it did," he said. "That's what it was supposed to do." Then he answered the question he was sure we would want to ask: How did it feel?

"The shock wave rocked us," he said quietly. "I went into a turn, to get back out to sea. I looked down. Under the cloud column the ground was a rolling cloud as black as tar that spread out for three or four miles in all directions. We were at 30,000 feet. In ten seconds the column was higher than that. I thought, 'My God—it works.' I had told the crew to check in with me on intercom, but not to talk until I told them to, starting with the tail gunner; then they all had something to say. We concentrated on getting back to Tinian."

"I get hate mail and hate calls," he mused. "But mostly I get people saying thanks. They come up to me and say, 'You saved my life.'"

40

Back to Fletcher: Leading and Teaching Leadership

"If leadership can't be taught,
it can be improved."

In the late fall of 1994, I was asked to help look for a new dean for the Fletcher School of Law and Diplomacy at Tufts University. I was happy to join in the search. After my fellowship at Fletcher I had served nineteen more years in the Army, eighteen of them outside the United States. I had kept in touch with the school, and it had had much to do with formulating my outlook on the wide world. While I was in the process of compiling a list of possible candidates for the deanship, I was surprised to receive an invitation from the school to consider the position myself. I thought about it, but not for long—I said yes. The idea of returning to Fletcher intrigued me, for many reasons. I saw it as a chance to put together what I knew about leadership and life in a last, full-time effort. And I could keep up with the Global Strategy Seminars in Washington, the trips to Bosnia, my chairing of the American Council on Germany, and other interests and commitments.

Returning to Fletcher would also take me back home to New England and close to my hometown, Wakefield. As always, it would be good to return to the Tufts campus. From the top of the hill, from the third-story deck of the school's building, you can see the skyline of Boston to the south and, closer in, the green-roofed buildings of Harvard, two miles away. Out to the west is Chestnut Hill, topped by the towers of Boston College, and far beyond are the rolling blue hills that Native Americans called Massachusetts. Close in on the north side are the fells, the rocky hilltops that hide Wakefield from sight six miles away. Eastward lie the towns of the Mystic River Valley, Paul Revere's road to Lexington. Viewing all this again, I assured myself that this step back into the academic world was a good fit for a Boston Irish lad.

I visited the school right away and talked to students, faculty members, staffers, and the university provost and president, and to a lot of alumni, trustees, and friends. I told everyone that if they picked me they would be getting a teaching dean. An early question I was asked in my first session with the students was "What changes do you think you would be making?" I gave the routine answer, saying that I would take time to learn more about the school before I made any changes— except that, of course, I would immediately call for reveille, taps, and uniforms. It took a couple of seconds before everyone laughed.

For Ginny and me, the new job meant another household move (our twentieth, nothing new). We were intrigued with the house offered us by the University, a venerable 1840s Greek revival mansion off campus at the foot of the hill, near where Alewife Brook runs into the Mystic River. There were still traces of the shipyards where Paul Curtis built magnificent high-speed clippers that sailed around South America in the China trade. Later in the century the house had been home to the family of Lydia Child, writer and emancipation activist, who wrote the Thanksgiving Day poem that takes us across the river and through the woods. Grandmother's house was in need of restoration to bring it back to its former self, including reconditioning of the marvelous pine floors and repair of the Ionic columns. Throughout the house showed signs—quirky features and pragmatic solutions—that suggested shipwrights had been active in its construction.

Over the next five years, I spent plenty of time on fund-raising and dealing with the usual problems of any organization, but I also wanted to share in the work of the faculty, to be a part of the educational effort in every way possible. Teaching leadership while leading the school was sure to be an interesting combination—theory and practice rolled into one. At Fletcher, not only did the teachers grade the students, but at the end of the course the students graded the teachers, so there would be a chance to measure the results of this dual-hatted job.

The faculty liked the idea of my dual role, pleased to have one more set of hands at the oars. There was a plus for me also, since it put us all in the same boat and made other school decisions a bit easier— the same as it was early in my career, when as an advisor to the Colombian Ranger School I volunteered to be one of the instructors. This time I ransacked my books and papers on leadership and pulled out some of my favorites (including works by James MacGregor Burns, Stephen Covey, and Joseph Rost); I also read Peter Flawn's good-humored, sometimes sardonic *A Primer for University Presidents* and Jane Smiley's novel *Moo*. In different ways, these books broadened my understanding of what I was getting myself into. I went over to Harvard and talked with two of the very best leadership teachers and writers, John Kotter and Ron Heifitz, to see how they were handling teaching on this topic; I hunted down leaders in all walks of life (including Dick Walters, retired from the State Department, and Robert Galvin of Motorola) and got them to visit and speak to the classes; I checked in with the Center for Creative Leadership (Chuck Palus, Bill Drath); and—with Ginny's concurrence, of course—I promised wine, dinner, and conversation with visiting speakers at the Curtis house for every student in my course.

Some of the students were forming a reading circle that they called "Leading Edge," so I joined them. We met once a week in the early evening to talk about books and articles. When I asked them to help me plan a regular course, they jumped in with great enthusiasm and all kinds of good ideas. Under pressure to create a good course, I thumbed through my note cards to find what I might use for teaching. From that review, I saw that I had the making of a philosophy of leadership based on:

1. self-knowledge,
2. the teaming model,
3. the art of communication, and
4. the recognition of change.

I mentioned that I would create a series of lectures—and got a thumbs-down from my colleagues in Leading Edge. The students didn't want this approach at all, so lectures went out the window and were replaced by group participation. I worked up a semester syllabus, twelve class sessions of two hours each, divided into the four themes above—a framework that would allow room for expansion, contraction, and digression, as well as some entertainment. I found, however, that the syllabus was going to be useful only as a starter for each classroom session. The first day began with a spontaneous overthrowing of the schedule. Then word spread around, and the class expanded each semester after that, so that we had to move through a series of ever larger classrooms, and finally to the auditorium.

Here is what happened. The opening class, first time around, began with a search for the qualities of leadership. We talked of *versatility, curiosity, reliability, personality, integrity, loyalty, sensitivity*, and *adaptability*. It was student participation, but it was slow going, as you can imagine. I scribbled on the blackboard as we continued, with *awareness, brightness, coolness, steadiness, thoroughness, selflessness, decisiveness, friendliness, articulateness*. I could tell that the students were drifting into the leadership doldrums. Then we addressed *organization, motivation, dedication*, and *communication*. To these, we said, we might add *confidence, experience*, and *prescience*. My arm was getting sore by the time we remembered *ability* and *flexibility*.

At some point we ground to a halt when I ran out of blackboard space, and I looked for something to revive the moribund students when we arrived at this point. I tried dividing the class into teams of three or four students, each to try to come to agreement on what is truly essential in the making of a good leader. After fifteen minutes or so, the first group said a leader is someone who can stand up for what is right, is willing to do the heavy lifting, and is able to pick up on what people are thinking and respond to it with action. The second group said that a leader motivates by satisfying basic human needs; conveying achievement and self-awareness; being a caring person with vision; and articulating high aspirations touched with realism—and by not being afraid of being wrong, and being humble enough to admit it when that happens. And so on with the rest.

Again, slow going.

I needed another angle, so I asked, "Have you ever had a bad boss?" This lit a fuse. There was instantaneous laughter, followed by a buzz of conversation; the students had taken over the class. After a few minutes I managed to regain a semblance of order and said, "I would like to have you once again form into some small groups of about four or five. I want you to do some group thinking here for a few minutes about leadership situations involving bad bosses. Be prepared to talk about things that for one reason or another just went wrong. Maybe you've had a situation where you found yourself sitting there thinking how much you could get done if the boss just understood. Maybe the problem was the teacher who didn't teach. I want each group to select an interesting bad boss that we can discuss. We don't have to name people and places. Almost every bad boss earns a nickname, so you can keep actual names out of this. There will be no retribution; nobody is going to jail. So talk it around among yourselves. Come up with a boss that made history in your life. If you've never had a bad boss, use the time to compare notes on a good one."

Off they went for fifteen hilarious minutes. Irony ran high, and class participation hit a peak. Listening to their discussions, I realized that using nicknames hid the boss and encouraged the students to speak candidly about their experiences. When I called the class together again, we began to list their bosses' nicknames and explain them. This became standard operating procedure in the course, and made for the most popular, and definitely the noisiest, hour in every one of the subsequent eight semesters that I taught. A sample of the nicknames will, I think, show why. The bosses on the list are a selection from various courses:

Sleaze—amoral, no standards
Speed Bump—slows the work
Ahab—single-minded
Gestapo—suspicious
Romeo—pats of "encouragement"
Dragon Lady—breathes fire
Oz—smoke and mirrors
Microman—overmanages
Kong—overbearing
Her Majesty—condescending
Benign—neglectful
Mr. Hyde—two people in one
Genghis—heads roll

The nicknames were characterizations in miniature, making it easy to compare and discuss the various bad bosses, and what invariably followed was a tumultuous series of critiques, abetted by me, in answer to the question "What do bad bosses have in common?" When, as always, we ran out of time, I asked the students to follow up with a one-page essay on "The Bad Boss." In the sessions that followed, we delved deeply into the components underlying good and bad leadership. We climbed up a ladder of questions and answers, each time more or less like this:

Question 1: What if I went to see the bad bosses one by one and said, "Some people who work for you consider you a bad boss." What would they think of that? What answer would I get from them?

Answer 1: Laughter. They would be insulted. They would deny that. They would ask who sent you. They would throw you out.

Question 2: Why wouldn't they know that I'm right, that they are indeed bad bosses?

Answer 2: They are wrapped up in themselves. They don't understand how they come across to others. They lack self-examination. (Someone added, "The unexamined life is prevalent.") They are not any longer open to learning, as they were in their early years.

Question 3: Why don't they just figure things out, read the maxims, and become a good leader? Given competence and knowledge of the job, what's the problem?

Answer 3: These leaders don't believe in people. They get the job done, satisfying the higher-ups, who don't question how it was accomplished. They don't relate well, and don't particularly care whether they do or not. They don't communicate—they can't read the signs. They're poor at self-analysis. (They don't understand themselves, but think they do.) They don't deal well with change. They're not team people. They have been catered to, and don't realize how much. They are insecure and overcontrolling, and they abuse the authority of hierarchy.

Question 4: Assuming all of that is an accurate picture, how did they get that way? Were they born like that?

Answer 4: Born that way maybe, but the real reason has to do with the work culture they came up in.

Question 5: Why don't the higher-ups correct them, train and develop them, or fire them? Don't they know?

Answer 5: They know. Maybe not all of it, but they know. The bad boss gets the job done, meets requirements. And besides, the higher-ups aren't into development. They want results. They'll say, "This is a tough business; we have goals to meet." That is why the bad boss will eventually be one of the higher-ups. That's the environment. In the climate they came up in, they look pretty good.

We laughed all the way, pummeling leaders that we found wanting. It was difficult to get away from the subject. When the fun was over, though, we recognized the sadness, the tragedy, of it all, the frustration, the waste of energy. The Bad Boss days in the classroom were both entertaining and productive—but why? Shared experiences and universal feelings; epiphanies galore; eager, active participation—and, of course, the importance of the subject. I should add that the makeup of every class at Fletcher was a composite of graduate students, half from the United States, half from the rest of the world, averaging twenty-eight years of age, balanced in gender and interested in global concerns. But among them there were wide differences in life experiences of all kinds. I adjusted my manner of teaching to recognize this, primarily by encouraging the interchange of ideas as a team effort both in and out of the classroom, aiming at providing room for many answers to any question.

Often the students wanted to dig into the delicate question of how to deal with a bad boss. The essence of the many answers over five years went something like this:

Make sure you understand the situation. Consider in what sense your boss's behavior is wrong, and if its level of importance is enough to require action on your part. Don't quit immediately, unless you don't like the job anyway, but start thinking about it. Keep up communication with the boss, and keep tabs on dates and times that things happen. Try to address the problem, but don't do a workaround that gets you in trouble. Stay out of the fray. Look carefully for help, advice, reinforcement. Don't do anything wrong yourself. Give the boss a chance to explain. Do your job the right way and see what happens. Assume that the right way is really what the boss wants. Don't wait too long to go higher, though, and be creative with your exit strategy if you see that you need one.

In each course we then turned to *good* bosses, and each time we agreed that indeed there are plenty of them, far more than bad ones. In a way it's like Milton's *Paradise Lost* or Dante's *Inferno*. The bad folks are more interesting than the good. I asked these questions: What can you say about the best bosses you have ever known—and especially, what do they know that the bad bosses *don't* know? Were they developed differently? Did they move up through an organizational culture that made them better leaders? What did they say about leadership? Were they born leaders? The answers, in one way or another, amounted to *"They know themselves."* To varying degrees, we tend to create a world of our own, a comforting bubble around ourselves. Good leaders know the existence of their bubble, so *they communicate well*; communication with them is much easier and more effective. My contributions to the discussion called out qualities I had come to recognize in strong leaders: *they know how to build and join a team*. And *they understand change*.

A surprising number of students also said that they have learned as much from bad leaders as from good ones. A variation of this comment was "Maybe there's a good boss and a bad boss in all of us." This led us to the inevitable question: How about *you*, in *your* times as boss? That in turn led both me and the students to judge ourselves. For the students to answer that most important question, I asked for journal entries—short notes near the beginning of the course and at the end. In between, we took some of the classic self-analysis tests like the Meyers-Briggs analysis and DISC profiling (Dominance, Influence, Steadiness, Conscientiousness).

Over the course of the semester, I divided the students into diverse teams and gave them tasks to be accomplished—preparing a concise analysis of a book on leadership, researching a particular leader and presenting a roundtable overview of facets of that leader's life experiences. We turned to fiction, reading Virginia Woolf, Walt Whitman, Joseph Conrad, and other poets and authors whose work can be as instructive as and more reliable than case studies.

The substance of our exchanges always carried these messages: finding one's self is part of understanding others, and essential to good leadership. Communication, when it's working right, is one of the great pleasures of life; but even in the best communication, something can be lost. One of the ways to get your people to talk to you is just to wait quietly, to give them a chance. Part of good communication is that short wait.

I taught these classes guided by my own definition of leadership, which is to act in such a way that others just don't want to let you down. They believe in you. And I had the sense the students came away with a better and more deliberate sense of leadership that we had fashioned together over the course of the semester.

I'm fond of a statement that General Andy Goodpaster told me Ike Eisenhower had said. Andy had worked for Ike in the White House. He said that once someone said to Ike, "I don't think that leadership can be taught, and I don't think that leadership can be learned." And Ike said, "Well, I think it can be improved."

While I was at West Point in 1993, I had accepted the chair of the American Council on Germany (ACG), an organization aimed at reestablishing postwar relationships; on a personal level, the five years I spent in this role kept me involved in a country where my family had lived at critical times in the country's growth and development. My tenure with the Council continued into the time I spent at Fletcher, giving me continuing opportunities to engage with global leaders. One of the several visits I made to Germany included a meeting with Chancellor Helmut Kohl in April 1996. Council President Carroll Brown and I met him in his office at the end of a long day and received a hearty welcome.

Kohl asked me if I wanted to speak English, if that would be more comfortable for me (I had begun speaking in German) and—as I had done in earlier visits—I said, "Herr Kanzler, wir sind hier in Deutschland und Ich muss Deutsch sprechen" ("Mr. Chancellor, we are here in Germany and I must speak German") or something like that, and he laughed and sat back with a big Helmut smile and said, "Sehr Gut, sehr gut" ("Very good, very good")—and we were off. With Kohl I felt perfectly comfortable in German, because I knew he was aware of my weaknesses in grammar and vocabulary, and I also knew he was not comfortable in English.

I had a list of things in mind I wanted to talk about, but instead I saw that he wanted to launch into areas that it pleased him to talk about, and in a kind of perhaps tired garrulousness he roamed across various fields of thought connected by only a loose association of ideas. He remembered very accurately the first time that we met, in Mainz in 1978 or 1979, when he came to visit the troops of U.S. 1st Brigade, 8th Division, and we talked about that. I told him that at heart I was an "echte Maanzer Viertelbube" (an old-time Mainzer boy), but he said that since I'd lived twice in Stuttgart I was really a "Schwob" (Swabian)—there was lots of this kind of banter. He noted that, compared with those days, American interest in Germany has died down a great deal, and he pointed to the visits of U.S. senators and congressmen, which had, he said, dropped off to close to zero. I replied that this was an unusual year, with extreme partisanship on the Hill, which resulted in—of all things—politicians criticizing each other for junkets, even when they knew that the trips involved were important. I added that congressional infighting on the budget had further inhibited travel: members were all staying close to Washington, knowing that their votes were needed. He responded that since the threat of the Soviets and Communism had disappeared, Americans were more interested in Pacific trade and less in Europe.

I switched subjects to the new work the American Council on Germany was doing, opening eleven "Niederlasserungen"—new chapters—in such U.S. cities as Boca Raton, Denver, Richmond, San Diego, Nashville, and Indianapolis. Kohl mentioned the visits by U.S. governors of various states, noting that they were smart enough to see the possibilities of increased trade, especially in the eastern Lander.

I was delighted that the translator brought in as a routine practice for our discussion made only one move to help out in the conversation: she gave me the right words for "opinion poll" (*öffentliche Umfrage*). I know she let me get away with some terrible grammar and roundabout vocabulary and some "Galvin dialect," but I saw that she knew that I was getting my meaning across and that Kohl was enjoying the exchange, since he doesn't like to stay very long in English. Like lots of folks, he is actually pretty good in light conversation in English, but he doesn't think he is. He is at least as good in English as I am in German, but I was, I must admit, very proud to be holding my own in discussing a relatively complex set of issues, *alles auf Deutsch* (all in German).

Kohl let me talk about the Russians for a while, and I told him of my conviction that peace in Europe depended on building up strong relationships of trust among the United States, Germany, and Russia and that we needed to get going *now*, which was already late enough. I praised Germany and told him how much I admired his determination to help the Russians, in addition to what he was doing in the eastern part of Germany as well as in the central European countries. Kohl agreed on the importance of all that, but I think he was in a mood to simply enjoy a good rambling chat, and after all, this was a talk about Germans and Americans and how things were going in that relationship. He wanted to hear why the new ACG chapters had caught on so well (I had mentioned that about half of the eleven were already self-sufficient, less than two years after we started the expansion). We talked about that.

I was my typical Celtic self, full of ideas and hot air, rolling along, leaving a trail of fractured German, but hopefully in a good way overall. I couldn't believe the hour (plus) had gone by so fast, and Kohl seemed refreshed by it all.

Teaching leadership, I was convinced, shouldn't stray far from leading. The coming together and overlapping of these various strands of work—as an administrator, teacher, and chairman of an international group—redoubled what I was able to do in any one of them individually. They kept me active in the mix, attuned to interests and concerns on several levels, and mindful of the broader context for the topics we were addressing. They helped cement my sense of what Fletcher represented in educating a new class of leaders. I settled on an informal motto for the school: "Fletcher—global perspective."

Epilogue

We are inhabitants of a changing world that will continue to surprise us in all kinds of ways. There is one aspect, however, that we can depend on: change itself. This book carries that message, I trust, along with some ways to respond to it. Most of the relationships that I have called to mind here are person to person, but the reader will, I hope, have seen in these pages that the words apply nation to nation as well. I therefore consider both perspectives together as defining a vision that allows us to see the workings of our daily lives on a larger scale than our back-yards. So as you put aside this book, I hope it is with our agreement—yours and mine—that our survival in the long run will depend on our recognition of this simple but powerful understanding: that we need a global perspective.

Acknowledgments

First, I am indebted to countless men and women who made my life and my career possible—encouraging, nurturing, counseling, and helping me at every step along the way: family, mentors, teachers, and friends, especially Bob Sorley, Bill Boucher, Ralph Puckett, Pete Taylor, Red Reeder, and Huck Cronin. Above all I am grateful to my father, Jack Galvin, and my grandmother, who lived next door, who loved books and talked about them always to me, along with my Aunt Margaret, completely blind by spinal meningitis who nonetheless worked as a secretary for General Electric and served as an editor for the Braille edition of *Reader's Digest*. This book was inspired by my sister, Barbara.

Turning to the writing of this book, I owe special additional thanks and recognition. First and foremost to my wife, Ginny, who typed, read, proofread, and was a sounding board for many versions of these chapters over many years. My daughter Kathleen assisted me in every stage of completing the book, along with cheers from her siblings, Mary Jo, Beth, and Erin. Robert L. Cohen edited a late draft of the book, tightening it in many valuable ways and offering astute suggestions. The staff at the National Defense University facilitated access to my archives—especially Scott Gower and Susan Lemke. A number of close friends read drafts and shared feedback over the years—including Paul and John Fargis, Walt Ulmer, and NATO historian Greg Pedlow. KC Brown helped me connect with the Association of the United States Army and the University Press of Kentucky. Roger Cirillo of AUSA shepherded us through that process, Donna Bouvier provided exceptional editing, and Allison Webster at the University Press of Kentucky helped in navigating the publishing waters.

Index

289, 342; NATO deployment of, 289, 341; nuclear arms reduction and, 349; number removed from Europe in 1990, 444
Pershing II plan, 152–53
Persian Gulf War of 1990–1991, 404–13, 416–17
Peru, 300
Petraeus, David: aide to Galvin at SACEUR, 349, 352–54; with Galvin in Panama, 301; as Galvin's aide-de-camp with the 24th Infantry Division, 263, 264–65; Galvin's CEPS speech on nuclear arms reduction and, 352–54; "Uncomfortable Wars: Toward a New Paradigm," 303; writings on low-level fighting, 303
petrified trees, 272
Pezl, Karel, 450–51
Phuoc Vinh, 126–28, 129, 130, 141, 177–78, 214
Pickering, Tom, 322, 433
Pilsen, 230
Pinochet, Augusto, 300, 318
plastering, 8, 9–11, 29–30
Pleasant Street Army, 17
plebe system, 40
poetry: by Galvin, 117; Galvin's postgraduate study of, 116–17, 122
Poindexter, John, 307
Pointe du Hoc, 290
Pointer, The, 46
Polk, James K., 171
Popular Forces of Liberation (El Salvador), 319
Portugal, 407
postgraduate education: Columbia University, 116–17, 121–22; Fletcher School of Law and Diplomacy, 221, 223; University of Pennsylvania, 122, 156

Potter, Dick, 431
Powell, Colin: 1991 meeting with Galvin on the new force structure in Europe, 445; Balkans conflict, 463; calls Galvin "Charlemagne," 347; conventional arms control and, 365–66, 374, 443; First Gulf War and, 405, 408, 409, 412–13; Galvin's 1985 communication on El Salvador, 325–29; Kurdish crisis and, 428–29, 430–31, 433, 436, 437; London Agreement and, 398; meetings with Galvin as SACEUR, 404; replaces Galvin with John Shalikashvili as SACEUR, 460, 464; Soviet Union coup against Gorbachev, 455, 456
Prague, 67, 171, 230–32
Prague Spring (1968), 171
Pravda, 378
press: Army views of, 158
"pretties," 180–81
Price, Charles, 374
Primer for University Presidents, A (Flawn), 482
Project Warrior, 282
promotions: to Brigadier General, 248; to Colonel, 239; to General, 295
Pryce, Bill, 305, 306
Puckett, Ralph, 57–58, 63, 65, 66, 269
Puerto Rico: with the 65th Infantry Regiment Combat Team, 55–58; at Antilles Command Headquarters, 58–60; observes a Marine Corps amphibious landing, 109–10; signs up with the 65th Infantry Division, 52; study of small-unit tactical experiences from World War II, 60–62
Pulido, Soldado, 69–70
Putnam, George, 201, 209